ELECTION
BROADCASTING
IN CANADA

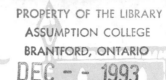

ELECTION BROADCASTING IN CANADA

Frederick J. Fletcher
Editor

Volume 21 of the Research Studies

ROYAL COMMISSION ON ELECTORAL REFORM
AND PARTY FINANCING
AND CANADA COMMUNICATION GROUP –
PUBLISHING, SUPPLY AND SERVICES CANADA

DUNDURN PRESS
TORONTO AND OXFORD

© Minister of Supply and Services Canada, 1991
Printed and bound in Canada
ISBN 1-55002-117-6
ISSN 1188-2743
Catalogue No. Z1-1989/2-41-21E

Published by Dundurn Press Limited in cooperation with the Royal
Commission on Electoral Reform and Party Financing and Canada
Communication Group – Publishing, Supply and Services Canada.

Canadian Cataloguing in Publication Data

Main entry under title:
Election broadcasting in Canada

(Research studies ; 21)
Issued also in French under title: La Radiodiffusion en période électorale
    au Canada.
ISBN 1-55002-117-6

   1. Electioneering – Canada. 2. Radio in politics – Canada. 3. Television in
politics – Canada. 4. Advertising, Political – Canada. 5. Elections – Canada.
I. Fletcher, Frederick J. II. Canada. Royal Commission on Electoral Reform
and Party Financing. III. Series: Research studies (Canada. Royal Commission on Electoral Reform and Party Financing) ; 21.

HE8689.7.P6E54 1991   324.7'3'0971   C91-090533-9

$29.95

Dundurn Press Limited   Dundurn Distribution
2181 Queen Street East   73 Lime Walk
Suite 301   Headington
Toronto, Canada   Oxford, England
M4E 1E5   OX3 7AD

CONTENTS

FIGURES

6. THE CBC NORTHERN SERVICE AND THE FEDERAL ELECTORAL PROCESS: PROBLEMS AND STRATEGIES FOR IMPROVEMENT

TABLES

5. POLITICAL BROADCAST ADVERTISING IN CANADA

FOREWORD

THE ROYAL COMMISSION on Electoral Reform and Party Financing was established in November 1989. Our mandate was to inquire into and report on the appropriate principles and process that should govern the election of members of the House of Commons and the financing of political parties and candidates' campaigns. To conduct such a comprehensive examination of Canada's electoral system, we held extensive public consultations and developed a research program designed to ensure that our recommendations would be guided by an independent foundation of empirical inquiry and analysis.

The Commission's in-depth review of the electoral system was the first of its kind in Canada's history of electoral democracy. It was dictated largely by the major constitutional, social and technological changes of the past several decades, which have transformed Canadian society, and their concomitant influence on Canadians' expectations of the political process itself. In particular, the adoption in 1982 of the *Canadian Charter of Rights and Freedoms* has heightened Canadians' awareness of their democratic and political rights and of the way they are served by the electoral system.

The importance of electoral reform cannot be overemphasized. As the Commission's work proceeded, Canadians became increasingly preoccupied with constitutional issues that have the potential to change the nature of Confederation. No matter what their beliefs or political allegiances in this continuing debate, Canadians agree that constitutional change must be achieved in the context of fair and democratic processes. We cannot complacently assume that our current electoral process will always meet this standard or that it leaves no room for improvement. Parliament and the national government must be seen as legitimate; electoral reform can both enhance the stature of national political institutions and reinforce their ability to define the future of our country in ways that command Canadians' respect and confidence and promote the national interest.

In carrying out our mandate, we remained mindful of the importance of protecting our democratic heritage, while at the same time balancing it against the emerging values that are injecting a new dynamic into the electoral system. If our system is to reflect the realities of Canadian political life, then reform requires more than mere tinkering with electoral laws and practices.

Our broad mandate challenged us to explore a full range of options. We commissioned more than 100 research studies, to be published in a 23-volume collection. In the belief that our electoral laws must measure up to the very best contemporary practice, we examined election-related laws and processes in all of our provinces and territories and studied comparable legislation and processes in established democracies around the world. This unprecedented array of empirical study and expert opinion made a vital contribution to our deliberations. We made every effort to ensure that the research was both intellectually rigorous and of practical value. All studies were subjected to peer review, and many of the authors discussed their preliminary findings with members of the political and academic communities at national symposiums on major aspects of the electoral system.

The Commission placed the research program under the able and inspired direction of Dr. Peter Aucoin, Professor of Political Science and Public Administration at Dalhousie University. We are confident that the efforts of Dr. Aucoin, together with those of the research coordinators and scholars whose work appears in this and other volumes, will continue to be of value to historians, political scientists, parliamentarians and policy makers, as well as to thoughtful Canadians and the international community.

Along with the other Commissioners, I extend my sincere gratitude to the entire Commission staff for their dedication and commitment. I also wish to thank the many people who participated in our symposiums for their valuable contributions, as well as the members of the research and practitioners' advisory groups whose counsel significantly aided our undertaking.

Pierre Lortie
Chairman

INTRODUCTION

THE ROYAL COMMISSION'S research program constituted a comprehensive and detailed examination of the Canadian electoral process. The scope of the research, undertaken to assist Commissioners in their deliberations, was dictated by the broad mandate given to the Commission.

The objective of the research program was to provide Commissioners with a full account of the factors that have shaped our electoral democracy. This dictated, first and foremost, a focus on federal electoral law, but our inquiries also extended to the Canadian constitution, including the institutions of parliamentary government, the practices of political parties, the mass media and nonpartisan political organizations, as well as the decision-making role of the courts with respect to the constitutional rights of citizens. Throughout, our research sought to introduce a historical perspective in order to place the contemporary experience within the Canadian political tradition.

We recognized that neither our consideration of the factors shaping Canadian electoral democracy nor our assessment of reform proposals would be as complete as necessary if we failed to examine the experiences of Canadian provinces and territories and of other democracies. Our research program thus emphasized comparative dimensions in relation to the major subjects of inquiry.

Our research program involved, in addition to the work of the Commission's research coordinators, analysts and support staff, over 200 specialists from 28 universities in Canada, from the private sector and, in a number of cases, from abroad. Specialists in political science constituted the majority of our researchers, but specialists in law, economics, management, computer sciences, ethics, sociology and communications, among other disciplines, were also involved.

In addition to the preparation of research studies for the Commission, our research program included a series of research seminars, symposiums and workshops. These meetings brought together the Commissioners, researchers, representatives from the political parties, media personnel and others with practical experience in political parties, electoral politics and public affairs. These meetings provided not only a forum for discussion of the various subjects of the Commission's mandate, but also an opportunity for our research to be assessed by those with an intimate knowledge of the world of political practice.

These public reviews of our research were complemented by internal and external assessments of each research report by persons qualified in the area; such assessments were completed prior to our decision to publish any study in the series of research volumes.

The Research Branch of the Commission was divided into several areas, with the individual research projects in each area assigned to the research coordinators as follows:

F. Leslie Seidle	Political Party and Election Finance
Herman Bakvis	Political Parties
Kathy Megyery	Women, Ethno-cultural Groups and Youth
David Small	Redistribution; Electoral Boundaries; Voter Registration
Janet Hiebert	Party Ethics
Michael Cassidy	Democratic Rights; Election Administration
Robert A. Milen	Aboriginal Electoral Participation and Representation
Frederick J. Fletcher	Mass Media and Broadcasting in Elections
David Mac Donald (Assistant Research Coordinator)	Direct Democracy

These coordinators identified appropriate specialists to undertake research, managed the projects and prepared them for publication. They also organized the seminars, symposiums and workshops in their research areas and were responsible for preparing presentations and briefings to help the Commission in its deliberations and decision making. Finally, they participated in drafting the Final Report of the Commission.

On behalf of the Commission, I welcome the opportunity to thank the following for their generous assistance in producing these research studies – a project that required the talents of many individuals.

In performing their duties, the research coordinators made a notable contribution to the work of the Commission. Despite the pressures of tight deadlines, they worked with unfailing good humour and the utmost congeniality. I thank all of them for their consistent support and cooperation.

In particular, I wish to express my gratitude to Leslie Seidle, senior research coordinator, who supervised our research analysts and support staff in Ottawa. His diligence, commitment and professionalism not only set high standards, but also proved contagious. I am grateful to Kathy Megyery, who performed a similar function in Montreal with equal aplomb and skill. Her enthusiasm and dedication inspired us all.

On behalf of the research coordinators and myself, I wish to thank our research analysts: Daniel Arsenault, Eric Bertram, Cécile Boucher, Peter Constantinou, Yves Denoncourt, David Docherty, Luc Dumont, Jane Dunlop, Scott Evans, Véronique Garneau, Keith Heintzman, Paul Holmes, Hugh Mellon, Cheryl D. Mitchell, Donald Padget, Alain Pelletier, Dominique Tremblay and Lisa Young. The Research Branch was strengthened by their ability to carry out research in a wide variety of areas, their intellectual curiosity and their team spirit.

The work of the research coordinators and analysts was greatly facilitated by the professional skills and invaluable cooperation of Research Branch staff members: Paulette LeBlanc, who, as administrative assistant, managed the flow of research projects; Hélène Leroux, secretary to the research coordinators, who produced briefing material for the Commissioners and who, with Lori Nazar, assumed responsibility for monitoring the progress of research projects in the latter stages of our work; Kathleen McBride and her assistant Natalie Brose, who created and maintained the database of briefs and hearings transcripts; and Richard Herold and his assistant Susan Dancause, who were responsible for our research library. Jacinthe Séguin and Cathy Tucker also deserve thanks – in addition to their duties as receptionists, they assisted in a variety of ways to help us meet deadlines.

We were extremely fortunate to obtain the research services of first-class specialists from the academic and private sectors. Their contributions are found in this and the other 22 published research volumes. We thank them for the quality of their work and for their willingness to contribute and to meet our tight deadlines.

Our research program also benefited from the counsel of Jean-Marc Hamel, Special Adviser to the Chairman of the Commission and former

Chief Electoral Officer of Canada, whose knowledge and experience proved invaluable.

In addition, numerous specialists assessed our research studies. Their assessments not only improved the quality of our published studies, but also provided us with much-needed advice on many issues. In particular, we wish to single out professors Donald Blake, Janine Brodie, Alan Cairns, Kenneth Carty, John Courtney, Peter Desbarats, Jane Jenson, Richard Johnston, Vincent Lemieux, Terry Morley and Joseph Wearing, as well as Ms. Beth Symes.

Producing such a large number of studies in less than a year requires a mastery of the skills and logistics of publishing. We were fortunate to be able to count on the Commission's Director of Communications, Richard Rochefort, and Assistant Director, Hélène Papineau. They were ably supported by the Communications staff: Patricia Burden, Louise Dagenais, Caroline Field, Claudine Labelle, France Langlois, Lorraine Maheux, Ruth McVeigh, Chantal Morissette, Sylvie Patry, Jacques Poitras and Claudette Rouleau-O'Toole.

To bring the project to fruition, the Commission also called on specialized contractors. We are deeply grateful for the services of Ann McCoomb (references and fact checking); Marthe Lemery, Pierre Chagnon and the staff of Communications Com'ça (French quality control); Norman Bloom, Pamela Riseborough and associates of B&B Editorial Consulting (English adaptation and quality control); and Mado Reid (French production). Al Albania and his staff at Acart Graphics designed the studies and produced some 2 400 tables and figures.

The Commission's research reports constitute Canada's largest publishing project of 1991. Successful completion of the project required close cooperation between the public and private sectors. In the public sector, we especially acknowledge the excellent service of the Privy Council unit of the Translation Bureau, Department of the Secretary of State of Canada, under the direction of Michel Parent, and our contacts Ruth Steele and Terry Denovan of the Canada Communication Group, Department of Supply and Services.

The Commission's co-publisher for the research studies was Dundurn Press of Toronto, whose exceptional service is gratefully acknowledged. Wilson & Lafleur of Montreal, working with the Centre de Documentation Juridique du Québec, did equally admirable work in preparing the French version of the studies.

Teams of editors, copy editors and proofreaders worked diligently under stringent deadlines with the Commission and the publishers to prepare some 20 000 pages of manuscript for design, typesetting and printing. The work of these individuals, whose names are listed elsewhere in this volume, was greatly appreciated.

Our acknowledgements extend to the contributions of the Commission's Executive Director, Guy Goulard, and the administration and executive support teams: Maurice Lacasse, Denis Lafrance and Steve Tremblay (finance); Thérèse Lacasse and Mary Guy-Shea (personnel); Cécile Desforges (assistant to the Executive Director); Marie Dionne (administration); Anna Bevilacqua (records); and support staff members Michelle Bélanger, Roch Langlois, Michel Lauzon, Jean Mathieu, David McKay and Pierrette McMurtie, as well as Denise Miquelon and Christiane Séguin of the Montreal office.

A special debt of gratitude is owed to Marlène Girard, assistant to the Chairman. Her ability to supervise the logistics of the Commission's work amid the tight schedules of the Chairman and Commissioners contributed greatly to the completion of our task.

I also wish to express my deep gratitude to my own secretary, Liette Simard. Her superb administrative skills and great patience brought much-appreciated order to my penchant for the chaotic workstyle of academe. She also assumed responsibility for the administrative coordination of revisions to the final drafts of volumes 1 and 2 of the Commission's Final Report. I owe much to her efforts and assistance.

Finally, on behalf of the research coordinators and myself, I wish to thank the Chairman, Pierre Lortie, the members of the Commission, Pierre Fortier, Robert Gabor, William Knight and Lucie Pépin, and former members Elwood Cowley and Senator Donald Oliver. We are honoured to have worked with such an eminent and thoughtful group of Canadians, and we have benefited immensely from their knowledge and experience. In particular, we wish to acknowledge the creativity, intellectual rigour and energy our Chairman brought to our task. His unparalleled capacity to challenge, to bring out the best in us, was indeed inspiring.

Peter Aucoin
Director of Research

PREFACE

IN MODERN DEMOCRACIES, election campaigns are contested to a large degree in the mass media. From the days of the openly partisan press to the contemporary multi-media environment, political leaders have relied upon mass media to mobilize electoral support. While the right to vote freely and the credibility of the ballot process are central to democracy, the conduct of campaigns and the flow of information to voters are also important. If campaigns are perceived to be conducted unfairly, the entire electoral process may become suspect. Concern for the legitimacy of the system is one of the primary reasons that most democracies have enacted regulations dealing with aspects of electoral communication. These regulations cover a wide range of media activities, including campaign advertising, election broadcasting and even some aspects of news and public affairs.

The Commission's research program on mass media and elections examined the major developments in electoral communication in Canada and other democratic countries in recent decades, in the context of electoral reform. The research studies were designed to cast light on major aspects of election media, whether amenable to regulation or not. Effective regulation requires an understanding of the entire system of campaign communication.

The results of the research program provided background for the Commission's report. Whatever their substantive focus, the studies examined issues such as fairness in electoral competition and public confidence in the electoral process, issues that are central to electoral reform. Some studies examined central elements in the campaign communication system, while others assessed its effectiveness in meeting the information needs of voters and the communication needs of parties. Several projects considered alternative forms of communication that might contribute to improved information for voters. The studies examined campaign media in the larger sense, including partisan advertising, free broadcast time, candidate communication strategies, new communication technologies and news and public affairs coverage, among other topics.

Research dealing directly with mass media and elections is reported in volumes 18 through 22. Volume 16, on opinion polling, and Volume 17, on the attitudes of Canadians toward the electoral system, also deal with campaign communication, but include material on other subjects as well. Taken together, the seven volumes provide a comprehensive overview of the issues of campaign communication.

Volume 21 examines some major aspects of election broadcasting in Canada: the history; the legal framework; the probable impact of the recently established Canadian all-news cable service, Newsworld, which has yet to cover a federal election; the potential of cable television in general, with special attention to the role of community and specialty channels; the regulatory issues surrounding political broadcast advertising; and the special problems of election broadcasting in the North. The studies examine important aspects of free time, paid time and, to a lesser extent, news and public affairs coverage of campaigns. The latter topic is examined in more detail in Volume 22. The influence of election broadcasting is discussed in Volume 18.

The Canadian system, with its unusual mix of public and private broadcasting and paid and free time, has been the subject of considerable debate since its inception in the 1930s. It was the first element to be developed in the system of "regulated competition" that prevails in Canadian federal elections. In recent years, European broadcasting has increasingly moved along the path taken by Canada and Britain earlier: permitting private broadcasting to develop alongside pre-existing public systems. This development raises the possibility of combining the free time traditionally provided by public broadcasters (and under regulation by private networks as well) with paid time. As Canada rethinks its own system, the appropriate mix of free and paid broadcasting time for parties and candidates during election campaigns is a growing issue in many countries. Even in the United States, where broadcasting is primarily private, there have emerged in recent years a number of proposals for some form of free time for candidates. New challenges and new opportunities for the electoral process and its key participants emerge with every new development in broadcasting. These studies provide a guide to these developments and some of the implications that flow from them.

David Spencer and Catherine Bolan present an overview of the evolution of the election broadcasting system in Canada. They examine the roots of current practices and regulatory structures in the struggle to create a place for political broadcasting on radio and, later, television as the broadcast media became the central focus of modern campaigns. They also discuss the influence of broadcasting on political campaigns and parties in relation to the tradition of partisan neutrality that emerged during this process. Pierre Trudel and France Abran examine, in some detail, the rationale for current legislation and regulations regarding electoral broadcasting and their compatibility with the *Canadian Charter of Rights and Freedoms*. They note that Canada's unique legal framework is a compromise between competing claims of fairness and of freedom of the press, and is reflected in the flexible approach taken by the CRTC's regulation of political broadcasting.

David Hogarth and William Gilsdorf studied the actual and potential impact of all-news services such as Newsworld and CNN on election coverage. The authors identify the probable contributions of these services – more regional coverage and extended live coverage of campaign events – but are concerned that the services will simply be an extension of existing television news services and not a real alternative. Peter Desbarats begins his examination of the potential of cable television for improving campaign communication by raising concerns about the increasing homogenization and managed nature of election coverage in the established media. He argues that cable television services could provide more diversity in election campaigns, especially for local candidates. Desbarats suggests that cable services could accommodate a wide range of candidates and opinions to counterbalance the narrowness of established media. Both of these papers express concern about the lack of diversity in campaign coverage.

Stephen Kline, William Leiss and their colleagues provide an overview of the development of campaign advertising and its growing importance in election campaigns. They note that in contrast to commercial advertising, partisan advertising is not subject to the scrutiny and self-regulation that constrain commercial advertising. The authors examine the evolution of the current regulatory structure for commercial advertising, exploring options for regulation of the content of political marketing. Campaign advertising is an area in which little work has been done in Canada and this study makes an important contribution. Related issues are discussed in Volume 12, *Political Ethics: A Canadian Perspective*, especially in the study on negative advertising.

Lorna Roth focuses on the special needs of the five northern ridings as they relate to the CBC's Northern Service. Her main findings address electoral issues in the northern and remote regions of Canada in their socio-economic and cultural uniqueness: the broadcasting regulatory structure, the allocation of electoral resources, the advertising allocation formula for free and paid time, and televised debates. Based on her extensive field work, she suggests that the electoral regulations should recognize the special needs of candidates in these ridings. Some related issues are addressed in the study by Valerie Alia in Volume 9.

Research in this volume was conducted in late 1990 and 1991 and is based on a variety of approaches and methods, including historical and legal analysis. While the 1988 federal election campaign was a point of departure for some of the studies, the general focus is broader. Several of the studies are pathbreaking in their systematic analysis of little-studied or emerging areas in election broadcasting. Others provide essential background information.

These studies raise important questions for future developments in election broadcasting in Canada with respect to its regulatory frame-work, the impact of new technologies and responses by party strategists. This volume will be of interest to students and scholars of the mass media, election campaigns and law, as well as policy analysts and others interested in regulatory structures, technological developments and party strategy. The studies bring to light a number of neglected issues and may well stimulate research and discussion on broadcasting issues in general.

The Commission's research program on mass media and elections drew on the expertise of a wide range of communication scholars and political scientists in addition to those whose work is published in these volumes. Their assistance is greatly appreciated. Among those who participated as peer reviewers and advisers, several deserve special recognition: Peter Desbarats, Dean of the School of Journalism, University of Western Ontario; David Taras, University of Calgary; Holli Semetko, University of Michigan; and Marc Raboy, Laval University. The research program also benefited from the advice of individuals from the parties and the media: John Coleman, President, Canadian Advertising Foundation; Terry Hargreaves, Elly Alboim and Colin MacLeod of the CBC; Geoffrey Stevens, political columnist; Lynn McDonald, sociologist and former MP; and others who prefer to remain anonymous. On behalf of the authors and the Commission, I must also acknowledge our debt to the practitioners from the media and the parties who attended our seminars or agreed to be interviewed and provided much valuable assistance and advice.

The administration of the research program depended heavily on the work of Cheryl Mitchell, who served as my assistant from the inception of the program, and our research assistants at York University:

Catherine Bolan, Claudia Forgas, Marni Goldman, Todd Harris, Sharon Johnston and Sheila Riordon. We were also assisted most ably by the Commission staff. Peter Constantinou and Véronique Garneau had particular responsibilities for research in this area. The staff of the Department of Political Science, the Faculty of Arts, Calumet College, and the Faculty of Environmental Studies at York University were very accommodating.

The authors themselves deserve special acknowledgement for their willingness to try to meet tight deadlines, complicated by their normal academic responsibilities, and in particular to respond with cheerfulness and despatch to our requests for revisions. The conscientious peer reviewers were of major assistance to the authors and ourselves in preparing these studies for publication.

The unfailing good humour and encouragement of Peter Aucoin, the director of research, made an important contribution to the work. It was a privilege to work with the Commissioners, whose willingness to bring their experience to bear on the most esoteric of formulations was an inspiration. Pierre Lortie's overall direction and, in particular, his suggestions for research and incisive comments on various drafts made a vital contribution, which is reflected in these research volumes as well as in the Final Report of the Royal Commission. Working with the other research coordinators was a genuine pleasure. Richard Rochefort and his staff were crucial in bringing these studies to publication.

On a personal note, I wish to thank my wife and frequent collaborator, Martha Fletcher, for encouraging me to undertake this task, which I have found very rewarding, and for her direct advice on many aspects of the work, as well as for bearing more than her share of the burden of domestic management. My son, Frederick, reminded me that work, however important, must be balanced with other aspects of life but also that the future of the democratic process is worth working for.

Cheryl Mitchell brought dedication and skill to the work and must have an ample share of the credit for whatever contribution the research program has made. In editing this volume, I was assisted by Catherine Bolan, Claudia Forgas and Todd Harris. For errors in design and execution, however, I remain responsible.

Fred Fletcher
Research Coordinator

ELECTION BROADCASTING IN CANADA

1

ELECTION BROADCASTING IN CANADA
A Brief History

David R. Spencer
Catherine M. Bolan

THE PRIMARY OBJECTIVE of this study is to examine the evolution of election broadcasting in Canada. We wish to trace its roots, the central principles and patterns that emerged with the advent of radio, and its evolution as radio matured and was challenged by television. What have been the major issues in this evolution? What interests and values has election broadcasting served? How have election campaigns been altered, first by radio, then by television and, more recently, by changes in the nature of television? We give special attention to radio, a medium often neglected in election research.

From its inception, election broadcasting has been viewed as a subcategory of political broadcasting. The fundamental issues surrounding political broadcasting – freedom of expression, fairness and equity in access, and appropriate regulatory structures – are applicable both during and between elections. Election broadcasting, however, compressed as it is during the brief period of electoral competition, raises special issues. Election broadcasting is usually seen as including news and public affairs coverage, party broadcasts and party advertisements. Our focus here is on how election broadcasting affects party competition during campaigns and the information available to voters. We trace the emergence of the new mass audience created by radio and television, which reached a peak at the height of network television, and its subsequent (and ongoing) decline through audience fragmentation.

If, as Harold Innis has argued, the printing press caused monastery walls to crumble with the spread of literacy in medieval Europe (Innis 1972, 143), the introduction of the radio in the 20th century fundamentally reshaped the way we communicate. In particular, radio was responsible for initiating a substantial redefinition of the relationship between ruler and ruled, and in the process, established the framework within which we conduct ourselves politically in contemporary times. The electronic media, first radio, then television, taught political personalities with a wide range of ideological convictions how to conquer geography and, in the process, diminished the importance of the whistle stop, the public meeting and the small town parade as the primary arenas for political campaigns (McAllister 1985).

Between 1920 and 1960, the print media, which were regional in character and distribution, were gradually forced to concede the immediacy of national issues to the first truly national medium – radio. Radio allowed the political professional to circumvent the reporters and columnists who dominated the pages of the daily press by speaking directly with constituents. From its beginnings, radio had a centralizing effect on political communication (Innis 1951, 60), and more and more public figures addressed their far-flung constituencies from radio studios in places like Toronto, Montreal, Ottawa and Vancouver, among others, as the medium grew in influence and acceptance. Consequently, election campaigners began to address more national issues at the expense of local or regional ones. Members of Parliament became identified more as dutiful members of a specific political party and less as representatives of a geographic territory with special and local interests.

Radio's involvement with elections began with the broadcasting of the results on election night. The first such broadcast took place in 1920, when Pittsburgh radio station KDKA joined with Detroit's WWJ to broadcast the returns of the Harding–Cox presidential race (Broadcasting Publications 1982, 1; Nolan 1989, 498). In 1923, Harding became the first American president to make a radio speech while in office (Clark 1962, 230). His successor, Calvin Coolidge, used radio to overcome the dour image that plagued his personal appearances (ibid.). Coolidge once remarked to Senator James Watson: "I am very fortunate that I came in with the radio. I can't make an engaging, rousing, or oratorical speech to a crowd as you can ... but I have a good radio voice, and now I can get my messages across to them without acquainting them with my lack of oratorical ability" (Cornwell 1957, 267–68). The introduction of radio thus changed not only the nature of political campaigning but also the skills needed for success.

Politicians, like other early observers, were concerned about what they viewed as the enormous potential influence of radio, and all the industrial democracies soon moved to provide a legislative framework for political broadcasting. In Canada, the concerns of the parties influenced the legislation (Kjosa and Paltiel 1970, 356) and thus the development of political broadcasting. The parties themselves were, of course, fundamentally changed by the introduction of radio. With attendance at political meetings down by at least half from the 1920s to the 1930s because voters could stay home and listen to the party leaders discuss their policies over the air (Nolan 1986, 105), the parties and, especially, their leaders were forced to try to master the new medium.

This study concentrates on the historical development of election broadcasting in Canada and its legislative framework, with references to comparable developments in the United States and Britain, the two countries with the most influence here. As well, it explores radio's altered role in election broadcasting in response to changes in technology and party strategy, and examines political broadcasting in the television age. Today, radio remains a secondary actor in political and election broadcasting with the possible exception of local coverage in the many smaller cities and towns across the country.

THE EMERGENCE OF POLITICAL BROADCASTING

Across the industrialized world, radio and film matured simultaneously. While cinema, and more specifically newsreels, had a significant impact on audience awareness of particular cultural and political events, they had little effect on elections because of their infrequent appearance. Radio and, later, television proved to be much more significant in the development of political broadcasting. In Canada, the United States and Britain, radio broadcasting was born as a purely private venture; until the first *Broadcasting Act* in 1932, the Canadian government, through the Department of Marine and Fisheries, did little beyond allocating licences and dial locations. Until the formation of the Canadian Radio Broadcasting Commission (CRBC) that same year, the majority of Canadian licences were held by private companies, and the stations were operated as ancillaries to larger, profit-making enterprises. Nonetheless, by 1932, Canada had 66 radio stations. Radio rapidly became an important part of the lives of Canadians. By the end of the Great Depression, three of every four Canadians owned a radio (Rutherford 1978, 79).

In 1927, eight years after the first station began regular broadcasting, Americans witnessed the birth of network radio. Under the direction of David Sarnoff, the Radio Corporation of America laid the foundation for the National Broadcasting Company (NBC), and under the entrepreneurial guidance of William Paley, the Columbia Broadcasting System (CBS) came into being the following year (Clark 1962, 231). Both networks emphasized entertainment programming, broadcasting a variety of comedy shows, live musical programs, mysteries and serialized dramas. That same year, the United States Congress passed the *Radio Act*, a largely technical bill which created a regulatory agency with a mandate to bring order to the chaotic radio spectrum. Four years later, 608 American radio stations were on the air. Aided by the growth of NBC and CBS, private radio eroded the virtual monopoly on advertising dollars enjoyed by the print media. The 1930 United States Census reported that 12 million of the country's 30 million homes were equipped with receiving sets (Broadcasting Publications 1982, 1). Both NBC and CBS enjoyed audiences in Canada as well as in the United States (Rutherford 1978, 80).

The British experience was similar. In February 1922, the Marconi Company of Great Britain was given a licence to undertake a broadcasting venture from a transmitter at Writtle, near Chelmsford. Prior to this official recognition by the British government, Marconi had conducted a number of experimental broadcasts. Later that year, a private firm, the British Broadcasting Company, was founded by six leading radio manufacturers. It received a government licence on 1 November and began broadcasting soon afterward (Briggs 1985, 363–64). British broadcasting remained in private hands until the publicly owned British Broadcasting Corporation (BBC) was established by Royal Charter on 1 January 1927. The BBC was given a broadcasting monopoly for at least 10 years. The private sector was expropriated, and its owners and operators were compensated by the British government. From this date on, British and American broadcasting experiences would have little in common for nearly three decades. The British model was purely public, the American exclusively private. The BBC's monopoly finally expired when independent television was licensed in the autumn of 1955 (ibid., 385). Canadian developments were influenced by both systems.

The Development of Programming

Unlike newspaper editors, whose primary mission was the collection and dissemination of news, radio programmers in the 1920s and early 1930s were aware that the growing popularity of the medium was due in large part to their widely accepted entertainment programs. Nevertheless, they were constantly searching for new ideas which they hoped would bring them larger audiences. Among other initiatives, they began to experiment with political broadcasting.

The case of CJGC (now CFPL), a station in London, Ontario, was typical. Its first identifiable political broadcast involved reporting the federal election results in 1925. Drawing on the resources of its owner, the *London Free Press*, the station broadcast up-to-the-minute results from local ridings with special emphasis on those held by cabinet ministers. In Montreal, the voice of the French-language newspaper *La Presse*, CKAC, also broadcast the results of the 1925 federal election to Quebeckers from an on-location site (Lavoie 1971, 19).

Institutionalized political broadcasting began in Canada in May 1929 when Sir Henry Thornton's Canadian National Railway (CNR) network broadcast the first episode of its series "The Nation's Business." The programs were to feature presentations by government ministers with replies by opposition members. The Conservatives, convinced that the series was designed to promote the governing Liberal party, persuaded their leader, R.B. Bennett, to withdraw his support. The uncooperative stance assumed by the Conservative party led to the cancellation of the series in December that same year (Kjosa and Paltiel 1970, 356; Weir 1965, 32).

In spite of the failure of "The Nation's Business," Canadian broadcasters continued to experiment with political broadcasting. Toronto radio station CKGW, owned by the distilling firm of Gooderham and Worts, broadcast the opening of Parliament in March 1931. The station, later to become the flagship in Toronto of the Canadian Broadcasting Corporation/Société Radio-Canada (CBC/SRC), set up a network of 27 stations and transmitted the broadcast over Canadian Pacific telegraph lines. Through its affiliation with NBC, the program was also carried on many stations in the United States (Nolan 1989, 511).

A series of broadcasts initiated by CNR stations in January 1932 highlighted the potential of political broadcasting. The network had retained Ottawa journalist Grattan O'Leary to participate in a series of 15-minute commentaries called "Canada Today." The programs were designed to address the serious political and financial problems that the nation was facing in the deepening crisis of the Great Depression. However, O'Leary, in concert with Grant Dexter, parliamentary correspondent for the *Winnipeg Free Press*, extended the mandate to include important international questions. In one broadcast, O'Leary used his electronic platform to appeal for the cancellation of reparations and war debts levied on Germany as a result of the *Treaty of Versailles*. O'Leary was convinced that German indebtedness and the rise of fascism were coincident events. American official circles were outraged by the suggestion and communicated their displeasure to Prime Minister Bennett. Despite intense pressure to the contrary, O'Leary and Dexter continued the series until the end of their contract (Weir 1965, 67–68).

These early political broadcasts in Canada, while subject to extensive debate in the House of Commons, were not subject to any form of regulation until the 1936 *Broadcasting Act*. They were treated as any other commercial programming carried by Canadian stations (Canada, Committee 1966, 362).

Americans had a colourful history of experimental political programming on radio before Congress passed the *Communications Act* in 1934. After the election broadcast of 1919, which could only be received by 40 000 radio sets (Mendelsohn and Crespi 1970, 256), New York Governor Al Smith used radio to appeal directly to the voters of New York State in 1924 when faced with an opposition attempt to thwart his legislative program. Smith's unsuccessful campaign for the American presidency in 1928 made heavy use of radio. That year, both major U.S. parties spent a record $10 000 000 on radio advertising.

From the outset, radio in the United States followed a more journalistic and commentary-oriented path, largely through its news commentary and round-table discussion formats. Daily radio commentators often extended their role as newscasters by introducing their own opinions, making a name for themselves and attracting a faithful listening audience (Peers 1969, 256). These commentaries were often sponsored by advertisers, and it was not unusual for regularly scheduled programs to feature speakers who espoused the views of their sponsors (ibid.).

In 1932, both NBC's 85 stations and CBS's 90 stations, along with many independent stations, broadcast the Democratic and Republican presidential nominating conventions live from Chicago (Broadcasting Publications 1982, 1). In spite of the Depression, the two parties spent a combined total of $5 million on radio time on the election campaign (Clark 1962, 236).

The emergence of political broadcasting in Western democracies was met with considerable resistance by the print media. This was especially the case in Great Britain. On 15 November 1923, one week after the opening of the British Broadcasting Company's first transmitter, the national election results were broadcast. Conservative Stanley Baldwin, the prime minister–elect, had used radio successfully in his campaign (Briggs 1985, 37). The broadcasting company retained the services of British press agencies to compile and transmit the results. Sir William Noble, a member of the company's board of directors, issued a memorandum requiring the cessation of broadcasting at 1:00 AM to ensure that the station did not reveal the final results before they appeared in the morning newspapers. Sir William declared, "We want to act in such a way that broadcasting may be an incentive to buy more newspapers" (ibid.). When, in 1924, John Reith, General Manager of the British Broadcasting Company, proposed to broadcast parliamentary debates, Prime Minister Bonar Law rejected the notion and referred to it as "undesirable" (ibid., 67). The editor of the journal *Popular Witness* also ridiculed the idea. An editor of another major newspaper accused Reith of "trying to take the bread out of our mouths" (ibid.).

As the use of radio by party leaders became more common, the British Broadcasting Company provided free time. As a result, the issue of allocation of time emerged. All three party leaders spoke on the radio in the 1924 general election. While the company was charged with deciding the number of these reserved periods, the allocation was to be the responsibility of the parties themselves. Apparently, the three parties could not agree, so the time was finally allocated by the company. The broadcasts enshrined the principle that the government and the Opposition must have access to approximately the same amount of air time prior to dissolution, and that each party must receive equal treatment during a campaign.

Successive British governments regularly imposed limitations on political broadcasting. When broadcasting was nationalized in 1927, the newly founded British Broadcasting Corporation (BBC) was forbidden to broadcast any editorial opinions of its own or any matter deemed controversial. Requests by the BBC in the 1920s to broadcast nonpartisan speeches by ministers, debates, and even the budget speech were denied by the minister in charge (Briggs 1985, 67–68). As will be seen, the CBC/SRC followed a similar policy of avoiding editorial comment.

The BBC won the right to schedule controversial material in 1929, although it was requested to be impartial in "admitting speakers to the microphone" (Peers 1969, 255). Initially, its cautious approach brought forth criticisms that it was too timid, especially over party broadcasts. In nonparty broadcasts, the Corporation proved more successful, airing debates by prominent speakers such as Bertrand Russell and dealing with many controversial questions, including those with international implications. Following complaints by the Foreign Office in 1936, the BBC became more cautious in the handling of its political questions in nonparty broadcasts (ibid., 256).

Political interference in the internal workings of the BBC and the continual frustration experienced by General Manager John Reith's attempts to institutionalize political broadcasts severely limited the coverage of political news well into the 1950s (Tunstall 1984, 9).

In addition, there appeared to be very little logic to the pattern. The limitations imposed on political coverage were arbitrary and apparently reflected the views of whoever happened to occupy the minister's office responsible for radio at any given point in time. Although the BBC covered election results, for many years campaign events did not appear on the daily news.

News and Information Programming

The dominance of entertainment programming in the early period of radio was accompanied by a general absence of information programming. For example, the CBC/SRC did not establish its own separate newsgathering and information service until 1941. One obstacle to broadcasters in developing their own programming was the competitive attitude of the newspaper industry, which resulted in limited access to its news service. For example, with the founding of the Canadian Radio Broadcasting Commission (CRBC) in 1932, the wire service Canadian Press (CP) had agreed to provide service only to the CRBC, and not to private broadcasters. The newspaper industry, which operated CP as a co-operative, seemed determined to curb the inroads being made by private broadcasters into its revenue base. In order to obtain the wire service, the CRBC and its successor, the CBC/SRC, agreed not to sell its newscasts to commercial sponsors. That same year, CP founded an exclusively broadcast service, Press News Limited (later Broadcast News), which it offered to both the CBC/SRC and private broadcasters (Nolan 1989, 506). Until the war years, the limited political news that most Canadians heard was designed in the editorial rooms of Canadian newspapers. As a result, many Canadian stations subscribed to American network services for international news coverage. For example, Montreal's French-language CKAC was a member of the CBS system as early as 1936 (Lavoie 1971, 36).

The development of broadcast news was also slow and cautious in Britain. It was not until 1930 that the BBC established a news operation. Under the leadership of Charles Siepmann, parliamentary events were cautiously reported in conjunction with the Reuters News Agency. Like the CBC/SRC, the BBC relied on the news agencies. A 1938 study of the British Press described BBC reports as "sober news ... which in the words of its news editor sets before itself the useful but nevertheless limited ideal of giving to the public a sober and accurate summary of the news which it receives from the four news agencies which are mentioned at least once a week by the announcer" (Political and Economic Planning 1938, 155).

Early Uses of Political Broadcasting

As a political medium, radio matured in the period between its founding and its first legislative controls in Canada, the United States and Britain. Most political broadcasts were treated as just one element in an increasingly expanding and sophisticated broadcasting environment. Beyond the formal transmission of political speeches and election results, several major political figures who realized the potential of this new medium exploited it successfully for their own specific agenda.

Alberta's William "Bible Bill" Aberhart forged his powerful Social Credit movement through his weekly radio broadcasts from the Calgary Prophetic Bible Institute, bypassing a hostile press. When he took power in 1935, his Social Credit movement had representatives in every corner of the province, although Aberhart had visited only a few of them personally. His success can be attributed to his radio presentation: "His sonorous voice rolled out from the radio each Sunday and it contained a message of hope, and what was more to the point, some sensible economics. The farmers who had a small radio would invite their friends and neighbours on a Sunday afternoon and the whole group would gather round and drink in his words like thirsty souls" (Irving 1972, 643). R.B. Bennett, the politician who withdrew from the CNR's early attempt at political broadcasting, had become a radio convert by 1935. Bennett, often suspected of being the ultimate economic conservative, announced his conversion to "New Deal" politics on national radio in January 1935 (Wilbur 1972, 586).

During the next decade, a steady stream of political leaders exploited the power of radio. William Lyon Mackenzie King succeeded not only to Bennett's prime ministerial office but also to his microphone at the national network. Franklin Delano Roosevelt's skilful mastery of his 84 "Fireside Chats," aired between March 1933 and January 1934, were significant events in radio broadcasting history (Mendelsohn and Crespi 1970, 259–60), as was Sir Winston Churchill's use of the BBC at the height of the Battle of Britain. In a more perverse way, radio aided the consolidation of two savage dictatorships in Germany and Italy. Commenting on Hitler and Mussolini, Churchill referred to them as "men of murder and the microphone" (Robbins 1971, 126). The highly partisan nature of the press spilled over into radio in the early years. The Quebec election of 1936 is a good illustration. The campaign was a battle between the long-ruling Liberal party and the Conservative–Reform–Liberal Alliance, which eventually became the Union nationale (UN). This alliance, led by Maurice Duplessis, had been experimenting with radio but found its access blocked by a well-entrenched newspaper and broadcasting cartel with strong Liberal connections. Nearly all of the private stations were owned by businesses (such as the CNR) or newspapers (such as *Le Soleil*) which were closely tied to the Liberal party. Nevertheless, Duplessis, a strong radio performer, gained enough access to the airwaves, especially through the CBC-French, to win. Radio had proved to be more open than the partisan press. Historians affirm that "the Union nationale owed its 1936 victory over the Liberals in significant measure to radio advertising, which had breached the wall of silence erected by a corrupt press, and that the establishment of Radio-Canada and the existence of private radio stations were responsible for the ultimate decline of the written press as a propaganda medium" [trans.] (Lavoie 1971, 42). The contest had been a wide-open and uncontrolled affair. The airwaves were filled with charges and counter-charges which led Liberal Louis-Alexandre Taschereau to suggest that political broadcasts be strictly regulated. He accused the Union nationale of conducting "une guérilla radiophonique" (ibid., 43).

Partisan advertising became a source of controversy during the 1935 federal election. A series of well-produced "soap opera" programs by the Conservative party pushed the issue of political broadcasting to the forefront. Of these broadcasts, the "Mr. Sage" series produced the most negative reaction. Six "Mr. Sage" programs were broadcast between 7 September and 11 October 1935. The Sage character was supposedly a small-town Ontario senior citizen who possessed ultimate political wisdom. A life-long Conservative, he invited his neighbours, many of whom held Liberal sympathies, to discuss politics on his porch. His obliging wife submissively agreed with his every word, especially when he offered suggestive remarks about Mackenzie King's personal and moral attitudes. Outraged, King protested to the chair of the CRBC, who in turn directed the Conservative party's advertising firm, the Gibbons Agency of Toronto, to inform listeners that the series was being sponsored by the Conservative party. The agency was also instructed to cease making judgements on the personal and moral character of Liberal politicians. The agency ignored the directive for its second broadcast, but the ensuing programs carried a disclaimer which declared that they were being sponsored by one R.L. Wright and "a group" of Conservatives. Direct connections to the federal Conservative party were never revealed to the public (Weir 1965, 202). The 1936 Quebec campaign and the 1935 Alberta campaign reinforced the 1935 federal experience to make clear the need for a framework of principles for political broadcasting.

All three countries whose political broadcasting histories are examined in this study shared some common dimensions. All faced severe hostility from newspaper owners and, with the exception of the Americans, conceded the reporting of the daily news to their print rivals. This severely hindered coverage of political events, with the result that political broadcasting was haphazard and ill-defined, and whatever images radio listeners formed about their political leaders were predetermined by newspaper editors and reporters. All broadcasters faced suspicious politicians and officials who wanted either to ensure that radio did not enter into any controversial activity or to retain some control over it. The watchdog role often played by the daily press was considered illegitimate in broadcasting. It was not until their respective governments decided to pass legislation to control the growth and influence of radio broadcasting that political broadcasting entered an era of legitimacy.

THE EMERGENCE OF REGULATORY STRUCTURES

When Canada, the United States and Britain chose to pass broadcast legislation, politicians defined the limits that they were prepared to tolerate when radio entered the political field. Although these countries shared some common experiences, more often than not their histories are peculiar to themselves. Canada, although the last to enact broadcast laws, defined the limits of political broadcasting more clearly than the others. The Americans viewed broadcasting as an extension of the private enterprise system. Britain viewed its public broadcasting system as an extension of the state structure. Canada opted for a mixed system. The tension between public service and private interests, therefore, was worked out in different ways in each country.

Canadian Legislation

In the initial stages, Canadian airwaves were dominated by American radio. Its shows and light programming had a proven audience appeal which was attractive to advertisers and was cost-effective for broadcasters. There were concerns, however, that Canadian radio was "flooded with programs expressing American experience, American ways of looking at themselves and the world, American popular culture and light entertainment" (Peers 1969, 254). At the same time, there were fears that free expression of opinion had less chance on private radio and that discussion of subjects with little popular appeal would be severely limited (ibid.). Thus began the extensive debate in Canada over the public and private uses of radio, especially with regards to political broadcasting.

The Royal Commission on Radio Broadcasting was established in 1928 to examine radio and to make recommendations as to the administration, management, control and financing of the Canadian airwaves. With Sir John Aird as Chair, the Commission submitted its Report in 1929: "While we are of the opinion that broadcasting of political matters should not be altogether banned, nevertheless, we consider that it should be very carefully restricted under arrangements mutually agreed upon by all political parties concerned" (Canada, Royal Commission 1929, 11). The Commission declared itself against the private use of what was considered a public domain. It envisaged a national radio network under public ownership and operation (Canada, Committee 1966, 361).

Following the recommendations of the Parliamentary Committee on Broadcasting in 1932, the Canadian Radio Broadcasting Commission was created through the *Broadcasting Act*. Its role was to provide for a national broadcasting service in Canada and to control all broadcasting while reserving an important place for commercial broadcasting (Peers 1969, 362). Initially, it was not deemed necessary to regulate political broadcasting as such. The question of "free access to the public air waves" (ibid.) subsequently became a subject of considerable debate as a result of the "Mr. Sage" incident during the 1935 federal election.

On 19 March 1936, immediately following the election, the House of Commons Committee on Radio Broadcasting was appointed to inquire into the operations of the Canadian Radio Broadcasting Commission and its administration of the *Broadcasting Act* of 1932, to investigate the extent of abuse of broadcasting privileges for political purposes, and to make recommendations on changes to the system (Peers 1969, 175). It was thought that the CRBC's regulations covering political broadcasting, which had been amended during the 1935 election, were too flexible: "No broadcasting station may broadcast any speech, printed matter or programme containing defamatory, libellous or obscene statements with regard to persons or institutions, or statements of a treasonable character or intended to promote change by unlawful means and which might lead to a breach of the peace, or any advertising matter containing false or deceptive statements" (Canada, Committee 1966, 363). Any political party following the regulations was entitled to use the Commission's stations, provided they had the money to pay for the air time (Foster 1982, 59). When the Committee reported to Parliament in 1936, it documented serious abuses of broadcasting for political purposes and concluded that the CRBC suffered from a lack of control in the administration of its affairs. Among other things, it recommended a more independent public corporation and more control over private broadcasters and the content of advertising (Canada, Committee 1966, 363).

As a result, the Canadian Broadcasting Corporation/Société Radio-Canada (CBC/SRC) was established through the 1936 *Canadian Broadcasting Act* as an independent statutory corporation which was to be impartial and non-controversial. (The CBC/SRC remained financially independent until 1952.) The clauses that related to political broadcasting, which continue to be the foundation of the legislative framework for political broadcasting today, were contained in section 22 of the Act:

(1) The Corporation may make regulations:

(*e*) to prescribe the proportion of time which may be devoted to political broadcasts by the stations of the Corporation and by private stations, and to assign such time on an equitable basis to all parties and rival candidates ...

(3) Dramatized political broadcasts are prohibited.

(4) The names of the sponsor or sponsors and the political party, if any, upon whose behalf any political speech or address is broadcast shall be announced immediately preceding and immediately after such broadcast.

(5) Political broadcasts on any dominion, provincial or municipal election day and on the two days immediately preceding any such election day are prohibited.

Subsequent to the legislation, the details of political broadcasting remained to be worked out. In addition to the allocation of paid and free time among the parties, there was the question of how the political broadcasts would be organized. The equitable allocation of time remained a delicate issue, leaving the CBC/SRC vulnerable to criticism from political parties (Canada, Committee 1966, 365). The CBC/SRC and the political parties set up a joint committee to study the problem and established the principle of free time for political parties during campaigns in 1939: "political broadcasting during a general election is to be on a sustaining or free basis ... Privately owned stations affiliated to the network are required to carry these broadcasts; and other private stations are *invited* to do so" (ibid.). In fact, the CBC/SRC allocated free time to the major political parties for the first time in the 1940 federal election (Nolan 1986, 170). Following the election, however, the Opposition charged that government ministers still had access to the airwaves for so-called nonpolitical speeches. To avoid charges of favouritism, in 1943 the CBC/SRC subsequently donated two hours of free time each month to all parties represented in the House of Commons (Canada, Committee 1966, 365; Kjosa and Paltiel 1970, 357).

The question of allocation of time remained unresolved. The policy was revised on 21 February 1944 to stipulate that if only two parties qualified for free time, it was to be divided equally between them. If more than two qualified, the government party was to receive two-fifths, and the remaining three-fifths was to be divided among the others. The CBC/SRC first gave free air time for provincial elections on 8 February 1943 (Canada, Committee 1966; Bird 1988). Thus a framework was established for party election broadcasts and for party broadcasts between elections.

With no legislative formula until 1974, the controversy over time allocation for free-time broadcasts continued. Until regulatory responsibilities were transferred to the new Board of Broadcast Governors (BBG) in the 1958 *Broadcasting Act*, the CBC/SRC controlled electoral broadcasting in negotiation with the parties. (In 1968, the BBG was replaced by the Canadian Radio–Television Commission, the CRTC.) In the 1944 amendments to the 1936 *Broadcasting Act*, the CBC/SRC was required to continue the free-time political broadcasts it had initiated on both of its national networks under the principles established with its first free-time allocations. All privately owned stations affiliated with CBC/SRC networks would be required to carry the broadcasts as part of their affiliation agreements. The CBC/SRC offered the programs to privately owned, independent stations on the condition that the broadcasts were self-sustaining and that all broadcasts in the series be transmitted. The CBC/SRC agreed to pay for hook-up and transmission charges (Bird 1988, 188).

Private stations were allowed to sell electoral advertising to parties and candidates. However, with the exception of cities in which only one radio outlet existed, all CBC/SRC stations stopped accepting paid political advertising (Bird 1988, 189). The 1944 amendments, which dictated the rules for the allocation of free time, among other things, remained virtually unchanged until the Report of the Royal Commission on Broadcasting in 1957 (Canada, Committee 1966, 365). At that time, the newly constituted BBG assumed the responsibility for both free-time and paid political broadcasts. The Board was given the legal right to make whatever regulations they deemed necessary. However, the BBG encouraged the parties and candidates to work out individual requirements with both local stations and networks, stepping in only when no agreement was reached (ibid., 369).

Regulation for free-time political broadcasts differentiated the broadcast media from the print media. Late in the winter of 1942, Glen

Bannerman, president of the Canadian Association of Broadcasters (CAB) which represented the private interests in the country, expressed deep resentment regarding the requirements imposed upon their industry. He reported that his 62 member stations had donated $760 291.43 worth of free time for political broadcasts in 1941 on a voluntary basis. The CAB was displeased with the enforcement of free-time broadcasts for stations affiliated with the CBC/SRC while the print media were not subject to any such requirements.

In addition to the free-time issue, radio was subject to consider-able pressure from interest groups. The CBC/SRC, conscious of its obli-gation as a public broadcaster, resisted the selling of advertising time for political broadcasting on the basis that commercial interests threat-ened the right of free expression: "We believe radio speech should be allowed to be forthright, provocative and stimulating ... We believe that national problems and international problems should be discussed by Canadian citizens without restriction or fear ... The free interchange of opinion is one of the safeguards of our democracy, and we believe we should be false to our trust as custodians of part of the public domain if we did not resist external control and any attempt to place a free air under the domination of the power of wealth" (Peers 1969, 261–62).

While the CBC/SRC was developing its policy of careful neutrality, some private broadcasters were moving into new areas of political broadcasting. For example, in 1942, Hamilton broadcaster Ken Soble, owner of radio station CHML introduced a program called "Inside Ottawa" which featured frequent appearances by local Liberal MP Colin Gibson, the Minister of National Revenue. In December 1943, the broad-cast was renamed "Report from Parliament Hill," and its local success convinced Soble that private broadcasting could benefit from political programming (*Canadian Broadcaster*, April 1944).

Soble took his concept to the annual convention of the CAB in Quebec City. The convention approved the idea and commissioned the CAB Public Relations Committee to meet with representatives of the three political parties in Ottawa. All parties agreed that private radio should receive equal recognition for its role in communicating political news with that of the daily press. The editor of the *Canadian Broadcaster*, Richard Lewis, endorsed the idea and urged all member CAB stations to carry such programs (*Canadian Broadcaster*, April 1944).

Private radio's involvement in political broadcasting was extended when Ottawa station CFRA began a daily series, "Today In Parliament." The broadcast, a summary of the day's events in the House of Commons, was written and delivered by Art McKenna, a member of the press gallery who was the correspondent for Canadian Dow Jones and the *Wall Street Journal*. Attention to election broadcasting continued to grow, but private broadcasters remained more interested in the drama of election night than in educating voters during the campaign. At the end of the decade, private broadcasters were subscribing to wire services which provided them with "live" election coverage. One service claimed to have provided live election background material: a complete list of candidates, biographies of members and leading contenders, feature-length sketches of party personalities, regional and national analyses of current political situations, histories of each riding, and firsthand pointers on critical contests (*Canadian Broadcaster and Telescreen*, 22 June 1949).

When politicians found themselves constrained by the regulations of the CBC/SRC, they often turned to the private sector. In January 1945, the Premier of Ontario, George Drew, assailed the CBC/SRC's political policy in a speech over Toronto radio station CFRB. Drew and the Ontario Progressive Conservative party believed that the CBC/SRC had censored a series of political broadcasts intended to discuss "matters of public interest." The CBC/SRC ruled that Drew's remarks were partisan, and as a result, should be treated as such. Drew, who intended to use the occasion to laud the performance of Canadian medical staff in treating war injuries in France and England, disagreed: "Freedom of speech cannot be half free and half muzzled. Either we have freedom of speech or we do not. This is something which affects every newspaper in this country. It affects every business organization in this country which advertises. It affects every individual who has the right to express his opinion and should express it on every possible occasion in regard to our public affairs" (*Canadian Broadcaster*, 20 January 1945).

American Legislation

The history of political broadcasting in the United States is characterized by the very strong judicial protection of freedom of the press under the First Amendment. The United States Constitution gave the mass media a strong legal basis for resisting government control. The crucial argument in support of regulation was that a broadcasting licence allowed private use of scarce public airwaves and that a public interest was involved (Graber 1991; Lichtenberg 1990). The *Communications Act* of 1934 has provided the legislative framework for American political and election broadcasting through principles set forth in section 315: the equal time rule, the fairness doctrine, and the right of rebuttal. Broadcasters who provided campaigning time to one candidate on their stations were obliged to provide the same opportunity to all other candidates. The fairness doctrine stipulated that

broadcasters who aired controversial issues must provide opportunities for conflicting viewpoints of the issues. The right of rebuttal ensured
a right of reply in cases of attack on the character, honesty or integrity
of a person or group.

Amid confusion and considerable debate over these clauses during
the 1940s and 1950s, in September of 1959 Congress amended the
Communications Act and enshrined two principles in American broadcast law as it affected political broadcasting. First, it removed the requirement for equal time provisions on news broadcasts and news interview
programs. Second, it embedded the fairness doctrine into law while
stating that the modification should not be interpreted as relieving
broadcasters of their responsibility to afford reasonable opportunity for
the discussion of conflicting views of public importance (Broadcasting
Publications 1982, 147–48). The concern was that the requirement of
fairness would discourage controversial broadcasting because groups
could claim their views had not been presented.

The amendment had an immediate impact on political broadcasts.
One year after Congress exempted news broadcasts and news interview programs from the equal-time provisions, the rule was waived
for the four Kennedy–Nixon televised debates in 1960. The net was
extended to include the vice-presidential contest as well, and in effect,
it excluded the nine other presidential candidates who ran that year
(Broadcasting Publications 1982). In a 1968 study, Thomas Guback
argued that the equal-time provisions had come to apply only to the two
major parties, the Democrats and Republicans. Minor parties were
virtually eliminated from the airwaves, and when they approached
broadcasting stations to purchase time, they were either refused or
offered rates higher than the two main parties (Guback 1968).

Throughout these challenges to section 315, the Federal
Communication Commission (FCC) maintained that it had an interest
in upholding the fairness doctrine. During the 1960s and 1970s, a series
of amendments required broadcasters to give equal time to persons
attacked in editorial comments. In addition, a broadcasting station that
sold time to a candidate's supporters was required to make available
for purchase on request an equal amount of time to the opponent's
supporters (Toohey 1974, 68).

Over the years, the fairness doctrine and right of rebuttal were criticized for impoverishing political debate by suppressing controversial
matters, while equal-time provisions were regarded as impeding
efficient election coverage (Graber 1991; Petrick 1976, 73–83). For
example, it was argued that FCC rulings on the question of equality
served only to confuse candidates and broadcasters alike, thus hindering

the development of controversial political broadcasting. Broadcasters were perceived as often denying access to certain groups and avoiding controversial subjects to escape requests to supply remedial access.

As a result, the FCC was under pressure to rescind section 315, especially the fairness provisions. The fairness doctrine was abandoned by the FCC under the Reagan Administration. Attempts by Congress to enact the provision as law in 1987 failed, with the FCC claiming that the rule was unconstitutional. The fairness rule remains unresolved at the present time (Graber 1991). Historically, however, this principle retains its significance for shaping the character of political broadcasting in the United States, as well as for providing examples of access rules for the emerging broadcasting system in Canada.

British Legislation

Developments in legislation in Great Britain reflected the continued desire of its politicians to regulate broadcasting activities. As in Canada and the United States, British legislative initiatives also prompted controversy and debate. On 10 February 1944, the government invoked the "fourteen-day rule" which prevented coverage of issues which were to be discussed in Parliament during the next fortnight (Briggs 1985, 292). The rule also prevented the discussion of any existing legislation or any issues deemed to be contentious (Tunstall 1984, 9). In part, the rule was invoked as a response to complaints by Conservative members of the House who felt that some BBC programs were giving more than the usual share of time to left-wing critics of the government. The Labour representatives were equally displeased because they felt that the programs were unusually kind to government perspectives (Briggs 1985, 216).

In 1947, a document named the "Aide Memoire" set out the BBC's political broadcasting obligations to the established parties. (The document was modified in 1948 to include the fourteen-day rule.) Political broadcasts were defined to include ministerial broadcasts for which a right of reply could be given to the Opposition with permission of the BBC, political public broadcasts (PPBs) during noncampaign periods and political education broadcasts (PEBs) during election campaigns. Both PEBs and PPBs were initially determined based upon the proportion of votes cast in the previous general election. A change to PPBs in 1974, however, ensured a time of 10 minutes for every two million votes cast for the party at the previous general election, with the government and the Opposition having the same number of broadcasts. Parties not represented in Parliament receive five minutes for PEBs if they contest 50 or more seats (Semetko 1991). An amendment to the

Aide Memoire in 1969 loosened the provisions somewhat by granting a right of reply to the Opposition and third parties in the case of controversial ministerial addresses without being subject to the approval of the BBC. A regular invoking of a right of reply resulted in many round-table discussions with Conservative and Labour party members and widened the spectrum of debate through the presence of Liberal party members (ibid.).

The fourteen-day rule issue was contested in 1955 when the host of the BBC's "In the News" complained that the program could not discuss the hydrogen bomb since a debate had been scheduled in Parliament within the fortnight. Backed by wide public support, the BBC announced that it would no longer observe the restriction. Nearly two years elapsed before Prime Minister Harold Macmillan suspended the rule indefinitely (Briggs 1985, 389). The fourteen-day rule has been the most prominent impediment to the development and acceptance of political broadcasting in Great Britain.

In Britain, political discourse on the air was discouraged, particularly if it showed a hint of partisanship, while many other industrial democracies such as Canada and the United States were encouraging its development. The BBC generally followed a cautious, conservative path (Boyle 1986), with the exception of broadcasts by government ministers which began during the war and continued until the advent of television in the early 1950s (Tunstall 1984, 11).

While matters such as the fourteen-day rule and the basic conservative approach of the BBC severely inhibited the growth of political broadcasting in Britain, it did encourage the reporting of political events on regularly scheduled newscasts, first on radio and later on television. Eventually, most Britons came to believe that BBC news reports and BBC-produced parliamentary summaries were capable of providing far more credible political news than the partisan PPBs.

Both the BBC and the Independent Television Authority (ITA) have been charged with the responsibility for enforcing the rules regarding political broadcasting in their own institutions. Although neither the BBC nor the ITA is required to carry party political broadcasts, they do respect the mutual need for both political parties and broadcasters to participate in such information programming. In addition to political public broadcasts, networks carry a range of interview shows and other programming dealing with political affairs.

In Canada, the United States and Great Britain, an overriding issue in the evolution of political and election broadcasting was the balance between free speech and fairness. Britain was perceived as too cautious under a heavy hand of government intervention. The American stations generally avoided broadcasting controversial issues initially, due to the uncertainty surrounding the *Communications Act*. The Canadian experience reflected continual debate between commercial and public interests. Similarly, the responses by these countries over the issue of the participation of minor parties in broadcasting have varied. In the United States, the free market approach favours wealthy parties and candidates over minor ones. In Canada, as in Great Britain, there is more scope given to minor parties, a result primarily of the commitment of the public systems to provide access to a wide range of viewpoints.

ADVENT OF TELEVISION

The years between 1952 and 1960 dramatically changed the role of radio in electoral and political broadcasting, marking the end of its brief period as the principal method of communication by which political leaders addressed their constituents. The growing importance of television not only changed the role of radio but also brought profound changes to the practices of political parties and journalisits. The changes had begun with radio but were dramatically accelerated by television.

The American Experience

Television's entry into political broadcasting occurred much earlier in the United States than in Canada, with coverage of the conventions of the Republican and Democratic parties in Philadelphia in 1948. While television coverage had limited impact on the election of Harry S Truman that year, only 12 years later, the Kennedy–Nixon debates confirmed the dominant role that television was to command in political broadcasting in subsequent years.

Television had begun to take an increasingly prominent role in American political broadcasting during the 1950s. Senator Joseph McCarthy exploited the medium to convince a good number of his fellow citizens that communists had infiltrated the infrastructure of American political life. Broadcaster Edward R. Murrow used the same medium to bring a halt to McCarthy's excesses (Merron 1988). Also during that time, the Republican presidential candidate, Dwight D. Eisenhower, shifted the bulk of his campaign media budget to television purchases. Eisenhower learned his role as a performer very well and, as the election result demonstrated, was far more comfortable with the medium than his opponent Adlai Stevenson, despite the latter's reputation as an outstanding public speaker (Gilbert 1986, 293).

In September 1960, the televised debates of presidential candidates John F. Kennedy and Richard M. Nixon were viewed in 75 million

American homes, reaching approximately three out of four eligible voters. Meanwhile, 30 million voters chose to listen to the debates on radio. Nixon suffered from the television exposure, although radio listeners felt that he was at least Kennedy's equal. Kennedy's success with the medium convinced campaign strategists of the power of television (Broadcasting Publications 1982, 149–50).

The British Experience
On 18 March 1947 from 10 Downing Street, Prime Minister Clement Attlee, leader of the Labour party, initiated the first broadcast dedicated to a party platform on radio (Briggs 1985, 380). In October 1951, Lord Samuel used television for the first time to solicit support for his Liberal party, and it marked the beginning of an emphasis on television at the expense of radio in political broadcasting in the United Kingdom (ibid., 382). Having lapsed after the experimental days of the 1930s and 1940s, full coverage of elections did not return to Great Britain until 1959, when the BBC and the independent television stations decided to broadcast electoral returns (Briggs 1985).

In 1952, 81 percent of the population of the United Kingdom could receive BBC television. While politicians had experimented with the medium in the early 1950s, several events throughout the latter part of the decade brought television into its own: a Conservative party conference in 1954, the first ministerial address in 1956, and debates over the nation's policy on the Suez crisis. On 28 October 1958, both the BBC and the independent ITV broadcast the opening of Parliament (Briggs 1985, 389).

The news coverage of the Suez crisis also marked the beginning of attempts by British broadcasters to operate at arm's length from government. In the spirit of fairness which had dominated the BBC since the days of John Reith, the network gave time for opposing opinions on the British-French invasion of Egypt. The government objected strenuously, but the BBC refused to budge. The decision was as much pragmatic as it was philosophical. The newer private network, ITV, which had begun telecasting in 1955, did not feel encumbered by the restrictions which dominated BBC thinking. Thus, the BBC found itself responding to ITV initiatives. It was ITV which brought electoral broadcasting back to Britain when it decided to cover a by-election in Rochdale in 1958. Shortly afterward, the 1959 general election received extensive coverage. The election was "the first one in which television took an active part and in which the politicians began building their campaigning around the television coverage" (Tunstall 1984, 9).

The Canadian Experience

For financial and regulatory reasons, television came later to Canada, enhancing American influences, since many Canadians were already receiving signals from south of the border. Political television began in 1953, when CBC/SRC television joined with radio to cover the federal election. It did not take long for television to eclipse radio and for election-night coverage to become a video production. Radio could not compete with the production values of television. As one observer noted after viewing the 1957 coverage: "On TV, continuous use was made of visual gimmicks like maps, charts and film inserts. Viewers were even able to watch the IBM Thinking Machine compute results for Norman DePoe to proclaim gloatingly. Commentaries, discussions, analyses and party leader statements left no dull moments between readings of results, and complete coverage was given in both English and French. Pick-up points for TV were Toronto, Winnipeg, Ottawa, Quebec, Montreal and Regina" (*Canadian Broadcaster and Telescreen*, 20 June 1957).

Although people in the industry expressed concern that radio was being overshadowed by television, politicians and political figures continued to use the Radio Bureau's "Report From Parliament Hill." In 1957, the series had recorded 146 members of Parliament, and their 15-minute broadcasts were sent to 90 stations from coast to coast. By the fall of 1957, however, it was reported that nearly two-thirds of Canada's four million households had purchased television sets. The election of John Diefenbaker as leader of the Progressive Conservative party in that same year was seen by millions of Canadians on CBC/SRC television (Peers 1979, 91). Within five years, programs with direct and indirect political messages were appearing on Canadian television screens. Viewers could choose political programs such as "Press Conference," "Cross Section," and "Ottawa Today," among others (Weir 1965, 398).

Policy Development

On 6 September 1958, the character and administration of Canadian broadcasting changed significantly with the passing of the new *Broadcasting Act*. The new legislation reflected the growing influence of the private sector (its rise in numbers and affluence) and the changed financial structure of the CBC/SRC. A deficit which had resulted from expansion after 1945 was exacerbated by the costly introduction of television, which had been delayed largely for financial reasons (Canada, Committee 1966, 365). The Act was intended to address one of the major complaints by Canada's independent broadcasters, who argued that the CBC/SRC should not be both a broadcaster and a regulator. The

CBC/SRC was relieved of its regulatory functions, which were assumed by the BBG, which had been created by the Act. In terms of political broadcasting, however, virtually nothing of significance was changed from the 1936 *Broadcasting Act* (Soderlund et al. 1984, 117).

In 1961, the BBG issued its *White Paper on Political and Controversial Broadcasting Policies*. It attempted to encourage the private sector while ensuring that broadcasting remained primarily a public service. The paper articulated four fundamental principles:

1. The air belongs to the people, who are entitled to hear the principal points of view on all questions of importance.
2. The air must not fall under the control of any individual or groups influenced by reason of their wealth or special position.
3. The right to answer is inherent in the doctrine of free speech.
4. The full interchange of opinion is one of the principal safeguards of free institutions.

In the spring of 1968, the new *Broadcasting Act* created the Canadian Radio-Television Commission (CRTC) to succeed the BBG. The amended Act was basically similar to the 1958 version, with one major exception. The new Act contained an explicit statement of the fundamental principles of political broadcasting (along with other statements of purpose):

(c) All persons licensed to carry on broadcasting undertakings have a responsibility for programs they broadcast but the right to freedom of expression and the right of persons to receive programs, subject only to generally applicable statutes and regulations, is unquestioned;

(d) the programming provided by the Canadian broadcasting system should be varied and comprehensive and should provide reasonable, balanced opportunity for the expression of differing views on matters of public concern. (Canada, *Broadcasting Act* 1968, s. 2(c), (d))

In 1974, a package of electoral reform included specific provisions for broadcasting. These included amendments to the *Canada Elections Act*, the *Broadcasting Act* and the *Income Tax Act*. Section 99 of the *Canada Elections Act* outlined the requirements for electoral broadcasting. First, all broadcasters were required to make six and one-half hours of paid time available to registered parties. Second, the formal definition of registered political parties led to recognition of parties not represented in the House of Commons. Third, network operators in both radio and TV were required to provide free time, with amounts differing among the networks. Fourth, an allocation formula which was applied to both paid and free time was established in law for the first time. While this formula favoured the major parties, it provided some time for new and minor parties.

The allocation of time to political parties not represented in Parliament remained contentious. In 1980, the federal political parties and the chief electoral officer agreed that the CRTC could resolve any disputes over the allocation of broadcast time for registered parties. As a consequence, the Social Credit party, the Communist party, the Libertarian party, the Marxist-Leninist party and the Parti Rhinocéros were each allocated a small amount of broadcast time (46 minutes in total). The CBC/SRC AM networks, Radio Mutuel, Telemedia, TVA Québec and CBC/SRC TV were required to donate free time to the parties in the same proportions which applied to purchased times (Soderlund et al. 1984).

The increasing participation of new parties in election campaigns was among the factors that led to creation of the position of broadcasting arbitrator in 1983. The arbitrator was responsible for having all registered parties work out a formula for broadcast time in the upcoming general election. In the event that an agreement could not be reached, the Arbitrator was authorized to render a decision (Canada, *Canada Elections Act* 1970, s. 99.15).

Canada has a more institutionalized system of election and political broadcasting than the United States or Britain. It involves not only the political parties and the broadcasters, both public and private, but also Elections Canada, the CRTC, which supervises many aspects of election broadcasting, and the Broadcasting Arbitrator. The system is one of regulated competition.[1] In the United States, in contrast, the ability of candidates to purchase air time determines their ability to communicate campaign messages to the public. The system is candidate-centred and money-driven.[2] Great Britain, while more committed to public enterprise, relies more on convention and consensus than formal regulation. The access to broadcast time by the minor parties, which have more legitimacy than in the United States, is a continuing issue in both the United Kingdom and Canada.

Journalistic Practices

The emergence of television in political broadcasting had a profound effect on journalistic practices and introduced a less partisan element in news reporting. In 1959, reporters working for the electronic media were admitted to membership in the parliamentary Press Gallery for the first time. Radio microphones and television cameras were not permitted in the chamber, but members could choose to appear on the electronic media by journeying to a room in the basement of the Parliament buildings where some limited broadcast facilities were available (Seigel 1983, 203–205). The move was significant on two accounts. It lessened the exclusive interpretative powers of the newspaper industry which had limited the scope of electronic reporting from its inception. As well, it assisted in the creation of the political reporters who became personalities in their own right, like the CBC's Norman DePoe. Political reporting reflected a more personal style without the overt partisanship that had characterized the print media.

The new technologies in political reporting found their way into Parliament after a decade of debate over the issue, when radio and television broadcast Queen Elizabeth opening a new session on 17 October 1977. The television coverage of both provincial and federal parliaments (the "Electronic Hansard") is currently transmitted to Canadian viewers on the parliamentary channels available to cable subscribers. These channels have considerable untapped potential to serve minority interests.

Political Parties
Political parties were profoundly altered by the advent of television, especially in the area of political advertising. The rise of political marketing based on mass advertising techniques coincided with the decline of traditional, localized, patronage-oriented, machine politics (Whitaker 1977, 218). This led to greater influence for advertising specialists and, later, market researchers (i.e., pollsters). Advertising agencies were utilized by political parties in political campaigns beginning in the 1920s and 1930s for radio and print campaigns. The development of broadcasting reduced the importance of newspapers as partisan instruments. The complexities of the new media led to an increasing reliance on "experts" who could advise the parties on the "exigencies of the electronic media" (Simpson 1988, 142).

The professionalization of political parties, resulting from their need for media experts, contributed to a decline in importance of volunteers to the campaign, thus distancing political parties from their supporters. This trend, along with the decline of the newspaper-dominated system before the advent of broadcasting, in which the party press and interpersonal networks connected political parties to their loyal voters, may have eroded the stability of people's political views and party identification (Smith 1981, 178). Television has played a central role in this destabilization by exposing viewers to numerous types of political viewpoints and arguments. Television audiences for news and public affairs have, in general, not been differentiated by partisan identification. These trends are now well established, as the coverage of elections is now dominated by television in all industrial democracies (Fletcher 1987). Political campaigns are organized around television because strategists are convinced that it is the best medium to reach the maximum number of voters at the minimum cost (ibid.).

In summary, a combination of the imperatives of television with the modern marketing techniques shaped by polling and new telecommunications technologies has dramatically altered election campaigns. Prior to the advent of television, political parties were the primary mediators between electors and politicians. Local candidates were a key part of the system of political communication, working through regional spokespersons in Parliament and constituency activists at home. Television enhanced the power of party leaders and party managers, shifting the balance of communication flows within the parties from bottom-up to top-down. Political marketing through television continued the trend begun by radio to regard elections as a national event, with the country seen as a single electoral district (or a few regions). There was, therefore, pressure to integrate local campaigns into the national one, an integration substantially aided by computers, electronic mail and fax machines (Lee 1989, 28–44). As will be seen, however, the era of the mass national audience appears to be coming to an end, suggesting that political parties will have to adjust to yet more changes in the communication structures they must use to seek public support.

RADIO IN THE AGE OF TELEVISION

Between 1952 and 1960, radio gave way to television as the predominant medium through which political figures in Canada, the United States and Great Britain addressed their constituencies. By 1966, when Canada began to consider revisions to its *Broadcasting Act*, television's dominance was apparent. In a survey taken that year, Canadians and Americans reported that their primary source of news was television (45 percent), but radio was close at 39 percent (*Canadian Broadcaster*, 14 December 1967). Television emerged as the dominant medium for advertisers, and politicians, advised by advertising executives, increasingly structured their campaign objectives around television.

Radio's decline in Canada as a vehicle for attracting mass audiences levelled off in the late 1960s with the advent of hit music stations and open-line shows. With the emergence of FM transmission in the early 1970s, the medium enjoyed higher audience shares. Although audiences continued to grow, they were shared among more and more outlets (Rutherford 1978, 86–87), and, as an advertising medium, its position against television has steadily declined. By 1973, total television advertising had moved ahead of that for radio,[3] and by 1989, television took in about twice as much advertising revenue as radio. Today, television attracts approximately two out of nine dollars spent on all forms of advertising in the country and remains the largest beneficiary of advertising allocations (Maclean-Hunter 1990).

In spite of commercial advertising trends to the contrary, politicians continue to spend significant sums on radio during election campaigns, although television remains the first choice of Canada's three major political parties. Spending does vary from election to election. Radio broadcasting accounted for over $3 million of election expenses in 1988 by the Progressive Conservative, Liberal, New Democratic and Christian Heritage parties. This is half the amount that was spent on television broadcasting. Radio advertising, as a percentage of total election expenses by the three mainstream parties, was second to television but not much larger than print. Individual candidates, however, spent more on print as a portion of their advertising budget and less on radio and television (Canada, Elections Canada 1988).

While the dominance of television in national campaigns has been established in recent years through leaders debates and extensive advertising campaigns, print and radio play a more prominent role at the constituency level. In a recent survey, 91 percent of local party strategists reported that newspapers played a somewhat or very important role in their campaigns. The figures for radio and television were 65 percent and 60 percent respectively (Carty 1991). Radio is of more importance to the local campaign in rural areas. In ridings that were predominantly rural, 78 percent of respondents reported that radio was a somewhat or very important feature of the campaign, as compared to 56 percent in urban ridings. One reason for this greater emphasis on radio could be that it is the source of more local news. People who are active in the community seem to pay somewhat more attention to radio news, possibly for this reason (MacDermid 1991).

There are differing opinions on the effectiveness of radio in political campaigns, with some observers arguing that radio's continuing presence in advertising campaigns has less to do with its effectiveness as a medium of influence and more to do with pure economics. Radio continues to be the cheapest form of advertising in Canada, and the most flexible, as it can normally be purchased on very short notice. As well, radio plays a largely supportive role in national campaigns, often as an "add-on" to print and television campaigns. Seldom, if ever, is radio treated as an advertising vehicle in its own right in national party strategies.

Radio's decline as an advertising medium is the result not only of the rise of television but also of audience fragmentation. The proliferation of stations in large centres where there are usually four to five times as many radio as television stations is compounded by the wide variety of radio formats in use. Cross-tuning in radio, where listeners sample several stations, preceded the "zapping" made possible by television remote controls. Among the problems created by these developments is the difficulty of conducting reliable audience analysis for radio, which makes advertising planning difficult.

Radio continues to be seriously challenged by new technological developments in television which erode radio's comparative advantages – music programming, immediacy and mobility. The portable Betacam and mobile satellite dish have made television news almost as immediate as radio. As well, small, battery-driven mini-television sets now permit viewers to take their favourite sporting event, news report or music program to almost any place where an off-air signal is available. In addition, television can now transmit high quality sound via cable, and music videos are cutting into the radio audience for popular music.

For a variety of reasons, however, political parties continue to allocate significant sums to campaign advertising on radio. The most important reason is that radio listening has remained for the most significant part a local experience, allowing effective targeting by riding, especially in smaller centres. In addition, radio is deemed by some strategists to be very effective in leaving general impressions with listeners whose primary attention is elsewhere. Radio serves as background to many other activities and can be used to promote images and impressions.

SUMMARY AND CONCLUSION

Despite its current role as a junior partner in Canada's media mosaic, radio was once the significant player in the development of this country's political broadcasting history. Current electoral practices and the laws that govern them in Canada, as in the United States and Great Britain, began with the introduction of radio as a centralizing mass medium in the second decade of this century. Radio changed the character and methods by which political campaigning took place, both during and between elections. Radio, and later television, turned the abstract politician whose activities were recorded in the daily press into a tangible human being. With the advent of the electronic carrier, every Canadian had the opportunity to be a spectator at an electronic whistle stop. However, the introduction of radio and television as an electoral vehicle reduced community participation in political life. Action became centralized in large communities across the nation. Issues became national issues, political life became professionalized, and communication took on a one-way character, from the centre to the periphery.

From humble beginnings with the reporting of election results, the broadcast media have become a dominant feature of modern election campaigns. The leader tours which were once a crucial link between local party activists and their parties are now little more than "pseudo-events" staged for television. Politicians had to come to terms with television as they had with radio, as they inevitably must with new communication technologies not yet imagined.

The "Mr. Sage" affair was a watershed in Canadian electoral and broadcasting history. It made the need for some form of regulation clear, underlining the potential for abuse. The state had an obligation to protect both politicians and the public from unscrupulous activity. The development of the public broadcasting system and of our approach to political and election broadcasting was influenced by the "fallout" from the "Mr. Sage" affair and its provincial counterparts. The fundamental principles of fairness and equity that govern political broadcasting today have their roots in the early days of radio. They derive especially from a concern that radio and, later, television might have enormous influence on public opinion, an influence that had to be regulated to ensure fairness in political competition.

Election broadcasting, through its evolution, has affected not only the strategies of politicians but also the information available to voters. Radio, like television and the print media, has suffered from continuing audience fragmentation. For television audiences, the fragmentation began with the advent of cable licensing of new broadcast enterprises and has been perpetuated by the increasing presence of national satellite channels (MuchMusic, The Sports Network, CBC Newsworld, Vision TV, Weather Now, YTV) and regional carriers. Emerging services such as pay-per-view and imported superstations promise to contribute to the fragmentation. Reaching appropriate audiences with appropriate information at convenient times is becoming increasingly difficult.

There is little doubt that we are again on the verge of important changes in the mass media. Even the large U.S. networks, such as ABC, NBC and CBS are being forced to "narrowcast" their programming in order to seek a formula for survival. Of course, this has major implications for the future of political and electoral broadcasting. Paid advertising on commercial television stations will become more costly and less effective. Yet, while advertising agencies and advertising planners remain unable to free themselves from an antiquated mass-media mentality, effective channels of communications go underutilized. A much more extensive political and electoral broadcasting system could be developed around the hundreds of community channels on Canadian cable systems or the cable channels assigned to both federal and provincial parliaments which lie vacant when these legislative chambers are not in session. In addition, the local and intimate communication provided by radio should not be ignored. The advent and growth of non-profit community broadcasting opens up new possibilities for alternative programming, including political programming.

The disintegration of the mass audience has prompted parties and candidates to turn to individualized methods of campaign communication such as direct mail and telemarketing. These methods have the advantage of providing well-timed, customized messages that address the concerns of targeted groups of electors. However, they remove important aspects of the campaign debate from the public arena. Public discourse would be better served if such targeted messages were channelled through appropriate public media, such as cable television or community radio, leaving open the possibility of debate and dialogue.

What is the future of radio in election broadcasting in Canada and other industrial democracies? Although the decline of radio as a dominant political medium began in the early 1950s, it still occupies a small role in contemporary political broadcasting. In the United States, radio enjoyed a brief revival during the Reagan years when the President returned to the medium following concerns about his treatment in the press and in television editing rooms. In a somewhat ironic case, it would seem that the most interested listeners to the President's radio broadcasts were the daily press and television, who covered the events widely.

Some observers of the industry see a very bleak future for radio. The demise of the financially unsuccessful radio news information network CKO raised questions about the viability of all-news radio, especially on FM. It seems clear that private radio is about to undergo significant restructuring, and it will take imagination and commitment to retain channels other than CBC/SRC for effective political broadcasting.

Consideration of the future of radio must take place in the context of the impact of communication technologies in general on political communication. The demise of the partisan press, promoted in part by radio, required political parties to find new channels through which to mobilize supporters and seek converts. The fragmentation of the mass audiences of radio and television requires new adjustments. The fact that "narrowcasting," especially through cable television, direct mail and telemarketing are increasingly important in the United States suggests that such trends are likely accelerating in Canada as well (Abramson et al. 1988, 14).

A resurfacing of "localism" in news coverage may mean increased importance for broadcasting services, such as cable television and radio, which can be easily localized (Abramson et al. 1988, 41). A great potential for radio lies in its capacity as an immediate and intimate medium to reconnect the links between the public and political figures. Radio continues to play a role in constituency-level campaigning, especially in rural areas where candidates engage in live radio debates and audience phone-in segments. As well, radio performs a vital role in national and regional issue debates. CBC-English programs such as "Morningside," "As It Happens" and "Cross-Country Check-up" provide a valuable connection between listeners, who often participate through telephone contact, and political personalities and leaders. While CBC/SRC programs rarely have a mass audience and some may have low ratings, they do appeal to the politically attentive segment of the population. In addition, it is the potential of the medium to rekindle meaningful, participatory, public debate which is our concern. As renowned political strategist Keith Davey put it in a nonpolitical context, "radio is not simply an afterthought to television, but a separate vital medium of communication" (Davey 1986, 124).

In short, our concern with radio is not simply with its past but also with the light that past experience casts on the likely influence of newer technologies and with the potential of radio and other new communication technologies to provide more effective links between candidates and electors. It is important that regulators and politicians consider the longer-term implications for the legitimacy of the electoral system – and, indeed, the political system – of the communications choices they make.

ABBREVIATIONS

am.   amended

c., ch.   chapter

en.	enacted
Pub. L.	Public Law (U.S.)
R.S.C.	Revised Statutes of Canada
S.C.	Statutes of Canada
s(s).	section(s)
Stat.	Statute

NOTES

This study was completed in July 1991.

The authors wish to thank the anonymous peer reviewers and Frederick J. Fletcher for their comments on an earlier version of this paper. Extensive revisions have been undertaken in response to their excellent suggestions. The authors, however, accept responsibility for the final version.

1. The *Broadcasting Act* of 1991 made no significant alterations in the structure of broadcast regulation or the rules and objectives of political broadcasting (Thompson-Pyper 1991).

2. It is important to note, however, that despite the predominance of private broadcasting, the United States has seen the emergence of a public broadcasting system. Originating in 1952 as an educational television system, it evolved slowly throughout the 1960s and 1970s until financial cuts in the 1980s. Currently there are calls for a new public broadcasting system which would strike a balance between commercial interests and state control (Kellner 1990, 201–207). Recent proposals suggest a possibly expanded role for the public broadcasting system in campaign communication.

3. In 1974, CBC/SRC radio stopped accepting advertising. However, it is required under the *Canada Elections Act* to make paid time available to registered political parties during the campaign advertising period (Canada, *Canada Elections Act* 1985, s. 307).

BIBLIOGRAPHY

Abramson, Jeffery, Christopher Arterton and Gary Orren. 1988. *The Electronic Commonwealth*. New York: Basic Books.

Bird, Roger, ed. 1988. *Documents of Canadian Broadcasting*. Ottawa: Carleton University Press.

Board of Broadcast Governors. 1961. *Political and Controversial Broadcasting Policies*. Ottawa: BBG.

Boyle, Alan E. 1986. "Political Broadcasting, Fairness and Administrative Law." *Public Law* (Winter): 562–96.

Briggs, Asa. 1985. *The BBC: The First Fifty Years*. Oxford: Oxford University Press.

Broadcasting Publications. 1982. *The First Fifty Years of Broadcasting: The Running Story of the Fifth Estate*. New York.

Canada. *Broadcasting Act, 1932*, S.C. 1932, c. 51.

———. *Broadcasting Act*, S.C. 1958, c. 22.

———. *Broadcasting Act*, S.C. 1968, c. 25.

———. *Broadcasting Act*, R.S.C. 1970, c. B-11, am. 1973–74, c. 51, s. 17.

———. *Broadcasting Act*, S.C. 1991, c. 11.

———. *Canadian Broadcasting Act, 1936*, S.C. 1936, c. 24.

———. *Canada Elections Act*, R.S.C. 1970, c. 14 (1st Supp.). s. 99, am. 1973–74, c. 51, s. 13; 99.15, en. 1980–81–82–83, c. 164, s. 17.

———. *Canada Elections Act*, R.S.C. 1985, c. E-2, s. 307.

———. *Income Tax Act*, R.S.C. 1952, c. 148, am. 1973–74, c. 51, s. 18.

Canada. Committee on Election Expenses. 1966. *Report*. Ottawa: Queen's Printer.

Canada. Elections Canada. 1988. *Report of the Chief Electoral Officer Respecting Election Expenses 1988*. Ottawa: Minister of Supply and Services Canada.

Canada. Royal Commission on Broadcasting. 1957. Ottawa: Queen's Printer.

Canada. Royal Commission on Radio Broadcasting. 1929. *Report*. Ottawa: King's Printer.

Canadian Broadcaster. 1942–90. (This includes the *Canadian Broadcaster and Telescreen*, the *Telecaster* and the *Broadcaster*.)

Carty, R.K. 1991. *Canadian Political Parties in the Constituencies: A Local Perspective*. Vol. 23 of the research studies of the Royal Commission on Electoral Reform and Party Financing. Ottawa and Toronto: RCERPF/Dundurn.

Clark, David G. 1962. "Radio in Presidential Campaigns: The Early Years (1924–1932)." *Journal of Broadcasting* 6 (Summer): 229–38.

Cornwell, Elmer E., Jr. 1957. "Coolidge and Presidential Leadership." *Public Opinion Quarterly* 21(2): 263–78.

Davey, Keith. 1986. *The Rainmaker: A Passion for Politics*. Toronto: Stoddart.

Fletcher, Frederick J. 1987. "Mass Media and Parliamentary Elections in Canada." *Legislative Studies Quarterly* 12(3): 341–72.

Foster, Frank. 1982. *Broadcasting Policy Development*. Ottawa: Canadian Radio-television and Telecommunications Commission.

Gilbert, Robert E. 1986. "The Eisenhower Campaign of 1952: War Hero as Television Candidate." *Political Communications and Persuasion* 3(3): 293–311.

Graber, Doris A. 1991. "The Mass Media and Election Campaigns in the United States of America." In *Media, Elections and Democracy*, ed. Frederick J. Fletcher. Vol. 19 of the research studies of the Royal Commission on Electoral Reform and Party Financing. Ottawa and Toronto: RCERPF/Dundurn.

Guback, Thomas H. 1968. "Political Broadcasting and Public Policy." *Journal of Broadcasting* 12:191–211.

Innis, Harold A. 1951. *Bias of Communication*. Toronto: University of Toronto Press.

———. 1972. "Paper and the Printing Press." In *Empire and Communications*. Toronto: University of Toronto Press.

Irving, John A. 1972. "The Social Credit Movement in Alberta." In *The Dirty Thirties*, ed. Michiel Horn. Toronto: Copp Clark.

Kellner, Douglas. 1990. *Television and the Crisis of Democracy*. Boulder: Westview Press.

Kjosa, Larry J., and Khayyam Z. Paltiel. 1970. "The Structure and Dimensions of Election Broadcasting in Canada." *Jahrbuch des Offetlich en Rechts der Genewart* 19:355–82.

Lavoie, Elzéar. 1971. "L'Évolution de la radio au Canada français avant 1940." *Recherches sociographiques* 12:17–49.

Lee, Robert Mason. 1989. *One Hundred Monkeys: The Triumph of Popular Wisdom in Canadian Politics*. Toronto: Macfarlane Walter and Ross.

Lichtenberg, Judith, ed. 1990. *Democracy and the Mass Media*. Cambridge: Cambridge University Press.

London Free Press. 17 August 1925.

McAllister, Ian. 1985. "Campaign Activity and Electoral Outcomes in Britain." *Public Opinion Quarterly* 49:489–503.

MacDermid, R.H. 1991. "Media Usage and Political Behaviour." In *Media and Voters in Canadian Election Campaigns*, ed. Frederick J. Fletcher. Vol. 18 of the research studies of the Royal Commission on Electoral Reform and Party Financing. Ottawa and Toronto: RCERPF/Dundurn.

Maclean-Hunter Research Bureau. 1990. *Advertising Revenues in Canada.* Toronto: Maclean-Hunter.

Mendelsohn, Harold, and Irving Crespi. 1970. *Polls, Television, and the New Politics.* Scranton: Chandler.

Merron, Jeff. 1988. "Murrow on TV." *Journalism Monographs* (July).

Nolan, Michael. 1986. *Foundations: Alan Plaunt and the Early Days of CBC Radio.* Montreal: CBC Enterprises.

————. 1989. "An Infant Industry: Canadian Private Radio 1919-36." *Canadian Historical Review* 70:496–518.

Peers, Frank W. 1969. *The Politics of Canadian Broadcasting 1920–1951.* Toronto: University of Toronto Press.

————. 1979. *The Public Eye.* Toronto: University of Toronto Press.

Petrick, Michael J. 1976. " 'Equal Opportunities' and 'Fairness' in Broadcast Coverage of Politics." *Annals of the American Academy of Political and Social Sciences* 427 (September): 73–94.

Political and Economic Planning. 1938. *Report on the British Press.* London: PEP.

Robbins, R. Cynewulf. 1971. "The Magnificent Music Box." In *A Media Mosaic,* ed. Walt McDayter. Toronto: Holt, Rinehart and Winston of Canada.

Rutherford, Paul. 1978. *The Making of the Canadian Media.* Toronto: McGraw-Hill Ryerson.

Seigel, Arthur. 1983. *Politics and the Media.* Toronto: McGraw-Hill Ryerson.

Semetko, Holli A. 1991. "Broadcasting and Election Communication in Britain." In *Media, Elections and Democracy,* ed. Frederick J. Fletcher. Vol. 19 of the research studies of the Royal Commission on Electoral Reform and Party Financing. Ottawa and Toronto: RCERPF/Dundurn.

Simpson, Jeffrey. 1988. *Spoils of Power: The Politics of Patronage.* Toronto: JCS Publications.

Smith, Anthony. 1981. "Mass Communications." In *Democracy at the Polls: A Comparative Study of Competitive National Elections,* ed. David Butler, Howard Penniman and Austin Ranney. Washington, DC: American Enterprise Institute for Public Policy Research.

Soderlund, Walter C., Walter I. Romanow, Donald E. Briggs and Ronald H. Wagenberg. 1984. *Media and Elections in Canada.* Toronto: Holt, Rinehart and Winston of Canada.

Thompson-Pyper, Cathy. 1991. "Implications of the 1991 Broadcasting Act for Election Broadcasting." Paper prepared for the Royal Commission on Electoral Reform and Party Financing. Ottawa.

Toohey, Daniel W., ed. 1974. *Legal Problems in Broadcasting*. Lincoln: Great Plains National Instructional Television Library, University of Nebraska.

Tunstall, Jeremy. 1984. *The Media in Britain*. London: Constable.

United States. *Communications Act of 1934*, June 19, 1934, ch. 652, 48 Stat. 1064 (Title 47, 35, 151–155, 201–221, 301–329, 401–416, 501–505, 601–609), s. 315.

———. ———. *Amendment of Sept. 14, 1959*, Pub. L. 86–274.

———. *Constitution of the United States*, 1788.

———. ———. *First Amendment*, 1791.

———. *Radio Act of 1927*, Feb. 23, 1927, ch. 169, 44 Stat. 1162 (Title 47, 81 et seq.).

Weir, E. Austin. 1965. *The Struggle for National Broadcasting in Canada*. Toronto: McClelland and Stewart.

Whitaker, Reginald. 1977. *The Government Party: Organizing and Financing the Liberal Party of Canada 1930–58*. Toronto: University of Toronto Press.

Wilbur, J.R.H. 1972. "R.B. Bennett as a Reformer." In *The Dirty Thirties*, ed. Michiel Horn. Toronto: Copp Clark.

2

THE LEGAL AND CONSTITUTIONAL FRAMEWORK FOR REGULATING ELECTION CAMPAIGN BROADCASTING

Pierre Trudel
France Abran

ELECTION BROADCASTING and radio and television campaign advertising have directly affected the development of Canadian broadcasting law. Rightly or wrongly, Canadian law has developed on the premise that political messages broadcast at election time can significantly influence results at the polls. Thus, a set of rules circumscribes the broadcasting of partisan advertising and other transmissions during election campaigns.

Theoretically, the general principles flowing from the *Broadcasting Act* apply to political messages broadcast at election time. The *Canada Elections Act* sets out specific rules concerning advertising broadcasts during federal election campaigns. During provincial and municipal elections, provincial legislation governs partisan advertising (i.e., advertising that promotes a political party or candidate).

Freedom of expression, of the press and of other communications media is affirmed in section 2(*b*) of the *Canadian Charter of Rights and Freedoms.* This principle has constitutional value and is set above all other laws.[1] That is why it is important to remember that laws and regulations pertaining to messages broadcast by radio and television must be compatible with the freedoms guaranteed by the Constitution. In

Canada, the courts have the ultimate responsibility for determining the compatibility of laws with the Constitution. Consequently, reference must be made to the criteria established by the courts for the interpretation of Charter rights in order to establish compatibility of state-initiated measures with constitutional provisions.

Regulation of electoral messages once raised only normative issues. The constitutionalization of freedom of expression, however, has made many of these issues legal ones. Laws and regulations governing matters of expression must henceforth be justified according to constitutional criteria. State intervention is not automatically acceptable under the Charter.

The legal framework for the broadcasting of election messages is based primarily on certain values and rationales and on demands to entrench aspects of these values in law. When the legal framework helps implement policies, it generally relies on the values that it is attempting to reflect. Such values are often contradictory. This framework cannot be analysed without looking at these values.

For the most part, these laws are aimed at reconciling the competing claims and values that arise for any issue. Thus, understanding the legal dimensions of an issue, such as the broadcasting of election campaign messages, requires a familiarity with the existing and potential rationales underlying the current legislation.

Moreover, before attempting to induce behaviour that conforms to the objectives underlying a given set of laws, one must be sufficiently familiar with the fundamental aspects and workings of available regulatory mechanisms.

The analysis of the legal framework of election campaign broadcasting in this study is the result of a combined review of both the "rationales" underlying the statutory and regulatory provisions for election campaign broadcasting and the instruments used to establish standards in an area such as campaign advertising.

It must be understood that this study presents a legal assessment, conducted according to legal methodology. It is neither a history of the regulation of election broadcasting nor a survey of those who work with the regulations. References to historical precedents and practices are intended only to enlighten the legal assessment.

Any assessment of the soundness of the rules governing election campaign broadcasting and advertising on radio and television gives rise to a number of questions. Should legislation be broadly drafted or should it provide for all necessary details? Should a regulatory agency impose a ban through regulation or by setting out conditions on an ad hoc basis? Or is it more advantageous to rely on self-regulation practised by the various "actors"? These are the types of technical and regulatory questions that must be answered by those in charge of developing instruments for policy implementation.

The various regulatory techniques likely to affect the election broadcasts must be examined. The adoption of one or another or a combination of regulatory techniques helps define the interplay between the rights, obligations and interests of the different actors involved in disseminating information.

Regulatory rationales and techniques come into play at many levels. Thus, there are reasons for taking different approaches to regulating radio and television and to regulating print media. There are also reasons that support the rules concerning the broadcasting of political programs during and outside election periods. Likewise, there are justifiable grounds for the legislative and regulatory choices regarding political and electoral advertising. These reasons, however, must be analysed in the light of the requirements dictated by the supremacy of fundamental rights and freedoms. The fact that a majority may advocate a measure does not necessarily mean that the measure conforms to constitutional standards. Nor is the conviction that certain messages or behaviours negatively affect certain groups sufficient to demonstrate that prohibiting such messages or behaviours is reasonable and justifiable under the Charter.

The first part of this study examines the fundamental rights that are most affected by the rules governing election campaign broadcasting. We identify the statements and reasoning used to justify the regulatory systems that deal with election campaign broadcasting. In the second part, regulatory approaches used to achieve more specific objectives are studied. Each approach is then examined by the test developed in Canadian law for evaluating its compatibility with the right of freedom of expression.

FUNDAMENTAL RIGHTS AND FREEDOMS GUARANTEED
BY THE CONSTITUTION

Radio and television election broadcasting calls into question a number of fundamental rights and freedoms. The production and dissemination of information obeys principles that, to a certain extent, are guaranteed by law. Freedom of expression is certainly at the heart of the laws that govern radio and television. Yet, this freedom has been the object of special interpretations that intended to take account of the specific nature of broadcasting. Limitations on this freedom have been based on these interpretations, as well as the practical significance these interpretations are to take. That is why the laws governing broadcasting in the electronic media differ from the laws that govern the press.

Other values and fundamental rights are relevant in an analysis of election messages. Among them, we must include the right to vote, the right to seek public office and the obligation to exercise democratic rights.

To gain a better understanding of the nature and scope of certain rights now guaranteed in our constitutional texts, recourse to American analyses and precedents can prove extremely useful. It is clear that these precedents are not binding under Canadian law. American laws are often quite different from Canadian laws. As well, these precedents are never used to set out what is or what should be. They serve essentially as indications of how to define fundamental rights. In *R. v. Keegstra* (1990), the Supreme Court indicated to what extent Canadian courts can rely on American jurisprudence. Then Chief Justice Dickson pointed out: "In the United States, a collection of fundamental rights has been constitutionally protected for over two hundred years. The resulting practical and theoretical experience is immense, and should not be overlooked by Canadian courts. On the other hand, we must examine American constitutional law with a critical eye" (ibid., 740). In *R. v. Committee for the Commonwealth of Canada* (1991, 178), Madam Justice L'Heureux-Dubé wrote that "it may be helpful ... to look at the American experience, not with a view to applying their decisions blindly but rather to learn from the process through which they were derived."

Thus, in our effort to glean principles applicable to election campaign broadcasting on radio and television, we shall be looking at analyses proposed in American jurisprudence. These precedents will not be analysed as if they reflected the state of Canadian law; rather, they will help us discern the subtleties of certain rights and notions in Canadian law.

Apart from freedom of expression, other fundamental rights are exercised in the electoral context, such as the right to vote and to seek public office. In the name of ensuring full enjoyment of these rights, it is conceivable that broadcasters will have less and less room to manoeuvre.

The Right to Vote and to Seek Public Office

Sections 3, 4 and 5 of the *Canadian Charter of Rights and Freedoms* deal with democratic rights. The right to vote and to seek public office is set out in section 3, which states: "Every citizen of Canada has the right to vote in an election of members of the House of Commons or of a legislative assembly and to be qualified for membership therein."

Gérald-A. Beaudoin underscores the importance of the right to vote, going so far as to write that "after the right to life and liberty, it is one of the most fundamental rights" (1989, 268). This right is explicitly recognized in the *International Covenant on Civil and Political Rights.* Article 25 of the Covenant states that:

> Every citizen shall have the right and the opportunity, without any of the distinctions mentioned in article 2 and without unreasonable restrictions:
> a) to take part in the conduct of public affairs, directly or through freely chosen representatives;
> b) to vote and to be elected at genuine periodic elections which shall be by universal and equal suffrage and shall be held by secret ballot, guaranteeing the free expression of the will of the electors;
> c) to have access, on general terms of equality, to public service in his [or her] country.

This Covenant was ratified by Canada on 19 May 1976 (Beaudoin 1989, 268).

As a result of the constitutional entrenchment of the right to vote, electoral legislation and the conditions imposed on the right to exercise the franchise are now subject to the criterion of "reasonableness," as set out in section 1 of the *Canadian Charter of Rights and Freedoms.*

Thus, members of the House of Commons are elected by universal suffrage. Electoral law also establishes the qualifications and conditions required to have the right to vote. A distinction is made between what qualifies a person to vote and the conditions of exercising that right. Because section 15 of the Charter opposes measures that would result in creating unequal voting rights among citizens, the measures that establish the conditions for exercising the right to vote must also meet the reasonableness test.

In *Dixon v. British Columbia (Attorney General),* Madam Justice McLachlin (then a judge of the Supreme Court of British Columbia) explains that: "It cannot be denied that Canadian society rests in large part on the traditional liberal ideal of equal respect for the dignity and worth of each individual. Where political rights are concerned, this ideal would accord equal rights to participate freely with one's fellow citizens in the establishment of the laws and rules which govern the conduct of all. The correlative of liberty is the assurance that each citizen is equally entitled to participate in the democratic process and that each citizen carries an equal voice in that process" (*Dixon* 1989, 259).

After considering the historical origins of American and British electoral systems, Madam Justice McLachlin concluded that the concept of equality is inherent in the Canadian concept of voting rights.

This concept of complete equality of voting rights has a substantive component. In *Reference re Provincial Electoral Boundaries* (1991), the Saskatchewan Court of Appeal based its findings on the American legal decision of *Reynolds v. Sims* (1964, 523–24) to affirm that an individual's right to vote cannot be diluted by measures that affect the relative weight of such a vote.

It may be presumed that true equality in the right to vote and in the exercise of that right is ensured by an electoral system designed so as not to favour unduly certain groups or political parties to the detriment of others. Brun and Tremblay observe that: "In a subtle way, an electoral system can be arranged in such a way that the vote of some people is worth more than that of others. This effect may be achieved either directly through unequal suffrage, such as familial suffrage wherein the male head of the household enjoys multiple votes, or indirectly ... by means of different polling methods or gerrymandering" (1990, 273).

Brun and Tremblay recognize that the right to vote, while still guaranteed in a formal sense, can become illusory or be diminished in scope as a result of how it is exercised. They add that:

> Even if the universal right to vote is recognized, it may be exercised in conditions whereby representativeness is diminished. Thus, depending on whether the vote is secret or public, it will represent more or less of a free vote and will translate with more or less accuracy the true opinion of the electorate. Similarly, an electoral system must be arranged so as to prevent undue pressure and voter-tampering as much as possible. Not only must it provide penalties for corrupt practices, but it must also ensure that such practices do not take place. The voter must have a real opportunity to express his or her opinion. (1990, 273)

It may be said that preserving the integrity of the right to vote and of the ability to exercise it effectively is a corollary of the constitutionally guaranteed right to vote. On that basis, therefore, it is possible to justify the restriction of practices that might deprive certain persons of the ability to exercise that right.

It is well established that the *Canadian Charter of Rights and Freedoms* opposes limitations to the right to vote inherent in the electoral system itself. However, it is less clear whether the Charter can be invoked to justify setting limits on practices that would erode the ability to exercise one's voting rights. Indeed, it seems that the Charter applies only to "governmental action," and may not be invoked on its own to directly sanction the activities of persons in the private sphere (*RWDSU* 1986). For example, section 3 of the *Canadian Charter of Rights and Freedoms* cannot be used to limit the free expression of non-candidates on the basis that advertising by third parties is likely to influence the electorate unduly.

Freedom to vote goes hand in hand with the right to seek public office. Brun and Tremblay warn that if we are not careful, the electoral process could be adjusted so as to "render insignificant the exercise of the right to vote, while unduly protecting the party in power ... or by somehow favouring this group over that group" (1990, 273). The authors add that it is "easy to understand the importance of impartiality on the part of electoral officers, who must not be working for any political party or candidate, as well as the importance of monitoring election spending, which could corrupt voters' motives" (ibid.).

The preservation of meaningful voting rights and a real chance to run as a candidate in elections is an essential component of the constitutionally guaranteed right to vote and to run for public office. These rights, however, would be rights in name only if their expressive component were ignored. Boyer (1990, 11) observes that, in one sense, the right to vote and to express one's point of view about the political parties, their platforms and the candidates is a natural extension of freedom of speech (see also *Brassard* 1877, 195).

To the extent that it is possible to show a connection between a given measure and the protection of these fundamental rights, it becomes necessary to reconcile the measure with the requirements of a much more general fundamental freedom: freedom of expression, of the press and of other communications media guaranteed by section 2(*b*) of the Charter.

Freedom of Expression
When thinking about the rules and principles of law affecting election campaign broadcasting, it is important to keep in mind that these rules and principles must be compatible with the freedoms guaranteed under the Charter. In most Western countries, radio and television have been treated differently from other communications media, especially the print media (Namurois 1980; Fallon 1987; Head 1985, 377ff.; Browne 1989). Indeed, the international agreements that proclaim the right to freedom of expression make provisions for special treatment of the electronic media and recognize the right of governments to make access to radio frequencies subject to a licensing scheme. For example, article 10

of the *European Convention on Human Rights* (1950) states that the right to freedom of expression does not prevent governments from requiring the licensing of broadcasting enterprises. However, as Pinto points out, any such system would have to respect freedom of expression (1984, 211). It is incumbent on any government that establishes a licensing scheme to guarantee that the rights recognized in article 10 of the Convention will continue to be protected (Fallon 1987).

Unlike the print media, it is generally thought that the broadcast media make use of a scarce resource, namely radio frequencies, which are considered public property. Moreover, the intrusive nature of the broadcast media and their allegedly superior persuasive ability have also been raised to justify their special treatment in relation to freedom of expression. For election campaign broadcasts, the need to guarantee that the various candidates and points of view will receive equitable treatment in the media of radio and television is generally recognized.

The Legal Supremacy of Freedom of Expression

Not only does Part I of the *Constitution Act, 1982* proclaim that everyone has freedom of opinion and expression, but section 52 of the same Act also affirms the primacy of the Constitution over all other laws. This section reads: "The Constitution of Canada is the supreme law of Canada, and any law that is inconsistent with the provisions of the Constitution is, to the extent of the inconsistency, of no force or effect." Consequently, measures that would effectively limit the ability to broadcast certain types of subject matter or deny access to the airwaves must henceforth be analysed in light of the major change brought about by the *Constitution Act, 1982*. From a merely interpretive principle with no defined legal force, freedom of expression has become a test for determining the validity of other laws. The well-established notion that the law dictates free expression must now be turned on its head: freedom of expression dictates the law (Trudel 1986, 174–75).

Free expression cannot be seen as a practice that is lawful only so long as no laws have been broken. Legal and regulatory schemes that contemplate expression-related violations must now be compatible with freedom of expression as guaranteed by the Charter and conform to the standard in section 1 of the *Canadian Charter of Rights and Freedoms* whereby one's rights and freedoms are guaranteed "subject only to such reasonable limits prescribed by law as can be demonstrably justified in a free and democratic society."

Freedom of expression has traditionally been dealt with in terms of its limits. Many studies, in fact, look at various provisions that limit the exercise of free expression (Tarnopolsky 1981; Skarsgard 1980–81;

Proulx 1985, 43ff.; Duplé 1986, 117ff.; A. Tremblay 1986). The courts have often spoken of freedom of expression when they were upholding measures to limit it.[2] This approach was quite understandable when free expression had a residual nature, that is, when it existed only insofar as the legislatures had not restricted it. Now that freedom of expression has attained constitutional status, it is no longer possible to be confined to such an approach (see Beckton 1989, 195–225; Magnet 1987, 287ff.). The mere adoption by Parliament or a legislature of a given measure does not make it ipso facto a valid limit on the now constitutionally entrenched freedom of expression.[3]

With regard to common law rules, in the *RWDSU v. Dolphin Delivery* decision, Mr. Justice McIntyre stated that "the courts are, of course, bound by the *Charter* as they are bound by all law" (1986, 600). He added that the courts ought to apply and develop common law principles in a manner consistent with the fundamental values enshrined in the Constitution. Consequently, there is no doubt that the principles of broadcasting regulation and the *Canada Elections Act* must be analysed in light of the guarantees set out in the *Canadian Charter of Rights and Freedoms*.

In *Quebec (Attorney General) v. Irwin Toy Ltd.* (1989), the Supreme Court of Canada pointed out that the matter of whether a governmental measure is consistent with freedom of expression first requires determination of whether the activity contemplated by the measure falls within the activities protected by the Charter guarantee.

There has been much discussion about the scope of freedom of expression. Specifically, it has been asked whether freedom of expression extends to communication such as commercial messages (Braun 1986; Binette 1987; Forest 1988).[4] The Supreme Court of Canada has tended to give a liberal interpretation of the protected sphere so that it encompasses all activities conducted to convey meaning. In *Quebec (Attorney General) v. Irwin Toy Ltd.*, the Court broadly interpreted the scope of freedom of expression, which "ensures that we can convey our thoughts and feelings in non-violent ways without fear of censure" (1989, 970). The Court explained that expression comprises both form and content, and that the two elements are inextricably linked. Expressive form and content are protected under the Constitution.

The message is the medium. A human activity cannot be excluded from the scope of guaranteed freedom of expression on the basis of its content or the meaning of the message it conveys. Therefore, where an activity transmits or tries to transmit a meaning, it conveys expressive content and falls, prima facie, within the scope of the guarantee of freedom of expression. Expressive content can be conveyed by a wide range of media such as print, speech and actions. Violence, however, although recognized by the Supreme Court of Canada as a form of expression, is not protected (*RWDSU* 1986). In its most recent decisions (*R. v. Keegstra* 1990; *Taylor v. Canada (Canadian Human Rights Commission)* 1990; *R. v. Committee for the Commonwealth of Canada* 1991) the Supreme Court of Canada upheld its approach based on a very liberal construction of the scope of free expression, which includes any expressive activity; the one exception is physical violence, but not mere threats of violence. The Court prefers to focus its judgements on the reasonable and justifiable nature of laws that place limits on freedom of expression.

Expression is the raison d'être of radio and television; prima facie, therefore, radio and television are protected by freedom of expression. If this argument is not entirely persuasive, it could be further argued that section 2(*b*) of the *Canadian Charter of Rights and Freedoms* guarantees freedom of expression, "including freedom of the press and other media of communication."

Political speech – or speech pertaining to government, or to the way in which the political leadership of the country is assumed and to the merits of those who wish to hold public office – is, of course, a central component of protected communication under freedom of expression. There is little doubt, therefore, that any law that limits freedom in these areas will certainly come into conflict with freedom of expression.

Election Broadcasting as an Expressive Activity

Election broadcasting is crucial to freedom of expression, as it has been traditionally understood in Canada. The free expression enjoyed by persons holding or intending to hold public office is considered the cornerstone of that freedom.

The right to discuss and criticize the acts and decisions of public office holders is well established. In *Reference re Alberta Statutes*, referring to the preamble of the *Constitution Act, 1867*, Chief Justice Duff stated that the Canadian Constitution should be similar in principle to that of the United Kingdom and that the existence of a parliament "working under the influence of public opinion and public discussion" is contemplated therein (1938, 133). The effectiveness of such institutions, he wrote, depends on the possibility for free discussion: "There can be no controversy that such institutions derive their efficacy from the free public discussion of affairs, from criticism and answer and counter-criticism, from attack upon policy and administration and defense and counter-attack; from the freest and fullest analysis and examination from every point of view of political proposals" (ibid.; see also Trudel 1984a, 29; Trudel et al. 1981, 196ff.).

For his part, in the same decision, Mr. Justice Cannon wrote, "Freedom of discussion is essential to enlighten public opinion in a democratic State; it cannot be curtailed without affecting the right of the people to be informed . . . concerning matters of public interest" (*Reference re Alberta Statutes* 1938, 145–46).

Mr. Justice Rand put forward the same ideas in the *Saumur v. City of Quebec* decision, writing that, under the *Constitution Act, 1867:* "government is by parliamentary institutions, including popular assemblies elected by the people at large in both provinces and Dominion: government resting ultimately on public opinion reached by discussion and the interplay of ideas" (1953, 330).

Before 1982, the courts had never struck down legislation solely on the grounds that it violated freedom of expression, freedom of the press or freedom of other media of communication. Instead, the courts were led to nullify measures conflicting with freedom of expression where it was demonstrated that such measures, because of their deleterious effect on the democratic process, fell outside the scope of property and civil rights. Despite this important nuance, there has never been any doubt that freedom of expression is one of the general principles included in the body of Canadian law (Tollefson 1968, 49; Barron 1963).

Grounds for Limiting Freedom of Expression

It seems well established that measures affecting broadcasting in Canada have an impact on freedom of expression. However, the reasonable and justifiable nature of such measures within the context of a free and democratic society remains to be examined. The criteria used to determine whether the measures adopted by Parliament are compatible with the *Canadian Charter of Rights and Freedoms* were set out by the Supreme Court of Canada in the *R. v. Big M Drug Mart Ltd.* (1985) and *R. v. Oakes* (1986) decisions. These criteria were applied to freedom of expression for the first time in *Quebec (Attorney General) v. Irwin Toy Ltd.* (1989).

According to the conditions contained in the test developed by the Supreme Court of Canada, the reasons that led the legislature to adopt the measure must be examined in addition to the means used to do so. This approach depends fundamentally on how freedom of expression is defined. How that freedom is interpreted will determine whether it should include certain acts or messages, and will often lead judges to consider certain limits to freedom of expression as "natural" limits that require no investigation into their compatibility with section 1.[5] However, with its decisions in *Quebec (Attorney General) v. Irwin Toy*

Ltd. (1989), *R. v. Keegstra* (1990), *Taylor v. Canada (Canadian Human Rights Commission)* (1990) and *R. v. Committee for the Commonwealth of Canada* (1991), the Supreme Court of Canada has rejected such an approach.

It is always necessary to indicate the values underlying guaranteed rights. In the decision *Re Edmonton Journal and Alberta (Attorney General)* (1989), Madam Justice Wilson identified two ways to apply the Charter and the fundamental freedoms it guarantees. According to a method that Madam Justice Wilson describes as "abstract," the underlying value that is protected by section 2(*b*) of the Charter is defined generally. With a contextual method, the primary function is to find a balance between the rights that are in conflict. Madam Justice Wilson added, regarding the contextual method, that one of the qualities of this method

> is that it recognizes that a particular right or freedom may have a different value depending on the context. It may be, for example, that freedom of expression has greater value in a political context than it does in the context of disclosure of the details of a matrimonial dispute. The contextual approach attempts to bring into sharp relief the aspect of the right or freedom which is truly at stake in the case as well as the relevant aspects of any values in competition with it. It seems to be more sensitive to the reality of the dilemma posed by the particular facts and therefore more conducive to finding a fair and just compromise between the two competing values under s. 1. (*Re Edmonton Journal* 1989, 1355–56)

An assessment of the reasons that justify limits to freedom of expression, as this freedom affects broadcast election messages, must be based on the context that characterizes these messages. A right or a freedom may have different meanings in different contexts. Freedom of expression is indisputably an essential condition of democracy and is the essence of the exercise of the franchise. But it is plausible that this freedom is equipped with a framework designed to balance its exercise more precisely to preserve the very existence of a true debate, that is, a situation in which all points of view have an opportunity to be heard. This contextual analysis is summarized by Madam Justice McLachlin in the case of *Rocket v. Royal College of Dental Surgeons* (1990, 251). This decision dealt with the reasonable and justifiable nature of a general prohibition against advertising by dentists. Madam Justice McLachlin assessed the values of the case, weighing the public interest in the information that could not be released because of prohibition. She wrote that "the public has an interest in obtaining information as to dentists' office hours, the language they speak, and other objective facts relevant to their practice" (ibid.). Because the measure under attack prohibited dentists from conveying such information without justification, she concluded that the measure includes harmful effects that defeat the desired advantages.

This type of assessment may be applied to most measures that limit freedom of expression to preserve balance and integrity of electoral debate. Insofar as some aspects of these measures are considered to be too far-reaching with regard to the desired objectives, these measures may be considered as failing to meet the section 1 test of reasonable and justified limits.

When evaluating the reasonable and justifiable nature of the limits imposed by a legislative measure (or other law), it is especially necessary to have a clear idea of the values that are conflicting with each other. Examining the grounds upon which legislators determined whether a measure addresses a pressing and substantial need in a free and democratic society involves examining the problems that are to be remedied and the desired objectives; in short, this means setting out a statement of the rationale underlying the measure under attack.

Parliament and the legislatures very rarely seek to eliminate a given freedom; the laws in force in Canada generally exist to serve legitimate ends. The laws relating to election campaign broadcasts on radio and television are no exception. Nevertheless, those who would uphold measures likely to conflict with freedom of expression must be able to make a strong case for those measures. This involves skilful argument, not only before the court judging the constitutional validity of the measure, but before public opinion, or even, broadly speaking, the legal community (Gold 1985a; 1985b; 1988). The courts that have to interpret fundamental rights evolve in a social environment and must render decisions that are legitimate in the opinion of the different audiences for whom their decisions are intended (Gold 1988, 5). The construction of rights and freedoms that can be extracted from various legal decisions is not the spontaneous creation of the judiciary.

The Canadian judiciary has yet to render a decision on the status of broadcasting as it relates to freedom of expression. In *Canadian Broadcasting Corporation v. R.* (1983), the Supreme Court of Canada took judicial notice of the will of Parliament to set up a broadcasting system that operated according to the principle of free expression.

Other than *New Brunswick Broadcasting Co. v. Canada (CRTC)* (1984), there have been no Canadian decisions rendered to date specifically covering the compatibility of broadcasting regulations with the right to freedom of expression. Chief Justice Thurlow concluded that refusing to renew a broadcasting licence pursuant to instructions issued by the Governor in Council under section 18 of the *Broadcasting Act* does not violate freedom of expression, basing his decision on the fact that broadcast frequencies are publicly owned: freedom of expression does not confer on anyone the right to use someone else's property. The same approach was favoured in the right to use municipal public property in *Canadian Newspapers c. Ville de Montréal* (1988).

There are a number of flaws in the reasoning of *New Brunswick Broadcasting Co. v. Canada (CRTC)* (1984). This decision entirely ignores the question of whether decisions regarding the use of public property should be made in accordance with the *Canadian Charter of Rights and Freedoms*. In fact, Mr. Justice Walsh excludes the use of public property from the scope of free expression. Zolf points out that the judgement "assumes, without any discussion of the purpose of section 2(b) of the Charter, that the Charter does not reach into public buildings or public facilities of any kind. It assumes further that when Parliament declares property to be public which previously was not, the reach of the Charter can thereby be impeded" (1988, 33). The author rightly questions the validity of postulates of this type.

Indeed, one wonders how far these guarantees contained in the Charter – freedom of expression in particular – would extend if they did not define the conditions under which the state may validly decide to allow public property to be used. Such a decision by state authorities should be subject to the obligation of ensuring that fundamental freedoms are not ignored. After all, it could be argued that every decision made by the state involves the use of someone else's property, namely state property. To say that freedom of expression does not carry with it the right to use state property is to disregard all the mechanisms the state uses to determine conditions for the use of frequencies. This statement also denies the need for those conditions to be tested for compatibility with constitutional guarantees. That is why such reasoning cannot hold.

Furthermore, in *Canadian Newspapers Co. c. Ville de Québec* (1986), the Superior Court of Quebec had no difficulty recognizing that constitutional guarantees extend to the conditions for the use of streets imposed on citizens by public authorities. In *Committee for the Commonwealth of Canada v. R.* (1987),[6] the Federal Court of Appeal held, in a majority decision, that the government's right of ownership over public property could not be used as the sole grounds for justifying any infringement of a fundamental freedom. Mr. Justice Hugessen developed his reasoning thus: "The government is not in the same position as a private owner ... as it owns its property not for its own benefit but for that of the citizen. Clearly the government has a right, even an obligation, to devote certain property for certain purposes and to manage 'its' property for the public good. The exercise of this right and the performance of this obligation may, depending on the circumstances, legitimize the imposition of certain limitations on fundamental freedoms" (ibid., 77). The Supreme Court of Canada upheld this view with its decision in *R. v. Committee for the Commonwealth of Canada* (1991) by unanimously recognizing that the government's right of ownership does not, of itself, mean that citizens cannot exercise their right to free expression on government property.

The fact that broadcast frequencies are publicly owned allows the state to regulate their use and even to prohibit unauthorized persons from using them. However, these measures must, like other state actions, be compatible with constitutional guarantees; in other words, they must constitute reasonable and justifiable limits within the meaning of section 1 of the *Canadian Charter of Rights and Freedoms*. Government regulation of broadcasting in Canada must be analysed from this perspective.

In *R. v. Oakes* (1986), Chief Justice Dickson explains that the purpose served by measures restricting a freedom guaranteed by the Charter must be sufficiently important to warrant overriding a right. Purposes that are "trivial" or inconsistent with the principles of a free and democratic society are not protected by section 1 of the Charter. To qualify as sufficiently important, the purpose must correspond to a pressing and substantial concern of a free and democratic society. How can such criteria be applied to measures that conflict with freedom of expression without having some notion of the values protected[7] by that constitutional freedom?

In this context, it is necessary to examine the reasoning in determining whether Canadian laws on broadcasting are reasonable and demonstrably justifiable in a free and democratic society, insofar as they limit rights established under the *Canadian Charter of Rights and Freedoms*. Thus, measures such as the inclusion of radio and television frequencies in the public domain must be considered in terms of this constitutional test.

In this respect, it has been argued that since the frequencies used by broadcast media are scarce, they should be publicly owned. Other arguments have been raised, such as the impact of broadcast media, as well as their intrusive and pervasive presence (see Evans 1979). From arguments such as those, the reasonable and justifiable nature of the limitations imposed on free expression in radio and television is determined.

Spectrum Scarcity   In the United States it is generally accepted that the broadcast media, because of their unique characteristics, are to be regarded differently from other media in terms of the constitutional guarantees of freedom of speech. The judicial reasoning that broadcasting regulations were in accordance with the guarantees of the First Amendment has developed around the notion of the scarcity of broadcast frequencies. This argument is sometimes used in Canada, but the courts have never had occasion to analyse it. Nevertheless, examination of regulatory history shows that spectrum scarcity has not been the only justification for the regulation of Canadian broadcasting.

   National Broadcasting v. United States (1943) was the first significant case in which the Supreme Court of the United States had to render judgement on the relationship between broadcasting and the First Amendment. The Court eventually decided that there was no constitutional right to obtain authorization either to use or to have a monopoly over electromagnetic frequencies. Consequently, where legislation denies the right to obtain a broadcasting licence, there is no prima facie negation of freedom of speech. The verdict in the case upheld a decision of the Federal Communications Commission (FCC), which concerned the types of programs to be aired by a company applying for a broadcasting licence. The role of the regulatory body, wrote the Supreme Court, is not limited to that of a "traffic officer," and the authorization mechanism set up by U.S. federal legislation was deemed constitutional. On that subject, Justice Frankfurter of the United States Supreme Court wrote:

> The Act itself establishes that the Commission's powers are not limited to the engineering and technical aspects of regulation of radio communication. Yet we are asked to regard the Commission as a kind of traffic officer, policing the wave lengths to prevent stations from interfering with each other. But the Act does not restrict the Commission merely to supervision of the traffic. It puts upon the Commission the burden of determining the composition of that traffic. The facilities of radio are not large enough to accommodate all who wish to use them. Methods must be devised for choosing among the many who apply. And since Congress itself could not do this, it committed the task to the Commission. (*National Broadcasting* 1943, 215)

Essentially, this analysis is based on the concept of scarcity. State control over the use of frequencies is deemed compatible with the constitutional guarantee of freedom of speech because these frequencies are scarce. Based on scarcity, American doctrine and jurisprudence have justified applying standards to the electronic media that differ from the standards applied to the print media. Rossini writes: "The spectrum scarcity doctrine constitutionally justifies extensive governmental regulation of the broadcast media. The doctrine, first adopted by the Supreme Court in 1933 and recently perpetuated in 1984, assumes that the absence of regulation would result in a crowded chaos of signals within the limited electromagnetic spectrum. The doctrine further assumes that regulation of the electromagnetic spectrum ensures that the few recipients of broadcast licenses will use this scarce national resource in the public interest" (1985, 827). Were it not for the spectrum scarcity justification, many U.S. regulations covering broadcasting would be deemed violations of the First Amendment.

United States Supreme Court case law states again and again the principle of analysing each medium in light of its particular characteristics when determining the extent to which it is protected by the First Amendment (*United States* 1948; *Kovacs* 1949; *Southeastern* 1975; *Metromedia* 1981; *City of Los Angeles* 1986). Thus, it is not surprising that U.S. judicial decisions distinguish between broadcasting and the print media (*Joseph* 1952, 503).

While the broadcaster's right to free expression may be extremely important, it does not extend so far that it overrides the rights of other citizens (*Associated* 1945). Moreover, the courts have recognized the right of Congress to set up a system of granting broadcasting licences and for revoking such licences, if necessary (*FRC* 1933). All these principles were already well established by the time the Supreme Court gave its landmark decision on broadcasting in *Red Lion Broadcasting v. FCC* (1969).

The Red Lion Broadcasting Company had contested the validity of the "fairness doctrine" rules established by the FCC, whereby candidates for public office were allotted a certain amount of reply time. The rules also required broadcasters to present programming in which matters of public interest were discussed fairly, while giving persons with differing points of view an opportunity to express themselves. To assess the constitutionality of these rules, the Court, once again, had to review the rationale for the distinction between broadcasters and print media with regard to First Amendment rights. It is far less likely that the FCC rules would have been deemed compatible with the print media's right to free expression.[8] Speaking for the majority of the Court, Justice White underscored the fact that use of the frequency spectrum would be virtually impossible without government intervention. Since the number of potential users exceeds the number of available frequencies, it is not possible, in his opinion, to recognize freedom of speech for broadcasters in the same way as for the print media. The crux of his argument is as follows:

> Because of the scarcity of radio frequencies, the Government is permitted to put restraints on licensees in favor of others whose views should be expressed on this unique medium. But the people as a whole retain their interest in free speech and their collective right to have the medium function consistently with the ends and purposes of the First Amendment. It is the right of the viewers and listeners, not the right of the broadcasters, which is paramount ... It is the purpose of the First Amendment to preserve an uninhibited marketplace of ideas in which truth will ultimately prevail, rather than to countenance monopolization of that market, whether it be by the Government itself or a private licensee ... It is the right of the public to receive suitable access to social, political, esthetic, moral and other ideas and experiences which is crucial here. (*Red Lion Broadcasting* 1969, 390; see also Wescott 1986, D-12)

The *Red Lion* (1969) decision emphasizes the rights of the public, in the light of which the rights of broadcasters are defined. The Court's analysis gave rise to the construction whereby broadcasters are, in a sense, public "trustees" and must accordingly use the frequencies entrusted to them in ways that serve the public interest.

This is not to say that freedom of speech does not apply to broadcast licensees. Rather, the reasoning in the *Red Lion* (1969) decision is oriented to recognizing limitations on the right to free speech enjoyed by persons entitled to use the airwaves; these persons cannot act without having regard for what the Court calls "the rights of the public" and of others to whom the use of electromagnetic frequencies is unavailable (Slansky 1985, 88).

The United States Supreme Court also put forward the argument that the rules being contested in the *Red Lion* (1969) case, namely, the fairness doctrine developed by the FCC during a 40-year period, were intended to increase opportunities for expression, not reduce them. That argument has been vigorously challenged.[9]

In 1973, the United States Supreme Court reaffirmed the principles of the *Red Lion* (1969) decision in *CBS v. Democratic National Committee* (1973), again in 1981 in *CBS Inc. v. FCC* (1981), and most recently in 1984 with the *FCC v. League of Women Voters* (1984) decision. In 1987, the FCC decided to scrap the fairness doctrine (*Syracuse* 1987, 5057–58) and opted instead to oversee the activities of broadcasters using an approach based on market forces to ensure diversity and equitable treatment of matters of public interest (*In the Matter of Inquiry* 1987).

Growing opposition to the spectrum scarcity rationale has characterized the U.S. experience during the past 20 years (Fowler and Brenner 1982; Rossini 1985; Evans 1979). Essentially, the critics assert that frequencies are no more scarce than any other resource, or that the scarcity is entirely relative if not, quite simply, the product of the regulatory scheme controlling the frequency spectrum.[10]

Whenever the spectrum scarcity argument is raised, it is important to define what type of scarcity is meant. The first type of scarcity stems from the impossibility of two or more broadcasts being carried on the same frequency at the same time within a specified region without causing intolerable interference. A receiver cannot pick up the signals of two or more transmitters using the same frequency. This phenomenon, referred to as "static technological scarcity," is raised to justify the administrative mechanisms in place for allocating frequencies (Spitzer 1985, 1359). It has been argued that the disadvantages caused by this form of scarcity are not unique to the spectrum. Theoretically, the same argument holds for newsprint. If it is certain that, in any given time period, two broadcasters cannot transmit on the same frequency, the same is true for paper: if two people write on the same page, the two messages will probably be obscured.

Another form of scarcity is characteristic of the frequency spectrum: technological scarcity in the dynamic sense. While the spectrum is a limited physical phenomenon, it is always possible to produce more paper. However, in any given period of time, the amount of paper and frequencies available are both constant. Over a longer period, one can increase the amount of paper available on the market. As a physical phenomenon, the spectrum cannot be expanded as such. On the other hand, it is possible to step up efforts in research and development to allow for a more efficient use of the spectrum.[11] These phenomena are not indicators of a greater scarcity of frequencies than of paper; rather, for frequencies and paper alike, these phenomena point out a need to develop mechanisms that could guarantee the exclusion of all those who are not entitled to make use of the resource.[12] In the case of paper, property rights play this role. As for determining who can use the spectrum, the opponents of government intervention in such decisions assert that property rights could constitute this exclusion mechanism as well (Minasian 1975; Webbink 1987).

A third type of spectrum scarcity is the result of excess demand. There are more people who want broadcasting licences than there are available frequencies. For authors like Spitzer (1985) and Coase (1959, 12–13), that proves nothing. The reason demand for frequencies is greater than the supply is that they are given away free, or, at most, for a price below their economic value, by licence allocation mechanisms. When a resource is supplied at no charge or at a price below its value, demand will often exceed supply.

A fourth type of spectrum scarcity results from the fact that it is extremely difficult to enter the market. Proponents of this view claim that launching a TV or radio station is more costly than securing access to printing facilities.[13] This is a much less compelling argument, especially when one looks at companies of similar scale. It is extremely expensive to launch a daily newspaper or a general interest magazine, whereas a small radio station can be started for just a few thousand dollars.

Finally, while both broadcast frequencies and paper are admittedly scarce resources, it is argued that frequencies are in shorter supply than paper. In practical terms, however, this relative scarcity depends on how each resource is used. For instance, paper is useless when it comes to broadcasting a live concert! To establish the relative scarcity of one resource in relation to the other, one would have to count the number of available frequency bands and pieces of paper, but this would require methods that have yet to be perfected.

The preceding review of the major arguments concerning spectrum scarcity shows that the doctrine's critics, for the most part, are of the opinion that scarcity problems are either imaginary or largely the result of the state-administered frequency allocation system. Critics conclude that a competitive market-place could ensure the efficient distribution of frequencies as it does for all other resources, such as paper, intended in whole or in part for the communication of information.

In Canada, a study team set up by the Task Force on Program Review recommended in 1986 the creation of a "permits market" for broadcasting licences (1986b, 190). Because this suggestion was generally not based on any known study conducted in a Canadian context, it had very little impact. While it is difficult to imagine the creation of a "permits market,"[14] the distribution of electromagnetic spectrum frequencies based on market forces does seem plausible.

It is significant that the grounds for public ownership of frequencies, and thus for limitations on the free expression of radio and TV station operators, is spectrum scarcity. Indeed, this has a normative impact. Spitzer writes that "assuming that a normative difference between the media exists, what specific regulatory treatment does this difference justify? For example, if only electromagnetic spectrum is scarce and scarcity is bad, then some administrative management of spectrum rights might be wise. However, if scarcity is the *only* relevant difference between print and broadcast, the prohibition of indecent but nonobscene broadcasts should be abolished" (1985, 1354–55).

Recognition of the constitutionality of state regulation of radio and television in the public interest raises another question: what is the public interest? In effect, it can be claimed that the scarcity of these frequencies may justify the existence of mechanisms designed to ensure that the spectrum frequencies may be used without interference. This scarcity does not, in itself, justify regulation bearing on the content of the programs that may be broadcast. Because of the concept of public interest and the character of the recognized public property of the spectrum, this type of intervention in broadcasting content may be justified. In *FCC v. WNCN Listeners' Guild* (1981), the United States Supreme Court held that the determination of what constitutes the public interest in a particular area falls within the jurisdiction of the FCC: it is the role of the Commission to decide, and any judicial intervention should be very limited. In this case, the Court ruled that the Commission's decision to allow market forces to promote diversity in radio station music formats was not unreasonable and, therefore, could not be reversed.

Thus, when we invoke spectrum scarcity to justify state control over spectrum use, we must admit the corollary, to the effect that Parliament, or the authorities to which it delegates such control, should be able to determine which spectrum uses will be in the public's best interest.

In its most recent decision on the constitutional validity of broadcasting legislation, *FCC v. League of Women Voters* (1984), the United States Supreme Court upheld its traditional approach based on spectrum scarcity. The Court declared unconstitutional section 399 of the *Public Broadcasting Act of 1967*, which banned editorials by broadcasters who received grants from the Corporation for Public Broadcasting. The five-member majority decision held that such a general prohibition was a violation of the First Amendment rights of public broadcasters.

The decision upheld the spectrum scarcity doctrine as the First Amendment basis for differential treatment of the broadcast and print media. In a footnote, the Court indicated that it was not convinced there was any need to review its traditional justification of broadcasting's special status based on spectrum scarcity:

> The prevailing rationale for broadcast regulation based on spectrum scarcity has come under increasing criticism in recent years. Critics, including the incumbent Chairman of the FCC, charge that with the advent of cable and satellite television technology, communities now have access to such a wide variety of stations that the scarcity doctrine is obsolete ... We are not prepared, however, to reconsider our long-standing approach without some signal from Congress or the FCC

that technological developments have advanced so far that some revision of the system of broadcast regulation may be required. (FCC 1984, 376)

For the past several years, the FCC has had the opportunity to make its position known concerning the rationales for broadcasting regulation. In its role of determining what is in the public interest, the Commission has already muted the spectrum scarcity rationale (*In the Matter of Inquiry* 1987). The future of this approach, based in large part on the convictions of the Reagan-appointed Commission members, depends on the course of political developments.

The Cable Industry The activities of cable television operators are significantly different from those of other broadcasting companies. In general, cable companies receive conventional broadcast signals and retransmit them via cable to their subscribers. How then can regulatory control of cable operations be justified? The rationales associated with public ownership of the airwaves – the basis for regulating conventional broadcasting – apply to cable regulation only in part, because Hertzian waves are used only to receive signals: cable television allows subscribers to *receive* an increased number of channels. Regulatory control of cable companies seems to be justified primarily by a concern for coherence and unity in Canada's broadcasting system.

As for the application of the Charter's guarantees of freedom of expression to cable operations, we must ascertain the nature of the cable industry and its activities.

In technical terms, a cable television system comprises facilities designed to receive signals and other facilities that allow these signals to be redistributed to its subscribers. The process involves a cable head-end as the hub of the distribution system, a relay system and an outlet in the subscriber's home. Signals are received at the head-end via microwave, satellite or other equipment. The relay system is made up of coaxial cables and amplifiers. Ducts and poles belonging to public utilities are used to carry coaxial cable and cable facilities are often located, in whole or in part, in public areas such as streets. Amplifiers are an important component of cable systems. The greater their capacity, the greater the potential for expansion of the cable system, in terms of the area served or the number of channels made available. The outlets in the subscribers' homes constitute the third and final component of cable systems.

Cable operators deal mainly with the reception of television signals. However, radio signals can also be received and relayed using existing cable facilities. In addition, cable companies produce their own programs and carry those of pay-TV and specialized companies over which they have no control. They also provide certain services such as community announcements, home shopping and advertising. Finally, cable operators distribute programs over which they exercise a certain amount of control and, sometimes, they also offer "interactive" services.

Many authors have tried to define the regulatory status of cable operations with respect to freedom of expression, keeping in mind that, in this area, the rationales based on scarcity and public ownership of the spectrum are less obvious. Should such companies receive the same treatment as radio and television stations that broadcast their programs exclusively over the airwaves? Would it not be possible to set different standards for different companies to assess whether the regulations governing these companies are compatible with the Charter guarantees of freedom of expression?

The status of cable companies has always been somewhat perplexing. They used to play only a passive role, retransmitting other stations' broadcasts. Coaxial cable capacity has increased to such a point today that cable companies have been able to develop many of their own exclusive services as well as offer their subscribers programs that would otherwise not have been available to them, except at much higher prices.

The multifaceted activities and services of cable companies have earned them an essentially hybrid status. At times they are treated like broadcasters, with everything that entails; at other times, because of certain aspects of their operations, it is more appropriate to deal with them in the same way as telecommunications companies.

This is more than just an academic question: whether the cable industry is treated like the press or like telecommunications carriers is significant. In the first scenario, a company would enjoy a high degree of editorial freedom to choose which services and programs are appropriate to broadcast to its clientele. On the other hand, if the company were dealt with in the same way as a telecommunications firm, it would be subject to more stringent duties in the area of rates, such as the obligation to treat its subscribers equitably.

In the United States, there have been many attempts to pin down the status of cable companies, in particular for the purpose of establishing standards by which to analyse the legislation governing their activities. To this end, there are two major schools of thought. The first regards the cable industry as a kind of electronic publisher to which the regulatory standards and principles of the print media ought to apply. Such an approach puts a great deal of emphasis on regulations that might affect the cable company's editorial freedom. The second school considers cable companies to be, in essence, natural monopolies, the type of service that cannot be run effectively by more than one company. Moreover, cable operators necessarily require the use of public property for their distribution equipment.

In *Quincy Cable TV Inc. v. FCC* (1985) the Court came to the conclusion that the spectrum scarcity rationale was no longer a valid justification for cable regulation. The Court pointed to the vast channel capacity of cable operations and, consequently, the impossibility of applying any "physical" scarcity argument to this medium.[15] Therefore, the Court refused to treat cable companies in the manner prescribed for over-the-air broadcasters by the Supreme Court in the *Red Lion* (1969) decision. The Court of Appeals for the District of Columbia offered the following reasoning: "The First Amendment theory espoused in *National Broadcasting Co.* and reaffirmed in *Red Lion Broadcasting Co.* cannot be directly applied to cable television since an essential precondition of that theory – physical interference and scarcity requiring an umpiring role for government – is absent" (*Quincy* 1985, 1449). This analysis led the Court to rescind a "must carry" rule under which cable operators would not be free to choose, on their own, which services to offer to their subscribers.

Justice Posner adopted a completely different position in *Omega Satellite Products Co. v. City of Indianapolis* (1982). In this case, the company was challenging an ordinance that the city had passed after discovering the company's cables in an underground culvert below a public way. According to the ordinance, the company was to have obtained a release from the city before installing its cables in municipal public property. The company sought an injunction prohibiting the city from removing the cable or enforcing the ordinance.

Justice Posner upheld the decision to deny the injunction, explaining that the technology involved in making cable services available to the public requires that the cable company have the status of a "natural monopoly." This requirement could justify the measures taken by the city. He explained the nature of the natural monopoly thus:

> The cost of the cable grid appears to be the biggest cost of a cable television system and to be largely invariant to the number of subscribers the system has. We said earlier that once the grid is in place – once every major street has a cable running above or below it that can be hooked up to the individual residences along the street – ... the cost of each grid will be spread over a smaller number of subscribers, and the average cost per subscriber, and hence price will be higher.

If the foregoing accurately describes conditions in Indianapolis ... it describes what economists call "a natural monopoly," wherein the benefits, and indeed the very possibility, of competition are limited. You can start with a competitive free-for-all – different cable television systems frantically building out their grids and signing up subscribers in an effort to bring down their average costs faster than their rivals – but eventually there will be only a single company, because until a company serves the whole market it will have an incentive to keep expanding in order to lower its average costs. In the interim there may be wasteful duplication of facilities. This duplication may lead not only to higher prices to cable television subscribers, at least in the short run, but also to higher costs to other users of the public ways, who must compete with the cable television companies for access to them. An alternative procedure is to pick the most efficient competitor at the outset, give him a monopoly, and extract from him in exchange a commitment to provide reasonable service at reasonable rates. (*Omega* 1982, 126)

Admitting that spectrum scarcity could not justify treating the cable industry differently from the print media, Justice Posner nevertheless cited reasonable grounds for state intervention that would not involve a violation of First Amendment rights. First of all, cable operations interfere with other users of public utilities such as telephone poles and underground ducts. As well, the natural monopoly characteristics of cable broadcasting justify regulation of entry into the market. Finally, since the majority of cable fare continues to originate from the broadcast media, the pervasive influence of such media along with the need to protect children, according to Justice Posner, warrants the application of standards similar to those governing radio and television.

Canadian cable undertakings are also natural monopolies and use public channels to send their signals, so it is possible to justify regulating their operations on the basis of obligations similar to those imposed on broadcasters and on telecommunications carriers.

It is important to observe, however, that rationales based solely on the public ownership of spectrum frequencies will sometimes be insufficient; in particular, if justifications must be found to monitor the contents of the broadcasts, other reasons must be invoked to justify limiting the industry's freedom.

The Intrusive Effect and Special Impact of Broadcasting   Besides spectrum scarcity, courts have occasionally advanced other grounds for regulating broadcasting, notwithstanding constitutional guarantees of freedom of expression.

The intrusive effect of the broadcast media was the basis of the United States Supreme Court's reasoning in *FCC v. Pacifica Foundation* (1978). In this decision, the Court upheld the FCC's censure of a radio station that had broadcast a monologue, by comedian George Carlin, consisting primarily of words generally considered to be vulgar (ibid., 751–55).[16] The FCC's declaratory order stemmed from the indecency of the words. Writing for the majority of the Court, Justice Stevens stressed the fact that the medium of radio is easily accessible to children, including children who are too young to read. Moreover, the Court stressed the pervasiveness of the broadcast media in the lives of all Americans. As the Court found that the words condemned by the FCC order were not obscene and would, in other contexts, have been protected by the First Amendment, it explicitly based its decision to uphold the order upon the particular context in which the monologue was broadcast. The Court implied that its decision would have been different had the broadcast been directed to a more restricted audience (Evans 1979, 883–84).

Thus, the special, sometimes intrusive nature of television and radio may justify infringements on freedom of expression that would be intolerable for the print media. Even recognizing the particular circumstances of the case, many commentators have been concerned about the impact of the decision. One wrote that: "By banning the broadcast [of George Carlin's monologue], the Court embarked on a new era in First Amendment controversies: 1) it set a precedent for the Supreme Court to be the judge of the value of words and 2) it prohibited the expression of an idea about attitudes of the public over a public medium without a showing of a significant countervailing public interest" (Parish 1979, 121; see also Hsiung 1987).

This statement clearly illustrates how difficult it is to determine grounds for limiting freedom of expression in the electronic media. The effects attributed to a given medium will often justify the limitations imposed. This stems from certain assumptions in case law about the supposed effects of broadcasts and the electronic media. There was no empirical proof in the *Pacifica* decision of any undesirable effects resulting from the broadcast of such words. A certain common sense seems to justify the attitude of the judges. It appears that the grounds for this decision lie in the inevitable concern roused by the fact that radio can be heard anywhere by people of various ages and walks of life.

The unique impact of broadcasting has also been invoked to justify rules limiting freedom of expression. In *Banzhaff v. FCC* (1968), the DC Circuit Court of Appeals upheld an FCC ruling that required broadcasters carrying cigarette advertising to air anti-smoking messages as well. To justify not imposing such a rule on other media, the Court underscored the greater impact of television arising from the fact that viewers are largely a captive audience; they are not always able to avoid the message. Whereas the written word necessitates an intellectual effort on the part of the reader, radio and television audiences have the message imposed on them without having to make any effort. This difference warrants state intervention to protect audiences or certain members thereof, such as children. This theory has won little support from the U.S. courts.[17]

Other Canadian Rationales   In Canada, as in the United States, spectrum scarcity represents one justification for public ownership and regulation of radio frequencies, but it is not the only one.

The very first Canadian statutes in this field were aimed at preventing interference.[18] The need to regulate not only ownership, but also the intellectual content of over-the-air transmissions was recognized once it was observed that these laws were inadequate to prevent uses of the airwaves that were contrary to the shared goals of Canadians.

In Canada, the *Report* of the Committee on Broadcasting (1965) recognized the importance of the limited number of radio frequencies as grounds for differential treatment of television and radio as opposed to other media. The Committee wrote that:

> A factor that distinguishes radio and television from the other media of mass communication is the necessity for some measure of public control over them. Because the number of available radio frequencies and television channels is limited, every nation in the world has found it necessary to exercise control over broadcasting. Newspapers, periodicals, film producers and the performing arts need no franchise from the State. It may be wise or desirable but it is not essential for the State to support any of the other mass media. But no radio or television station can come into existence without the grant of a scarce public asset for its use. State intervention in the field of broadcasting is thus inescapable; the only issue is how far it should go in controlling and directing the media it has brought into existence. (Canada, Committee 1965, 6–7)

The 1951 *Report* of the Royal Commission on National Development in the Arts, Letters and Sciences also invoked the special nature of the broadcasting industry: "Radio broadcasting is akin to a monopoly. Any man who has the impulse and the means may produce a book, may publish a newspaper or may operate a motion picture theatre, but he may not in the same way operate a radio station. The air-channels are limited in number and normal competition in any air-channel is impossible. Throughout the world these channels are recognized as part of the public domain; and radio stations may operate only with the permission of the state" (Canada, Royal Commission 1951, 276).

The development of Canadian broadcasting law does not mean, however, that spectrum frequencies have been kept in the public domain solely on the basis of their scarcity. The establishment of the Aird Commission on 6 December 1928 was motivated not so much by the chaotic interference that resulted from too many unregulated users of the airwaves, but rather by a controversy over broadcast content (Ellis 1979, 2ff.). At that time, broadcasting was done by private businesses that, for the most part, aired American programs. For its part, the Canadian National Railway decided to initiate a radio broadcasting service for its passengers (ibid.). The mandate of the Aird Commission was to determine how broadcasting could best serve Canadian interests. G. Tremblay (1986, 80) points out that, while spectrum scarcity may have been one of the grounds for state control of broadcasting, it was never the only one. In this regard, the prevailing situation in Canada differs significantly from that in the United States.

This was also the finding of the Task Force on Broadcasting Policy (1986a). Its report states that:

> Unlike American communications legislation which was designed primarily for co-ordination purposes, Canadian broadcasting policy has always pursued social and cultural objectives. It was never just because radio frequencies were scarce, but also because the Canadian presence on the airwaves was weak, that since 1929 commissions of inquiry into broadcasting have recommended strengthening the system. The assignment of radio frequencies for broadcasting in Canada is an essential component of national sovereignty. (Canada, Task Force 1986a, 147)

The Task Force report adds:

> Because of the urgency of the issue, Canada has always expected broadcasting to reflect the country's identity. From the outset radio and television were considered instruments for creative expression, education and information by and for Canadians rather than simply as entertainment media. The availability of a larger number of channels will do little or nothing to guarantee access or to ensure that the airwaves will reflect the Canadian identity and culture. (Canada, Task Force 1986a, 147)

Thus, in Canada, there are other reasons besides scarcity that explain or justify public ownership of the airwaves. Some authors, noting the similar findings of a succession of inquiry commissions and task forces examining broadcasting policy, have pointed to the "Canadian culture and unity doctrine" (Finkelstein 1985, 71): the protection of Canadian sovereignty, far more than spectrum scarcity, has been the justification for state control over broadcasting and, at the same time, for public ownership of the airwaves (Canada, Task Force 1986a, 146–47).

It cannot be denied that the limitations on free expression that flow from public ownership of radio frequencies are amply justified by the need to safeguard our national identity, as well as by spectrum scarcity and the special impact and intrusive presence of the broadcast media. Nevertheless, the same issue must be addressed for all the other provisions that regulate the activities of the Canadian broadcasting system (see McPhail 1986).

Clearly, it is reasonable for Parliament to conclude that the defence of our national identity, along with the protection of listeners, justifies keeping radio frequencies in the public domain. However, whether the objectives served by the legislation in question are reasonable must be determined based on the other rights and freedoms set forth in the *Canadian Charter of Rights and Freedoms (Singh* 1985).

In situations where freedom of expression is severely constrained, it is even more necessary that the objective be one of substantial importance (*R. v. T.R.* 1984):[19] the required importance of the objective increases in direct proportion to the prejudicial consequences of the limitation.

In addition to these general rationales for limiting freedom of expression in radio and television, there are other rationales related more specifically to the context of elections.

Freedom of Expression and Broadcast Election Messages
In *Quebec (Attorney General) v. Irwin Toy Ltd.* (1989), the Supreme Court of Canada described the sequence of steps for analysing whether a state-imposed measure infringes on the guarantee of free expression. Once it is established that an activity comes within the sphere of protection, the next step is to determine whether the purpose or effect of the government action was to restrict freedom of expression.

If the government has aimed to control an attempt to convey a meaning, either by directly restricting the content of expression or by restricting a form of expression tied to content, or if the government has aimed to control access to or communication of the message, then its action abridges freedom of expression.

A measure may effectively limit freedom of expression even if that is not its primary purpose. In such a case, the regulated activity must first be examined. If the regulated activity furthers one of the major goals of freedom of expression, namely the search for truth, participation in the decision-making process or personal growth and self-realization, then by regulating the activity the measure effectively restricts freedom of expression (*Quebec (Attorney General)* 1989, 971).

It cannot be denied that the purpose of legislation governing Hertzian waves and the broadcasting of messages on radio and television is to control attempts to convey meaning, either by directly restricting the content of expression or by restricting a form of expression tied to content; such legislation, therefore, restricts freedom of expression.

Once it is established that a measure effectively constitutes a limitation of freedom of expression, the next step is to analyse whether the limit is reasonable and justifiable in a free and democratic society. This process essentially asks: how can such restrictions be justified? Thus, it is necessary to examine the rationales that support broadcasting legislation.

The Protection of Editorial Freedom   Freedom of the press has been officially recognized since 1960 by section 1 of the *Canadian Bill of Rights*. However, mere recognition in a federal Act of Parliament did not bring about any major change in the judiciary's attitude toward freedom of expression.

Before it achieved constitutional status, freedom of the press was usually used as an interpretive principle (Trudel 1984b, 16; *Re Pacific* 1977). The decision in *Gay Alliance Toward Equality v. Vancouver Sun* (1979; on this decision see also Black 1979; Kopyto 1980; Richstone and Russell 1981) is one of the clearest indications of judicial appreciation of freedom of the press. It represents by far the most elaborate decision by the Supreme Court of Canada on the nature and consequences of using the right of freedom of the press for purposes of statutory interpretation.

The *Gay Alliance Toward Equality v. Vancouver Sun* (1979) decision delimited editorial freedom for the first time in Canada, that is, the nature and scope of the powers of media executives to set their own editorial policies. This conception of editorial freedom is derived from the rights of ownership that media executives exercise over the press industry and, in this sense, editorial freedom may be construed as a variation of freedom of commerce.

The facts of the case were simple. The *Vancouver Sun* had refused to print a small advertisement promoting a Gay Alliance publication.

A complaint was filed with the B.C. Human Rights Commission, which found that the *Sun* had broken the law by denying the Alliance, on discriminatory grounds and without reasonable cause, the same service that it customarily offers to any other member of the public, namely the publication of classified advertising.

A majority of the Court ruled that the *Human Rights Code* section, which prohibits discrimination in the offer of services normally offered to the public, must be interpreted in a manner so as not to limit freedom of the press. The purpose of the statutory provision at issue was not to prescribe the nature and scope of public services. Therefore, where a newspaper – the *Vancouver Sun* in this case – happens to disapprove of homosexuality, it is that newspaper's right to decide what services it will offer to the public and to define them in accordance with its editorial policy.

The dissenting judgement of Mr. Justice Dickson distinguishes between the actual news or editorial content of a newspaper and the content of its advertising: classified ads are more akin to public services offered by the newspaper, which cannot be denied to anyone on the basis of prohibited grounds of discrimination.

Before 1982, very few judgements dealt with the regulatory framework of broadcasting through the lens of freedom of the press. In the majority judgement in *CKOY v. R.*, Mr. Justice Spence wrote that he was "ready to assume that the broadcasting media may be presumed to be defined within the word 'press'" (1979, 14). Stressing that freedom of the press is not absolute, Mr. Justice Spence pointed out that the regulation at issue in the case upheld an interviewed person's freedom of speech by requiring radio stations to obtain that person's consent prior to broadcasting the interview. Having concluded that the regulation in question did not restrict a broadcaster's freedom of expression, Mr. Justice Spence was of the opinion that this regulation did not violate the *Canadian Bill of Rights*.

Rules that force a broadcaster to broadcast certain messages, as in the *Canada Elections Act*, are prima facie limitations of the broadcaster's editorial freedom, making it necessary to consider the conflict between two forms of freedom of expression.

The Conflict between Electoral Expression and Editorial Freedom   Freedom of expression is essential to the continuance of our democratic institutions. For the democratic process to work, citizens must enjoy considerable latitude for expressing themselves on all matters conceivably relating to the administration of public affairs. If the constitutionally entrenched freedom to vote and to run for public office is to have anything more than purely formal significance, then the genuine possibility for candidates to address the electorate must be ensured.

Figuring among the central elements of freedom of expression of the press and other communication media is the principle of editorial freedom or, in other words, the freedom of a media executive to determine what to publish or broadcast, how much time to devote to the various issues, and how to deal with and present those issues.

Canada's unique legal framework for election broadcasting grew out of the need to create a cohesive system that could reconcile the requirements of free expression and political debate during election campaigns with the requirements of freedom of the press (*Trieger* 1989, 280).

To clarify the reasoning behind the rules for election broadcasting, we have identified the major rationales for imposing certain limitations on free expression in the electronic media generally. It remains for us to examine rationales for limiting the editorial freedom of broadcasters in the specific context of election campaigns.

THE RULES FOR ELECTION CAMPAIGN BROADCASTING

We propose to analyse the rules for election campaign broadcasting in light of the requirements inherent in the fundamental rights and freedoms guaranteed under the Charter. To that end, we must first identify what factors are taken into account when assessing the constitutional compatibility of the various regulatory techniques used. Next, we shall apply those factors to each of the rules and measures brought to bear on election campaign broadcasting.

Criteria for Analysis of Regulatory Measures

A typology of regulatory approaches will enable us to categorize the rules according to their principal characteristics; that, in turn, will allow us to apply to each rule the test designed by the Supreme Court of Canada to determine whether each rule constitutes a reasonable and justifiable means of achieving the desired ends. The first step, however, is to describe the major features of the test.

When it assesses whether given limitations to freedom of expression are reasonable and justifiable, the Supreme Court of Canada applies a test that asks, first, whether the measure in question responds to a pressing and substantial need in society. If so, one must next determine whether the means used are proportional to the desired ends. Proportionality depends on whether the measure is rationally connected to the objective it is intended to serve and whether the means chosen by the legislature impair the freedom as little as possible.

A Pressing and Substantial Concern

All measures to control the broadcasting of expressive content during election campaigns must be carefully analysed to ascertain their intended purpose. It is essential at all times to be able to specify the needs that a statutory or regulatory measure is designed to serve or the ills it is designed to cure. As well, sufficient information must be provided to demonstrate that the ill one seeks to remedy is not pure fiction; in certain situations, the measure must be seen in its larger context within the regulatory framework of election broadcasting. For example, a measure preventing electoral advertising by third parties may initially seem pointless or arbitrary. However, if the measure can be placed in the overall context of regulating election spending, it will certainly appear more rational.

Proportionality of Means in Relation to the Objective

As a rule, the means employed by the legislature must impair constitutionally protected freedoms as little as possible. The *R. v. Oakes* (1986) and *Quebec (Attorney General) v. Irwin Toy Ltd.* (1989) tests require that the means selected be reasonable and demonstrably justifiable. This, in turn, requires the application of a proportionality test to ensure that the means are fair and not arbitrary, are carefully designed to achieve the objective in question and are rationally connected with that objective. In addition, there should be a proportionality between the effects of the limiting measure and the objective, and, finally, the means should impair the Charter freedom as little as possible.

For example, vague measures are naturally more likely to be considered excessive, even if such measures were designed to serve legitimate ends. Even so, there is no need to provide original, arguably constraining, definitions of "law" for future purposes, as the parties in *Re Ontario Film and Video Appreciation Society and Ontario Board of Censors* (1983) tried to do. It is sufficient to observe that for the production and dissemination of information, when measures are so broad or so vague that it is impossible to determine their scope of application with any degree of certainty, such measures are very harmful to the effective exercise of free expression.[20] This does not prevent Parliament, however, from dictating broad guiding principles and objectives of the broadcasting industry; but it must be precise when drafting rules and regulations that are adopted to achieve those objectives.

As underscored previously, the measure must infringe as little as possible on Charter rights and, moreover, its consequences must not be so severe that the infringement of individual rights outweighs the government's pressing and substantial objective.

A Rational Connection between a Measure and Its Objective

Evidence that a rational connection exists between a measure and its objective must be persuasive. In broadcasting, this means that one needs to identify the desired objective and demonstrate that the regulatory measure approved by Parliament is rationally connected to that objective.

A majority of the Court in *Quebec (Attorney General) v. Irwin Toy Ltd.* (1989) found sufficient evidence to establish the existence of such a connection. The prosecution was seeking a limited ban on commercial advertising directed at children to prevent advertisers from exploiting children's inability to differentiate between reality and fiction, and to grasp the persuasive intent behind the message. The Court stressed that, "In the *Ford* judgement, by contrast, no rational connection was established between excluding all languages other than French from signs in Quebec" and the need to preserve the French "visage linguistique" of Quebec (ibid., 992).

Minimal Impairment

The means selected should impair the right or freedom in question as little as possible. The standard of proof is the balance of probabilities applicable in civil cases. The party seeking to uphold the limiting measure has the onus of proving, on a balance of probabilities, that the means selected impairs the Charter freedom as little as possible.

The notion of minimal impairment is difficult to define. According to the majority in *Quebec (Attorney General) v. Irwin Toy Ltd.* (1989), it means that the legislature has to "strike a balance" between the claims of competing groups.

The choice of means and objectives requires assessment of conflicting scientific evidence. Democratic institutions are meant to let us all share responsibility for making difficult choices. When the courts are called on to review the results of the legislature's deliberations, particularly for the protection of vulnerable groups, they must be mindful of the legislature's representative function. While there may be evidence of other less intrusive options, the Supreme Court of Canada will not compel legislatures to choose the least ambitious means to protect vulnerable groups from powerful groups exercising their freedoms under the Charter.

For example, in *Canadian Newspapers Co. v. Canada (Attorney General)* (1988), the Supreme Court of Canada applied the proportionality test and weighed the various competing interests. The Court found without any difficulty that there was a rational connection between the measure and its objective. The case concerned provisions of the *Criminal Code* prohibiting disclosure of the identity of a sexual assault victim. On the question of whether a mandatory ban on publication of the complainant's identity caused the least possible impairment of the freedom of the press, the Court found, keeping in mind the objectives sought, that only the certainty that their names would not be published could guarantee victims that reporting a sexual assault would not lead to disclosure of their identities. This certainty must exist when the victim decides to make the complaint. Consequently, a provision granting a discretionary power to the trial judge on whether to impose the ban would be inappropriate, since such a provision would not satisfy the victim's need for certainty.

Thus, the minimal infringement requirement is not stated in absolute terms. It is not a matter of restricting legislatures to methods that will infringe only nominally on Charter freedoms: they are given a certain amount of latitude to weigh the various options.

The regulatory framework of election campaign broadcasting is, in some ways, the result of a compromise between the competing claims of the various participants. Candidates cite freedom of expression to demand access to the airwaves to convey their platform to the public. Lobby groups want to use the media to make their views known regarding the platforms of parties and candidates. Both naturally invoke their right to free expression in support of their demands. For their part, broadcasters invoke their uncontested legal right to freedom of expression provided for in the *Broadcasting Act* and, especially, the programming responsibilities incumbent on them. The tension that exists between broadcasters, and candidates and political parties is reflected in the interpretation of the *Broadcasting Act* that the Canadian Radio-television and Telecommunications Commission (CRTC) has developed by upholding the public's right to receive balanced programming of high standard.

Classification of Measures Used to Regulate Election Campaign Broadcasting

Election campaign broadcasting on radio and television is controlled by regulations falling under two major categories. The first category is derived from broad principles legislating balanced programming of high standard. The second category, which is far more limited, consists of various rules pertaining to the conditions for broadcasting certain kinds of messages.

General Obligations Flowing from the Broadcasting Act

The *Broadcasting Act* was promulgated in February 1991. The passage of this new law was the culmination of more than 20 years of discussion and reflection on the policies governing radio and television in Canada. In 1986, the *Report* of the Task Force on Broadcasting Policy (137ff.) laid the groundwork for a new broadcasting act designed to replace the *Broadcasting Act, 1968*. The Task Force recommendations were studied by many parliamentary committees and the majority were approved. In 1988, Bill C-136 was tabled in the House of Commons. It was adopted by the House of Commons, but could not be adopted by the Senate before the general election of 1988. Bill C-40 was tabled in the House of Commons in October 1989 and finally received royal assent on 1 February 1991.

The new Act retains the same structure as the 1968 Act. However, it contains more statements regarding Canadian broadcasting policy. While the statements contained in the *Broadcasting Act, 1968* were confined to 12 paragraphs, the *Broadcasting Act, 1991* sets out Canadian broadcasting policy in 46 paragraphs.

The structure of the *Broadcasting Act* of 1991 is relatively simple. It sets out the principles underlying Canadian broadcasting policy (s. 3), and it empowers a regulatory body, the Canadian Radio-television and Telecommunications Commission,[21] to regulate and supervise broadcasting companies (ss. 5, 6, 9, 10, 12, 14, 16, 21, 24) with a view to implementing that policy. In addition, the 1991 Act charges the Canadian Broadcasting Corporation with the responsibility for providing a national public broadcasting service (s. 35ff.).

The 1991 *Broadcasting Act* contains few substantive provisions[22] and consists mainly of enabling provisions. For example, the Act empowers the CRTC to make regulations (ss. 10, 11), to set conditions for all broadcasting licensees under the Act (s. 9), to enforce its rulings and decisions (ss. 12, 13) and to hold public hearings, through edicts, about complaints related to matters within its powers (s. 18(3)).

The CRTC uses the statement of Canadian broadcasting policy set out in the Act as the rationale for its actions. The CRTC is acting under the terms of a mandate – in principle, a wide-ranging mandate[23] – to implement broadcasting policy. The Commission has recourse to a set of regulatory techniques to fulfil its mandate.

The CRTC performs its regulatory duties through the use of four main instruments, of varying legal weight. These are: adoption of statutory instruments; policy statements, which it makes public periodically; rulings and edicts for broadcasting operations; and rulings and decisions that it issues after considering complaints against broadcasting operations.

The *Broadcasting Act* is a statutory framework based largely on vague concepts, and general principles and standards (Trudel 1989b).

By creating a broad mandate, Parliament delegated to government and to regulatory and supervisory authorities the power to adopt rules and to render decisions that will create a broadcasting policy. Constitutional markers frame the actions the government and the CRTC may take in the areas not clearly defined in their mandates.

The extent to which the law relies on objectives, general concepts and technical standards gives a great deal of leeway to administrative authorities responsible for supervising and regulating the broadcasting system. The principle of interpretation contained in the *Canadian Charter of Rights and Freedoms* creates the frameworks within which public organizations must exercise their powers and duties, especially those organizations with a great deal of discretionary power. Freedom of expression and the other rights guaranteed by the Charter may be limited only by "law," and only by what is reasonable and demonstrably justified in a free and democratic society. Consequently, those measures that are likely to affect fundamental rights and freedoms should be formulated in a sufficiently intelligible manner that those individuals potentially affected by the measures can determine the extent of their rights and obligations.

The application of a particular standard in a particular instance always includes an element of assessment. But when a rule serves only to grant absolute power for applying a standard, so that an individual or group can do whatever appears most appropriate in a given situation, then this is not a "rule of law" (*Re Ontario Film* 1983). However, as soon as it is reasonably possible for someone affected by legislation to know the contents of a law, we are dealing with a rule of law. In this respect, even those laws that are often considered to be vague and polymorphous, such as those governing contempt of court (Popovici 1977), have been considered as laws and not as the exercise of discretion or absolute power (*R. v. Kopyto* 1987; see also Trudel 1989a). In the *Sunday Times* (1978) decision, the European Court of Justice found that contempt of court, a violation under the terms of common law, was a "rule of law" under the terms of the Convention[24] because it is possible for a reasonably informed person to determine those actions that are prohibited under the terms of this law (see Pinard 1991). In *R. v. Therens* (1985, 645) the Supreme Court of Canada, in a judgement written by Mr. Justice Le Dain, stated what constituted a rule of law:

> The limit will be prescribed by law within the meaning of s. 1 if it is expressly provided for by statute or regulation, or results by necessary implication from the terms of a statute or regulation or from its

operating requirements. The limit may also result from the application of a common law rule.

By contrast, a public officer's manner of acting is not, in itself, a rule of law (*R. v. Simmons* 1988, 531; *R. v. Therens* 1985; see also *R. v. Thomsen* 1988, 650).

R. v. Committee for the Commonwealth of Canada (1991) illustrates the two schools of thought of Supreme Court justices on the question of determining what constitutes rule of law under the *Canadian Charter of Rights and Freedoms*. For Madam Justice L'Heureux-Dubé, it must be determined whether the text of a law or regulation that restricts a guaranteed freedom is sufficiently exact to allow the person affected to determine what is permitted and what is forbidden. Madam Justice McLachlin considers that it is not appropriate to require such a high degree of precision for laws and regulations because, as she writes, the state would then be obliged to adopt detailed regulations bearing on all imaginable possibilities before it could justify its conduct under section 1 of the Charter. That is why she considers that, as soon as the restriction results from the application of a rule of law, in the instance where this decision is made by a civil servant, the decision is likely to be analysed in the light of the standards of reasonableness set out in section 1 of the Charter. This latter position is doubtless much more realistic – it is detached from a formal approach that makes it virtually impossible for the law to rely on the standards of good conduct. Over the long term, viewing legislation formally could lead to a situation where laws are analysed in the same way as municipal by-laws.

In *Slaight Communications v. Davidson* (1989, 1079–80), the Supreme Court of Canada, in a judgement written by Mr. Justice Lamer,[25] had to stipulate the steps that must be followed to determine the validity of an order from an administrative court and consequently from rules adopted under general powers. The principles stated are sufficiently broad to include most of the decisions made by the government, the minister of communications or the CRTC under the *Broadcasting Act* of 1991.

First, Mr. Justice Lamer stated two important principles:

- an administrative tribunal may not exceed the jurisdiction it has by statute; and

- it must be presumed that legislation conferring an imprecise discretion does not confer the power to infringe the *Charter* unless that power is conferred expressly or by necessary implication. (*Slaight Communications* 1989, 1079)

Mr. Justice Lamer added that the application of these two principles to the exercise of discretion leads to one of the following two situations:

1. The disputed order was made pursuant to legislation which confers, either expressly or by necessary implication, the power to infringe a protected right.

   – It is then necessary to subject the **legislation** to the test set out in s. 1 by ascertaining whether it constitutes a reasonable limit that can be demonstrably justified in a free and democratic society.

2. The legislation pursuant to which the administrative tribunal made the disputed order confers an imprecise discretion and does not confer, either expressly or by necessary implication, the power to limit the rights guaranteed by the *Charter*.

   – It is then necessary to subject the **order** made to the test set out in s. 1 by ascertaining whether it constitutes a reasonable limit that can be demonstrably justified in a free and democratic society;

   – if it is not thus justified, the administrative tribunal has necessarily exceeded its jurisdiction;

   – if it is thus justified, on the other hand, then the administrative tribunal has acted within its jurisdiction. (*Slaight Communications* 1989, 1080)

The Duty of Broadcasters regarding Program Quality   The *Broadcasting Act*, 1968 declares that "the programming provided by each broad-caster should be of high standard" (section 3(*d*)).[26] The new *Broadcasting Act* of 1991 repeats that objective in the same terms. It states in paragraph 3(*g*) that "programming originated by broadcasting undertakings should be of high standard." In the 1968 Act, this objective is part of a provision that also covers programming provided by the broadcasting system as a whole. However, this objective of high standard is intended to cover the programming provided by each broadcaster;[27] the same holds true in the new Act.

In the CRTC public notice *Concerning a Complaint against CKVU Television, Vancouver, British Columbia by Media Watch* (1987b), the Commission stated that "the right of freedom of expression on the public airwaves cannot supersede the public's right to receive broadcast programming of high standard."

The CRTC decision regarding the renewal, for a short period, of the operating licence of CHRC in Quebec City summarizes and explains the views of the CRTC regarding the imperatives of high quality programming in the context of freedom of expression. Recognizing the superior status of freedom of expression, the CRTC affirms that:

> Section 1 of the Charter makes it readily apparent that the rights and freedoms listed therein are not absolute in this country, nor have they ever been for that matter. Freedom of expression in Canada is thus not without restriction. The ... provisions of the Act unequivocally attest to Parliament's intent that, in supervising the use of radio frequencies, which are public property and limited in number by the radio spectrum, the greatest possible emphasis be given to the affirmation of the right to freedom of expression, subject to the requirement for programming of high standard and subject to achieving an intelligent harmony with the requirement for balance in the discussion of matters of public concern. (*Les entreprises* 1990, 6)

Further on in the document, the CRTC concedes that "the right to freedom of expression is to be favoured as much as possible in view of the requirements of high quality and balance." But this should not mean that men and women who bear the brunt of the exercise of freedom of expression are unprotected from those who control a station's airwaves.

The CRTC's concept of "high standard" is often confused with other concepts like "balance." High standard (Trudel 1989b) is invoked more liberally, however, because it can apply to matters on which two legitimate viewpoints do not exist. In the *Media Watch* (CRTC 1987b) case, for example, the CRTC agreed that the issue of whether women ought to be raped does not lend itself to "balanced" debate. Similarly, in the Nishga Tribal Council Complaint (CRTC 1985), the CRTC stated that "abusive comments cannot be justified by offering equal time to the abused." In such situations, the regulatory body relies on the high standard notion for justifying decisions to sanction or to censure.[28]

The concept of high standard also refers to good programming and journalistic practices. In its 1974 decision concerning the renewal of the CBC's network licence (*Radio* 1974; see also *Renewal* 1979), the CRTC emphasized that such things as accurate reporting and presenting informed commentary on all aspects and all points of view of any given issue should remain the central concerns of journalism. Likewise, when it renewed Rogers Cable's licence in 1985, the CRTC reminded broadcasters that: "With regard to high-standard programming, the Commission has a continuing expectation that high editorial standards are carefully adhered to by the licensee, and emphasizes the licensee's responsibility for the programs that it broadcasts" (*Rogers* 1985, 7).

This approach is much the same as the approach taken in the *Media*

Watch (CRTC 1987b, 6) case, where the CRTC explained that to determine whether a broadcaster has discharged its duties in the area of programming quality, the circumstances of each case must be considered, including the context of the programming, "the extent to which the broadcaster had an opportunity to determine, prior to broadcast, whether a statement did not merit airing and, failing that, its willingness to accept responsibility and offer an apology for the airing of a statement which failed to satisfy acceptable standards of broadcasting." In this case, the CRTC also noted that "broadcasters fall short of discharging their responsibilities and of attaining the high standard of programming required when the frequency entrusted to them is used, not to criticize the activities of a particular group but to advocate sexual violence against its members" (ibid., 6–7).

The public notice of 28 June 1984 (CRTC 1984b) was issued as a result of complaints against Montreal radio station CFCF. It concerned the use of a telephone survey (Instapoll) in which listeners, by calling the station, were able to indicate whether they sympathized with Corporal Denis Lortie's motives when he opened deadly fire in the Quebec National Assembly on 8 May 1984. Emphasizing the woefully flawed methodology of such a poll, the CRTC came to the conclusion that the requisite high standard of programming had not been met. In this regard, the Commission wrote that "asking listeners to answer a question with a 'yes' or 'no' may be acceptable or at least harmless when the question relates to matters not crucial to the well-being of society, but is inappropriate and even dangerous in the case of fundamental public issues" (ibid., 6). Furthermore, in this case, there was no system for controlling the number of times the same person could vote. Also mentioned were certain situational factors such as the lack of consideration for the victims' loved ones and the possibility that, after such an event, people would be encouraged to express extreme sentiments. Thus, the CRTC concluded that by conducting and broadcasting the Instapoll, CFCF had failed to discharge its obligation to maintain a high standard of programming.[29]

The obligation to cover election campaigns is seen as an inherent part of the broadcaster's duty to inform the public so as to ensure that it has sufficient knowledge to make an enlightened choice from among the various parties and candidates. It is also a fairly obvious application of the consideration of balance contemplated in section 3(*d*) of the 1968 Act and section 3(*i*)(ii) of the 1991 Act. Also invoked in support of the broadcaster's obligation to cover elections within its broadcast area is the high standard of programming principle. In Circular No. 334, *Political Broadcasting – Complaints re: Free Time and Editorial Time*

Allocations, the CRTC noted that, "bearing in mind the licensee's duty found in section 3(d) of the Broadcasting Act to provide 'high standard' programming, it is difficult to envisage a situation where a licensee would not ensure such coverage" (CRTC 1987a, 8–9). The notion of high standard, therefore, constitutes the foundation of applicable rules regarding partisan broadcasting.

Programming of high standard surely justifies the requirement that the licensee identify the sponsor and, as the case may be, the political party on whose behalf an announcement is broadcast. The obligation to identify the sponsor is an express provision of the 1968 *Broadcasting Act*. There is also no doubt that the CRTC has the authority to impose the obligation even though the provision is not included in the new Act.

In the 1968 Act, this requirement is valid for federal as well as provincial and municipal elections (section 19(2)). Sponsor identification must be made both immediately before and after the broadcast if it exceeds two minutes. If air time is under two minutes, identification can be made either immediately before or after the broadcast.

The 1991 *Broadcasting Act* retains the CRTC's authority to make regulations and to prescribe conditions of licence. In *CKOY v. R.* (1979), the Supreme Court of Canada had to determine the validity of a section in the *Radio (A.M.) Broadcasting Regulations* (now *Radio Regulations, 1986*), which at the time prohibited stations or network operators from broadcasting telephone interviews unless the interviewee had consented to such a broadcast or had telephoned the station for the purpose of participating in a broadcast. Writing for the majority, Mr. Justice Spence established the test for determining the nature of the connection between the policy in section 3 of the *Broadcasting Act* and the CRTC's authority to enact regulations.

To that effect, Mr. Justice Spence wrote that "the validity of any regulation enacted in reliance upon s. 16 must be tested by determining whether the regulation deals with a class of subject referred to in s. 3 of the statute and ... in doing so the Court looks at the regulation objectively" (*CKOY* 1979, 11).[30] However, as the wording of section 3 is very general, Mr. Justice Spence believed that Parliament obviously intended to give the CRTC considerable latitude in exercising its regulatory power to implement the policy and objectives that it was created to pursue. Accordingly, the Court held that whether "the impugned regulation will implement a policy or not is irrelevant so long as we determine objectively that it is upon a class of subject referred to in s. 3" (ibid., 12).

After finding that the purpose of the CRTC regulation was to prohibit any "undesirable broadcasting technique which does not reflect the high standard of programming which the Commission must, by regulation of licensees, endeavour to maintain," Mr. Justice Spence added that it was "self-evident" that such a technique might well lower the high standard of programming (*CKOY* 1979, 13). Therefore, we can presume that, when it enacts regulations, the CRTC has a duty to strive for programming of high standard and that this objective determines the extent of its powers.

The CRTC's mandate is to oversee and regulate all aspects of the broadcasting system with a view to implementing the Canadian broadcasting policy as described in section 3 of the *Broadcasting Act.* Consequently, it is by referring to that section that we may identify what areas the CRTC has the authority to regulate. The section is not restricted to subjects of regulation; it also enunciates principles, goals and standards.

It is necessary to make a specific connection between the regulatory authority provided in the *Broadcasting Act* (section 10 of the 1991 Act) and the provisions of section 3. The principles and objectives contained in section 3 identify a purpose for the standards that the regulatory body is empowered to adopt. In effect, the standards become valid once it is possible to establish a connection between them and the principles and objectives set out in section 3.

Section 3 also delimits the scope of the CRTC's power to impose licensing conditions on radio, television and cable companies. The power is granted by section 9 of the *Broadcasting Act* of 1991:

> Subject to this Part, the Commission may, in furtherance of its objects:
>
> ...
>
> (*b*) issue licences for such terms not exceeding seven years and subject to such conditions related to the circumstances of the licensee,
>
>> (i) as the Commission deems appropriate for *the implementation of the broadcasting policy set out in subsection 3(1).*[31] [emphasis added]

In *CTV Television Network v. CRTC* (1981, 254), the Federal Court of Appeal, in a decision subsequently upheld by the Supreme Court of Canada (*CTV* 1982, 543), found that the power granted in section 17 of the 1968 Act is very broad; the new Act confers the same broad power. Both courts gave the following analysis of the 1968 Act: "it seems to be well within the power of the committee under section 17 ... to impose a condition designed to further one of the objects of the broadcasting policy, provided the condition is one that is related to the circumstances of the appellant [applicant for a licence or for renewal thereof] and provided that its imposition is not contrary to the Act or to regulations that have been made in exercise of the power to make regulations contained in section 16" (ibid.).

The assessment of this aspect of the *Broadcasting Act*, 1968 holds true for the 1991 Act, which repeats the same terms. The extent of the CRTC's powers to set licensing conditions is delimited by the terms of section 3. In addition to providing a foundation for the specific and regulatory decisions of the CRTC, these principles form a general framework for broadcasting in Canada. By offering both an ideal and a purpose for the CRTC's regulatory role, the high standard concept helps define the extent of the CRTC's powers and, as such, the extent of its discretionary power. The standard also affects the direction that the CRTC may take in the exercise of its discretion.

The authors of the 1966 *White Paper on Broadcasting* included an empowering aspect in their definition of programming of high standard: "In programming, high quality is more a matter of general excellence than of mere content. So called 'high-brow' programs can be artistically or technically poor, while light entertainment can be excellent. High quality does not necessarily flow from high cost, and standards of quality cannot readily be made a condition of a licence. However, judgements about quality can quite legitimately be made in retrospect on the basis of actual observed performance, and should carry a great deal of weight when an application for the renewal of a licence is being considered" (Canada 1966, 11).[32]

The authors of the 1966 white paper intended that the regulatory body should, to a certain degree, be able to take into account the quality of programs provided by licensees when considering renewal applications. They also recognized the inherent difficulty of passing judgement on the quality of radio and television programs.

In the name of pursuing high standards, it is permissible for the CRTC to evaluate the performance of broadcasters in terms of the quality of their programming. The CRTC's exercise of this power is legitimized, to some extent, by its connection to the high standard criterion. Notice the standard's enabling role: it acts to legitimize discretionary decisions. The rhetorical function of the standard, therefore, is not present only when Parliament enunciates it by passing the legislation; the norms established by the rhetoric form an integral part of the standard's enabling role. It helps to enhance and delimit the enabling effect of the standard. Thus, the high standard is an enabling criterion that is both general and specific.

The symbolic meaning contained within the standard is even more indicative of its comprehensive nature. The "high standard of programming" requirement encourages efforts to exceed this standard. The criteria that the CRTC develops in the future may go beyond current practices. Such a formulation helps to widen the discretionary power of those enforcing the Act. The Act itself is even strengthened by the legitimizing nature of the standard, which is expressed in such a way that it can do little else than inspire support for this principle.[33]

The delimited nature of the standard helps to make it a regulatory instrument that is versatile yet sufficiently specific. At any given time, the accepted standards of television and radio professionals place limits on what CRTC standards can effectively demand. The semantic limits of "high standard programming" will correspond to what the industry is ready to accept. Gifford (1971, 429) explains that when contextual forces are opposed to a broad interpretation of the standard, the legitimacy of this standard – its major strength – is impaired.

In other words, any attempt to persuade the broadcasting industry, in the name of high standard programming, to adopt practices out of step with generally accepted ones would probably fail. This fact is illustrated more clearly by examining how the CRTC enforces the high standard when it assesses the conduct of broadcasters. The CRTC is flexible in its approach: it makes recommendations and encourages stations to adopt internal policies less likely to give rise to regrettable incidents. Only when it comes up against a station that is clearly unwilling to change its attitude will the CRTC resort to censure.

Balanced Treatment of Candidates   The integrity of the electoral process requires that all candidates have an equal opportunity to address the electorate. Indeed, it is vital that each candidate be given the opportunity to outline his or her platform to the voters and to solicit their vote.

However, there is good reason to fear that the disparity in resources available to the various candidates and political parties is such that only the wealthy will be in a position to secure sufficient advertising space and time to communicate their point of view.

By definition, time available on radio and television is limited. The amount of time that can be devoted to advertising is determined either by regulation or by the tolerance threshold of those members of the audience who simply change the channel if the programming does not hold their attention. Because broadcasting time is a scarce resource, much is at stake in deciding how to distribute it: relying solely on the rules of supply and demand would give an unfair advantage to those who can afford to pay large sums of money for broadcasting time.

In short, there is nothing to ensure that a conventional, market-driven distribution of advertising time would guarantee all candidates and political parties access to the airwaves. This situation has led to the development of measures to ensure balanced treatment of the various candidates.

Section 3(d) of the *Broadcasting Act*, 1968 enunciated the principle of balance when it declared that "the programming provided by the Canadian broadcasting system should be varied and comprehensive and should provide reasonable, balanced opportunity for the expression of differing views on matters of public concern." The 1991 *Broadcasting Act* no longer deals with the subject of balance in relation to the treatment of issues of public interest. However, section 3(1)(*i*)(i) states that the programming provided by the system should "be varied and comprehensive, providing a balance of information, enlightenment and entertainment for men, women and children of all ages, interests and tastes." According to Thompson-Pyper (1990, 30), the intention behind this new wording is to uphold the general principle of balance, as found in the *Broadcasting Act*, 1968, but to back away from the too specific reference to matters of public interest.

Undoubtedly, balance is the oldest and most recurring principle of broadcasting policy and regulation in Canada. Balance is sometimes seen as the counterpart of the American "fairness doctrine." At times, it is considered the basis of licence allocation policies and, at other times, as the guiding ethical principle for programming decision makers: in any case, balance is most certainly the sine qua non of the legal framework for broadcasting in Canada. The 1965 *Report* of the Fowler Committee on Broadcasting maintained that balanced programming rejects the notion that broadcasters may limit themselves to "giving the public what it wants" (Canada, Committee 1965, 4). By the same token, the concept of balance is used to prevent broadcasters from advocating one cause to the exclusion of every other point of view opposed to it.

Under section 3(d) of the *Broadcasting Act*, 1968, the programming provided by the Canadian broadcasting system should provide a reasonable, balanced opportunity for the expression of differing views on matters of public concern. According to Hammond (1982), this objective was inserted into the *Broadcasting Act*, 1968 after the controversy created by the program "This Hour Has Seven Days." The new *Broadcasting Act* renews this system.

Balanced audiovisual programming can be achieved in various ways. One could deduce from the general principle that balance ought to be found in each broadcaster's programming. Or, one might consider balance in reference to the broadcasting system as a whole and conclude that it is sufficient that the system be organized and regulated to assure a reasonable and balanced opportunity to express differing points of view. Of course, one can infer that if each broadcaster respects the principle of balance in his or her programming, it will be respected in the whole system. This last perspective is endorsed by the CRTC. (See CRTC 1970, 1972, 1977, 1987d; *Les entreprises* 1990; see also Squire and Stepinac 1969; Cook 1982.)

In *National Indian Brotherhood v. Juneau (No. 3)*, Mr. Justice Walsh maintains that the provisions of section 3 of the *Broadcasting Act*, 1968 are not intended "to apply to each and every programme but to broadcasting policy as a whole" (1971, 513). He points out that section 3(*d*) of the 1968 Act is merely part of one section

> providing that the programming should be varied and comprehensive and provide reasonable balanced opportunities for the expression of differing views on matters of public concern and be of high standard, using predominantly Canadian creative and other resources. Here again it is apparently the general programming that is being referred to and not any individual programme and, in any event, as already stated, the only sanction provided would be the revocation, suspension or refusal to renew the licence if a programme did not comply with this regulation. (*National* 1971, 514)

The *Broadcasting Act* of 1991 covers a station's programming as a whole and does not authorize the CRTC to intervene for any one specific program. Decisions about specific programs fall within the broadcaster's editorial discretion. This interpretation, arising out of the *National Indian Brotherhood v. Juneau (No. 3)* (1971) decision, is confirmed in the new Act, because section 2(3) states that: "This Act shall be construed and applied in a manner that is consistent with the freedom of expression and journalistic, creative and programming independence enjoyed by broadcasting undertakings." However, when it comes to setting ethical guidelines for programming dealing with controversial subject matter, balance is the key concept.

Even today, the treatment of controversial issues on radio and television is still governed by a series of principles that originated in the early years of radio. Although they have been somewhat refined through years of experience, debate and analysis, the principles handed down to us concerning controversial programming have stayed remarkably constant.

The Aird Commission was appointed in 1928 as a result of controversy surrounding certain broadcasts by four stations belonging to a religious group. One of the Commission's recommendations – the adoption of a regulation prohibiting the broadcast of controversial remarks – was to become a fundamental principle of the balanced programming standards of Canadian broadcasting policy (Canada, Royal Commission 1929, 12–13).

More debate and commentary was touched off by the radio broadcast of political advertisements entitled "Mr. Sage," sponsored by the incumbent Conservative party. The 1936 Act that was passed by the Liberal government, which came to power despite the opposing party's unflattering broadcasts, included provisions prohibiting dramatizations in political and electoral advertising (Canada, *Canadian Broadcasting Act* 1952, s. 21(3)).

In its first years, the Canadian Broadcasting Corporation (CBC) experienced a number of events that ultimately led to the adoption of measures to deal with controversial programming. In early 1937, the Corporation's Board of Governors, which at the time was responsible for regulating all radio operations including those in the private sector, took Toronto station CFRB to task for broadcasting programs concerning birth control for and sterilization of persons with intellectual disabilities (Cook 1982, 12). In autumn of the same year, the CBC passed a regulation prohibiting the broadcast of "anything in contravention of the law" or offensive to any race or religion. The same regulation forbade the broadcast of false or misleading news, as well as programs about birth control and venereal diseases unless such programs were presented in a manner appropriate for radio. Defending itself against charges of restricting freedom of expression and equitable treatment of controversial issues, the CBC declared that since radio was an "intimate medium" that entered into people's homes, some control was necessary (Peers 1969, 260).

In 1938, two more controversies were recorded in the annals of radio. A weekly CBC public affairs program had broadcast criticisms of British foreign policy. Debate ensued in Parliament and the press about whether Parliament should exercise tighter control over the CBC's activities and whether the Corporation ought to reflect official government policy. Cook (1982) writes that: "In an exchange of letters between chairman of CBC Board of governors, Leonard Brockington, and Prime Minister King, King expressed some misgivings about the particular program in question, but did give an assurance that the government would not interfere in the internal programming policies of the CBC. The CBC, however, became more cautious. The weekly commentary program, which broadcast the viewpoint of one speaker each week, was replaced with a new forum series where several speakers debated in each program" (ibid., 13–14; see also Peers 1969, 266–67).

There was also heated discussion during this period on the issue of buying radio time to broadcast opinions about a controversial topic. The ensuing debate revealed a number of inconsistencies in the CBC's policy concerning the sale of air time to individuals (Cook 1982, 13–14; Peers 1969, 266–67). The deliberations sparked by these events eventually led to the 1939 publication of the CBC Statement of Policy with respect to Controversial Broadcasting. This document established a lasting distinction between political programming, around which an entirely separate body of regulation developed, and controversial programming in general (Boyer 1983).

Published in July 1939, the CBC statement (cited in Baum 1970, 164) repeated many of the standards upon which prior decisions had been based. It is a significant document in that it sets out the principles that still apply today to the treatment of controversial topics. Among them is the idea that the airwaves are an appropriate medium to use to stimulate the discussion of controversial issues. The policy statement stressed that the most effective way to preserve freedom of expression is to allow the greatest number of diverse and conflicting opinions to be voiced. Therefore, according to the document, all the major viewpoints should be presented in an equitable, if not equal, manner. It is not surprising, then, that the statement rejects the idea of selling air time to individuals and warns the CBC to resist any attempt to regiment programming.

The war years were marked by a number of debates about whether the CBC should espouse government policy in all respects during wartime (Ellis 1979, 25). Similarly, the frequent attacks on the CBC by the Quebec clergy gave rise to much debate in Parliament throughout the 1950s (Beke 1970, 110).[34] None of the reports on these matters, however, resulted in any amendments to the basic principles enunciated in the 1939 policy statement.

With the passage of the *Broadcasting Act* of 1958, the power to oversee and regulate broadcasting was transferred to the Board of Broadcast Governors (BBG), an organization independent of the CBC.

In 1961, the Board of Broadcast Governors published Circular No. 51 – *White Paper on Political and Controversial Broadcasting Policies*, which essentially restated the principles of the 1939 policy developed by the directors of the CBC. Following that example, the BBG policy was based on the following four principles:

1. The air belongs to the people, who are entitled to hear the principal points of view on all questions of importance.
2. The air must not fall under the control of any individual or groups influenced by reason of their wealth or special position.

3. The right to answer is inherent in the doctrine of free speech.
4. The full interchange of opinion is one of the principal safeguards of free institutions. (BBG 1961, 7)

From these principles, the Board drew the corollary that the best safeguard of freedom of discussion is a policy that permits opportunity for the expression of varying points of view. The general nature of the Board's policy is clear in the following excerpt from Circular No. 51:

> In accordance with its policy of resisting any attempts to regiment opinion or to abuse freedom of speech, the Board lays down no specific rulings covering controversial broadcasting. The Board itself supports the policy of the fullest use of the air for:
>
> (a) Forthright discussion of all controversial questions;
> (b) Equal and fair presentation of all main points of view;
> (c) The discussion of current affairs and problems by informed author- itative and competent speakers.
>
> Broadcasting is a changing and evolving art and no fixed and perma- nent criteria can be set down for the best method of presenting contro- versial material. (BBG 1961, 8)

Circular No. 51 continues to be an essential text in the field of policy governing controversial programming in Canada (CRTC 1977).[35] Some of its principles were later adopted and refined by the CRTC.

The Board of Broadcast Governors was not directly involved in the furore surrounding the program "This Hour Has Seven Days." Undoubtedly one of the most controversial shows ever broadcast, "This Hour Has Seven Days" was a public affairs program that distinguished itself by incisive, satirical and occasionally irreverent discussion of current events. Interviews were conducted with a powerful dose of emotion, and the writers sought to break free from the CBC's prevailing programming code. The Crown corporation's management had expe- rience mainly in radio and were ill at ease with the visual coverage of delicate subjects; when they decided to cancel the program, it was consid- ered an act of censorship on their part. As well, CBC management seemed more than anything to be concerned about the debates that certain episodes of the series had touched off in Parliament (Cook 1982, 25).

For their part, the writers and hosts of "This Hour Has Seven Days" believed that CBC public affairs programs should present a critical view of Canadian culture and society (Cook 1982, 25). The parliamentary committee studying the matter criticized the senior administration of the CBC, reminding them that neutrality does not have to add up to dull programming. Program producers were encouraged to retain their own style while at the same time watching out for any biases that might creep into the discussion of controversial issues (Peers 1979, 347–48).

"This Hour Has Seven Days" heralded the introduction of a notion of balance that was quite distinct from the objective treatment standard understood to mean "fairness" in reporting and broadcast commentary. Carscallen describes the new concept of balance that took root during this period:

> The interpretation of "balance" in public affairs programming therefore became more relative and contingent than the ideal-type balance which senior management imagined could be achieved. The concept of "fair comment" was substituted for "balanced comment." The staff conceived of the public affairs program as balanced over a period of time but not necessarily within one program series. They believed that the Establishment's values should be challenged; hypocrisy should be revealed; the underdog should sometimes be championed; illusions should be stripped away; that the individual Canadian had a right to see what was happening in the society in which he lived so that he might more realistically make social and political decisions. (Carscallen 1966, 140–41 in Cook 1982, 25)

In time, another program provided an opportunity to set out guidelines for producing and broadcasting reports on controversial topics: it was called "Air of Death" (Squire and Stepinac 1969).

On 22 October 1967, the CBC English television network broadcast a program dealing with pollution in the Dunnville–Port Maitland region of Ontario, near Hamilton. The documentary dealt with fluoride emissions from the Electric Reduction Co. plant. The program showed that the fluoride emissions were responsible for killing hundreds of cattle, destroying crops and endangering human lives. The tone and content of the broadcast sparked public debate. From its inception, the CRTC undertook to inquire into the way the CBC assumed its responsibilities during the production and broadcast of "Air of Death." The Committee appointed by the CRTC[36] was given the mandate not only to hold public hearings in connection with the program itself, but also to assist the CRTC in developing a policy for controversial programming. The terms of reference stated that the Committee "would determine measures taken by the CBC for the maintenance of high standards of public information in preparation, production and broadcasting of the program" (CRTC 1970, 1). According to the CRTC, one of the purposes of the hearing was to allow the CRTC to help develop standards of public information in broadcasting, "including the need of balanced opportunity for the expression of differing views on matters of public concern" (ibid.).

The Committee expressed its general opinions in the form of "thoughts" in connection with several important aspects of informational programming on radio and television.[37] For example, the Committee observed that the concepts of "high standard" and "balance" expressed in the 1968 *Broadcasting Act*, and the CRTC's supervisory powers must not, "in the case of informational programming, result in a curb or limitation in the television medium's search for ways and means of describing those problems which are of common interest and concern to the public" (CRTC 1970, 14). The Committee recommended to the CRTC that it make every effort to encourage station managers, producers and directors to put their talent toward creating such programs. The Committee also suggested that broadcasting organizations should adopt their own policies relating to the preparation, production and broadcast of documentaries; in view of the visual impact of television broadcasts and the intense response they evoke from their audience, the Committee stated that broadcasters might want to rethink their internal supervision procedures.

Such procedures should enable station management to perform internal checks and monitoring of the progressive phases of production before the documentary becomes a fait accompli and changes can no longer be made. The Committee goes so far as to say that: "It is not sufficient for a broadcasting organization to satisfy the collective responsibility which it freely acknowledges it has with respect to all programming, unless, in the course of production of a program, senior officials are available to act in the dispassionate role of a referee, to balance the natural involvement of persons identified with a particular program" (CRTC 1970, 15).

The concept of balance set out in section 3 of the *Broadcasting Act*, 1968, as interpreted by the CRTC Committee, does not mean that every program must present all sides of an issue. What is important is that controversial issues be dealt with fairly and honestly within programming as a whole. Nor did the Committee see the concept of balance as implying any duty to give equal attention to all viewpoints contrary to the one advanced in a given program. The Committee's concern was that any controversy regarding the existence or gravity of a problem dealt with in a broadcast be identified clearly and explained fairly.

After issuing several warnings against the use of certain methods in the presentation of controversial subjects, and after urging broadcasters to bring matters of public interest to the audience's attention without resorting to hyperbole, the Committee concluded that such matters should not be resolved by over-regulation, but by the recognition by broadcasters that their audience is sophisticated and willing to hear a range of opinions.

In its public notice concerning a complaint lodged against radio station CHNS Halifax, the CRTC censured a broadcast licensee for not having taken steps to allow opposing points of view to be expressed on a matter of public concern (CRTC 1972). CHNS had broadcast an editorial during the course of which certain organizations, allegedly funded by money collected in a fund-raising march called Miles for Millions, were compared to the Front de libération du Québec (FLQ). It was even suggested that some of the funds so raised would end up in the hands of supporters of Cuba's Fidel Castro. These comments were made a few days after the FLQ had committed acts that threw the country into a serious political crisis and led the government to invoke the *War Measures Act.*

At 8:20 AM on the same day, five minutes after the editorial, the station invited the organizers of the march to debate the matter with the author of the editorial in an open-line show scheduled to begin at 8:30 AM. During the program, the organizers of the march expressed their views. The CRTC said in its announcement that: "Where a broadcast commentary constitutes an attack on an organization which will have an immediate and profound effect on the plans or objectives of the organization, exceptional care will be required to ensure that the organization is given an equitable opportunity to present its views" (CRTC 1972, 3).

In addition to granting air time to the organizers, the station should have provided the organizers with "a copy of the material to be broadcast and a notice of the times it was to be aired" (CRTC 1972, 3) before the broadcast. The Committee concluded that, in failing to take "these or similar measures," CHNS had breached its duty to provide equitable opportunity for the expression of differing views regarding matters of public interest. In this case, therefore, not only should the station have granted air time to the organization it was criticizing, which it did, it should have gone further and given the organizers the opportunity to know the substance of the attack in advance. The impact of the decision is, of course, tempered by the fact that the CRTC reminds licensees that "whether a breach of this duty [imposed by the *Broadcasting Act*] has occurred will depend on the circumstances of each case" (ibid.). Nevertheless, the decision expands to a surprising degree the notion of balance and even the "right of reply," as it is referred to in some jurisdictions.

The public notice concerning CHNS determined a duty a posteriori.

Until that time, none of the regulations or public notices and decisions of the regulatory agencies had ever mentioned a duty to warn a person or organization about the tenor of an editorial comment before it is broadcast. It is possible, however, to infer such a duty from the terms of section 3(d) of the 1968 *Broadcasting Act*, wherein broadcasters should provide a reasonable, balanced opportunity for the expression of differing views on matters of public concern. The Commission very likely relied on this principle to come to its conclusion that, in the CHNS case, the station had not fulfilled its duty. Unfortunately, this fact is not made clear. Morris criticizes this aspect of the decision:

> Another disturbing aspect of the CHNS announcement is that the CRTC saw fit to censure a licensee for violating general and somewhat vague principles, not stipulated standards of conduct. Licensees in the U.S. at least have the guidance of a fairly specific doctrine and a long series of decisions to guide them, even though unexpected quirks ... are occasionally inflicted upon them ... The BBG-CRTC refusal to set out definite but flexible guidelines worked to the detriment of a licensee in this case. (1972, 34–35)

Broadcasters worried about the impact the outcome of the CHNS case would have on their programming decisions. There was a debate on this matter at the 1972 conference of the Canadian Association of Broadcasters (ibid., 46, appendix B).

In its 1974 CBC network licence renewal decision (*Radio* 1974), the CRTC reiterated the importance of paying great attention to standards of professional broadcast journalism, including the rules of debate, the right to reply and the requirement of evidence in support of assertions broadcast in public. The Commission repeated that the Canadian people had the right to receive accurate information and informed commentary on all sides of important questions of public concern. Since then, the CBC has consolidated its program policies and has even published statements of "journalistic policy" (CBC 1982).

The 1977 *Report on Issues Raised by CFCF's Anti Bill 22 Campaign* (CRTC 1977) was published in response to a Montreal radio station's active campaign against Quebec's language legislation. Following an analysis of CFCF's programming, in which the CRTC found that the station had failed to provide adequate balance in its programs dealing with the controversy over the legislation, the Commission called CFCF to a licence renewal hearing to allow it to explain how it perceived its programming responsibilities during the campaign and how it considered that it had met its responsibilities.

The objective of the *Report on Issues Raised by CFCF's Anti Bill 22 Campaign* was "to encourage and stimulate broadcasters to experiment with and find new approaches, formats and standards for controversial programs" (CRTC 1977, 1). Broadcasters were reminded that final responsibility for programming rests with them. The report was intended to outline some general issues arising from that particular case and to recall a number of fundamental principles that "apply to all broadcast licensees in the exercise of their responsibility when dealing with controversial subjects requiring a reasonable and balanced opportunity for the expression of differing points of view" (ibid., 2).

Although it was in line with previous policies relating to controversial programming, the CFCF-Bill 22 report is certainly the most complete statement issued by the CRTC on these matters.

The first argument advanced by the CRTC was that radio frequencies are public property: "the operation of a broadcasting undertaking constitutes a public trust that must be used in the public interest and on behalf of the public which the undertaking is licensed to serve" (CRTC 1977, 8). In return for conferring this trust on a private enterprise, the public expects to receive full information on matters of public concern. Before setting the corollaries of this basic principle, the CRTC states further that: "The broadcaster's duty which flows from this is twofold: to devote a reasonable amount of broadcast time to the coverage of public issues; and to cover controversial issues of public importance fairly by providing an opportunity for the presentation of contrasting points of view. The proper exercise of this duty is critical to the democratic process" (ibid.).

According to the CRTC, the public's right to receive programming that provides a reasonable, balanced opportunity for the expression of differing views on matters of public concern supersedes the licensee's right to freedom of expression. This is so even though, subject to the evaluation of the supervisory agency, the licensee is responsible for determining what is reasonable, what constitutes balance, which matters are of public concern and which views deserve to be aired. The CRTC reserves its right to review the broadcaster's decisions when it writes that: "The Commission may require reconsideration on the basis of the public's right to receive programming which deals fairly and adequately with controversial issues. It is the denial of this right by a broadcaster which is a form of censorship" (CRTC 1977, 9).

However, it is up to the broadcaster to judge, according to his or her editorial policy, what constitutes controversy. Deeming them of continuing relevance, the Commission reiterates the words of the Board of Broadcast Governors, according to whom broadcasting is a changing and evolving art for which no fixed criteria and methods can be established.

The broadcaster's duty as described in the CFCF-Bill 22 (CRTC 1977) report is very similar to the description of the twofold American fairness doctrine. Therefore, it is safe to conclude that the fundamental principles of the fairness doctrine apply in Canada. They are not enforced in Canada, however, in the same way as they are in the United States.

The CRTC recalled the fundamental principles on controversial programming in its 23 September 1987 public notice, *Election Campaign Broadcasting*. It set out the premises of its various policy statements in that regard:

(a) CRTC regulation, as a general rule, should not constrain or inhibit the ways and means of presenting controversial issues.

(b) Broadcasters have a responsibility to become involved in controversial issues of public concern.

(c) Broadcasters should devote a reasonable amount of air time to the coverage of controversial public issues and should provide an opportunity for the presentation of differing points of view.

(d) The public, through the presentation by broadcasters of the various points of view in a fair and objective way, should be placed in a position to make its own informed judgement on controversial issues.

(e) It is for the broadcaster in the first instance to determine what is a reasonable balanced opportunity for the expression of differing views, subject to review by the Commission. (CRTC 1987d, 7–8)

These general principles have occasionally been analysed, as in the case of the concept of controversy and the responsibilities of broadcasters when dealing with controversial subjects. Some kinds of broadcasting, like political programs and political party messages, are by definition controversial and are subject to specific regulations.

In its 23 September 1987 notice covering election campaign broadcasting, the CRTC explained that: "Throughout the history of broadcasting in Canada, licensees, as part of their service to the public, have been required to cover elections and to allocate election campaign time 'equitably' to all political parties and rival candidates" (CRTC 1987d, 1).

This obligation is perceived as an inherent part of the duty to ensure that the public is fully informed so that it can make an enlightened choice from among the various parties and candidates. It is a fairly obvious application of the balance principle in paragraph 3(*d*) of the *Broadcasting Act*, 1968, and section 3(1)(*i*)(i) of the *Broadcasting Act* of 1991.

The CRTC's approach to election campaign broadcasting is based on the principles of flexibility and recognition of the fundamental responsibility of broadcasters. This approach is a flexible regulatory technique that allows the broadcasters the discretion to exercise their responsibilities, even if this means that the regulatory authority has to intervene to suggest guidelines or to assess conduct a posteriori. The Commission's most recent policy statement on election campaign broadcasting attests to that fact: "It is desirable to vest in its individual licensees the widest possible responsibility for determining and achieving fair treatment of issues, candidates and parties during elections in their respective service areas" (CRTC 1988a, 2).

In addition to flexibility, the CRTC favours an approach characterized by reference to the rights of the public.

In addition to its general power, under paragraph 10(1)(*c*) of the 1991 *Broadcasting Act*, to make regulations respecting "standards of programs and the allocation of broadcasting time for the purpose of giving effect to the broadcasting policy set out in subsection 3(1)," the CRTC may make regulations respecting: "the proportion of time that may be devoted to the broadcasting of programs, including advertisements or announcements, of a partisan political character and the assignment of that time on an equitable basis to political parties and candidates" (Canada, *Broadcasting Act*, 1991, s. 10(1)(*e*)).[38]

The concept of a "partisan" broadcast has been studied in *R. v. CFRB Ltd.* (1976). According to Mr. Justice Arnup of the Ontario Court of Appeal, it is not necessary for a program to be explicitly sponsored for it to qualify as partisan; he explained that it is sufficient that the message conveyed by the broadcast be intended to favour a particular party or candidate: "In my view, a partisan broadcast is one intended to favour one candidate over the other or others, in an election, or to favour one point of view over another, in a referendum. The broadcast need not have a political sponsor, nor need there be a connection between the speaker and any political party or recognizable faction" (ibid., 390–91).

This case dealt with an editorial that favoured a particular candidate. It must be concluded that the title and nature of a program do not determine its partisan character. Instead, the partisan content of the program must be deduced from the remarks broadcast.

In *R. v. CBC, CTV and Global* (1991), the court concluded that a televised leaders debate is not a partisan broadcast.

The golden rule in this area, it would appear, is the principle of equitable treatment. The *Radio Regulations, 1986* (s. 6) and *Television Broadcasting Regulations, 1987* (s. 8) state: "During an election period, a licensee shall allocate time for the broadcasting of programs, advertisements or announcements of a partisan political character on an equitable basis to all accredited political parties and rival candidates represented in the election or referendum."[39]

In federal and provincial elections, the CRTC publishes guidelines intended basically to remind licensees of their statutory duties and to convey to them the CRTC's interpretation of the following principles:

- Radio and television station licensees shall log as advertising material any paid broadcast of a partisan political character which, including the identification of the sponsor and the party, if any, is two minutes or less in duration ...
- Licensees are not obligated to offer free time for broadcasts of a partisan political character to political parties and candidates.
- The allocation of time among political parties and candidates for broadcasts of a partisan political character is to be arranged between political parties and candidates and licensees on an equitable basis both qualitatively and quantitatively ...
- For the purposes of the above-mentioned sections, in reviewing the allocation of time, the Commission will take into account all broadcasts in which political partisans may have appeared.
- Any broadcasting personality who is a candidate for election and continues his or her broadcasting during the campaign is considered by the Commission to be receiving an inequitable advantage unless the licensee of the broadcasting undertaking on which such candidate appears agrees to provide similar opportunity to the candidate's opponents. If similar facilities are not provided, the Commission considers that such candidates receive publicity that is not available to their opponents and therefore requires that these candidates discontinue their broadcasting activities until after the election. (CRTC 1987c, 1–2)

In Circular No. 334 – *Political Broadcasting – Complaints re: Free Time and Editorial Time Allocations*, the CRTC stressed that "once a licensee chooses to give free time, it must allocate some time to all political parties which are duly registered under the applicable legislation" (CRTC 1987a, 7).

The principle of equitable allocation is the crux of all the CRTC's related directives and recommendations, but it does not mean "equal time." As Mr. Justice Walsh pointed out in *Turmel v. CRTC*, "certainly, if it had been intended that all applicants be given equal time, the word [used in legislation] would have been equal" (1981, 415). In the *Turmel* case, the applicant sought to obtain information regarding the process used by broadcasters to determine the allocation of free air time to candidates.

In *Turmel v. CRTC* (1983), the plaintiff applied for a mandamus order against the CRTC to force it to prevent Bushnell Communications from broadcasting, free of charge, a political debate in which only three of the four candidates were invited to participate. The application was made on the grounds that such an allocation of time was contrary to paragraph 9(1) of the CRTC's *Television Broadcasting Regulations*. The plaintiff claimed that, if there were insufficient time for every candidate to be heard, the equitable solution in that case would be to draw lots rather than allow the broadcaster to decide which candidates were worthy of air time and to exclude the others.

While admitting that such an approach had its merits, Mr. Justice Walsh stated that the court was in no better position to judge what is a fair allocation of the time than a broadcaster, and was in fact probably less so and less likely to be well informed as to the political trends in any given election (*Turmel* 1983, 7). Indeed, the courts regularly express their reluctance to assume the role of the regulator in such matters (*Trieger* 1989, 277).

Using policy directives, the CRTC can regulate the means of determining whether the treatment of a particular candidate corresponds to the fairness standard, and has also designed its policies to ensure that this standard is upheld.

Despite the more demanding nature of their mandate, community stations do not enjoy the benefits of any relaxation of the rules, and have a responsibility that is identical and equal to conventional broadcasters for balance in programming (CRTC 1988b, 9–12).[40] In its statement of policy, *Balance in Programming on Community Access Media*, the CRTC recognized that the special mandate that has been imposed on community radio stations to develop the maximum number of innovative programs that differ from those provided by other broadcasting operations in the community is such that these stations should also "seek out differing views more frequently even though they often operate with limited resources" (ibid., 7).

Community television operates via the community channel distributed by the cable television operation. Cable television operation is subject to the same obligations as other broadcasting operations, especially those set out under section 3(1)(*h*) of the *Broadcasting Act*, 1991, which states the principle of responsibility to be held by businesses that hold licences for the programming they broadcast.

Cable broadcasters consequently assume responsibility for the messages they transmit (CRTC 1979, 6). The hybrid character of cable companies, however, poses special problems regarding the designation of responsibilities. Telecommunications operations, with which cable operations are sometimes affiliated, are essentially not responsible for the content of their messages. However, from their status as broadcasting operations, cable operations have inherited responsibility for the messages they transmit through community channels.

As a result, cable operators are responsible for the content of community programming, even if the CRTC defines community television in terms of public participation, advocating equitable public access, and attempts to establish a spirit of cooperation among those involved. The ultimate and effective control of a community channel belongs to the cable operator.

Starting in 1971, the CRTC stated that "the licence holder for a cable television system must assume responsibility for the services provided by a channel reserved for local programming" (CRTC 1971, 16). In 1975, the CRTC reiterated its policy. It required the formation of consultative groups of citizens to advise and assist the licence holder in operating the community channel "without diminishing the licensee's ultimate responsibility for the programming being distributed" (CRTC 1975, 5).

The CRTC has consistently refused to modify this policy, despite pressure from some groups. In 1984, the Canadian Cable Television Association (CCTA) asked the CRTC "to explore means by which the ultimate responsibility for access programming could be shared with community producers" (CRTC 1984a, 1). The CRTC rejected this request because "responsibility for all licensee-originated programming, including access programming, must rest with the holder of the licence, and that this responsibility is not one which can be transferred or shared" (ibid., 5). This position was reiterated in 1988 in the policy statement regarding balance in programming in community media (CRTC 1988b).

Section 14 of the 1976 regulations, which required licence holders to provide a reasonable and balanced opportunity for the expression of differing opinions on matters of public concern, has not been taken up in the *Cable Television Regulations, 1986*. The deletion of this section does not, however, release licence holders from this obligation, because the terms of section 3(1)(*i*)(i) of the *Broadcasting Act, 1991* still cover this principle. Generally, each broadcasting operation must conform to the requirement of balance within its own programming; however, only that portion of programming dealing with issues of public concern must be balanced. This balance must be achieved throughout the programming as a whole provided by the operation during a "reasonable" period, rather than during a particular broadcast. Moreover, achieving balance does not necessarily mean granting an equal amount of time to each point of view. It means, rather, that various points of view should be presented during regular programming, during a "reasonable" period of time (CRTC 1988b, 3–4). The CRTC considers that each licence holder is responsible for deciding whether an issue is of public concern, as well as how to attain balance in programming.

In September 1988, the CRTC also devoted its attention to the issue of applying its policy regarding balanced programming to community media, such as community and student radio stations, as well as community channels distributed by cable operators (CRTC 1988b). The CCTA wanted "to apply to community programming a slightly less onerous interpretation of the words of subsection 3(d) of the Act relating to balanced programming than it applies to programming produced by, or for the account of, over-the-air broadcasters" (ibid., 6). The CCTA considers that the CRTC, by encouraging community access through a community channel, assigns a role to a cable television operator that is essentially different from the role assigned to a conventional broadcaster. According to the CCTA, this requirement for access to community interests implies that "persons presenting points of view on matters of public concern are 'volunteers,' or persons who have requested access to the facilities in order to express their views, whereas for over-the-air stations the on-air personnel are usually employees" (ibid.).

However, the CRTC refused to modify its balance requirements for community media, given that all licence holders have an equal and identical responsibility imposed on them by the *Broadcasting Act* of 1991, and that this responsibility was accepted, from the beginning, when licences were granted. The CRTC does recognize that striking a balance on issues of public concern is more difficult for those licence holders whose mandate is to provide community access to the airwaves. But this difficulty does not, however, necessitate different treatment for these licence holders at the cost of restricting access to the airwaves. The CRTC describes its position: "Nonetheless, while not wishing in any way to discourage access to the broadcasting system by a wide variety of community groups and individuals, the Commission wishes to stress that it expects these licensees to continue to play an important role in providing a forum for the expression of differing views on matters of public concern" (CRTC 1988b, 8).

The CRTC also suggests certain mechanisms to encourage the achievement of balance by licence holders whose programming is based on community access, as well as by all broadcasters dealing with controversial issues (CRTC 1988b, 9–12). The CRTC reiterates, first of all, that the licence holder is responsible for determining which questions are of public concern, and for producing programs that will guarantee that the questions will be dealt with in an equitable manner. The licence holder can remind the public of the role played by access to the station or the channel through a regularly broadcast notice and at times when there is a large audience; the notice can state the responsibilities of the broadcaster regarding community access to programming, and the means used to achieve this.

Registration for scheduled "platform" or "public comment" broadcasts may provide the public with an opportunity to express various opinions on controversial issues dealt with during other broadcasts produced by the licence holder, but without releasing the licence holder from the responsibility regarding balance, if no individual takes the opportunity to respond. Even if licence holders are not responsible for doing so, they may choose to provide access to the airwaves to persons with complaints, so that such persons may present their viewpoints at a time when there is a reasonable possibility to be heard. Even there, the licence holder is not released from responsibility for balance if the complainant refuses the offer. The licence holder must seek groups or persons who have opinions that differ from the opinions expressed during a broadcast dealing with questions of public concern and provide them with an opportunity to express their point of view. If these mechanisms do not provide balance regarding a particular question, the CRTC suggests that the licence holder use his or her own resources to produce or purchase programming that meets the requirement of balance. The use of one of these mechanisms does not, however, release licence holders from their obligation regarding balance.

Cable broadcasting operations also have specific regulatory obligations regarding partisan political programming distributed on community channels. Section 15 in the CRTC's *Cable Television Regulations, 1986* stipulates that: "Where a licensee provides time on its community channel during an election period for the distribution of programming of a partisan political character, the licensee shall allocate that time on an equitable basis to all accredited political parties and rival candidates."

Cable operators are, in consequence, responsible for providing equitable access to community television channels.

The Commission imposes on cable operators – with respect

to the community channel – the same programming obligations as conventional broadcasters, namely, final responsibility for program content, including the requirements of balance and high quality. For programming in general, however, the CRTC assigns a different mandate to cable broadcasters than to conventional broadcasters. Unlike conventional broadcasters, cable operators, through the community channel, have an obligation to ensure community access and control this access. It can be claimed that, owing to this fact, cable television operators have greater programming obligations than do conventional broadcasters; however, there is a certain degree of risk that a cable operation might sacrifice access to the community channel, claiming the need to fulfil its responsibility for balance, quality and liability for content.

The CRTC's policy regarding responsibility for community channels might appear contradictory in some ways. On the one hand, access to community channels is encouraged, and the CRTC tries to make these channels a special facility for expression by citizens and even fringe groups, but on the other hand, the CRTC resists efforts to implement this policy effectively. In the 1975 statement, for example, the CRTC encouraged "the use of [community channels] for unusual ideas and opinions on the broadest range of subjects" (CRTC 1975, 5). This policy loses some of its force when it is contrasted with the ultimate responsibility for the content of the message. Would a cable distributor risk broadcasting a program dealing with a controversial subject? Distributors would instead prefer to broadcast a game played by the local hockey team. There are also doubts as to the real impact of the CRTC's policy designed to ensure that cable broadcasters provide "the maximum opportunity for the community to see *live* programming" (ibid.). With this policy, the CRTC intended that community channels broadcast live reports on sessions of municipal councils, community debates and public discussions. The intent was to provide the community with a democratic instrument, but the cable operator retained a veto, a right of censorship over the programming. The cable operator judges the content of the broadcasts, and may refuse access to the airwaves, on the grounds that it has legal responsibility for all program content.

Examination of the decisions rendered by the CRTC reveals some contradictions regarding responsibility. In 1987, when an application to renew the broadcasting licence of a cable operator was being considered, the Commission asked the operator to attend a public hearing in response to allegations that the CRTC felt were "serious" (*K-Right* 1987). The operator had proposed charging an access fee of $100 to a citizens' club that wanted to broadcast its annual bingo game over the community channel. The club refused payment, as it had already made several contributions to the licence holder, and intervened before the CRTC to oppose the renewal of the broadcasting operator's licence. Even though the operation could not provide suitable information regarding its activities and its performance, the CRTC renewed the licence for a six-month period. The Commission required that the broadcaster submit a report concerning "details of its community programming expenses and the use of volunteers, the programming schedule of the community channel, whether presentations on that channel are live, tape-delayed or repeats, and projected capital expenditures related to its proposed system upgrade and improvements in service, as well as a firm timetable for the implementation of such improvements" (ibid., 4). As for the allegations concerning the restrictions on the community channel, the CRTC clearly affirmed that there had been a violation of its regulations and its policies: "With respect to the intervention and the issue of community channel access, the Commission wishes to reaffirm that the imposition of a fee for access by any individual or community group to the community channel is unacceptable and contrary to its cable television policies and regulations" (ibid., 4–5).

In this decision, the CRTC mentioned that it was powerless to control the content of broadcasting: "At the same time, the Commission notes that the programming distributed on the community channel is at the licensee's discretion and that the Commission has no power to dictate to licensees the specific programming to be carried" (*K-Right* 1987, 5). The CRTC subsequently encouraged the licence holder to come to an agreement with the community group to settle their differences on the basis of goodwill.

This decision reflects the contradictions between the policy covering access to the community channel and the principle of responsibility. Responsibility has devolved to the licence holders, and the licensees have, as we have seen, the obligation to "provide local community information," "permit the expression of ideas" and "seek out individuals who have common interests." The CRTC itself noted, however, that it was not within its powers to control access to the media. The cable operator could justify its failure to meet an obligation on the grounds that it was responsible for the content of the broadcast. If this shortcoming is combined with other violations of the cable operator's obligations, the licence held by the operator may, in the worst case, be renewed for only a short term. In any event, by holding a licence, the operator would retain its status and right of censorship.

Some cable distributors, however, show initiative and dare to get involved in controversial programming. A 1985 decision is a case in point. Rogers Cable TV Ltd., one of the biggest cable television distributors in Canada, regularly broadcasts an open-line television program over its community channel. The Mayor of North York, a municipality in Metropolitan Toronto, hosts the show. During a public hearing, one participant, a member of the Municipal Council of North York, was very concerned about how the host dealt with controversial issues and issues of public interest (*Rogers* 1985, 529). According to the intervener, the Mayor presented a partisan point of view: "The Mayor chooses to use his show for personal abuse and partisan political purposes, not community discussion of civic issues" (ibid.). She referred to the licence holder's obligations arising from section 3(*d*) of the *Broadcasting Act*, 1968 and sections 13(1) and 14 of the old *Cable Television Regulations.* These regulatory obligations dealt with the equitable distribution of time devoted to partisan political programming and balance in the expression of various opinions on subjects of public concern.

At the hearing, Rogers Cable assured the CRTC that, during the 11 years that this very popular broadcast had been on the air, it had "made every reasonable effort to provide the community of North York, and particularly City Council members, with an opportunity for rebuttal, to ensure presentation of a balanced viewpoint" (*Rogers* 1985, 529–30). The CRTC based its response on the concept of high standard: "the Commission considers that controversial issues which are debated on an open-line program demand exceptionally careful treatment on the part of the licensee to ensure fairness, balance and high standard of programming in accordance with paragraph 3(d) of the Broadcasting Act" (ibid., 530).

In this decision, the CRTC stated that it was satisfied by the commitment on the part of Rogers Cable to allow for the expression of differing viewpoints, when necessary. The Commission also emphasized, as a warning, the responsibility of the licence holder for the programs it broadcasts.

Because community television has become a community cable channel, its status is dependent, to some degree, on cable operators. Through its choice of medium, the CRTC made this decision. The cable operator holds the broadcasting licence, along with the legal responsibility that this involves. We are still a long way from defining a third sector in the *Broadcasting Act.* In the absence of official recognition of the community sector, it might be useful to recognize community television associations, which have been attempting to survive for years. There were 33 such associations in Quebec at the beginning of 1986, and four were in the process of being formed (Canada, Task Force 1986a, 496). This is still a very low number, considering that there are currently 144 cable television operations in Quebec. Recognizing these associations could help to stimulate the development of community television.

The Caplan-Sauvageau report noted the urgency of reviewing regulations "to put community television on a firmer footing" (Canada, Task Force 1986a, 502). During public hearings before the Caplan-Sauvageau Task Force, the Regroupement des organismes communautaires de communication du Québec called for the granting of licences to associations. It wanted each community television association to be granted "official beneficial and legal status distinct from that of cable operators" (ibid.). The Task Force recommended that "the CRTC ... license community television associations on terms similar to those developed for community radio stations" (ibid., 502). However, the Task Force does not deny the potential contribution by cable television broadcasters, and it recommends that "cable system operators who themselves program community channels ... be licensed as community broadcasters" (ibid., 503).

These two recommendations would have shaken up the community television sector and would certainly have given it a boost. With regard to responsibility, and hence, public access, nothing has been resolved, because the awarding of a cable distribution licence very often signifies the granting of a "true right of censorship over all community programs" (Trudel 1984a, 360).

Parliament has favoured an approach to broadcasting based on the enunciation of very general standards, intended to guide the authorities in charge of regulating the day-to-day activities of the media. Many provisions invoke concepts such as "balance" and "comprehensive and varied" programming of "high standard." The regulatory authorities rely on these nebulous concepts and then proceed to take various measures such as adopting regulations and determining licensing conditions. Since these concepts are not defined anywhere, or are ill-defined at best, and since they are always invoked implicitly, it has been suggested that the courts and the Commission are liable to render arbitrary judgements (Finkelstein 1985, 90ff.).

Clearly, the danger is not as great as it was believed to be during the first years of the application of the *Canadian Charter of Rights and Freedoms*. It is now established that even though decisions of regulatory bodies, taken by virtue of broad enabling provisions, may be subject to Charter review, such provisions will not thereby be invalidated.[41]

When determining the proportionality of the means in relation to the ends sought, the nature and operation of a regulatory mechanism must be assessed, which is more complex than the required standards set out in the legislation. In a complex field characterized by creativity and innovation, such as radio and television, it is reasonable to assert that only regulatory mechanisms founded on the enunciation of standards accompanied by sweeping powers to a specialized organization will be able to cope with the numerous requirements and fundamental rights involved.

It would be inaccurate to say that the use of legislative standards is too vague a technique to meet the requirements flowing from the respect of fundamental rights. By examining the legal nature of standards and coming to a more precise understanding of their operation in the context of the *Broadcasting Act* of 1991, one observes that they do constitute a mechanism that is proportional to the multiple, complex goals of this type of legislation (Trudel 1989b).

Al-Sanhoury attempted to define these standards in terms of what they accomplish: "standards give an average measure of the extent to which social conduct is likely to adapt to the particular circumstances of any given hypothesis" (1935, 145). In an attempt to define the characteristics of standards, Rials (1984, 44) notes that they do not constitute the rule itself, but a means of formulating the rule in law. This approach is perfectly suited to situations in which it might be difficult to formulate a priori rules of conduct to be followed by those covered by the legislation.

Characterized by its rapid development and essentially creative nature, broadcasting is ill-suited to detailed regulation. By using standards, the law tries to provide an ideal measure of proper social conduct for, say, the programs of each broadcaster. But such a measure must be constantly adapted to circumstances so that it will be as proportional as possible to the purposes it is meant to achieve. An imperative, universal rule could prove so inadequate and arbitrary that it would be useless in certain situations.

Standards, according to Rials, are "yardsticks of the norm" (1984, 43). Therein lies their specificity, but as well, their ambiguity. Normality is in fact ambiguous. For instance, programming of high standard prescribes what should be, or more precisely, the characteristics of what should be. Legislators hope that, by using the standard, what they want to see become the norm will prevail.

This is why standards, which are fundamentally undefinable, provide a way of identifying the basic objectives the regulatory body will try to embody in the norms that it develops. In radio and television, these norms might relate to various issues such as the proportion of advertising, journalistic standards and ways of presenting controversial material. In any case, the regulatory body is ultimately responsible for determining what constitutes, for example, balance, variety and programming of high standard.

Rials (1984) noted that it is not the indeterminateness of standards that opens the door to discretionary power, but their indeterminability. In other words, he showed that standards do not give rise to discretionary power: the authorities in charge of enforcing them are going to have to interpret them anyway. The lack of definition of standards gives rise to interpretation.

The interpretation of concepts like balanced programming of high standard necessarily involves passing some kind of judgement on the conduct of broadcasters. Such judgements could not be made without taking the facts of each case into account. Most standards are intended to govern behaviour in complex situations; they are not, and probably never can be, formulated with any precision. That does not make them impossible to determine in given situations. How they are determined will vary with time and circumstances, so a determination made on one occasion will not necessarily constitute a valid precedent in other circumstances.

Regulatory bodies must, therefore, go beyond the realm of law to find criteria for good conduct as prescribed by standards. When the reader is trying to ascertain the prescribed characteristics of certain behaviours, the standard will often refer him or her to a different kind of standard. For instance, when the *Civil Code of Lower Canada* states that the "depositary is bound to apply in the keeping of the thing deposited the care of a prudent administrator" (art. 1802), it refers the reader to the norms and practices that prevail in the environment where the contract is signed. In the same breath, the standard demands that codes of proper behaviour from a specific environment be introduced into the legal realm.

By prescribing standards, Parliament asks the regulatory body to refer to the best professional practices of the industry to determine the best ways of producing and presenting radio and television broadcasts to the public. These are the practices that the standard must introduce into broadcasting regulation.

Access to the Airwaves for Various Points of View Election campaign broadcasting brings to the fore a classic dilemma in the law of electronic media in North America. Who has the ultimate duty of deciding what shall be heard over the airwaves? Who can have access to the airwaves? What events should the electronic media cover?

Lange illustrates the various facets of access in the electronic media:

> The access question is nothing less than an inquiry into the proper structure and purpose of the American press. More recently, however,

the question has arisen in the narrower context of immediate confrontations between the owners of the media and their gatekeepers, on the
one hand, and individual members of the public on the other. Thus,
a group of businessmen organized against the war in Vietnam demand
the right to air their views in sixty-second broadcast editorials.
Members of a clothing workers union propose to buy a page of advertising space in a metropolitan daily newspaper to protest the impor-
tation of foreign-manufactured clothing. Individual citizens insist that
they be allowed to use the origination facilities of their community's
cable television system to express their personal views on any subject.
In each case proponents of a point of view seek direct access to a
communications medium that they do not generally control. If access
is to be granted, some accommodation obviously is required among
interests that are likely to conflict. (1973, 1)

The rules of electoral broadcasting are the result of measures designed
to guarantee a certain amount of access to the airwaves for political
parties and candidates. Consequently, these rules circumscribe the
editorial freedom of broadcasters.

In *Red Lion Broadcasting v. FCC* (1969), the United States Supreme
Court found that such measures enhance and promote freedom of expression. Writing for the Court, Justice White explained that the public's
right to freedom of expression and the broadcaster's right to editorial
freedom can be reconciled by invoking the public's right to hear different
points of view on the many aspects of life in society. Upholding the FCC's
deregulation measures, the Court's most recent decisions in cases similar
to *Red Lion* relied mainly on the power of the Commission to decide
what was in the public interest (Slansky 1985).

Thus, in its decision in *FCC v. League of Women Voters*, the U.S.
Supreme Court reiterated the principles of *Red Lion Broadcasting v. FCC*
(1969):

> Finally, although the government's interest in ensuring balanced
> coverage of public issues is plainly both important and substantial,
> we have, at the same time, made clear that broadcasters are engaged
> in a vital and independent form of communicative activity. As a
> result, the First Amendment must inform and give shape to the
> manner in which Congress exercises its regulatory power in this area.
> Unlike common carriers, broadcasters are "entitled under the First
> Amendment to exercise 'the widest journalistic freedom consistent
> with their public [duties]' " ... Indeed, if the public's interest
> in receiving a balanced presentation of views is to be fully served,

we must necessarily rely in large part on the editorial initiative and judgment of the broadcasters who bear the public trust. (FCC 1984, 378)

Nevertheless, subject to measures that might be justified on the grounds of the special nature of frequencies or the medium, the principle of the editorial freedom of broadcasters continues to form the basis of the legal framework of broadcasting. Consequently, there is no general right of access to the airwaves. Canadian law seems to follow the same pattern. In *Trieger v. CBC* (1989), Mr. Justice Campbell of the High Court of Ontario observed that the U.S. courts have never recognized the existence of a general right of access to the airwaves based on the constitutional guarantee of freedom of speech. In the context of a motion for an injunction, he added that: "There is enough doubt on these points to require a full trial to determine whether or not the right to free speech carries with it in the circumstances of this case, the right to force the media to carry anyone's message to the public" (ibid., 282).

In *CBS v. Democratic National Committee* (1973), Justice Douglas of the United States Supreme Court delimited the scope of state measures that infringed on the editorial freedom of broadcasters: "Licensing is necessary for engineering reasons; the spectrum is limited in wavelengths and must be assigned to avoid stations interfering with each other ... The Commission has a duty to encourage a multitude of voices but only in a limited way, *viz.*, by preventing monopolistic practices and by promoting technical divisions that will open up new channels. *But censorship or editing or the screening by Government of what licensees may broadcast goes against the grain of the First Amendment*" (ibid., 157, emphasis added).

In Canada, Mr. Justice Walsh expressed himself in the same way in *National Indian Brotherhood v. Juneau (No. 3):*

> Reading the Act as a whole and in particular the sections to which I have referred, I find it difficult to conclude that Parliament intended to or did give the Commission the authority to act as a censor of programmes to be broadcast or televised. If this had been intended, surely provision would have been made somewhere in the Act giving the Commission authority to order an individual station or a network, as the case may be, to make changes in a programme deemed by the Commission, after an inquiry, to be offensive or to refrain from broadcasting same. Instead of that, it appears that its only control over the nature of programmes is by use of its power to revoke, suspend or fail to renew the licence of the offending station. (1971, 513)

The editorial freedom of broadcasters is upheld in sections 2(3) and 3(c) of the *Broadcasting Act* of 1991. Section 3(c) also states that those who hold licences to operate broadcasting facilities assume responsibility for what they broadcast. We cannot find any authoritative judgement that recognizes the right of government to interfere with programming decisions (see, however, *Federal Liberal Agency* 1989).[42] Although public authorities are qualified to regulate use of the airwaves, they cannot supplant the licensees when the time comes to decide what to broadcast.

With that general proposition in mind, there is nothing prohibiting Parliament from prescribing, in favour of candidates for election, more specific rights to air time. In *CBS Inc. v. FCC* (1981, 2825), the United States Supreme Court held that it was possible to grant a legislative right of access in opposition to broadcasters without infringing on the First Amendment.

In summary, it is possible to delimit the rights of broadcasters and candidates in relation to a candidate's request for air time. However, the regulatory mechanisms used to delimit these rights must not unduly infringe on broadcasters' editorial freedom.

In *CBS Inc. v. FCC* (1981), the order was formulated permissively. It provided, in effect, that a station could be penalized if it repeatedly refused to give reasonable attention, in good faith, to access requests from legally qualified candidates. The order prevented broadcasters from adopting across-the-board policies that, although precise, are likely to be arbitrary. The United States Supreme Court described the way the order in question was interpreted and applied:

> Broadcasters are free to deny the sale of air time prior to the commencement of a campaign, but once a campaign has begun, they must give reasonable and good-faith attention to access requests from "legally qualified" candidates for federal elective office. Such requests must be considered on an individualized basis, and broadcasters are required to tailor their responses to accommodate, as much as reasonably possible, a candidate's stated purposes in seeking air time. In responding to access requests, however, broadcasters may also give weight to such factors as the amount of time previously sold to the candidate, the disruptive impact on regular programming, and the likelihood of requests for time by rival candidates under the equal opportunity provisions of § 315(a). (*CBS* 1981, 2825)

However, the Court noted that such factors may not be invoked as pretexts for denying access. To justify a negative response, broadcasters must cite a realistic danger of substantial program disruption. To make it easier for the FCC to review such decisions, broadcasters must explain their reasons for denial.

In Canada, candidates and representatives of political parties have a right of access to the airwaves. The *Canada Elections Act* gives candidates a right to paid or free advertising time. The duty to make political broadcasting time available to political parties and candidates at no charge flows from the principle that the airwaves are public property and from the will to give candidates access to them.

As early as 1934, Mackenzie King had this to say about free access to the public airwaves:

> Radio ... plays such an important part in all matters affecting public opinion that it would be quite proper that some provision should be made whereby, for example, each political party which has a representative following should be entitled to have broadcast, at the expense of the state one or two addresses which would set forth its platform or policies before the people. That I believe is the custom in Great Britain itself and it might well be followed here. Apart from that I think there ought to be some definite understanding that radio where it is to be used for political purposes will be used in a manner which will not give to one party which may happen to have more in the way of financial backing than other parties, a larger use of that national instrument. (Canada, Committee 1966, 362)

The Committee on Election Expenses (1966, 43) underscored the fact that the use of radio and television constituted "the greatest contributing factor to rising costs of campaigning" and that political parties and candidates ought not to have to pay all these costs. Broadcasters, in compensation for using the public airwaves, should encourage the expression of political viewpoints by providing some free air time as a public service.

The duty to make time available to parties is twofold: it is different depending on whether it is offered at no charge or made available for purchase.

Every broadcaster must, subject to the conditions of its licence, "make available for purchase by all registered parties for the transmission of political announcements and other programming produced by or on behalf of the registered parties an aggregate of six and one-half hours of broadcasting time during prime time on its facilities" (Canada, *Canada Elections Act*, s. 307(1)).

Prime time is defined specifically in the *Canada Elections Act* (section 2). In the case of a radio station, it means the time between the hours of 6 AM and 9 AM, 12 PM and 2 PM, and 4 PM and 7 PM. In the case of a television station, it means the hours between 6 PM and midnight.

Where a broadcaster is affiliated with a network, the portion of broadcasting time to be made available to the parties, as may be agreed between the broadcaster and the network operator, must be made available by the network operator during the portion of the broadcaster's prime time broadcasting schedule that has been delegated to the control of the network operator (Canada, *Canada Elections Act*, s. 307(2)).

Time allocation is determined by unanimous agreement. The process of allocation is presided over by a broadcasting arbitrator.

The broadcasting arbitrator, who has the duty to allocate broadcasting time when unanimous agreement is not reached, is designated at a meeting convened by the chief electoral officer.

The meeting may be convened when Parliament is dissolved or 90 days after polling day at every general election. It may also be convened 14 days from the day the broadcasting arbitrator dies, becomes incapacitated or resigns from office, except when that day occurs during a general election (Canada, *Canada Elections Act*, s. 304(1)). Should any of these events occur during a general election, the chief electoral officer is to appoint a new broadcasting arbitrator as soon as possible (ibid., s. 306).

The leader of each registered party designates two representatives to attend the meeting. The chief electoral officer convenes the meeting and designates a person to chair it. The representatives make the result of their consultations known to the chief electoral officer in a written report signed by each of them. The report must be submitted no later than six weeks after a meeting convened on the dissolution of Parliament and not later than 90 days after election day. In all other cases, the report is submitted within four weeks of the meeting.

It is the chief electoral officer's duty to appoint, as broadcasting arbitrator, the person selected by the representatives. When there is no unanimous agreement among the representatives, the chief electoral officer selects and appoints the broadcasting arbitrator (Canada, *Canada Elections Act*, s. 304(4), (5)).

The broadcasting arbitrator's term of office expires six months after polling day at the general election following his or her appointment. He or she is eligible for reappointment (Canada, *Canada Elections Act*, s. 305) and receives a salary to be determined by the chief electoral officer. The chief electoral officer may remove the broadcasting arbitrator from office only for just cause.

On request, political parties receive the names and addresses of all broadcasters and network operators from the broadcasting arbitrator (Canada, *Canada Elections Act*, s. 313(2)).

The broadcasting arbitrator must inform the CRTC of every allocation of broadcasting time made under sections 309 and 310 of the *Canada
Elections Act* and every entitlement under section 311, as soon as possible
after the allocation is made or after the CRTC requests it.

The CRTC must notify every broadcaster and network operator of
every allocation and entitlement to broadcasting time, and do so once
more immediately after the writs for the next general election are issued
(Canada, *Canada Elections Act*, s. 313(1)).

The 6.5 hours of broadcasting time are shared among the registered political parties. The allocation is made at a meeting attended by
representatives of the parties. If the meeting ends in unanimous agreement among the parties, the allocation agreed on is binding (Canada,
Canada Elections Act, s. 309(2)).

If the representatives cannot reach unanimous agreement within
four weeks following the meeting, the broadcasting arbitrator will
decide on an allocation of broadcasting time that is binding on all registered parties.

The meeting is convened on the request of the official agent of any
registered party to the broadcasting arbitrator (Canada, *Canada Elections
Act*, s. 308(1)). That request may be made at any time after the broadcasting arbitrator has been in office for 60 days. Within 30 days after
such a request is received or, if no such request is received, within six
months after the commencement of the broadcasting arbitrator's term
in office, the broadcasting arbitrator contacts the parties[43] and convenes
the meeting.

A registered party that informs the broadcasting arbitrator in
writing that it does not wish to be allocated any of the broadcasting
time to be made available under section 307 of the *Canada Elections Act*
or that fails to communicate its intentions on time allocation to the
broadcasting arbitrator is not entitled to receive any such broadcasting
time under the mechanism provided. The same is true for any party
that fails to have its representative attend the consultative meeting
concerning the allocation of broadcasting time (Canada, *Canada Elections
Act*, s. 309).

In addition to the 6.5 hours to be made available under section
307, all broadcasters must make a maximum period of 39 minutes available (Canada, *Canada Elections Act*, s. 311(4)) to any political party whose
application for registration was accepted by the chief electoral officer
either before or after the allocation of broadcasting time.

Every new party is entitled to purchase broadcasting time in an
amount equal to the smallest portion of broadcasting time to be made

available, under section 307, to any registered party. The amount of time purchased must not exceed six minutes (Canada, *Canada Elections Act*, s. 311(1)).

Where a party is deleted from the register, after an allocation of the broadcasting time under section 307, the broadcasting arbitrator distributes that party's allocated broadcasting time among the remaining registered parties. This distribution is conducted during a meeting convened by the broadcasting arbitrator within two weeks of the deletion. The deleted party's time will not be reallocated if the deletion occurs after the writs for a general election are issued (Canada, *Canada Elections Act*, s. 312).

Section 310 of the *Canada Elections Act* provides for the allocation criteria to be used by the broadcasting arbitrator when the registered parties fail to reach unanimous agreement.

The first criterion imposes a ceiling on broadcasting time available to each eligible party: the broadcasting arbitrator may not, under any circumstances, allocate to any one party more than 50 percent of the total broadcasting time to be made available.

The broadcasting arbitrator considers the following factors: equal weight to the percentage of seats obtained by each registered party in the House of Commons in the previous general election; equal weight to the percentage of the popular vote obtained by each registered party at the previous general election; and half the weight given to the other factors is given to the number of candidates endorsed by each registered party in the previous general election, expressed as a percentage of all candidates endorsed by all registered parties in that election.

The following equation represents the weight given to the allocation criteria:

2 [percentage of seats obtained by each registered party in the House of Commons in the previous general election]

+

2 [percentage of the popular vote obtained by each party in the previous general election]

+

1 [number of candidates endorsed by each registered party in the previous general election, expressed as a percentage of the total number of candidates endorsed at that election]

= **percentage of time granted to the registered political party**

Where the allocation thus calculated results in one of the parties receiving more than 50 percent of the broadcasting time to be made available, the broadcasting arbitrator allocates the excess time among the other registered parties entitled to broadcasting time.

The broadcasting arbitrator enjoys some discretion: if he or she considers that the allocation calculated according to the prescribed formula would be unfair to any of the registered parties or contrary to the public interest, the broadcasting arbitrator may, subject to the 50 percent ceiling and the requirement to allocate excess time, modify the allocation to resolve the problem (Canada, *Canada Elections Act*, s. 310(4)).

In each of the calendar years following the one in which broadcasting time has been allocated under sections 309 and 310 of the *Canada Elections Act* or a political party has requested and is entitled to broadcasting time under section 311, the broadcasting arbitrator convenes and chairs a meeting of the representatives of all registered parties to review the allocation (Canada, *Canada Elections Act*, s. 314).

Where the total broadcasting time allocated or requested exceeds 6.5 hours, the broadcasting arbitrator must reduce the time to 6.5 hours proportionately among the parties.

Not later than 10 days after the writs for a general election have been issued, each political party entitled to purchase broadcasting time must send a notice to the broadcasters and network operators (Canada, *Canada Elections Act*, s. 315), setting out its preference for the proportion of advertising time and program time to be made available to it and the days and hours in which that time is to be made available.

Every broadcaster who receives such a notice must, within three days after receiving it, consult with representatives of the parties that sent the notice so they can reach an agreement on the requests. Where there is no agreement, the matter is referred to the broadcasting arbitrator who must decide on the requests as soon as possible and notify the broadcaster and representatives of the decision.

In making that decision, the broadcasting arbitrator must take into account the principles set out in section 315(4) of the *Canada Elections Act*, to the effect that each political party should have the freedom and flexibility to determine the proportion of commercial and program time to be made available to it. The broadcasting arbitrator must also strive to make such time available fairly throughout prime time.

The broadcasting arbitrator's decision is binding on political parties, broadcasters and network operators, if applicable.

Provision for the right of political parties to obtain advertising time would be of no effect if such a provision were not accompanied by a limit on the rates that can be charged for such time.

The *Canada Elections Act* stipulates that it is an offence to charge a registered party, other political party or a candidate, or any person acting on their behalf, a rate for broadcasting time allocated to them that exceeds the lowest rate charged for an equal amount of equivalent time on the same facilities made available to any other person.

Conventional radio and television networks – that is, those licensed for more than a particular series of programs or type of programming and not involving any operation that receives broadcasts – have a duty to make time available at no cost to registered political parties.[44] Section 316 of the *Canada Elections Act* imposes such a duty on network operators that reach a majority of those Canadians whose mother tongue is the same as that in which the network broadcasts.

The amount of free broadcasting time a network is to make available to registered parties must be no less than the free broadcasting time it made available to them in the 29 days before polling day at the last general election.

The allocation of free time among the parties is as follows:

- two minutes is to be given to every registered party and to every political party that waives its right to paid time made available under section 307 of the *Canada Elections Act*;
- two minutes is to be given to each party that has indicated that it does not want any of the paid broadcasting time made available under section 311(1) of the Act; and
- the remainder must be distributed among all registered parties that have been allocated paid time in the same proportion established under section 310 of the Act.

Prohibitions

The regulation of election campaign broadcasting is often ensured by recourse to prohibitions. The *Canada Elections Act* and *Broadcasting Act, 1968* contain a number of prohibitions that require analysis.

Blackout Periods Applicable to Broadcasters, Candidates and Parties   Section 19 of the *Broadcasting Act, 1968* prohibits broadcasters from broadcasting, and broadcast-receiving licensees from receiving, programs, advertisements or announcements of a partisan character in relation to a provincial or municipal election or a referendum on the day before and the day of a referendum or election. The blackout applies to elections, except as provided by any law in force in a province and, in addition, to any election or referendum that is being held in the areas normally served by the broadcast operators. This provision is not repeated in the *Broadcasting Act* of 1991. As Thompson-Pyper notes, "it was the assessment of the Bill's drafters that these provisions were possibly in conflict with the Charter" (1990, 32). In other respects, it appears that Department of Communications authorities believed that this type of provision was better covered under the terms of electoral legislation (ibid.). Also, all provincial legislation bearing on elections allows for a period during which election broadcasting is prohibited. Generally, this prohibition covers the day before and the day on which provincial elections are held. Keeping such a prohibition in the *Broadcasting Act* of 1991 would have been redundant, at least for provincial elections.

In federal elections, sections 48 and 213 of the *Canada Elections Act* limit the period in which candidates and political parties can engage in certain campaigning activities.

For example, during certain periods, every registered party and every candidate that advertises on the facilities of any broadcasting operation or obtains an advertisement for publication in a periodical for promoting or opposing a particular party or candidate is guilty of an offence (Canada, *Canada Elections Act*, ss. 47(1)(*a*), 213(1)). The limitation applies to three specific periods: between the day the writs for an election are issued and the Sunday that falls 29 days before polling day, on polling day and the day before polling day.[45]

A notice of a meeting to be held for the principal purpose of nominating a candidate at an election, a notice of a function, meeting or other event that the leader of a registered party is scheduled to attend or a notice of invitation to meet or hear the leader of a party at a specific place is not considered to be an advertisement for promoting or opposing a party or candidate (Canada, *Canada Elections Act*, ss. 48(2), (3), 213(2)).

Thus, the *Canada Elections Act* imposes a blackout on partisan political advertising outside the prescribed campaign period beginning on the Sunday 29 days before polling day and ending on the second day before polling day. It should be emphasized that an election campaign must be of a minimum duration of 50 days (Canada, *Canada Elections Act*, s. 12(4)). The Act also limits the amount of paid time that can be made available to registered federal parties within the prescribed period (ibid., s. 307). Section 320 of the *Canada Elections Act* makes it an offence to charge a registered party, during that period, any amount in exchange for broadcasting time that exceeds the time required to be made available to it under any allocation of broadcasting time established under sections 309, 310 and 311 of the *Canada Elections Act* (i.e., additional time must be free and made available to all registered parties in accordance with the allocation).

Blackouts of political broadcasts in the hours preceding voting originated at the same time as radio first appeared and people became aware of the potential this medium had to reach a great number of voters at election time (Boyer 1983, 329).

The 1928 Royal Commission on Radio Broadcasting, chaired by Sir John Aird, was created "to examine into the broadcasting situation in the Dominion of Canada and to make recommendations to the Government as to the future administration, management, control and financing thereof" (Canada, Royal Commission 1929, 5). Following the recommendations of the Aird Commission, Parliament passed the *Canadian Radio Broadcasting Act* in 1932, which established the Canadian Radio Broadcasting Commission. This Commission's major functions were to provide a national broadcasting service and to regulate all broadcasting in Canada. At that time, political broadcasts were considered the same as any other commercial broadcasts; the only existing control was to prohibit stations from broadcasting any speech or program containing defamatory, slanderous or obscene statements about persons or institutions, or treasonable statements or statements intended to promote change unlawfully and that might lead to a breach of the peace (Canada, Committee 1966, 362–63).

The 1935 federal election thrust the issue of regulating political broadcasting to the forefront of the news. In 1936, the Special Committee on Radio was appointed to inquire into the operation of the Canadian Radio Broadcasting Commission, its administration of the *Canadian Radio Broadcasting Act, 1932* and the use of broadcasting for political ends. The Committee reported serious political abuses of broadcasting and lack of proper control by the Radio Commission during the 1935 election (Boyer 1983, 329). It therefore recommended that dramatized political broadcasts be prohibited, that full identification of sponsorship of all political broadcasts be required, and that the limitation and allocation of time devoted to political broadcasts be placed under the control of an agency, part of whose mandate would be to allot time to parties and candidates fairly and equitably. Finally, the Committee recommended that no political broadcasts be allowed on election day or on the two days immediately preceding election day.

The Special Committee's recommendations became part of the *Canadian Broadcasting Act, 1936*, which established an independent public body, the Canadian Broadcasting Corporation, and gave it the mandate of regulating the Canadian broadcasting system, including the limitation and allocation of time devoted to political broadcasts.

A statutory requirement for a blackout of political broadcasting during the days preceding an election appeared for the first time in Canada in section 22(5) of the *Canadian Broadcasting Act, 1936*. It provided that "political broadcasts on any dominion, provincial or municipal election day and on the two days immediately preceding any such election day are prohibited." The *Broadcasting Act* of 1958 and then the *Broadcasting Act* of 1968 retain a similar prohibition. However, section 19 of the 1968 Act shortens the blackout time to the one day before and the day of the election and extends the blackout to include referendums (s. 19(1)(*a*)) and the election of a member of the House of Commons, the legislature of a province and the council of a municipal corporation (s. 19(1)(*b*)).

In 1966, the Committee on Election Expenses (the Barbeau Committee) concluded that one way to limit the cost of elections would be to make election campaigns shorter. Since, in the opinion of the Barbeau Committee, "the campaign period need not coincide with the period needed for the establishment of the election machinery" (Canada, Committee 1966, 48), it was recommended that "parties and candidates be prohibited from campaigning on radio and television, and from using paid print media including newspapers, periodicals, direct mailing, billboards and posters, except during the last four weeks immediately preceding polling day" (ibid., 49).

Following this recommendation, in 1974, Parliament passed the *Election Expenses Act*, which amended the *Canada Elections Act* by introducing sections 13.7 and 61.2 (now sections 48 and 213). These provisions limit the broadcasting of partisan advertising by candidates and political parties to the prescribed campaign period, that is, between the Sunday 29 days before polling and the second day before polling. Because party spending has increased mainly because of advertising costs, campaign communication expenditures should be concentrated within a 28-day period.

Certain members of the Standing Committee on Privileges and Elections saw this authorized period of 28 days for campaign advertising as an unfair restriction on candidates' and political parties' freedom of speech. Whereas the news media have the right to make comments and editorials at any time, "there are candidates and political parties who have an immediate and direct interest in what is taking place, but [who] have no opportunity to reply to comments from ... news media or anybody else who wants to run advertisements about it. They are prohibited from advertising to reply during those periods of time" (Canada, House of Commons 1973, 37). Restricting partisan advertising to a specific period of time raises the question of the extent to which political parties and candidates have the right to freedom of speech.

In addition, the *Election Expenses Act* transferred the blackout provisions for federal elections to the *Canada Elections Act* from the *Broadcasting Act*, 1968 (Canada, *Election Expenses Act*, s. 17). Boyer (1983, 339) points out that the provisions limiting the advertising period for candidates and parties underwent certain transformations as a result of this move.

- The blackout period for political broadcasts during a federal election now applies only to partisan political advertising by parties and candidates and not to editorials, comments and commentaries under the editorial control of broadcasters. The intention was to accord broadcasting operators the same privileges as the print media, which can publish editorials up until the day before and the day of an election. Broadcasters are still subject to the *Broadcasting Act*, which requires fair and balanced treatment of all points of view.
- The restricted period for advertising applies as much to broadcasting as to publication in the print media.
- The provisions only apply to federal general elections.

Section 19 of the *Broadcasting Act*, 1968 differs in that:

- The blackout period extends to advertisements, announcements and programs of a partisan character.
- It applies only to broadcasting, not to the print media.
- It applies only to coverage of referendums and provincial elections.

The blackout provisions do not appear in the 1991 *Broadcasting Act*. However, the blackout remains in force for federal elections and referendums under the provisions of the *Canada Elections Act*.

The objectives of sections 48 and 213 of the *Canada Elections Act* differ from those of section 19 of the *Broadcasting Act*, 1968. The restriction on periods during which candidates and parties may advertise must be placed in the overall context of regulating election spending. The measure seeks to reduce the cost of campaigning; for it to qualify as rational, therefore, it must be shown that increased election spending is the result of the high cost of broadcast advertising. Studies, notably those commissioned by the Committee on Election Expenses, appear to confirm that causal link.

As for blackouts on the advertisements of parties and candidates, is this measure the least possible infringement on guaranteed rights and freedoms? It could be argued that it is not a complete ban, as it applies only to three specific periods: between the day the election writs are issued and the Sunday 29 days before polling, on polling day and on the day before polling day. Candidates and parties have 28 days to expound their platforms. Still, the proportionality between the effects of the limitation and its objectives is debatable. The measure reduces the electorate's access to information and limits the right to reply: parties and candidates, for example, are prevented from taking a stand or justifying themselves regarding events that might occur during the blackout. These various interests, however, must be balanced against the need to control campaign expenses.

As for the 48-hour advertising blackout provided for in section 19 of the *Broadcasting Act, 1968*, the intention was to allow voters a chance to reflect on their choice in peace and calm without being inundated by partisan information. Boyer writes that the underlying rationale of this provision was that "voters should not be unduly influenced by a rush of publicity or promotion in the last hours before polling" when they have had ample time "to carefully consider and assess the policies of the candidates and the parties" (1983, 338).

To establish a rational connection between the measure and the objective, it must be demonstrated that broadcasting political messages one day before or on the day of an election influences the electorate; an impression or fear of such an influence does not suffice to make the measure rational. If the rational connection can be shown, then the limited duration of the blackout may be considered an indication that the measure infringes on the rights and freedoms under the Charter as little as possible. Furthermore, a blackout may be seen as the only way to alleviate the erosion of the right of reply caused by the broadcast of a partisan message just before polling.

Restrictions on Advertising by Third Parties   Section 259(1) of the *Canada Elections Act* provides that every person who incurs election expenses between the date of the issue of the writs and the day immediately following polling day, other than a candidate, the candidate's official agent, a registered agent of a party acting within the scope of his or her authority or any other person acting on behalf of a candidate with the candidate's knowledge and consent, is guilty of an offence.

"Election expenses" are defined in section 2 of the *Canada Elections Act* as being, among other things, "for the purpose of promoting or opposing, directly and during an election, a particular registered party, or the election of a particular candidate ... the cost of acquiring the right to the use of time on the facilities of any broadcasting undertaking, or of acquiring the right to the publication of an advertisement in any periodical publication."

When a person is found guilty of the above offence, and the violation was committed with the knowledge and consent of a candidate, an official agent or the registered agent of a registered party, that candidate, official agent or registered agent is also guilty of a corrupt practice.

In the period between the issue of the election writs and the day after polling, third parties are thus prohibited from engaging in any form of expression, by broadcasting or by publication, for the purpose of promoting or opposing a party or the election of a candidate without the knowledge or consent of the party or candidate.

In 1964, Maurice Lamontagne, Secretary of State, announced the creation of an advisory committee to "inquire into and report upon the desirable and practical measures to limit and control federal election expenditures" (Canada, Committee 1966, 5). Lamontagne stressed that it was a complex problem that touched the very heart of life in a democracy, and one that was becoming increasingly complex with the proliferation of means of communication and especially with the advent of television.

The Committee on Election Expenses, chaired by Alphonse Barbeau, published its report in 1966. The Committee recognized the need for Canadian legislation to regulate campaign spending and revenues to ensure the proper functioning of the democratic system. The Committee was convinced that campaign expenses were essential to the democratic process but also that they needed to be regulated to control abuse:

> The elector cannot make a sensible choice unless he [or she] is well informed. Keeping the electorate well informed means using the great communications media: radio, television, newspapers, printed flysheets, billboards, etc. If these media are to be used well, parties and candidates must spend very considerable sums of money. The sums are essential expenditures incurred in informing the public. It may be alleged that political expenditures do not always meet the aim of informing the elector and one may criticize the wrong or foolish use of money by parties or candidates; but one cannot dispense with the use itself. It may also be alleged that the financial means of the different parties and of their candidates are disproportionate, and the lack of proportion may likewise be criticized. From this, one can argue that measures should be taken to limit the expenses of parties and candidates that are too lavish in their expenditures, and to encourage the development of new sources of money for those who have not enough, so that they, too, may be able to use informational media to the full. (Canada, Committee 1966, 29)

The Barbeau Committee considered that the way to reduce the cost of election campaigns was to shorten them and to limit expenditures by candidates and parties on media.

The most practical and efficient means of controlling candidates' campaign expenses and reducing the cost of elections is to limit those expenditures that are easily traced and documented, such as money spent on campaign advertising. The Committee did in fact recommend spending limitations for candidates on the use of communications media, setting a ceiling of $0.10 per voter whose name is registered on the voters list in the candidate's constituency (Canada, Committee 1966, 49).

However, the limitation on candidates' spending would be meaningless, said the Committee, if other committees and organizations were permitted to campaign in the name of and on behalf of the candidates:

> The Committee is aware that many corporations, trade unions, professional and other groups take a lively interest in political activity and political education. To a large extent these organizations lie outside the structure and control of the political parties which they directly or indirectly support. Many have public educational programs and projects which attempt to create a climate either in support of, or opposition to, a political party. The Committee has no desire to stifle the actions of such groups in their day-to-day activities. However, the Committee has learned from other jurisdictions that if these groups are allowed to participate actively in an election campaign any limitations or controls on the political parties or candidates become meaningless. (Canada, Committee 1966, 50)

The Barbeau Committee thus recommended that third parties be prohibited from incurring expenses to support or oppose parties or candidates from the day the election writs are issued until the day following the election: "That no groups or bodies other than registered parties and nominated candidates be permitted to purchase radio and television time, or to use paid advertising in newspapers, periodicals, or direct mailing, posters or billboards, in support of, or opposition to, any party or candidate, from the date of the issuance of the election writ until the day after polling day" (ibid., 50). The Committee was careful to emphasize that this limitation was in no way meant to restrict the normal news and public affairs programs of broadcasting operators or the news reporting and editorial opinions of any established newspaper or periodical.

In 1970, a House of Commons Special Committee was appointed to study the limitation and control of election expenses in Canada and to submit a report on these matters (Canada, House of Commons 1971). The Special Committee on Election Expenses, chaired by Hyliard

Chappell, agreed with the recommendation in the Barbeau report prohibiting the use of advertising media by candidates before the 29th day leading up to an election, but recommended that such prohibition be extended to parties as well (ibid., recommendation 24). The Chappell Committee also proposed limiting the campaign spending of parties and candidates (ibid., recommendation 23). However, it made no recommendation on the need to limit the freedom of expression of third parties to achieve the objective of any legislative provision limiting the campaign spending of parties and candidates. The Special Committee suggested that the government should incorporate the Committee proposals in a bill to amend the *Canada Elections Act*.

In 1974, the law governing federal election finances was modified by the passage of the *Election Expenses Act*, which amended the *Canada Elections Act*, the *Broadcasting Act*, 1968 and the *Income Tax Act*. Boyer (1983) points out that the political context of the time had considerable impact on the system put in place to regulate election finances; the author was referring to the tabling of the Barbeau report and the substantial research it commissioned, as well as the elections of 1970 in Quebec, 1971 in Ontario and 1972 in the United States, in which campaign expenses "mushroomed beyond anything anyone had conceived of previously" (ibid., 57–58).

The *Election Expenses Act* was based in large part on the recommendations of the Barbeau Committee. Among other things, it provided for greater financial equality among candidates and parties by putting a ceiling on election expenses and prohibiting anyone from incurring expenses above this level.

Section 70.1, the basis for section 259 of the current *Canada Elections Act*, provided – for the first time in Canadian legislation – a prohibition against any person, other than a candidate or a political party, incurring election expenses between the day the writs are issued and the day immediately following polling day. "Election expenses" was defined in the same way as in the current section 2 of the *Canada Elections Act*. Section 70.1(4), however, provided that it constituted a defence to any prosecution to establish that a person incurred election expenses:

(a) for the purpose of gaining support for views held by him on an issue of public policy, or for the purpose of advancing the aims of any organization or association, other than a political party or an organization or association of a partisan political character, of which he was a member and on whose behalf the expenses were incurred; and

(b) in good faith and not for any purpose related to the provisions of this Act limiting the amount of election expenses that may be incurred by any other person on account of or in respect of the conduct or management of an election.

The rationale for the prohibition, in terms of limiting freedom of expression, can be found by placing it in the context of the system for capping expenditures made on behalf of parties and candidates. This prohibition is designed to ensure the integrity of the system.

Boyer (1983, 79) gives the example of the 1980 U.S. presidential election between Jimmy Carter and Ronald Reagan, in which Reagan held at least a $6 million advantage in financing his campaign, thanks to Republican supporters who had conducted a parallel advertising campaign. In the 1976 case, *Buckley v. Valeo* (1976), the United States Supreme Court ruled that a law limiting election expenditures made by third parties was unconstitutional because it restricted their freedom of speech. The Court stressed that any limitation on the amount of money that a person or group could spend on political communication during an election campaign would, by definition, reduce available means of expression and inhibit the opportunity for in-depth debate because having recourse to communications media necessarily involves spending money.

The purpose of section 70.1 of the *Canada Elections Act* was to prevent parallel election campaigns by third parties. As Boyer points out, "in exchange for a closed-system for election finances, a measure of freedom of speech for individual citizens is forfeited" (1983, 79).

In practice, section 70.1 of the *Canada Elections Act* proved difficult to enforce because a person could invoke section 70.1(4) and avoid prosecution by maintaining that, in good faith, he or she was promoting his or her views on a matter of public policy or advancing the aims of his or her organization. The decision in *R. v. Roach* (1978) illustrates the problem. The accused was president of a union local and was charged with unlawfully incurring an election expense during a 1976 federal by-election. Opposed to the anti-inflation program of the Liberal government then in power, he rented an airplane that towed a banner urging members of the local not to vote Liberal. Roach was acquitted on several grounds, one of which was that he was clearly expressing, in good faith, the views of his association on an issue of public policy. This acquittal raised a number of concerns among members of the House of Commons. How can the law maintain the effectiveness of the system controlling election finances if lobby groups and others can so easily justify themselves by claiming that their money was spent on promoting their views on matters of public policy or on advancing the aims of their organization? In the words of MP Lorne Nystrom, speaking in 1977,

> I do not quarrel, of course, with the judgment of His Honour, but I do think we as parliamentarians should concern ourselves with plugging the loopholes in the act so that this type of activity is not permitted, because if we were to allow what I would call third party advertising, we would be inviting nullification of the act. Not only would we be allowing private citizens to put advertisements in the media campaigning for a certain point of view during an election campaign, but we would also be allowing citizens' committees of all sorts to be formed, committees of concern, citizens in defence of freedom, citizens in defence of God knows what. We would also be allowing the Canadian Manufacturers Association, trade unions, mining associations, insurance companies, and so on, to get involved in election campaigns and campaign for certain ideas or for certain philosophies and not come under the scope of election expenditures. That could distort the whole intent of the act. (Canada, House of Commons 1977, 639)

In his 1983 statutory report (Canada, Chief Electoral Officer 1983, 73–74), the Chief Electoral Officer of Canada, Jean-Marc Hamel, bemoaned the ineffectiveness of section 70.1 as drafted and the abuses it had occasioned. For example, some individuals had spent substantial sums to promote or oppose the election of a particular candidate or party without having to account for those sums in terms of sources or amount. Hamel proposed that persons who are not acting on behalf of candidates or parties should be bound by the same rules during an election as are the candidates and parties, meaning:

- the freedom to contribute funds or services to official candidates and parties of their choice;
- the ability to register as a party and nominate candidates dedicated to the aims of their organization; and
- the ability to obtain written authority from candidates or parties to incur election expenses on their behalf, the said expenses being chargeable against the expenditures of the candidate or the party.

The chief electoral officer recommended repealing the defences provided in section 70.1(4) of the *Canada Elections Act* and adding a new provision whereby if a person or organization is found guilty of incurring unlawful election expenses with the sanction or connivance of a party or candidate, that party or candidate is guilty of a corrupt practice. In the opinion of the chief electoral officer, such amendments would not limit the right of individuals or organizations to speak out during an election for or against a particular party or candidate, nor would such amendments limit the right of citizens to promote their views on issues of public policy; the only restriction would be on their right to spend money for the primary purpose of opposing or promoting the election of a candidate or party. Thus, the chief electoral officer makes a distinction between the right to express oneself and the right to spend money to express oneself. The prohibition covers only spending that leads to the direct support of, or opposition to, a candidate or party; it does not target expression per se.

In 1983, Parliament passed the *Act to Amend the Canada Elections Act (No. 3)* (s. 14), which integrated the chief electoral officer's recommendation that the defence of good faith be repealed. During the debates in the House of Commons, members were aware that the amendment would encroach on the rights of citizens to express themselves freely, but also that it was necessary, to respect the spirit of the Act, to "equalize the chances of all candidates in all parties, by setting reasonable limits on election expenses and by guaranteeing reimbursement of a considerable part of those expenses" (Canada, House of Commons 1983, 28295). In the words of one member of the Progressive Conservative party, representing a minority view at the time:

> There is, I suppose, only one controversial amendment. I say it is controversial because I think it will undoubtedly end up being tested in the courts. This amendment would eliminate third party or special interest group advertising during the election period unless the third party had the express consent of a party or candidate for such advertising. In that case, the party or candidate would have to include the cost of that advertising as an election expense. As well, if the third party ceases to be a special interest group by registering as a political party and nominating candidates in at least 50 electoral districts, it could advertise.
>
> This amendment is more severe than is realized and is more severe than the proposals discussed at the ad hoc meetings with the Chief Electoral Officer, but we agreed to it on the basis that it will be much easier to police. However, I suspect that any number of groups in the country may wish to challenge that provision as it strikes me as somewhat of an interference with the rights of an individual to lobby on behalf of a political party or candidate. (Ibid., 28297)

That is exactly what happened in 1984 in the case of *National Citizens' Coalition Inc. v. Canada (Attorney General)*, where the plaintiffs challenged the validity of section 70.1, claiming that it violated freedom of expression as provided in section 2(*b*) of the Charter, as well as the democratic right to vote, which includes the right to an informed choice. The attorney general argued that the provision ensured equality and fairness among the participants in a federal election; if it did indeed limit the rights and freedoms of citizens, such limits were reasonable and justifiable.

Mr. Justice Medhurst of the Alberta Court of Queen's Bench declared that section 70.1, which prohibits spending by third parties, violates the guarantee of freedom of expression in section 2(*b*) of the *Canadian Charter of Rights and Freedoms* because it limits the ability of every person, other than a candidate or a registered party, to incur election expenses during a prescribed period. The restriction must be examined in the light of section 1 of the Charter, which involves balancing the individual's right to free expression against the collective societal benefits of having an effective system to elect members of Parliament.

According to Mr. Justice Medhurst, the restriction was not reasonable in a free and democratic society. The proper test is this: can the government empirically prove that the limitation is justified? After studying the legislative history of the *Canada Elections Act* provision, and in particular the repeal of the good faith defence as requested by the chief electoral officer in 1983, the judge came to the conclusion that there was insufficient evidence of abuse of section 70.1 to have warranted the chief electoral officer's recommendation. Mr. Justice Medhurst stated that fears or concerns of mischief that may occur are not adequate reasons for imposing a limitation on freedom of expression; there should be actual demonstration of harm or a real likelihood of harm to societal values. The attorney general, in the judge's opinion, had not established to the degree required that freedom of expression needed to be limited. Even if the objective was valid, he could not believe that no other means were available to achieve it.

As Hiebert (1989–90) emphasizes, the *National Citizens' Coalition* decision was rendered before the *Oakes* (1986) judgement, in which the Court specified the criteria to be met for a limitation on a Charter right to be deemed reasonable and justifiable. Those criteria do not include empirical evidence of harm.

Hiebert underscores the wave of media comment generated by the case. The prohibition on third-party election expenses was branded a disgrace to the democratic process (Hiebert 1989–90, 77). However, she says "few reports acknowledged that the legislation does not affect interest groups' ability to financially promote issues; neither did they address the implications of having no restrictions on what interest groups spend" (ibid.). The *National Citizens' Coalition* decision has never been appealed. For the 1984 election, the Commissioner of Canada Elections decided not to prosecute alleged violations of section 70.1(1) of the *Canada Elections Act* anywhere in Canada (Canada, Chief Electoral Officer 1984, 24).

In her article, Hiebert (1989–90) observes that spending by interest groups reached unprecedented levels in the 1988 general election. This can be explained partly by the issues raised in that election, namely free trade and abortion. These expenditures were channelled in two directions: either to negative or positive advertising that would name a candidate or party, or to general informational advertising regarding the issues at stake. According to Hiebert, "Estimates of campaign expenses by the three largest spending groups other than political parties are about $3.5 million, and this figure does not include the more modest spending by dozens of smaller organizations" (ibid., 80). The Commissioner of Canada Elections at that time was bothered by the flurry of last-minute advertising campaigns on the eve of the election when candidates and parties are incapable of responding because of legal blackouts (ibid.). Despite his concerns, however, he has decided to continue the policy of not prosecuting offenders.

The wording of section 70.1 (now section 259) is difficult to enforce in practice, according to Hiebert:

> The regulations provide that any money spent during a federal campaign to promote or oppose a candidate or party, other than those funds which are formally associated with the candidate's or party's allowable expenses, [is] unlawful. The *Act* does not prohibit interest groups from financially promoting an issue, as long as that issue is not associated with a particular candidate or party. While it is obvious that those advertisements which promoted or opposed a specific candidate or party violate the *Act*, it is not as clear whether the ads which promoted or opposed free trade but did not identify any candidate or party are unlawful. (1989–90, 81)

Hiebert (ibid., 81) believes that the trend toward increased independent spending is here to stay and, in the future, will only become more entrenched. In her view, this is not an isolated phenomenon resulting from the free trade issue that characterized the 1988 election.

It could be argued that the aim of the ban on independent expenditures, which consists of ensuring the fairness of the electoral process, is important enough to override a Charter guarantee. However, nothing prevents a third party from incurring election expenses so long as they are attributed to the party or candidate on whose behalf they were incurred.

It is also possible to establish a rational connection between the measure and its objective if the prohibition on third-party advertising is seen in the broader context of the regulation of election spending. Given the obvious difficulty of maintaining limits on candidates' and parties' expenses without limiting expenses incurred by third parties, it is likely that the Court will be flexible in its application of the proportionality test to determine whether the limits are reasonable.

However, it appears that the means chosen is one that infringes the least on freedom of expression. The government can assert that only a ban on spending by third parties will ensure that the regulation of candidates' and parties' expenses is effective and fair. But is it necessary to impose a complete prohibition on third parties for such a long period of time when candidates are entitled to four weeks of advertising? If the aim of the limit is to ensure total equality in the area of election expenses, then why not shorten the prohibition on third parties so as to make it identical to the one imposed on candidates and parties? But even if the blackout on advertising by third parties is shortened, the problem of monitoring their spending remains.

The goal should be to preserve the right of third parties to express themselves and still uphold the spirit of the law. Freedom of expression can be used in accordance with law by third parties and interest groups. For example, they can publish material outlining the priorities of their organization, describing their stand on certain issues, urging members of the organization to identify the candidates who support these issues before the vote, and so on.

In 1984, the chief electoral officer recommended:

> That the question of third party advertising be looked at with a view to striking a proper balance between the adequate control of election expenses and the freedom of expression of Canadians. In my opinion, the solution should probably lie in the imposition of certain restrictions on third parties not amounting to a total prohibition. In this way, third parties would be free to participate fully in the election campaign in a manner that would strive to ensure fairness in the system. However, news items and regular editorials should be specifically excluded from the application of any new provision. (Canada, Chief Electoral Officer 1984, 24)

Premature Publication of Election Results   Under section 328 of the *Canada Elections Act*, persons, companies and corporations are forbidden to publish the results of voting in any constituency in Canada, by means of radio or television broadcast, by newspaper, news-sheet, poster, billboard or handbill or in any other manner, before the hour fixed by or pursuant to the Act for the closing of the polls in that constituency. Anyone who contravenes that provision is guilty of an illegal practice and an offence.

Boyer (1983, 587) relates that this type of provision appeared for the first time in 1938 to stop Canadian Press (CP) from publishing election results before the official reports came out. Armed with provisional results, CP was able to make certain predictions about the outcome of the election even before all the electors had cast their vote. At the time, however, the voting period could extend over several days.

Today, voting is confined to one day; however, Canada is split into six separate time zones. The prohibition aims to avoid the danger that the publication of early election results might influence voters in ridings where the polls are still open. Apparently, in some previous federal elections, after the Liberal party had won enough seats outside British Columbia to form the government, many voters in that province were left with the impression that it would be futile to go to the polls (Boyer 1983, 589), hence, the feeling of western alienation.[46] Considering the possible consequences of a portion of the electorate feeling that their vote counts for nothing, this issue truly jeopardizes the constitutionally guaranteed right to vote.

The difficulties involved in enforcing this section have often been decried by various chief electoral officers (Canada, Chief Electoral Officer 1980, 20). In the 1980 election, some Alberta and BC cable operators transmitted U.S. network broadcasts that revealed the Canadian election results before the polls had closed in those provinces. However, section 18 of the *Cable Television Regulations* prohibited licensees from modifying or suppressing broadcasts during their transmission. Thus, by conforming to the provision in the *Canada Elections Act* that prohibited early publication of election results, cable operators were in potential breach of the *Cable Television Regulations*. No charge, therefore, was laid under the *Canada Elections Act*. Today, section 19(*c*) of the *Cable Television Regulations, 1986* forbids a licensee from modifying or withholding programming service "except in accordance with section 105(1) [now section 328] of the *Canada Elections Act*."

Some argue that the prohibition discriminates against Canadian broadcasters: voters in western Canada can still find out the result of the election before their polls close by tuning in to U.S. radio stations

(Canada, Chief Electoral Officer 1983, 30).

Furthermore, the *Canada Elections Act* is vague as to the chief electoral officer's responsibilities in a case where polling hours in one or several constituencies have to be extended (e.g., due to electrical failure) (Canada, Chief Electoral Officer 1980, 20): is the blackout on broadcasting extended accordingly? If so, it would be difficult to reach all the broadcasting stations and inform them of the extended voting hours so that they would delay announcing the results. Such a situation occurred in the 1980 election, but no charges were laid against stations that could not be informed about the extended voting hours.

The aim of the ban on premature publication of election results is to avoid influencing voters who have not yet cast their ballots. But does premature publication of the results really have any influence on the electorate? The reality of the risk must be proved. However, the absence of any such provision could affect some people's attitudes about the usefulness of voting, while its presence offers some assurance of the guaranteed right to vote. The existence of a rational connection between the measure and its purpose can thus be seen.

As for minimal infringement on a guaranteed freedom, broadcasters are not required to delay announcing the results indefinitely. For example, nothing says that broadcasters have to wait until voting results are announced officially, but only until the polls have closed in constituencies that can receive the broadcast.

It has been argued that the provision created inequality between Canadian and American broadcasters since the latter publish Canadian election results as soon as they receive them. In the past few years, several solutions have been proposed to alleviate some of the problems experienced in enforcing section 328 of the *Canada Elections Act.*

Bill C-237 proposed making voting hours the same across the country, so that polling stations in every time zone would open and close at the same time. This proposal responded to two concerns derived from Canada's time zones: (a) reports of voting results from eastern Canada might affect voting and turnout in the West, and (b) the perception of voters in the West that national elections have been decided before their votes are counted. Under the proposed rules, results from across the country would be announced at about the same time. To avoid late-night closings in certain regions like Newfoundland, it was proposed that polling stations should be open for only eight hours, down from eleven. However, as some members of the Standing Committee on Privileges and Elections stressed, such a measure would run the risk of congesting polling stations (Canada, House of Commons 1981, 4). More important, reduced voting hours (resulting, for example, in the closure of polling stations at 4:00 PM in British Columbia) could lead to reduced voter turnout.

Another proposed solution was to refrain from counting the votes in eastern Canada until all polling stations across the country had closed. This alternative would also cause problems: "poll workers could hardly be expected to have put in their 12 or 13 hours and then have to sit around for another three hours before they started counting, or even four hours in some cases. Heaven knows what they might do to amuse themselves during that period, and the effects on the count might be catastrophic" (Canada, House of Commons 1981, 6).

All the solutions proposed rested on the hypothesis that the results from eastern Canada influence the results in the West. One member of the Committee pointed out that very little evidence exists to support that premise:

> With almost a regular pattern, certainly since the election of 1962, there have been more Liberal votes in the east and more Conservative votes in the west. The fact that the east has been voting Liberal has not influenced the west; much to the regret of some, I might say. If you look at 1980, the fact that the Liberals were winning fairly solidly in the east obviously did not make a single dent in the minds of western voters. If you look at the United States, where, unlike the way it is in Canada, as soon as the polls close in the east the television stations start broadcasting the results, so that you can sit and watch election results in California for three hours before the California polls close – notwithstanding that, it is not unusual for western states to vote in a different direction from the way in which they vote in the east. So I am just wondering if I am correct in assuming your premise is that somehow eastern results, if they are known, influence western voters, and if you have any evidence to base that on. (Canada, House of Commons 1981, 7–8)

These various solutions stand to create even more significant issues of discrimination than are already raised by the current provision. All in all, the problems caused by section 328 as drafted are fairly limited.

Broadcasting from outside Canada   Section 303 of the *Canada Elections Act* makes it illegal and an offence for anyone to use a broadcasting station outside Canada, during an election, to broadcast any matter having reference to an election if done with the intent to influence persons to cast or refrain from casting their votes. The section also makes it an offence to aid, abet or counsel anyone to commit such acts.

Where any person, with the knowledge and consent of a candidate, broadcasts outside Canada a speech or any entertainment or advertising program during an election, in favour or on behalf of any political party or any candidate at an election, the candidate who knew about and consented to the broadcast is guilty of an offence.

This concern about the use of foreign stations is far from theoretical: 90 percent of the Canadian electorate live no more than 200 miles north of the U.S. border (Boyer 1983, 371). Therefore, it is possible for messages in violation of Canadian election broadcasting rules to be transmitted into Canada from an external source not subject to Canadian law.

The *Report* of the Committee on Election Expenses revealed that, at the end of the 1957 election campaign period, local candidates used American facilities near the Canada-U.S. border to broadcast spot announcements and programs to the area around Vancouver (Canada, Committee 1966, 379). In 1962 and 1963, the Liberal party used a station in Buffalo to broadcast programs into Canada. Broadcasting from outside Canada was even reported during the official blackout period.

The objective of the prohibition on the use of foreign broadcasts is to prevent candidates, parties or any other person from evading Canadian rules concerning everything from limiting election expenses to regulating access to the airwaves for the purpose of broadcasting political messages. As well, the intention is to avoid situations that could create de facto inequality between those parties that are financially strong and those that have less money. The measure also works in favour of effective rules for the control of election campaign expenditures and political broadcasts. Here, the objective seems to be sufficiently important to meet the constitutional test.

The means employed – a prohibition – is perhaps the most effective but not necessarily the best to meet the criterion of minimal infringement on freedom of expression. Prohibitions have significant scope, cover a wide variety of acts and expression and provide for penalties and criminal proceedings. However, this prohibition is circumstantial, limited in time and requiring intent. It could be argued, therefore, that the legislature, in seeking to adapt the means employed to the purpose of the measure, could find no more reasonable method to achieve that purpose. The effects of such a measure are no doubt harmful, in a general sense, but it cannot be denied that the objective is of proportional importance.

CONCLUSION

To conclude, let us summarize the main points that arise from our examination of the provisions governing election campaign broadcasting.

Broadcasting during election campaigns is a multifaceted activity. As a battleground for a wide range of competing interests, it cannot be understood in a unidimensional context. Broadcasting presents a situation in which the need for fair and harmonious discussion during election campaigns must be reconciled with the equally fundamental requirement of free expression. This reconciliation cannot be achieved by pronouncements that ignore one side of the issue in favour of another; it requires recourse to complex regulatory techniques.

That is why the rules that have been developed in Canada in this area are marked by subtlety. The Canadian Radio-television and Telecommunications Commission and the authorities that preceded it shunned regulatory techniques that were based on inflexible rules and prohibitions. Instead, they took into account the fact that the electronic broadcasting field is characterized by rapid change and a multitude of possible situations. The adoption of overly specific rules might have led to additional inflexibility that would in no way improve the quality of campaign-related broadcasting at election time.

With freedom of expression as one of a number of principles that have achieved constitutional status, it is more crucial than ever to construct a legal and regulatory framework for election broadcasting, founded on the will to find solutions to clearly defined problems. When any given rule is adopted that limits free expression, the need for an explicit justification for such a rule cannot be overemphasized. It is also essential to find the means with the least potential to trample on editorial freedom.

For all that lies outside the solution or prevention of identifiable ills, it should be sufficient to adhere to the general principles of balance and programming of high standard. These principles have resulted in a whole set of subtle and flexible rules, rules that, although sometimes lacking in precision, have nevertheless contributed to creating a media environment that is the envy of many countries around the world.

ABBREVIATIONS

Alta. Q.B.	Alberta Queen's Bench
am.	amended
art.	article
c.	chapter
C.A.	Court of Appeal
C.C.C.	Canadian Criminal Cases
Co. Ct.	County Court
C.R.C.	Consolidated Regulations of Canada
C.S.	Rapports judiciaires de Québec, Cour Supérieure
D.L.R.	Dominion Law Reports

F.	Federal Reporter
F.C.	Federal Court Reports, Canada
F.C.C. Record	Federal Communication Commission Record
F. Supp.	Federal Supplement
H.C.	High Court of Justice (Ont.)
L. Ed.	Lawyers' Edition, United States Supreme Court Reports
M.P.L.R.	Municipal and Planning Law Reports
O.R.	Ontario Reports
R.	Rex/Regina
R.J.Q.	Recueils de jurisprudence du Québec
R.S.C.	Revised Statutes of Canada
S.C.	Statutes of Canada
S.C.R.	Supreme Court Reports
S. Ct.	Supreme Court Reporter
SOR	Statutory Orders and Regulations of Canada
s(s).	section(s)
Supp.	Supplement
T.D.	Trial Division
U.S.	United States Supreme Court Reports
U.S.C.A.	United States Code Annotated
W.W.R.	Western Weekly Reports

NOTES

This study was completed in May 1991.

The authors would like to thank Anne Mailfait and Julie Bergeron, trainees at the Centre de recherche en droit public, who helped make this work a reality.

Pierre Trudel is a professor of law at the Université de Montréal and a director of the Centre de recherche en droit public. France Abran is a lawyer and research officer at the Centre de recherche en droit public. The Centre de recherche en droit public neither agrees nor disagrees with the opinions expressed in the work of its researchers; the opinions expressed herein should be attributed solely to the authors.

In this study, quoted material that originated in French has been translated into English. The original draft of the study used standard legal citation form and has been edited to conform with Commission style.

1. Section 52 of the *Constitution Act, 1982*, enacted as Appendix B of the *Canada Act 1982* (U.K.), 1982, c. 11, stipulates that "The Constitution of Canada is the supreme law of Canada, and any law that is inconsistent with the provisions of the Constitution is, to the extent of the inconsistency, of no force or effect."

2. For example, *L. c. Editions de la cité* (1960) where the judge wrote at page 489, "freedom of the press and freedom of information, like all freedoms, are limited by the principles of civil liability."

3. Subject to the ability of Parliament and the legislatures to pass legislation derogating fundamental freedoms in accordance with section 33 of the *Constitution Act, 1982*.

4. Excluding commercial speech from the prima facie Charter guarantee of freedom of expression entails the enormous difficulty of having to define commercial speech. See Simon (1984–85, 216).

5. For a critique of this tendency, see Mackay (1989, 726).

6. [1987] 2 F.C., 68, reversing the decision in [1985] 2 F.C., 3.

7. The constitutional guarantee of freedom of expression can be interpreted many ways. See Baker (1986, 75).

8. The Supreme Court of the United States refused to allow a rule that would compel an editor in the print media to publish a story. See *Miami Herald Publishing v. Tornillo* (1974); Barron (1981, 1–9).

9. See, for example, Krattenmaker and Powe (1985).

10. The very scheme, that is, whose alleged reason for existence is spectrum scarcity.

11. By the same token, it is conceivable that research and development of improved forest-harvesting techniques might yield a higher quantity of available paper. In this sense, it is not an exaggeration to say that, in any given period of time, all resources are limited. Going beyond the limitations requires greater skill or greater intensity in the development of those resources.

12. Such mechanisms would encourage investment in more efficient uses of the spectrum by, among others, broadcast licensees.

13. One could argue that this kind of scarcity does not really pertain to the spectrum as such.

14. The Study Team's recommendation reads as follows: "Adoption of a 'permits market' licensing process where the value of a license reflects the competitive impact of a new broadcaster and the tastes and desires of consumers are better served as existing licensees attempt to increase their economic value, which is transferable" (Canada, Task Force 1986b, 190).

15. The Court added that the natural monopoly situation of these companies arises from economic conditions.

16. The words at issue are: "shit," "piss," "fuck," "cunt," "cocksucker," "motherfucker" and "tits."

17. Nevertheless, it is mentioned in *Robinson v. American Broadcasting Co.* (1971); *Capital Broadcasting v. Mitchell* (1971); see also Evans (1979, 883–84).

18. The legislation did not prescribe rules pertaining to intellectual content of programs. It simply set conditions for frequency allocation. See Bird (1988).

19. In *R. v. T.R.* (1984), the judge found that the rehabilitation of young offenders was a substantial concern. Consequently, banning publication of the iden-

tities of accused youths constitutes a minor infringement of freedom of information compared with the importance of the objective it is meant to serve.

20. The same analysis is offered in *Luscher v. Deputy Minister, Revenue Canada, Customs and Excise* (1985, 89–90).

21. The status of the CRTC changed dramatically in 1975 when it acquired authority over telecommunications falling under federal jurisdiction. See the *Canadian Radio-television and Telecommunications Commission Act*, S.C. 1974-75-76, c. 49. In connection with the structure and operations of the Commission, see Bouchard et al. (1986, 11–81).

22. In the *Broadcasting Act*, 1968, there is a provision concerning partisan broadcasts, which were prohibited on the day an election or a referendum was to be held, or on the day before the day an election or a referendum was to be held. See the *Broadcasting Act*, R.S.C. 1985, c. B-9, s. 19. This provision was not included in the 1991 Act.

23. According to the wording contained in the *Broadcasting Act*, the functions of the CRTC take on two meanings. Strictly speaking, they consist of the Commission exercising the powers of being able to adopt regulations, conferred by sections 10, 11 and 12 of the Act. This activity relates to setting standards to establish rules that apply under most circumstances. The CRTC's regulatory function also assumes a wider mandate, and includes the establishment of rules to govern particular cases, by decision or by order. This, then, is a control function.

24. On page 30 of the decision, the Court indicated that in the expression "provided for under the law," the word "law" covers both written and unwritten law. For studies comparing the European Convention with the *Canadian Charter of Rights and Freedoms*, see Hovius (1985); Mendes (1982); Turp (1984).

25. In this case, Mr. Justice Lamer dissented in part; however, the majority accepted his analysis of the judicial principles involved.

26. In the Canadian legal context, the expression "broadcasting" designates radiophonic communication intended for the general public. Since television stations use Hertzian waves for broadcasting purposes, these stations are broadcasting operations and are designated as such, even though the expression "telecasting" would be a more precise term to designate this activity in English.

27. This is different from the 1958 Act, which prescribed that the Board of Broadcast Governors should regulate broadcasting to create "a varied and comprehensive broadcasting service of a high standard that is basically Canadian in content and in character" (*Broadcasting Act*, S.C. 1958, c. 22, s. 10). The French version spoke of "un service de radiodiffusion vaste et varié qui atteigne un haut niveau et soit fondamentalement canadien par son contenu et sa nature" (ibid.). See Beke (1970, 127). See also *Broadcasting Act 1981*, 1981, c. 68, U.K. Section 2 of this Act establishes the Independent Broadcasting Authority and provides that "the function of the Authority

shall be to provide, in accordance with this act and until 31st December 1996, television and local sound broadcasting services, additional in each case to those of the BBC and of high quality ... as may from time to time be reasonably practicable."

28. There is a link between the balance concept and other principles that the CRTC cites on controversial programming. The CRTC does not seem willing to define "high standard" or other fundamental principles of the *Broadcasting Act*. In the CRTC's defence, though, one has to admit that the high standard concept is so broad that, if necessary, it could be used to deal with controversy, sexist or racist comments and many other issues.

29. The CRTC did, however, note certain mitigating circumstances, in that the station admitted its error and apologized.

30. Section 16 (now section 6 of the *Broadcasting Act*) sets out the regulatory powers of the CRTC.

31. The rest of paragraph (a) concerns the licences given to the CBC.

32. This document, which was tabled in Parliament a short time before the bill that became the *Broadcasting Act*, explained the government's approach.

33. Indeed, it carries greater legitimacy to intervene in the name of the quest for high-standard programming than on behalf of interest groups active in the Canadian broadcasting industry.

34. Beke (1970) relates how the numerous parliamentary inquiries seriously endangered the independence of the CBC and at the same time required the directors of the Corporation to devote considerable energy to "witch hunts," energy that could otherwise have been channelled toward better management of the Corporation.

35. In CRTC (1977), *Controversial Programming in the Canadian Broadcasting System – Report on Issues Raised by CFCF's Anti Bill 22 Campaign*, the Commission refers to *Circular 51*, which is appended to the notice.

36. The hearing was announced on 4 February 1969.

37. Only those principles pertaining directly to the treatment of controversial issues are mentioned.

38. In the *Broadcasting Act*, 1968, the CRTC could also regulate the use of production techniques in advertising messages, political announcements or broadcasts of a partisan nature. The origin of the provision concerning dramatizations was a particular event that left its mark on the history of Canadian broadcasting: the airing of dramatized radio spots, sponsored by the Conservative party, which denounced the policies of the Liberal party. These six broadcasts, entitled "Mr. Sage," heaped praise on Conservative policies and criticized those of the Liberals. When the Liberals won the election in 1935, they introduced the provisions in the *Canadian Broadcasting Act, 1936*. In 1968, they became the enabling provisions for the CRTC.

39. "Election period" means: (a) in the case of a federal or provincial election or of a federal, provincial or municipal referendum, the period beginning on the date of the announcement of the election or referendum and ending on the date the election or referendum is held; (b) in the case of a municipal election, the period beginning two months before the date of the election and ending on the date the election is held.

40. The CRTC suggests a number of means designed to facilitate attainment of the requirement for balance for operators dealing with controversial issues (*Vancouver Co-operative Radio* 1987, 7).

41. See the developments on this point in the section describing general obligations derived from the *Broadcasting Act*.

42. In this decision, the judge did not deal with the substantive issues, but granted an interlocutory injunction ordering the broadcast of an advertisement containing material that the defendants alleged belonged to them by copyright. The Court decided that the balance of convenience lay in favour of the plaintiffs. To our knowledge, this is the first time a court has ordered the broadcast of a program. If such a trend continues, it might have considerable impact on the fundamental principle that broadcasters are responsible for what they broadcast.

43. He can contact the leader or chief agent of the party; see section 308(2) of the *Canada Elections Act*.

44. The definition contained in section 2 of the *Broadcasting Act* is much more wide-ranging. This definition states that a "network" is "any operation involving two or more broadcasting undertakings where control over all or any part of the programs or program schedules of any of the broadcasting undertakings is delegated to a network operator."

45. Every registered party, through the agency of a person acting on its behalf, that advertises for such purpose and within such period "is guilty of an offence and liable on summary conviction to a fine not exceeding twenty-five thousand dollars" (section 47 of the *Canada Elections Act*).

46. It has also been a problem in the United States; see Polsky (1984).

REFERENCES

Al-Sanhoury, A.-A. 1935. "Le standard juridique." In *Recueil d'études sur les sources de droit en l'honneur de François Gény*. Vol. II. Paris: Librairie du Recueil Sirey.

Associated Press v. United States 326 U.S. 1 (1945).

Baker, Edwin. 1986. "Limitations on Basic Human Rights – A View from the United States." In *La limitation des droits de l'homme en droit constitutionnel comparé*. Montreal: Éditions Yvon Blais.

Banzhaff v. FCC 405 F.2d 1082 (1968); petition for review denied on appeal 396 U.S. 842 (1969).

Barron, Jerome A. 1963. "The Constitutional Status of Freedom of Speech and Press in Canada: The History of a Quiet Revolution." *Northwestern University Law Review* 58:73–106.

———. 1981. *Public Rights and the Private Press*. Toronto: Butterworths.

Baum, Daniel J. 1970. "Controversial Broadcasting in Canada." *Osgoode Hall Law Journal* 8:159–70.

Beaudoin, Gérald-A. 1989. "Democratic Rights." In *The Canadian Charter of Rights and Freedoms*, ed. Gérald-A. Beaudoin and Edward Ratushny. 2d ed. Toronto: Carswell.

Beckton, Clare. 1989. "Freedom of Expression." In *The Canadian Charter of Rights and Freedoms*, ed. Gérald-A. Beaudoin and Edward Ratushny. 2d ed. Toronto: Carswell.

Beke, A. John. 1970. "Government Regulation of Broadcasting in Canada." *Canadian Communications Law Review* 2:104–44.

Binette, André. 1987. "La liberté d'expression commerciale." *Cahiers de droit* 28:341–66.

Bird, Roger. 1988. *Documents of Canadian Broadcasting*. Ottawa: Carleton University Press.

Black, W.W. 1979. "Case Comment – Gay Alliance Toward Equality v. Vancouver Sun." *Osgoode Hall Law Journal* 17:649–75.

Board of Broadcast Governors. 1961. *White Paper on Political and Controversial Broadcasting Policies*. Circular No. 51, 18 December. Ottawa: BBG.

Bouchard, Marie-Philippe, Michèle Gamache and Mireille Beaudet. 1986. "La réglementation des entreprises de radiodiffusion et des télécommunications canadiennes." Study prepared for the Task Force on Broadcasting Policy. Montreal: Centre de recherche en droit public.

Boyer, J. Patrick. 1983. *Money and the Message – The Law Governing Election Financing, Advertising, Broadcasting and Campaigning in Canada*. Toronto: Butterworths.

———. 1990. "Freedom of Expression and the Electoral Process, Power of Speech; Power over Speech." Speech given at the Centre for Constitutional Studies Conference, 21 April, Edmonton.

Brassard v. Langevin, [1877] 1 S.C.R. 145.

Braun, Stefan. 1986. "Should Commercial Speech Be Accorded Prima Facie Constitutional Recognition Under the Canadian Charter of Rights and Freedoms?" *Ottawa Law Review* 18:37–53.

Browne, Donald R. 1989. *Comparing Broadcast Systems*. Ames: Iowa State University Press.

Brun, Henri, and Guy Tremblay. 1990. *Droit constitutionnel.* 2d ed. Montreal: Éditions Yvon Blais.

Buckley v. Valeo 424 U.S. 1 (1976).

Canada. *Act to Amend the Canada Elections Act (No. 3),* S.C. 1980–81–82–83, c. 164, s. 14.

———. *Broadcasting Act,* S.C. 1958, c. 22, s. 10.

———. *Broadcasting Act,* S.C. 1967-68, c. 25.

———. *Broadcasting Act,* R.S.C. 1985, c. B-9, ss. 2, 3, 16, 17, 19.

———. *Broadcasting Act,* S.C. 1991, c. 11, ss. 2, 3, 5, 6, 9–14, 16, 18, 21, 24, 35.

———. *Cable Television Regulations, 1986,* SOR/86-831, 1 Aug. 1986, ss. 15, 18, 19.

———. *Canada Elections Act,* R.S.C. 1970, c. 14 (1st Supp.), s. 70.1.

———. *Canada Elections Act,* R.S.C. 1985, c. E-2, ss. 2, 12, 47, 48, 105, 213, 259, 303–316, 320, 328.

———. *Canadian Bill of Rights,* S.C. 1960, c. 44, s. 1.

———. *Canadian Broadcasting Act, 1936,* S.C. 1936, c. 24, s. 22.

———. *Canadian Broadcasting Act,* R.S.C. 1952, c. 32, s. 21.

———. *Canadian Charter of Rights and Freedoms,* ss. 1, 2, 3–5, 15, 33, Part I of the *Constitution Act, 1982,* being Schedule B of the *Canada Act 1982* (U.K.), 1982, c. 11.

———. *Canadian Radio Broadcasting Act, 1932,* S.C. 1932, c. 51.

———. *Canadian Radio-television and Telecommunications Commission Act,* S.C. 1974–75–76, c. 49.

———. *Constitution Act, 1982,* being Schedule B of the *Canada Act 1982* (U.K.), 1982, c. 11, ss. 33, 52.

———. *Election Expenses Act,* S.C. 1973–74, c. 51, s. 17.

———. *Income Tax Act,* R.S.C. 1952, c. 148, am. S.C. 1970–71–72, c. 63.

———. *Radio (A.M.) Broadcasting Regulations,* C.R.C. 1978, c. 379.

———. *Radio Regulations, 1986,* SOR/86-982, 18 September 1986, s. 6.

———. *Television Broadcasting Regulations, 1987,* SOR/87-49, 9 January 1987, ss. 8, 9.

Canada (Canadian Human Rights Commission v. Taylor). See *Taylor v. Canada (Canadian Human Rights Commission).*

Canada. 1966. *White Paper on Broadcasting.* Ottawa: Queen's Printer.

Canada. Chief Electoral Officer. 1980. *Report of the Chief Electoral Officer of Canada as per subsection 59(1) of the Canada Elections Act.* Ottawa: Minister of Supply and Services Canada.

————. 1983. *Report of the Chief Electoral Officer of Canada as per subsection 59(1) of the Canada Elections Act*. Ottawa: Minister of Supply and Services Canada.

————. 1984. *Report of the Chief Electoral Officer of Canada as per subsection 59(1) of the Canada Elections Act*. Ottawa: Minister of Supply and Services Canada.

Canada. Committee on Broadcasting. 1965. *Report*. Ottawa: Queen's Printer.

Canada. Committee on Election Expenses. 1966. *Report*. Ottawa: Queen's Printer.

Canada. House of Commons. 1977. *Debates*. 7 November, 3rd sess., 30th Parliament.

————. 1983. *Debates*. 25 October, 1st sess., 32d Parliament.

Canada. House of Commons. Special Committee on Election Expenses. 1971. *Report*. Ottawa: Queen's Printer.

Canada. House of Commons. Standing Committee on Privileges and Elections. 1973. *Minutes of Proceedings and Evidence*. 11 October, 1st sess., 29th Parliament.

————. 1981. *Minutes of Proceedings and Evidence*. 7 June, 1st sess., 32d Parliament.

Canada. Royal Commission on National Development in the Arts, Letters and Sciences. 1951. *Report*. Ottawa: King's Printer.

Canada. Royal Commission on Radio Broadcasting. 1929. *Report*. Ottawa: King's Printer.

Canada. Task Force on Broadcasting Policy. 1986a. *Report*. Ottawa: Minister of Supply and Services Canada.

Canada. Task Force on Program Review. 1986b. *Management of Government: Regulatory Programs – Report*. Ottawa: Minister of Supply and Services Canada.

Canadian Broadcasting Corporation v. R., [1983] 1 S.C.R. 339.

Canadian Broadcasting Corporation (CBC). 1939. *Statement of Policy with Respect to Controversial Broadcasting, CBC Board of Governors*. Ottawa, 8 July.

————. 1982. *Journalism Policy*. Ottawa.

Canadian Human Rights Commission v. Taylor. See *Taylor v. Canada (Canadian Human Rights Commission)*.

Canadian Newspapers Co. c. Ville de Montréal, [1988] R.J.Q. 482 (C.S.).

Canadian Newspapers Co. c. Directeur des services de la voie publique et de la circulation routière de la Ville de Québec (1986), 33 M.P.L.R. 28 (C.S. Qué.).

Canadian Newspapers Co. v. Canada (Attorney General), [1988] 2 S.C.R. 122.

Canadian Radio-Television Commission (CRTC). 1970. *Report of the Special Committee Appointed in Connection with the CBC Program "Air of Death."* Public Notice, 9 July. Ottawa.

———. 1971. *Canadian Broadcasting: "A Single System."* Policy Statement on Cable Television, 16 July. Ottawa.

———. 1972. *Inquiry by the Radio-Television Commission into a Complaint Against Radio Station CHNS, Halifax, by the Halifax-Dartmouth Committee of Miles for Millions.* Public Announcement, 28 March. Ottawa.

———. 1975. *Policies Respecting Broadcasting Receiving Undertakings (Cable Television).* 16 December. Ottawa.

Canadian Radio-television and Telecommunications Commission (CRTC). 1977. *Controversial Programming in the Canadian Broadcasting System – Report on Issues Raised by CFCF's Anti Bill 22 Campaign.* Public Announcement, 24 February. Ottawa.

———. 1979. *A Review of Certain Cable Television Programming Issues.* Public Announcement, 26 March. Ottawa.

———. 1984a. *Community Channel Policy Review.* Circular No. 297, 12 June. Ottawa.

———. 1984b. *Controversial Broadcasting – Complaints Against Radio Station CFCF, Montreal.* Public Notice 1984-159, 28 June. Ottawa.

———. 1985. *Complaints by the Nishga Tribal Council and Musqueam Indian Band Against CKNW New Westminster, B.C.* Public Notice 1985-236, 4 November. Ottawa.

———. 1987a. *Political Broadcasting – Complaints re: Free Time and Editorial Time Allocations.* Circular No. 334, 4 June. Ottawa.

———. 1987b. *Concerning a Complaint Against CKVU Television, Vancouver, British Columbia by Media Watch.* Public Notice 1983-187, 17 August. Ottawa.

———. 1987c. *Broadcasting Guide – Provincial General Elections.* Circular No. 337, 8 September. Ottawa.

———. 1987d. *Election Campaign Broadcasting.* Public Notice 1987-209, 23 September. Ottawa.

———. 1988a. *A Policy with Respect to Election Campaign Broadcasting.* Public Notice 1988-142, 2 September. Ottawa.

———. 1988b. *Balance in Programming on Community Access Media.* Public Notice 1988-161, 29 September. Ottawa.

Capital Broadcasting v. Mitchell 333 F. Supp. 582 (1971).

Carscallen, Helen. 1966. "Control in a Broadcasting System." Master's thesis, University of Toronto, Faculty of Graduate Studies.

CBS Inc. v. FCC 101 S. Ct. 2813 (1981).

CBS v. Democratic National Committee 412 U.S. 94 (1973).

City of Los Angeles v. Preferred Communications Inc. 106 S. Ct. 2034 (1986).

CKOY v. R., [1979] 1 S.C.R. 2.

Coase, R.H. 1959. "The Federal Communications Commission." *Journal of Law and Economics* 2:1–40.

Committee for the Commonwealth of Canada v. R., [1987] 2 F.C. 68 (C.A.), reversing [1985] 2 F.C. 3 (T.D.); (sub nom. *R. v. Committee for Republic of Canada*, [1991] 1 S.C.R. 139).

Cook, Peter G. 1982. "The Concept of Balance in the Supervision and Regulation of Canadian Broadcasting: Public Issues and CRTC Policies." Master's thesis, Simon Fraser University, Department of Communication.

CTV Television Network v. CRTC (1981), 2 F.C. 248 (C.A.); affirmed [1982] 1 S.C.R. 530.

Dixon v. British Columbia (Attorney General) (1989), 59 D.L.R. (4th) 247 (B.C.S.C.).

Duplé, Nicole. 1986. "La liberté de la presse et la Charte canadienne des droits et libertés." In *Qu'est-ce que la liberté de la presse?*, ed. Alain Prujiner and Florian Sauvageau. Montreal: Boréal.

Edmonton Journal and Alberta (Attorney General), Re [1989] 2 S.C.R. 1326.

Ellis, David. 1979. *Evolution of the Canadian Broadcasting System: Objectives and Realities 1928–1968*. Ottawa: Minister of Supply and Services Canada.

Les entreprises de radiodiffusion de la Capitale Inc., CRTC Decision 90-772, 20 August 1990.

Evans, Anne C. 1979. "An Examination of the Theories Justifying Content Regulation of the Electronic Media." *Syracuse Law Review* 30:871–92.

Fallon, Marc. 1987. "La radio et la télévision face au juge européen." *Annales de droit de Louvain* 47:153–91.

FCC v. League of Women Voters 468 U.S. 364 (1984).

FCC v. Pacifica Foundation 438 U.S. 726 (1978).

FCC v. WNCN Listeners' Guild 450 U.S. 582 (1981).

Federal Liberal Agency of Canada v. CTV Television Network Ltd., [1989] 1 F.C. 319 (T.D.).

Finkelstein, Marie Alison. 1985. "Selected Social Issues in Programming: The Legal, Constitutional and Policy Implication of the Equality Provision in Bill C-20." Background study prepared for the Task Force on Broadcasting Policy. Ottawa.

Ford v. Quebec (Attorney General), [1988] 2 S.C.R. 712.

Forest, Réal. 1988. "Liberté d'expression dans le domaine économique." In *Application des Chartes des droits et libertés en matière civile* (Formation permanente du Barreau du Québec). Montreal: Éditions Yvon Blais.

Fowler, Mark S., and Daniel L. Brenner. 1982. "A Marketplace Approach to Broadcast Regulation." *Texas Law Review* 60:207–57.

FRC v. Nelson Bros. Bond & Mortgage Co. 289 U.S. 266 (1933).

Gay Alliance Toward Equality v. Vancouver Sun, [1979] 2 S.C.R. 435.

Gifford, Daniel J. 1971. "Communication of Legal Standards, Policy Development, and Effective Conduct Regulation." *Cornell Law Review* 56:409–68.

Gold, Mark E. 1985a. "The Mask of Objectivity: Politics and Rhetoric in the Supreme Court of Canada." *Supreme Court Law Review* 7:455–510.

———. 1985b. "The Rhetoric of Constitutional Argumentation." *University of Toronto Law Journal* 35:154–82.

———. 1988. "La rhétorique des droits constitutionnels." *Revue juridique Thémis* 22:1–35.

Hammond, R. Grant. 1982. "Embedding Policy Statements in Statutes: A Comparative Perspective on the Genesis of a New Public Law Jurisprudence." *Hastings International and Comparative Law Review* 5:323–76.

Head, Sydney W. 1985. *World Broadcasting Systems – A Comparative Analysis.* Belmont: Wadsworth.

Hiebert, Janet. 1989–90. "Fair Elections and Freedom of Expression Under the Charter." *Journal of Canadian Studies* 24 (Winter): 72–86.

Hovius, Berend. 1985. "The Limitation Clauses of the European Convention on Human Rights: A Guide for the Application of Section 1 of the Charter." *Ottawa Law Review* 17:213–61.

Hsiung, James C. 1987. "Indecent Broadcast: An Assessment of *Pacifica's* Impact." *Communications and the Law* 9 (February): 41–56.

In the Matter of Inquiry into Section 73.1910 of the Commission's Rules and Regulations Concerning Alternatives to the General Fairness Doctrine Obligations of Broadcast Licensees, [1987] 2 F.C.C. Record 5272.

Joseph Burstyn Inc. v. Wilson 343 U.S. 495 (1952).

Kopyto, Harry. 1980. "The *Gay Alliance* Case Reconsidered." *Osgoode Hall Law Journal* 18:639–52.

Kovacs v. Cooper 336 U.S. 77 (1949).

Krattenmaker, Thomas G., and L.A. Powe, Jr. 1985. "The Fairness Doctrine Today: A Constitutional Curiosity and an Impossible Dream." *Duke Law Journal*: 151–76.

K-Right Communications Ltd., CRTC Decision 87-337, 7 May 1987.

L. c. Éditions de la cité, [1960] C.S. 485.

Lange, David L. 1973. "The Role of the Access Doctrine in the Regulation of the Mass Media: A Critical Review and Assessment." *North Carolina Law Review* 52:1–91.

Luscher v. Deputy Minister, Revenue Canada, Customs and Excise, [1985] 1 F.C. 85 (C.A.).

MacKay, A. Wayne. 1989. "Freedom of Expression: Is It All Just Talk?" *Canadian Bar Review* 68:713–64.

McPhail, Brenda M. 1986. "Canadian Content Regulations and the Canadian Charter of Rights and Freedoms." *Canadian Journal of Communication* 12 (Winter): 41–53.

Magnet, Joseph Eliot. 1987. *Constitutional Law of Canada: Cases, Notes and Materials*. 3d ed. Toronto: Carswell.

Mendes, Errol P. 1982. "Interpreting the Canadian Charter of Rights and Freedoms: Applying International and European Jurisprudence on the Law and Practice of Fundamental Rights." *Alberta Law Review* 20:383–433.

Metromedia Inc. v. City of San Diego 453 U.S. 490 (1981).

Miami Herald Publishing v. Tornillo 418 U.S. 241 (1974).

Minasian, Jora R. 1975. "Property Rights in Radiation: An Alternative Approach to Radio Frequency Allocation." *Journal of Law and Economics* 18:221–72.

Morris, Robert J. 1972. "The CHNS Case: An Emerging Fairness Doctrine for Canada?" *Canadian Communications Law Review* 4:1–54.

Namurois, Albert. 1980. "Aspect du droit de la radio et de la télévision dans le monde, en rapport avec la liberté d'expression." *Études de radio-télévision*. No. 27 (May): 1–42.

National Broadcasting v. United States 319 U.S. 190 (1943).

National Citizens' Coalition Inc./Coalition nationale des citoyens inc. v. Canada (Attorney General) (1984), 11 D.L.R. (4th) 481 (Alta. Q.B.).

National Indian Brotherhood v. Juneau (No. 3), [1971] F.C. 498.

New Brunswick Broadcasting Co. v. Canada (CRTC), [1984] 2 F.C. 410 (C.A.).

Omega Satellite Products Co. v. City of Indianapolis 694 F.2d 119 (1982).

Ontario Film and Video Appreciation Society and Ontario Board of Censors, Re (1983), 41 O.R. (2d) 583, 147 D.L.R. (3d) 58 (Div. Ct.); affirmed (1984), 5 D.L.R. (4th) 766 (Ont. C.A.).

Pacific Press and R., Re (1977), 37 C.C.C. (2d) 487 (B.C.S.C.).

Parish, P. William. 1979. "Case Note: FCC v. Pacifica Foundation." *University of Detroit Journal of Urban Law* 57:95–121.

Peers, Frank W. 1969. *The Politics of Canadian Broadcasting 1920–1951.* Toronto: University of Toronto Press.

———. 1979. *The Public Eye: Television and the Politics of Canadian Broadcasting 1952–1968.* Toronto: University of Toronto Press.

Pinard, Danielle. 1991. "Les seules règles de droit qui peuvent poser des limites aux droits et libertés constitutionnelles protégés et l'arrêt Slaight Communications." *National Journal of Constitutional Law* 1:79–136.

Pinto, Roger. 1984. *La liberté d'information et d'opinion en droit international.* Paris: Economica, Collection d'études juridiques comparatives internationales.

Polsky, Jeff. 1984. "Turning Out the Electorate: Early Network Projections and Decreased Voter Turnout." *Comm/Ent Law Journal* 6:865–85.

Popovici, Adrian. 1977. *L'outrage au tribunal.* Montreal: Éditions Thémis.

Proulx, Michel. 1985. "Le droit de s'exprimer." In *Justice Beyond Orwell,* ed. Rosalie S. Abella and Melvin L. Rothman. Montreal: Institut canadien d'administration de la justice and Éditions Yvon Blais.

Quebec. *Civil Code of Lower Canada,* art. 1802.

Quebec (Attorney General) v. Irwin Toy Ltd., [1989] 1 S.C.R. 927.

Quincy Cable TV Inc. v. FCC 768 F. 2d 1434 (1985); petition for review denied on appeal 106 S. Ct. 2889 (1986).

R. v. Big M Drug Mart Ltd., [1985] 1 S.C.R. 295.

R. v. CBC, CTV and Global, oral judgement, Toronto, Kerr J., 27 March 1991.

R. v. CFRB Ltd. (1976), 30 C.C.C. (2d) 386 (Ont. C.A.).

R. v. Committee for Commonwealth of Canada. See *Committee for Commonwealth of Canada v. R.*

R. v. Keegstra, [1990] 3 S.C.R. 697.

R. v. Kopyto (1987), 47 D.L.R. (4th) 213 (Ont. C.A.).

R. v. Oakes, [1986] 1 S.C.R. 103.

R. v. Roach, (1978), 78 C.C.C. (2d) 405 (Ont. Co. Ct.).

R. v. Simmons, [1988] 2 S.C.R. 495.

R. v. Therens, [1985] 1 S.C.R. 613.

R. v. Thomsen, [1988] 1 S.C.R. 640.

R. v. T.R. (1984), 7 D.L.R. (4th) 205 (Alta. Q.B.).

Radio Frequencies Are Public Property, CRTC Decision 74-70, 31 March 1974.

Red Lion Broadcasting v. FCC 395 U.S. 367 (1969).

Reference re Alberta Statutes, [1938] S.C.R. 100.

Reference re Provincial Electoral Boundaries, [1991] 3 W.W.R. 593 (Sask. C.A.).

Renewal of the Canadian Broadcasting Corporation's Television and Radio Network Licences, CRTC Decision 79-320, 30 April 1979.

Reynolds v. Sims 12 L. Ed. 2d 506 (1964).

Rials, Stéphane. 1984. "Les standards, notions critiques du droit." In *Les notions à contenu variable en droit*, ed. Chaim Perelman and Raymond Vander Elst. Brussels: Travaux du Centre national de recherches en logique.

Richstone, Jeff, and J. Stuart Russell. 1981. "Shutting the Gate: Gay Civil Rights in the Supreme Court of Canada." *McGill Law Journal* 27:92–117.

Robinson v. American Broadcasting Co. 441 F.2d 1396 (1971).

Rocket v. Royal College of Dental Surgeons, [1990] 2 S.C.R. 232.

Rogers Cable TV Ltd., CRTC Decision 85-496, 28 June 1985.

Rossini, Murray J. 1985. "The Spectrum Scarcity Doctrine: A Constitutional Anachronism." *Southwestern Law Journal* 39:827–43.

RWDSU v. Dolphin Delivery, [1986] 2 S.C.R. 573.

Saumur v. City of Quebec, [1953] 2 S.C.R. 299.

Simon, Todd F. 1984–85. "Defining Commercial Speech: A Focus on Process Rather than Content." *New England Law Review* 20:215–45.

Singh v. Minister of Employment and Immigration, [1985] 1 S.C.R. 177.

Skarsgard, Anne. 1980–81. "Freedom of the Press: Availability of Defences to a Defamation Action." *Saskatchewan Law Review* 45:287–318.

Slaight Communications v. Davidson, [1989] 1 S.C.R. 1038.

Slansky, Paul. 1985. "Program Regulation and the Freedom of Expression: Red Lion's Alive and Well in Canada?" *Canada–United States Law Journal* 9:81–112.

Southeastern Promotions Ltd. v. Conrad 420 U.S. 546 (1975).

Spitzer, Matthew L. 1985. "Controlling the Content of Print and Broadcast." *Southern California Law Review* 58:1349–1405.

Squire, Ronald, and Steve Stepinac. 1969. "The CRTC Hearing into 'Air of Death': Comments on the Regulation of Controversial Broadcasting." *Canadian Communications Law Review* 1:132–59.

Sunday Times, European Court of Justice, Series A, no. 30, 27 October 1978.

Syracuse Peace Council, [1987] 2 F.C.C. Record 5043.

Tarnopolsky, Walter Surma. 1981. "Freedom of the Press." In *Newspapers and the Law*. Vol. 3 of the research studies of the Royal Commission on Newspapers. Ottawa: Minister of Supply and Services Canada.

Taylor v. Canada (Canadian Human Rights Commission), [1990] 3 S.C.R. 892.

Thompson-Pyper, Catherine. 1990. "Implications of Bill C-40 for Election Broadcasting." Background study prepared for the Royal Commission on Electoral Reform and Party Financing. Ottawa.

Tollefson, E.A. 1968. "Freedom of the Press." In *Contemporary Problems of Public Law in Canada, Essays in Honour of Dean F.C. Cronkite*, ed. O.E. Lang. Toronto: University of Toronto Press.

Tremblay, André. 1986. "La liberté d'expression au Canada: le cheminement vers le marché libre des idées." In *Perspectives canadiennes et européennes des droits de la personne*, ed. Daniel Turp and Gérald-A. Beaudoin. Actes des Journées strasbourgeoises de l'Institut canadien des études juridiques. Montreal: Éditions Yvon Blais.

Tremblay, Gaétan. 1986. "Le service public: principe fondamental de la radiodiffusion canadienne." Study prepared for the Task Force on Broadcasting Policy. Montreal.

Trieger v. Canadian Broadcasting Corporation (1989), 66 O.R. (2d) 273 (H.C.).

Trudel, Pierre. 1984a. *Droit de l'information et de la communication – Notes et documents*. Montreal: Éditions Thémis.

———. 1984b. *La liberté d'information – Règle supralégale et principe d'interprétation*. Ottawa: Canadian Bar Foundation.

———. 1986. "Liberté d'information et droit du public à l'information." In *Qu'est-ce que la liberté de la presse?*, ed. Alain Prujiner and Florian Sauvageau. Montreal: Boréal.

———. 1989a. "Liberté de presse ou procès public et équitable? À la recherche du fondement au droit d'accéder aux audiences et de diffuser des informations judiciaires." *Revue du Barreau* 49:251–81.

———. 1989b. "Le standard de programmation de haute qualité dans la législation sur la radio et la télévision." *McGill Law Journal* 34:203–32.

Trudel, Pierre, Jacques Boucher, René Piotte and Jean-Maurice Brisson. 1981. *Le droit à l'information*. Montreal: Presses de l'Université de Montréal.

Turmel v. CRTC, [1981] 2 F.C. 411 (C.A.).

Turmel v. CRTC, Federal Court, Trial Division, No. T-2884-83, 16 December 1983.

Turp, Daniel. 1984. "Le recours au droit international aux fins de l'interprétation de la Charte canadienne des droits et libertés: un bilan jurisprudentiel." *Revue juridique Thémis* 18:353–411.

United Kingdom. *Broadcasting Act, 1981*, 1981, c. 68, s. 2.

———. *Constitution Act, 1867*, 30 & 31 Vict., c. 3, preamble.

United Nations. *European Convention of Human Rights*, 1950, 213 United Nations Treaty Series 221, art. 10.

———. *International Covenant on Civil and Political Rights*, 1976, 999 United Nations Treaty Series 187, art. 25.

United States v. Paramount Pictures Inc. 334 U.S. 131 (1948).

United States. *Constitution of the United States*, 1788. *First Amendment*, 1791.

———. *Public Broadcasting Act of 1967*, 47 U.S.C.A. § 390–399.

Vancouver Co-operative Radio, CRTC Decision 88-694, 29 September 1987.

Webbink, Douglas W. 1987. "Radio Licenses and Frequency Spectrum Use Property Rights." *Communications and the Law* 9 (June): 3–29.

Wescott, Grace. 1986. "Broadcast Regulation and the Canadian Charter of Rights." *Communications Law Conference Programs Materials*. Toronto: Law Society of Upper Canada.

Zolf, Dorothy. 1988. "The Regulation of Broadcasting in Canada and the United States: Straws in the Wind." *Canadian Journal of Communication* 13 (Spring): 30–44.

3

THE IMPACT OF ALL-NEWS SERVICES ON ELECTIONS AND ELECTION COVERAGE

David Hogarth
William O. Gilsdorf

Eᴠᴇʀ sɪɴᴄᴇ ɪᴛ ʙᴇɢᴀɴ ʙʀᴏᴀᴅᴄᴀsᴛɪɴɢ as a basic cable service in July 1989, Canada's news channel – ᴄʙᴄ Newsworld – has covered a number of political and nonpolitical stories of considerable national importance. These include (and this is a partial list) reports on the proceedings of the Dubin Inquiry; Manitoba's provincial hearings on native justice; the summer conflicts at Oka-Kanesatake; the proceedings of the Meech Lake federal-provincial negotiations; the events of the recent Gulf War; and, as well, extended coverage of recent provincial election campaigns in Ontario and Manitoba.

It seems probable, however, that the full political impact of cable news has not yet been felt in Canada. As one official at the Canadian Broadcasting Corporation (ᴄʙᴄ) told us, Canadian all-news television will only receive its political "road test," its real "test of strength," in a federal election campaign: in a campaign yet to come. In short, the new service does have a record as a political broadcaster in Canada, but it is an incomplete record and hence a rather difficult one to assess. If only for this reason, this study of the political impact of cable news – specifically the impact of all-news television on Canadian elections and election coverage – is perhaps premature and, without doubt, speculative to a considerable degree.

Nonetheless, there is a record of sorts to go on and we have chosen to proceed with this study as follows. The first section examines the history of all-news broadcasting in North America, a history that largely takes place in the United States, where the Atlanta-based Cable News Network (CNN) has been in service for over 10 years (long enough to have covered three American federal campaigns). Documentation in Canada concerning the Newsworld service is somewhat more scarce, limited mostly to newspaper accounts and corporate statements of intent issued following the CBC's publication of a formal proposal for a Canadian all-news service in the spring of 1987. Throughout, these written records are supplemented with the more current views of cable broadcasters whom we interviewed at CNN bureaus in Atlanta and Washington, and at CBC Newsworld offices in Toronto, Ottawa and Calgary. In the same vein, we will be drawing upon our discussions with a number of political party strategists who have dealt with these services during election campaigns in Canada and the United States at the federal and regional levels. Our overall aim in this section will be to examine all-news services as North American media institutions; that is, as organizations with regularized patterns of resources and constraints, and with historically established procedures for covering social events, political and otherwise.

With this historical background in mind, we turn to the Canadian all-news service's plans for covering the next federal election campaign. Our impression is that those plans are far from certain. In its first year of service, the all-news service was, understandably, concerned with more pressing issues than elections of uncertain date. In fact, Newsworld seems to have drawn up only a preliminary campaign coverage strategy, and that partly in response to our request for an interview. In our analysis of what that strategy may be, we draw on the views of a number of CBC reporters who will provide the new service with most of its regional and national news footage in the next federal election campaign. Also of interest to us are forecasts by cable journalists, CBC officials and party strategists as to what we might expect from Newsworld in the way of "differentiated" news service in the coming election. Out of this material, we conclude with a working list of policy recommendations concerning the role of all-news broadcasting in future Canadian election campaigns.

One final note concerning the overall mandate of cable news in this country is suggested by our reading of the licensing documents. The CBC's promises of performance for Newsworld, as set out in the November 1987 licence decision of the Canadian Radio-television and Telecommunications Commission (CRTC), are, in a long-standing tradition of Canadian broadcast policy, both modest and extremely ambitious. The modesty has to do with the material resources claimed for the service – which are, to be sure, nothing extravagant (allowing, for instance, for a first-year budget for Newsworld that is less than one-tenth that of its American counterpart, CNN, in 1989). In fact, in Canada, cable news has essentially been chartered as a news "delivery service": a service that produces little news footage of its own but operates as a "second window" for reports, mostly regional, that are available on the parent CBC network.

At the same time, corporate and regulatory documents make some rather ambitious claims for the new service which we think are of direct relevance to this study and to any assessment of cable news in Canada, whatever its specific interest or intent. First, cable news has been licensed and promoted as an essentially neutral information medium, a medium that can reflect Canadian society free of the distortions – commercial, political or otherwise – which affect regular news broadcasts in this country. These documents suggest that, free of direct advertising and ratings pressures, the cable news channel will have more time to tell its stories, more time to make sense of these stories for its audience and more time to provide access to a range of "distinct and different voices from across the country" (CRTC 1987a, 228). A great deal of the analysis in this study is concerned with the substance of these claims, particularly those concerning the so-called public access dimensions of the new channel.

Secondly, cable news has been promoted and developed as a technological medium for cultural sovereignty in Canada. This is a rather unusual claim, particularly within a Canadian context where cable technology has generally been used to bring metropolitan (mostly American) broadcast signals to areas that could not receive them over the air. Most of the Newsworld licensing documents that we examined suggest that the all-news service will reverse the "metropolitanizing" tendencies of cable in a number of ways. At a national level, cable news promises to help Canada retain control of its information resources within a larger North American communications market by providing a full-time service of "news and views from a Canadian viewpoint" (the corporate history places cable news squarely within Canada's long-standing struggle for "information sovereignty"). At a regional level, cable news is seen to reverse cable's traditional one-way flow of information by allowing regional communities to speak for themselves and make their views known to a larger national audience. At a more generic popular level, cable promises to open the airwaves to a variety of views, political and nonpolitical, which may not be well represented on regular Canadian broadcast channels. In the words of former director Joan

Donaldson, Newsworld will provide a "river of information giving a variety of perspectives" (*Toronto Star* 1989).

In Canada, then, cable news has been mandated to provide "news without filters" (CRTC 1987b, 2882): unmediated communication, communication in which Canadians from all walks of life can speak for themselves on roughly their own terms to a national audience; and communication which stands as a free pool of information to which Canadians can turn with confidence in a time of national decision. In this study, we essentially try to assess these broader claims in a specific political context: to determine, in other words, how Newsworld might operate as a communications medium in a national election campaign.

ALL-NEWS SERVICE IN THE UNITED STATES (CNN)

All-news broadcasting is relatively new to North America. The first full-time news and information service sponsored by advertisers was established by a New York radio station, WINS, in the 1960s; flagship stations for the major broadcasting networks, such as WCBS in New York, have followed the format with some degree of financial success since that time (though the Canadian CKO radio network went bankrupt with the all-news format in 1989 after 13 years of service). The Independent Television News Association (ITNA), a cooperative of nonaffiliated local American broadcasters, made some efforts to produce a 24-hour television news schedule in the 1970s; but it was Atlanta businessman Ted Turner's Cable News Network (CNN) which established the idea of an all-news cable television service on a commercial basis in 1980. According to its first president, Reese Schonfeld, CNN was founded on the idea that network television news had stolen the "birthright of journalism." In Schonfeld's view, cable news would be an antidote to network news, an "electronic newspaper" against the "news as entertainment medium" being offered by the American television networks (Whittemore 1990, 28).

CNN's major innovation as a cable news programmer was its extensive use of live footage, mostly of press conferences and other prescheduled news events. This sort of programming has become a very prominent feature of all-news public-affairs schedules in North America – see, for example, the program formats submitted by the main competitors for a Canadian all-news service (CRTC 1987b). For CNN, live coverage served to fill the 24-hour news line-up (a major problem for the network in its first years of service); it offered the network its largest audiences (who have tuned in to CNN's "breaking stories" in steadily growing numbers since 1980); and, most importantly, network officials claimed, it fitted in with the general CNN "philosophy of news," a philosophy which, according to CNN owner Ted Turner, called for newscasters to "get out of the way of the news" and "provide more words of people and less pre-packaged editorializing." CNN should be what Turner called a "network of record": a network in which "comments come from people making events happen" (*New York Times* 1988).

CNN programmers plainly view "unmediated news" – particularly the coverage of political events as a matter of record – as a singularly important contribution to American television journalism. Network officials cite their decision to break with the other networks and provide full coverage of the 1984 Democratic and Republican party conventions as a "turning point" in CNN's development. In fact, the cable network has provided virtually full coverage of the major party conventions in all three campaigns in which it has been involved (in 1984 it spent over U.S.$6 million of its total U.S.$12 million campaign budget on convention coverage (*New York Times* 1984); "gavel to gavel" coverage was also CNN's "major spending item" in the 1988 campaign (Belkin 1987)). Gaining equal access to the U.S. president and key American policy makers has been another long-term goal of the network, and the determination with which CNN has pursued this goal (launching, for instance, a four-year law suit to break up the White House-network cartels governing access to special presidential events) gives some indication of the extent to which regularly scheduled political events – party conventions, presidential tours, press conferences – have become the staple fare of the network's public affairs schedule during and between elections.[1]

CNN has made some efforts to provide independent investigative reporting in recent years, and this shift in policy may have some substantive effect on the way the network covers future elections (see below); but its emphasis still seems to be on record coverage in the public affairs schedule. Tom Hannon, CNN's political director, told us that such coverage is the "most important type of report CNN does in the long run," a sort of ongoing historical record of political events which the regular networks cannot or will not provide for their viewers (Hannon interview).

This approach to news coverage has provoked considerable criticism from those (including some CNN staffers) who maintain that CNN has come to rely far too heavily on press releases and staged events to fill its line-up. "Too much duty coverage of official Washington" says *Newsweek* in its 10th anniversary assessment of the network. "CNN has certainly not reinvented the formula of political news" (Alter 1990b, 48). CNN's original investigative unit director, Ted Kavanau, has similarly criticized CNN's political bureau in Washington for "years of putting out standard stuff, not real news" (Whittemore 1990, 299). (Kavanau's plans to "turn Washington upside down" were cut short when his special investigative unit was disbanded shortly before the last U.S. presidential election.) CNN has recently established new investigative units to cover political affairs, and we were told they would play a "prominent" (though as yet imprecise) role in the next campaign. Still, Turner's promise to provide "electronic sunshine" on the political process by making politicians accountable for their actions seems to have been treated with a considerable degree of scepticism by most of the journalists and party strategists who were interviewed for this study.

It also seems that CNN has not fully used the extra broadcast time at its disposal to air alternative points of view on political issues. A 1982 content study of the network has found some evidence that CNN "relies on a wider variety of sources and presents a better balanced mix of viewpoints" than its competitors, relying for instance on more "non-partisan experts" and fewer government sources in its political and economic stories (Maines 1984). That study, however, seems to have included current affairs programming in its sample (where outside experts are normally heavily represented in debate formats such as CNN's "Crossfire") and excluded live coverage where the views of public officials are generally more heavily represented, often without journalistic comment. Moreover, this report and further research work by Womack (1989) suggest that CNN does not provide wider access in proportion to the extra news time it has at its disposal.

Similarly, CNN's attempts to provide air time for minor parties or social movements have been notable but rather sporadic. In the 1980 political campaign, the network caused something of a sensation by including independent candidate John Anderson in a presidential debate, against the wishes of the sponsoring League of Women Voters and the other Republican and Democratic candidates. Anderson's statements were edited into the tape at CNN's Washington bureau. Stu Loory, a political reporter at CNN, claimed that the network had "blazed a new trail in journalism" with its coverage (Whittemore 1990, 180), and John J. O'Connor (1980) of the *New York Times* viewed the CNN broadcast as an "intriguing glimpse into a possible future when all third party candidates ... will have access to a national forum," access that is "impossible on limited over the air network television." The network has not repeated the experiment in subsequent campaigns, however, and apparently has no immediate plans to do so. The CNN officials interviewed for this study stressed that their organization was not a "public access" channel and that the network had no responsibility to make special efforts for candidates from smaller parties. According to one official,

CNN's policy on this matter is essentially that of the other networks; that is, it will provide special access for minor-party candidates "if and only if they have clear public support."

There is also some question as to whether CNN's 24-hour format provides viewers with a more adequate understanding of complex social issues. Research concerning the relative depth of CNN's political coverage, however that is defined, is almost nonexistent, but a comparative study by the Media Institute of Washington, DC, concerning television coverage of economic issues (focusing on reports about a 1983 stock market rally) found that only 7 percent of CNN stories bothered to define key economic terms as compared to 17 percent of stories carried on CBS, NBC and ABC. Similarly, only 31 percent of CNN's stories dealt with the causes and implications of the stock market rally as against 39 percent of stories covered by the networks. In this case, CNN does not seem to have used its extra time to provide "comprehensive" coverage of the economic issues concerned, leading the researchers to conclude that "more news time and superior news performance do not seem to be related" (Maines 1984, xv). Again, we know of no comparable study of CNN's political or election coverage.

In closing, we should note that a surprising number of the journalists and party respondents interviewed said that CNN's impact on the general public would be minimal in the next U.S. national election. Some recent demographic research suggests that the audience for American cable news is influential but limited, concentrated mainly among affluent, educated Americans, many of whom already participate quite regularly in American politics (Lamb 1988). Brian Lamb has argued that CNN's coverage of political events has "potential democratic value" by "showing the democratic process at work," though he concedes that the network may be "preaching to the converted" in this respect (ibid., 29). Interestingly, much of the source material we examined concerning CNN's election role emphasizes its impact on American politicians and policy making, rather than its influence on American voters and their involvement in the political process. One American party strategist we spoke with insisted that the latter impact is probably insignificant: American cable news programming is, in his view, "news by politicians and for politicians," a medium through which newsmakers can convey their message at greater length and with less journalistic mediation than on regular television. Other strategists we spoke with suggested that CNN and the American public affairs information channel C-SPAN allow newsmakers to gauge public responses to their political initiatives.[2] Cable news thus seems to be viewed by this group primarily as a tool for policy makers: an information resource for those who

already have a stake in the political process. A number of these findings are supported by the Canadian research, as described in the
next section.

ALL-NEWS SERVICE IN CANADA

Comparing the development of all-news service in Canada and the
United States is somewhat problematic. It should be noted at the
outset that Canadian cable news programmers essentially see themselves in an altogether different business from their American counterparts. Their task, they say, is not simply to make news for profit
(though it is partly that) but to provide a reflection of Canadian society
as set out in their conditions of licence with the Canadian Radio-
television and Telecommunications Commission (CRTC). The Canadian
all-news mandate and its implications for Newsworld's role as a political broadcaster will be discussed at some length later, but in the
remainder of this section we want to examine the Canadian service in
a more general historical context: as a media organization with regularized patterns of resources and constraints, and with a more or less
established set of procedures for covering Canadian social events,
political or otherwise.

The CBC reports that it first drew up plans for a specialty news
channel in 1985, partly in response to the availability of CNN on Canadian
cable channels, which began in 1984. The idea for a CBC news channel
received some support in the Caplan-Sauvageau report on broadcasting
(Canada, Task Force 1986, 301–304), and in April 1987 the CBC submitted
to the CRTC a formal proposal for such a service. Competing bids were
received from the Rogers Cable Company affiliate, the Public Affairs
Channel (which subsequently withdrew its proposal), and from the
Allarcom corporation, an Edmonton-based private broadcaster. In
November 1987 the Commission awarded the three-year licence for an
English-language news and information service to the CBC; the CBC's
application for a separate French-language service was denied, though
a new Radio-Canada proposal for a French-language service was being
prepared for the CRTC as this study was being written.

The Newsworld licence was controversial from the start. Within
days of its announcement, 17 of 20 Alberta Conservative MPs publicly
criticized the ruling as an affront to the interests of western Canada
and the nation's private broadcasting community, and gave their official support to Allarcom's appeal to the Commission (and subsequently
to the federal Cabinet) to have the decision overturned. The licence
was also opposed by most of the Quebec wing of the federal
Conservative party, because of its lack of provision of a French-language

news channel. Communications Minister Flora MacDonald criticized the decision for having effectively licensed a unilingual service, and she described as "premature" the CRTC's various rulings on pay television, which had awarded licences for national sports and music networks as well as for a news service. The proposed *Broadcasting Act*, which MacDonald made public within days of the CRTC's licensing decisions, had envisaged a very different institutional structure for pay television in Canada, specifically calling for a second public channel to deal with specialty broadcasting concerns such as "in-depth news." Ultimately, the CRTC cable news decision was simply set aside by the Cabinet, as a "sensitive area of Canadian culture whose provisions need more consideration" (*Gazette* 1987).

Newsworld's licence was eventually given final approval by Cabinet in October 1988 but with two substantial conditions of service attached. First, 70 percent of cable news programming was to be based outside Toronto, mostly at regional headquarters in Halifax, Winnipeg and Calgary. Newsworld was to be a regional service against the "central Canadian broadcasting monopoly" which was then seen to exist (*Globe and Mail* 1988e). Second, the government moved against what it called the "danger of absolute public control" of all-news broadcasting in Canada (ibid.). CBC's 1987 cable proposal had envisaged what was essentially a publicly operated cable news service; but by 1988, in response to the new directions from Cabinet, the corporation had arranged for fully 25 percent of programming to come from private sources such as the *Globe and Mail* and the *Financial Times of Canada*. Moreover, Newsworld programming would be marketed to cable companies by Toronto's privately owned Cancom service. In later statements, CBC President Pierre Juneau described the Newsworld project as a "joint venture between public and private broadcasters" (ibid.). As a result of these negotiations, Newsworld was essentially established as a "parallel but differentiated" service in the Canadian broadcasting system. What this means is that the news channel draws quite heavily on CBC news and current-affairs programming – airing regular broadcasts from the CBC's national newsroom and repeats of CBC current-affairs programming such as "The Journal" and "The Fifth Estate" – while at the same time producing a considerable amount of its own (mostly current affairs) programming. Newsworld thus uses its own facilities and those of the CBC to produce a range of interview, discussion and debate formats, most of which are organized and produced by Newsworld's own production team, sometimes in collaboration with private media outlets such as the Southam corporation. Newsworld's morning show produced out of Halifax and its afternoon line-up from Winnipeg, Toronto and

Ottawa essentially consist of this type of original current-affairs programming, as does much of the weekend schedule: the native current affairs program "Nedaa" is a case in point. Newsworld also produces daily news digests such as the Ottawa-based "Capital Report" and Calgary's "Cover Story."

However, as far as news itself is concerned, Newsworld essentially operates as a "second window" on material already available within the Canadian public broadcasting system. That is, Newsworld draws heavily on footage produced by local, regional and national CBC news teams, making some of that material – particularly local and regional news reports and extended footage from the national news – available to a new national audience (CRTC 1987b, 2880). This strategy for a parallel but differentiated service is essentially the foundation of all-news television service in Canada. Newsworld was never conceived by its various organizational handlers as a full-fledged "alternative" news and information service. In fact, the CBC and CRTC regulators established cable news service as, first and foremost, a second "delivery system" for the public network. Newsworld is meant to be a "complement" to the CBC rather than a "second adversarial team" (McQueen interview).

Operating as such, the Canadian news channel has largely been spared the tremendous start-up costs which the independent service CNN incurred in its first years of operation; CNN lost over U.S.$175 million before it started operating at a profit in 1985. CBC established Newsworld with a first-year budget of Cdn.$19.3 million, less than one-tenth of that spent by CNN in 1989. Much of this money has been spent for extended coverage of reports already available on the parent network – footage which had, in the past, been taped but had not always been aired for regular newscasts. The extra cost of processing this material, if any, has been incurred as an "incremental cost" (to ensure a separation of service as called for in the parent network's condition of licence). The news channel has only incurred direct costs for news when it has had occasion to order up special reports from the CBC – reports which CBC officials have stressed will be kept to a minimum for budgetary reasons, at least in Newsworld's first years of service (CRTC 1987b, 2881 and 3039). Thus, while producing its own schedule of current-affairs programming, Canada's news channel relies almost totally on the infrastructure of the regular public network to gather, process and transmit news.

"A national all-news service was only available to Canadians on this basis," said a CBC official, who explained "there just wasn't enough money for a completely independent news channel" or for a competitive service such as the Turner network in the United States. The next section examines more closely how this cable "production and delivery" system might operate in a federal election campaign. More specifically, it questions whether, and to what degree, such a role is compatible with the cable channel's promises of performance as a public-affairs broadcaster.

PROMISES OF PERFORMANCE AND THE NEXT ELECTION

Justification for the establishment of a specialty cable news service in Canada has encompassed a range of potential benefits (CBC 1987; CRTC 1987c). From our reading of the licensing documents, these include:

- increased regional representation (with cable news production and processing to be based in areas outside central Canada);
- greater variety of news sources ("interested communities," including social movements, multicultural groups and political parties); and
- extended coverage of news events.

These are certainly not the only claims made for the service (CBC 1987, 1988; CRTC 1987c); but in our view they are the most pertinent to public-affairs coverage and will have a direct bearing on the news channel's possible performance in a federal election campaign. Each of them will be discussed in turn.

Regional Representation

In Canada, cable news has been promoted first and foremost as a medium for regional representation. The news channel is mandated to "reflect each part of Canada to itself and to other regions" (CRTC 1987c, 245) and to "draw upon the incredible wealth of material [within the Canadian broadcasting system] previously not given opportunity to be seen outside place of origin" (ibid., 247). Cable news broadcasters interviewed for this study stressed that the Canadian all-news service goes beyond the mere transmission or retransmission of regional data to "communicate the richness and wealth of local experience in this country" (Donaldson interview).

Although networking arrangements are far from settled, CBC spokespersons have given us a general picture of how Newsworld might cover the regions in the next election. It seems that most local election reports will be prepared by CBC regional bureaus or affiliates and processed by Newsworld producers in Halifax, Toronto, Winnipeg and Calgary. Via this network, Newsworld will receive regular satellite reports from each of Canada's regions, including northern Canada, which was supplied with a satellite up-link when the cable service was established; regional reports will also, of course, be included in the regular newscasts of "The National." CBC officials expect that over 80 percent of Canadian federal ridings will be covered in this fashion.

What Newsworld will do with this material is still somewhat unclear. In a federal election, Newsworld producers would apparently have the job of presenting the regional reports as a "continuous stream" of programming to a national audience (CBC 1987, 30–31). But Newsworld officials insist that they will make few or no changes to individual stories as such. That is, producers will package the local material on the assumption that it has already been vetted at some level by the parent network. "We assume it conforms [to the fairness and balance standards set out in the corporation's code of journalistic policy], so, as much as possible, we show it 'as is' to a national audience" (Donaldson interview). In this way, it seems, the integrity of regional programming will be maintained.

More closely monitored – and perhaps more problematic for the service – will be the maintenance of a partisan balance in regional stories received from the parent network. A structure to monitor overall balance as such has apparently not yet been established, though in the Manitoba and Ontario elections Newsworld developed a logging and entry system to keep track of how parties and interests were being represented in the regional program packages, and this system may well remain in place for the federal election. Other than these basic measures regulating the flow of local campaign material, we were told that corporate "filters" on the regional material would be kept to a minimum. Newsworld, said Donaldson, will allow the regions to "speak directly about issues which concern them to a national audience" – through the CBC affiliate system. Moreover, Newsworld will apparently use its own current-affairs programming – specifically the interview, analysis and debate formats (largely produced out of the region) – to reflect regional concerns and issues with "as little distortion as possible" (Donaldson interview).

Local producers in Ontario and Manitoba who provided the news channel with campaign reports in the last provincial elections mostly confirm this organizational scenario. "There was no editing, no direction, no feedback from them," says a Manitoba CBC reporter. "Newsworld simply told us they wanted to pick up our election night coverage and they did." Producers in Ontario and Manitoba told us they received no requests for extended reports or special analysis from the news channel. "There were no conditions," said a CBC reporter in

Toronto. "They just took what we gave them. As long as they stuck with us, what Canadians saw was what our local audience saw."

There have been some discussions within Newsworld and the parent network, however, concerning the proper balance between regional and national material in the news schedule and the overall propriety of Newsworld's regional mandate. Some Newsworld journalists interviewed seemed to support the *Toronto Star* journalist Antonia Zerbisias' assertion that the channel produces too many "features on fish, potatoes and wheat" (1990). "There's just no sense of proportion for the regional stuff," said one Newsworld producer. "You get the sense that it's there to fill time or to fill a quota." On the other hand, at least some CBC journalists interviewed felt that the news channel had not given regional issues enough time during the Manitoba and Ontario elections. According to a CBC reporter in Toronto, Newsworld "stuck with us until decision time, then cut to a commercial and switched to their own analyst from Quebec. We had a whole discussion panel on local issues which they missed because of that." However, the Manitoba producers interviewed seemed quite impressed with the breadth and sensitivity of Newsworld's coverage of local issues, in both its news reports and its own current-affairs programming.

In whatever way the regional representation issue is resolved, CBC officials insist that the regional network will form the backbone of its all-news federal campaign coverage. "It's not a perfect or complete system but we believe it will reflect Canadian political reality better than anything Canadians are likely to see in the next election," says one Newsworld official in Calgary. "It's a regional alternative. You won't be getting that type of programming anywhere else in the Canadian broadcasting system."[3]

Access for Social Movements

CBC officials say the news channel will serve as a forum for "distant and different voices from all parts of the country" during and between elections (CRTC 1987c, 228). Moreover, Newsworld can be expected to represent social and multicultural groups in a manner "that realistically reflects their participation in Canadian society" (ibid., 252). These were explicit promises of performance tabled at the CRTC licensing hearings in July 1987 (see, for example, CRTC 1987b, 3066) in the CBC's proposal for a specialty news service (see, for example, CBC 1988, 17). These promises have been reaffirmed in recent public statements by service officials. For instance, Newsworld's first chief, Joan Donaldson, speaks of a 24-hour "river of information" providing a "greater variety of perspectives on issues of importance to Canadians" (*Toronto Star* 1989).

Canadians have essentially been told that more news means more diverse news, news that draws upon a variety of perspectives that are not fully represented within the regular Canadian broadcasting system.

The corporation has not always been clear as to its responsibility toward social movements or minority parties, but officials have pledged to ensure some degree of public access to the news channel through a number of procedures. First, the corporation seems to suggest that Newsworld's regional schedule will, as a matter of course, offer Canadians a range of local viewpoints which are underrepresented on Canada's regular broadcasting channels. It is at least partly on this basis that the news channel can be seen as a "differentiated service."

This is a plausible but, in our view, somewhat problematic position. As a "second window" on the regular network, for instance, the news channel will be relying on news programming, both national and local, in which the constraints of time and conventional journalistic notions of balance are probably in full force. These factors, which have traditionally excluded minority parties and interests from being fully represented on the regular channels of the Canadian broadcasting system, will continue to govern much of Newsworld's election programming – at source.

These constraints may be somewhat relaxed in Newsworld's original election programming, specifically in news analysis shows such as "Inside Politics" and "Cover Story," which will apparently be prominently featured in the network's election schedule. But the Newsworld officials interviewed said that, throughout the campaign, they will emphasize repeat news headlines (provided by the parent network), the sort of news wheels and headline formats on which all-news services have traditionally relied during and between elections. In other words, the amount of extra broadcast time available on the news channel to minority interests and small political parties may be rather less than corporate statements have indicated. Moreover, and this is a point we would stress, access provided to minority social movements will almost certainly not be in proportion to the amount of extra broadcast time available to Newsworld producers. In other words, if Newsworld does "open the airwaves" to alternative news and views in the next election, it may not open them much, and even then only within its limited original program schedule.

Finally, and perhaps most importantly, the Newsworld organization does not recognize any "special obligations" to provide public access under its current charter. That is, even assuming Newsworld producers do have full 24-hour days with which to reflect the "full balance" of Canadian viewpoints in a general election, they accept no special responsibility to do so above and beyond the CBC's normal operating procedures in this area. Trina McQueen said that Newsworld will "act like any other broadcaster" to ensure that its coverage is fair and balanced in a federal election (McQueen interview); that is, its coverage will be governed by the CBC's 1988 regulations concerning party political broadcasts and in particular by the corporation's code of journalistic policy (which, among other things, calls for CBC reporters to represent a balance of opinion on social issues, taking into account the "weight of opinion" behind a point of view).

Most of the minor-party representatives interviewed felt that the news channel would not offer them a significant forum in which to present their views to the Canadian electorate.[4] "Newsworld will be worse than any other news organization," says Greg Vézina of the Green Party of Canada, "because with all the time it has to cover political affairs it will end up doing what the CBC and all the other regular broadcasters do – covering the same old three party platforms." Vézina, who is challenging the regular networks' "minor party" policies in an Ontario court (including their refusal to adhere to the CRTC regulation (CRTC 1987a) calling for the "equitable coverage" of minor party positions, as determined by the provincial courts), claims that Newsworld's news and current-affairs treatment of the smaller parties during the Ontario election was particularly deficient. In particular, he cites the CBC's refusal to provide the smaller provincial parties with air time after they were excluded from the regular leaders debates.

Some journalists argued that Newsworld's policies in this area may be more flexible than current corporate statements indicate, that the service may not settle on a precise fairness and balance policy until its own corporate infrastructure is in place with regular levels of funding secured. Then, we have been told, Newsworld may offer Canadians more differentiated coverage of political affairs. "It may really go its own way in the next few years," says one CBC journalist. "There's definitely the will here to provide Canadians with something completely different in news and current affairs." That may be the case, but the assertion that more air time will as a matter of course "provide for a greater diversity of opinion" (CBC 1988, 17), an assertion which stood as a founding premise in the service's early licensing statements, seems rather implausible in hindsight. Judging by existing corporate statements of policy and by the allocation of resources and present allotment of time on the news channel, we believe the equation of more news with more diverse news is inherently problematic in Canada.

It should be noted that some of Newsworld's current-affairs programming is considered both capable and unique by many of the journalists and party activists interviewed, and that it may have risen above some of the corporate constraints listed above. Many of our sources, for instance, pointed to weekend programming such as "The Week Starts Here" and "Focus North" which sometimes offer a wide variety of perspectives on politics and social issues otherwise unfamiliar on Canadian television. However, our analysis suggests that such programming has emerged in spite of the founding structure of all-news television service in Canada, not because of it. Unfortunately, in many respects Newsworld seems to have been developed and conceived as a service offering Canadians "more of the same" at election time; that is, familiar news sources and news perspectives – in a new cable package.

Extended Coverage of the Campaign

In the remainder of this study we want to examine the possible benefits of extended election coverage for Canadian voters and politicians. For many, extended coverage is the defining feature of cable news, the most important programming that it can offer its viewers as citizens. Rightly or wrongly, North American cable programmers have generally equated live (usually lengthy) coverage of scheduled political events with public service, a service which they and only they can provide on a regular basis. Perhaps not surprisingly then, Canadian cable news programmers have already promised to carry "live and total" coverage of party platforms, speeches and policy statements for the next federal election. They will probably make good on this promise. Newsworld has already provided over 450 hours of live event coverage in its first year of service, including over 20 hours of live coverage of the first ministers' conference on the Meech Lake Accord in June 1990 (Stevens 1990), and it will probably continue to emphasize such programming in years to come, both during and between elections.

Extended public-affairs coverage has been justified as a public service on several grounds: it is designed to inform Canadians of their options in the election campaign and to expose them more generally to the workings of the government and media during a modern day election campaign (Donaldson interview). "People want to be in on the process unedited," says Michael Harris, Newsworld's current director. "They want the whole press conference including the boring parts where reporters stumble on their questions" (Zerbisias 1990). The CBC's director of English-language television programming has promised that Newsworld will make a "major effort" to provide lengthy coverage of party platforms in the next campaign, coupled with a range of current-affairs programming which might

Toronto. "They just took what we gave them. As long as they stuck with us, what Canadians saw was what our local audience saw."

There have been some discussions within Newsworld and the parent network, however, concerning the proper balance between regional and national material in the news schedule and the overall propriety of Newsworld's regional mandate. Some Newsworld journalists interviewed seemed to support the *Toronto Star* journalist Antonia Zerbisias' assertion that the channel produces too many "features on fish, potatoes and wheat" (1990). "There's just no sense of proportion for the regional stuff," said one Newsworld producer. "You get the sense that it's there to fill time or to fill a quota." On the other hand, at least some CBC journalists interviewed felt that the news channel had not given regional issues enough time during the Manitoba and Ontario elections. According to a CBC reporter in Toronto, Newsworld "stuck with us until decision time, then cut to a commercial and switched to their own analyst from Quebec. We had a whole discussion panel on local issues which they missed because of that." However, the Manitoba producers interviewed seemed quite impressed with the breadth and sensitivity of Newsworld's coverage of local issues, in both its news reports and its own current-affairs programming.

In whatever way the regional representation issue is resolved, CBC officials insist that the regional network will form the backbone of its all-news federal campaign coverage. "It's not a perfect or complete system but we believe it will reflect Canadian political reality better than anything Canadians are likely to see in the next election," says one Newsworld official in Calgary. "It's a regional alternative. You won't be getting that type of programming anywhere else in the Canadian broadcasting system."[3]

Access for Social Movements

CBC officials say the news channel will serve as a forum for "distant and different voices from all parts of the country" during and between elections (CRTC 1987c, 228). Moreover, Newsworld can be expected to represent social and multicultural groups in a manner "that realistically reflects their participation in Canadian society" (ibid., 252). These were explicit promises of performance tabled at the CRTC licensing hearings in July 1987 (see, for example, CRTC 1987b, 3066) in the CBC's proposal for a specialty news service (see, for example, CBC 1988, 17). These promises have been reaffirmed in recent public statements by service officials. For instance, Newsworld's first chief, Joan Donaldson, speaks of a 24-hour "river of information" providing a "greater variety of perspectives on issues of importance to Canadians" (*Toronto Star* 1989).

Canadians have essentially been told that more news means more diverse news, news that draws upon a variety of perspectives that are not fully represented within the regular Canadian broadcasting system.

The corporation has not always been clear as to its responsibility toward social movements or minority parties, but officials have pledged to ensure some degree of public access to the news channel through a number of procedures. First, the corporation seems to suggest that Newsworld's regional schedule will, as a matter of course, offer Canadians a range of local viewpoints which are underrepresented on Canada's regular broadcasting channels. It is at least partly on this basis that the news channel can be seen as a "differentiated service."

This is a plausible but, in our view, somewhat problematic position. As a "second window" on the regular network, for instance, the news channel will be relying on news programming, both national and local, in which the constraints of time and conventional journalistic notions of balance are probably in full force. These factors, which have traditionally excluded minority parties and interests from being fully represented on the regular channels of the Canadian broadcasting system, will continue to govern much of Newsworld's election programming – at source.

These constraints may be somewhat relaxed in Newsworld's original election programming, specifically in news analysis shows such as "Inside Politics" and "Cover Story," which will apparently be prominently featured in the network's election schedule. But the Newsworld officials interviewed said that, throughout the campaign, they will emphasize repeat news headlines (provided by the parent network), the sort of news wheels and headline formats on which all-news services have traditionally relied during and between elections. In other words, the amount of extra broadcast time available on the news channel to minority interests and small political parties may be rather less than corporate statements have indicated. Moreover, and this is a point we would stress, access provided to minority social movements will almost certainly not be in proportion to the amount of extra broadcast time available to Newsworld producers. In other words, if Newsworld does "open the airwaves" to alternative news and views in the next election, it may not open them much, and even then only within its limited original program schedule.

Finally, and perhaps most importantly, the Newsworld organization does not recognize any "special obligations" to provide public access under its current charter. That is, even assuming Newsworld producers do have full 24-hour days with which to reflect the "full balance" of Canadian viewpoints in a general election, they accept no put this material into some kind of a perspective for voters (McQueen interview).

How such programming will appeal to the general electorate is rather uncertain. Newsworld officials seem to have concluded that the audience for run-of-the-mill speeches and news conferences in toto may be dedicated but is almost certainly small, with little growth potential beyond its current "narrowcast" levels (Nunes 1990). A.C. Nielsen figures collected for the CBC are of little help here as they include only standard variables such as geography, age, sex, education, occupation, household income and language. According to these studies, Newsworld's viewers tend to be overrepresented in Ontario and underrepresented in Quebec; many are retired and generally they are better educated than most Canadians; they seem to be fairly evenly divided among the sexes and among income groups (CBC Newsworld *Audience Profile, 1989/90*, weeks 29–41). But these figures tell us little about the political involvement of Newsworld viewers; in this area we must speculate. What we do know is that the cumulative audience for Canada's news channel consists of about 15 000 viewers per minute. The figures supplied to us by the CBC were calculated only on a cumulative basis and excluded the final weeks of the Meech Lake negotiations when ratings were a good deal higher.[5] Moreover, the almost unanimous perception among the journalists and party strategists interviewed is that those who tune in to entire speeches, news conferences and political events are probably already interested and active (either as journalists or politicians) in this country's political process. None of the broadcasters we spoke with regarded "record" coverage as having even a potentially wide audience. In fact, like their American counterparts, many of our Canadian journalist and party respondents seemed to view extended coverage of this material as a service for politicians more than for voters at election time. Thus, unedited election events – speeches, campaign events and press conferences which will often be televised in their entirety by Newsworld during the next election – are seen to be chiefly of interest to those who make a living either giving or going to those events, namely journalists and politicians.

This issue will be looked at later in the discussion of the relative public service merits of extended coverage of this sort. At this point, we would simply note our impression that the benefits of cable news service in Canada have been most clearly defined in the policy-making area. According to our sources, such benefits for politicians might include reaching the voters, reaching voters without mediation and monitoring political events.

Reaching the Voters

As has been noted, most of the party strategists and broadcasters were somewhat pessimistic in their assessment of the potential impact of a cable news service on the general electorate. Most believed that the all-news service's audience is irredeemably small and select, and that it is probably already active and decided in its political preference (though, as noted previously, there are no hard data to bear this out).

Newsworld's utility as an advertising medium is seen to be further limited by its inability to accept local commercial announcements, political or otherwise. Many of the party strategists interviewed believed that this policy had eliminated the news channel's competitive advantage as a "narrowcasting" medium through which the parties might, at a reasonable cost, reach a specific audience in a target riding. Moreover, strategists point out that the free time provided to the parties could be of limited utility since the news channel cannot guarantee its clients regular time slots because live news coverage often pre-empts a regular advertising schedule. "There's just no predictability in cable news," said a strategist for the Conservative party.

Reaching the Voters without Mediation

Most of our party respondents believed that Newsworld would provide them with more time to get their message across to the voters with little or no journalistic mediation. Few, however, foresaw the live format having any impact on the way regular broadcasters covered the campaign, and even fewer believed that the news service would force them to reorganize their campaigns in any significant way. Most journalists we spoke with accepted this view. The all-news service, we were told, would probably cover the same campaign events as the networks: press conferences, stump speeches and timed announcements; Newsworld would be tied to the traditional campaign sites simply because it lacked the human and technological resources – the investigative staff or the portable satellite up-links, for instance – to do otherwise.

Moreover, the assertion that Newsworld's ongoing "complete record" of campaign events might allow the regular network to experiment with new and perhaps more analytical types of coverage was dismissed by many of our sources. "They [Newsworld] do what they do because they have to. They won't change the way we cover campaigns," said a CBC producer. One of the strategists agreed: "They're new to the game and they'll have to adapt to us because we have no plans to adapt to them."

Monitoring Political Events

Politicians might use an all-news service to monitor and respond to campaign events, regional issues and party platforms, according to some of our small-party respondents. There is a story, told by many, of Jean Chrétien's use of the channel in this way during the Liberal leadership convention. Chrétien is reported to have ordered the Newsworld service installed in his Calgary hotel in order to keep up with developments at the Meech Lake conference in Ottawa. Whether apocryphal or not, these reports are perhaps suggestive of the way the news service is perceived as a strategic resource by this country's policy élite. To be sure, some of our sources were rather more cautious in their assessment of cable's strategic utility as such, pointing out, for instance, that the major parties have their own intelligence-gathering systems, and suggesting that the news channel might actually be of more use to journalists, particularly reporters for smaller newspapers who have no other access to political events. Most of our party respondents, however, stated that they watched Newsworld, that their colleagues watched Newsworld, and that the all-news service would probably help them monitor the campaign, because it would be going to "places we can't go," as one strategist put it. Provincial campaign strategists for the New Democratic, Liberal and Conservative parties, for instance, said that the news channel helped them keep track of their competitors during the Ontario election.

Nevertheless, our general impression from these conversations was that, inasmuch as strategists have given cable much thought, they do not believe it will force them to alter their traditional media strategies in any significant way. There may, however, be one exception to this rule, one way in which cable news service could decisively change campaigns in years to come – and not necessarily to the advantage of Canada's regular political players. There is no certain trend to identify here, but a surprising number of our party respondents told us that Newsworld might change the timing of campaigns. That is, by televising the campaign on a full-time basis, Newsworld might speed up the process of communications amongst politicians, in effect reducing their collective control over the pacing and shaping of election messages. If strategists had any fear about cable news, this was it. "It could be like a 24-hour open line for politicians," said an NDP organizer. "It could force us to respond to announcements and come up with a policy position within the hour, whereas in the past we had all day." We received no reports of such an effect in the Ontario and Manitoba elections, but we were told that federal politicians had had to scramble to keep up with, and respond to, the flurry of statements coming out of the Meech Lake negotiations, and that the CBC's all-news instant coverage made the political pace of the talks all the more punishing and unpredictable for party leaders. In the words of one Conservative party consultant, the full-time televising of Canadian elections could "add a measure of unpredictability in campaigns, and no politician likes unpredictability."

CONCLUSIONS

The foregoing are just some of the views that respondents shared with us concerning the possible impact of all-news broadcasting in the next election campaign. What was most evident to us in these discussions was that Canadian journalists and party strategists have not given cable news much thought. Newsworld programmers, preoccupied as they are with day-to-day management in these first years of service, seemed rather taken aback by our questions concerning their plans for an as yet abstract and distant campaign. Our party sources, on the other hand, seemed largely indifferent to cable, it being a new and untested medium. In short, there was little conventional wisdom on which to base the conclusions for this study. What we offer here is a tentative list of features that might govern all-news campaign coverage in the next Canadian election campaign – barring a radical change in mandate and/or funding.

1. Canada's all-news service will probably rely upon the production facilities, technical equipment and distribution technologies of its parent network to cover the election while offering some original current-affairs programming to put this material into perspective for its viewers. Newsworld will also air regional reports and extended national footage which has not yet been viewed by a national audience. As far as news coverage goes, this arrangement may result in a fair amount of duplicated service.

2. Newsworld will not accept any special responsibilities as a public-affairs broadcaster. Its standards concerning fairness, balance and overall quality control of incoming election material will not differ significantly, if at all, from those of the parent network. In this sense at least, Newsworld will not be offering alternative election coverage in the next campaign. Its news reports will probably cover the same political events as the regular networks: press conferences, stump speeches and timed announcements. Newsworld will be tied to traditional campaign sites simply because, under its present constitution as an adjunct news service to the CBC, it lacks the human and technical resources – the investigative staff and the portable satellite uplinks, for instance – to do otherwise. Moreover, Newsworld accepts no responsibilities to provide special public access in its

original current-affairs programming where time constraints on alternative perspectives would seem to be more relaxed.

3. Whether Newsworld can meet its promises of performance, organized as such, is at least questionable. Most of the journalists and party strategists we interviewed felt that the service could provide Canadian voters with a valuable "second window" on regional events and issues, though these forecasts may have to be revised somewhat in the wake of the corporation's recent cuts in local programming. Moreover, most respondents expected that the news channel would provide extended coverage of election events, though again the precise benefits of such a service to the viewing public have, in our view, been rather ill-defined. More problematic may be Newsworld's performance as a forum for minority parties and minority interests which have generally not been well represented on Canada's regular broadcasting channels. In our view, the standards and procedures that have traditionally excluded minority parties and minority interests from regular television will probably continue to exclude them from the new all news channel in the next election. More news will not necessarily mean more diverse news or news from new political perspectives in Canada. Nor will more time necessarily result in a more varied cable current-affairs schedule.

4. Whether all-news service will alter the way politicians do business during the elections is also somewhat uncertain. Most of the respondents said the new medium had not made them change their campaign style in the Ontario and Manitoba elections; nor would it make them change their ways in the coming federal campaign. The three large national parties, we were told, would continue to put their emphasis on the usual leader tours, the usual three-event days, the usual sound bites for the usual evening newscasts. All-news service, we were told, will not change all that.

Nonetheless, cable might affect campaign communications in more amorphous ways. Specifically, the news channel might have three distinct effects: it might allow the parties to get more of their message across to a limited audience; it might let them monitor and respond to regional and national campaign events; but it might also force them to respond to those events as they develop, thereby reducing their collective control over the shaping and pacing of campaign messages. However, there was not even much of a consensus on these points. Most of the party strategists we spoke with felt that cable would not have a very wide impact in the next campaign; the remainder were, for the most part, not sure what that impact would be.

5. What was most evident in our conversations with party strategists was that, whatever their views concerning cable's impact on Canada's regular political players, the benefits of such a service for the general electorate remained somewhat ill-defined. Public impact was simply not an issue in most of our discussions. Even the designers of the all-news system, those officials who might be expected to be best able to articulate the public service benefits of the new service, were far from specific in their forecasts of how it might help Canadians understand or participate in an election campaign: how, for instance, the new service might enable Canadians to express their current dissatisfaction with the major political parties through concerted political action; or how it might simply help them act as voters and make up their minds about a given candidate or platform at election time. Perhaps our major conclusion about the importance of an all-news service in an election campaign is this: in many respects, cable news in Canada seems to have been constructed as what one party strategist calls "a very expensive tool to make politicians' and journalists' jobs a lot easier at election time." Cable's democratic utility, in our view, remains somewhat uncertain at this stage in its history.

RECOMMENDATIONS

We believe there are several features of the CBC Newsworld service that should be re-examined if Canadians are to receive the sort of all-news election coverage they deserve. In the discussion that follows we have tried to be sensitive to Newsworld's budgetary constraints, which are clearly a basic condition of possibility for an all-news service in Canada. In fact, we believe that a reform package that takes into account these limits is quite feasible. Our reading of the history of North American all-news services suggests that more money does not necessarily mean better news. With these considerations in mind, our recommendations are as follows.

Development of a Differentiated Regional Service

According to most of our respondents, Newsworld provides a valuable service by showcasing regional news and information that was previously unavailable to a national audience. We believe, however, that the service could do a better job in this regard by developing at least the beginnings of a parallel regional network, staffed by its own reporters and drawing upon more mobile technology (portable satellite up-links, for instance), all of which might cover regional campaign stories that have not been aired on regular channels of the parent network. The CBC has resisted the idea of a differentiated cable service as such because of the start-up costs involved. We believe, however, that such a policy could be considered as a long-term goal, mainly by reducing the amount of duplication of services already available on the news channel. Specifically, the service might reduce spending on extended coverage of election stories already covered by the networks, since such coverage can often be seen on the CBC and on other television services; and it might accept a loosening of the technical broadcast standards which Canadians have come to associate with regular television news (standards which, by most accounts, have never been the cable service's strong point). In our view, what a differentiated regional all-news service requires is not so much a change in budget as a change in operating philosophy, a change in the conception of the kind of public-affairs coverage Newsworld can and should offer its audience during and between elections. As a first recommendation, then, we suggest that Newsworld make a concerted effort to include some form of differentiated news programming in its regional election schedule.

Inclusion of Minor Parties in Campaign Coverage

According to the CBC's promises of performance, a 24-hour news channel should air alternative points of view, should "provide airtime for more programs of opinion" (CBC 1988, 17) and should relax conventions of balance within news and current-affairs programs – conventions which have often served to exclude minority interests from the regular networks' public-affairs schedules (CRTC 1987b, 3066). In our view, current operating procedures are often at odds with these original statements of intent. The CBC's pledge to "rigorously enforce" its standard procedures for fairness and balance in political programming, coupled with its insistence that Newsworld adhere to current CBC policies concerning the "equitable" coverage of minor parties, suggests to us that the news channel has little to offer in the way of an alternative public access strategy. Such a strategy was certainly not in evidence during the Ontario and Manitoba campaigns. We would advise the CBC to re-examine its current policies in this regard. To remain wedded to traditional public access formats (which were essentially developed for 22-minute news and current-affairs programs) would, in our view, represent a very regrettable lost opportunity in Canadian political broadcasting. As a second recommendation, then, we suggest that the all-news service use its extra election broadcast time to provide a forum for Canada's minor parties and social movements, both in its news and in its current-affairs schedules.

More Political-Advertising Time

As a related recommendation, we urge the CBC to provide more free and paid political-advertising time on the news channel, particularly for minor parties whose views may not have been adequately aired on the regular network.

Context for Coverage

In a recent public statement, the CBC's director of English-language programming called on Canadian journalists to report the "methodology behind journalism," to be more explicit, for instance, about attempts by politicians to manipulate the news and the role these attempts have played in news organizations' subsequent strategies of coverage. We agree with this view and would further suggest that the news channel use its particular broadcast resources to provide Canadians with more election coverage "in context": coverage, that is, which makes the rules of the electoral process and the media's role within that process more explicit to viewers.[6] This would not just be an exercise in media literacy (in essence, letting viewers in on the work, effort and choice that go into a news line-up). It might also contribute to a more general political understanding, an understanding of campaigns in which the media have come to play an increasingly important role in shaping political messages. In short, we recommend that the news channel make a more concerted effort to provide a more "self-reflexive" type of campaign coverage that would indicate the degree to which the Canadian media have themselves become part of the campaign stories they report.

Review of the Policy concerning Extended Coverage of Traditional Campaign Events

We believe that, in the next election, Newsworld may have to make some tough choices between live programming – extended coverage of political events already being covered by the regular network – and issue analysis designed to put these events into some sort of context. CBC officials do not acknowledge such a trade-off, and we believe they are mistaken in this regard. We are not privy to the services' current accounts, but we do know that the American CNN network has only recently been able to develop its own investigative newsgathering infrastructure because of the cost of maintaining live coverage on its regular schedule. (CNN's investigative and political "issue" units have only begun full operation after nearly 10 years of service in the United States.) We see no reason why Newsworld should not be faced with the same constraints in this area.

At the same time, we believe that Canadian cable programmers do retain a good degree of discretion concerning what goes into their public-affairs schedule. In other words, there is nothing inevitable about a live event schedule on cable news. Such a format is, in our view, the result of programming choices, and we feel that the grounds for these choices should be made explicit to Canadians during and between elections. As a fifth recommendation, then, we suggest that the cable news service develop a clear and consistent set of guidelines and principles regarding the appropriate balance between live programming and issue analysis in its election schedule.

We would note, in closing, our own reservations concerning the news channel's planned emphasis on extended event coverage in the next election. We do believe there is considerable value in letting viewers see political events unedited and in their entirety – be they press conferences, speeches or some other variety of campaign event – particularly as the regular CBC network currently files a maximum of 45 seconds on such stories. Voters should be given the opportunity to hear the leaders and other political figures at length and in fuller context, should they wish to do so.

The problem is that perhaps they don't. Audience ratings are by no means conclusive here; Canadians may want to get the whole picture, complete and unedited, of the various stump speeches, press conferences and scheduled events that will take place in the next election. But none, we repeat none, of our sources believed this. As was noted earlier, unedited election events are seen by party activists and journalists to be chiefly of interest to those who make a living either giving or going to such events, namely, party activists and journalists.

Even if more people do tune in, it would seem incumbent on the news channel to help them make some sort of sense of that raw coverage. In other words, it may not be enough (though it may often be necessary) just to bring entire political statements and sales pitches to Canadian voters at election time. We believe that voters should also be presented with as wide a variety of perspectives as possible to help them understand the Canadian political process and also their immediate options in the next election. With some notable exceptions, such as "The Week Starts Here" and "Focus North," such diversity of viewpoint seems to be somewhat lacking in Newsworld's original program schedule, not, perhaps, through the fault of Newsworld's producers but because of the CBC's refusal to relax access restrictions on the 24-hour news channel. In short, our criticisms are directed not just at extended event coverage per se but at the lack of critical perspective that Newsworld will be bringing to enhance such coverage in its regular program schedule. For these reasons, we believe that Newsworld's current strategy for covering elections – extended conventional campaign reports coupled with extended conventional campaign analysis – is inherently flawed and in need of review. At the very least, it is difficult to see how such programming will either bring more Canadians into the political process or make that process more comprehensible to them as voters.

There is at least some agreement among academic researchers, journalists and politicians that traditional journalistic formats have failed to clarify political issues in recent Canadian election campaigns (see, for example, Fletcher 1981, 1985; Fletcher and Everett 1989; Gilsdorf, 1981a, 1981b, 1990). Newsworld, in our view, presents Canadian broadcasters with a considerable opportunity to experiment with these formats, to tell the campaign story in "other than traditional" ways – whatever those may be. Our belief is that Canadians are familiar with the conventional terms by which broadcasters have made sense of Canadian elections and that these terms have already been well represented within the Canadian broadcasting system. Our hope is that the all-news service will provide Canadians with a new set of terms to understand elections in years to come.

NOTES

This study was completed in 1991.

1. Not all of the record is as ponderous as it sounds. To cite one famous example, CNN provided over 60 hours of live coverage of millionaire Claus Von Bulow's trial for manslaughter in 1984. But CNN officials insist that the network "does not try to sensationalize its [live] coverage." As one spokesperson notes, "For every hour of a crime trial, we have tenfold carried dull hearings. We have paid our dues" (Whittemore 1990, 270).

2. Some observers view C-SPAN – the Cable Satellite Public Affairs Network – far less cynically. Peter Kaplan, for instance, suggests that C-SPAN has shed "electronic sunshine" on the U.S. electoral process by putting politicians on the record and holding them accountable to their constituents (Kaplan 1983; see also Becker 1981). During the 1988 election, C-SPAN went beyond its usual 24-hour coverage of political party functions, lobby briefings and daily proceedings of the U.S. Congress to follow a number of presidential candidates – live and unedited – through the Iowa and New Hampshire primary caucuses.

The public education benefits of such election coverage may be laudable, but they are somewhat limited. C-SPAN reaches only 11 million households in the United States, many of whose members are already active in politics (Lamb 1988). Moreover, even if the audience for this sort of programming grows, C-SPAN's days as a "show-it-all" network may be numbered. Even during the 1988 election, many candidates were reported to be playing for the cameras, keeping both nonedited and edited-for-C-SPAN speeches on hand for even the most trivial campaign events (Corry 1988, H31). These developments led one of C-SPAN's most prominent supporters, John Corry of the *New York Times*, to wonder whether "TV was running the system or the system was running TV" on public-affairs television (ibid.).

3. When the research was being done for this study in the fall of 1990, Newsworld officials had little to say about the possible role of cross-country phone-in shows and citizen forums in the next election. Since that time, a prominent CBC news producer has told us that phone-in shows will be used extensively by Newsworld during the next election campaign. Programs of this type are featured quite prominently on the news channel's schedule and have been cited in the licensing statements as exemplary forums for public discussion and regional representation.

4. Representatives of the Green, Libertarian and Family Coalition parties were all critical of Newsworld's public access policies in this regard. The Reform Party, however, told us that its candidates had received "triple the amount of coverage" on Newsworld as on the regular networks under the present access rules. Interviews with party leader Preston Manning on various all-news current-affairs programs were particularly noteworthy in this regard, offering the party an opportunity to explain its policies that was "unavailable anywhere else in the Canadian broadcasting system" (Hill interview). In fact, the Reform Party does not support the legal challenge by the other minor parties to the CBC's (and Newsworld's) public access policies. "We don't need a law to get equitable coverage [as called for in the CRTC regulation (CRTC 1987a)]," says Reform spokesperson Ron Hill. "The CBC ignores us at their peril" (ibid.).

5. The news channel "cumulatively reached" over 4 million Canadians during the last week of the Meech Lake hearings in June 1990; it reached 5 332 000 viewers during the final week of the Oka crisis, and 7 400 000 viewers during the first week of the Gulf War (memo from Philip Savage, Research Officer, CBC, 29 April 1991).

6. Depending on one's point of view, the open newsroom format pioneered by cable broadcasters has either "demystified" the news or intimidated viewers with an opening barrage of technology, thereby reinforcing the idea that news organizations are uniquely capable of reporting on the world thoroughly and objectively.

INTERVIEWS

A number of interviewees preferred to remain anonymous. We have felt it necessary to respect the wishes of these journalists and party strategists who did not want to be identified or have certain comments for attribution. The interviews were conducted in October 1990.

Journalists

CNN
Dassauer, Karen, Political Unit, CNN, Washington.
Hannon, Tom, political director, CNN, Atlanta.
Anonymous (three interviewees), CNN, Washington.

Newsworld
Donaldson, Joan, director, Newsworld.
McKean, Sandy, executive producer, Newsworld, Halifax.
McQuaker, John, executive producer, Newsworld, Calgary.
Anonymous (two interviewees), Newsworld, Ottawa.
Anonymous (two interviewees), Newsworld, Toronto.
Anonymous, Newsworld, Winnipeg.

CBC
Alboim, Elly, CBC, Ottawa.
Hargreaves, T., CBC senior adviser.
Kiefl, Barry, research officer.
McQueen, Trina, CBC director of News and Current Affairs.
O'Neill, Pierre, Radio-Canada, Montreal.
Savage, Philip, research officer.
Anonymous, CBC, Calgary.
Anonymous, CBC, Ottawa.
Anonymous (four interviewees), CBC, Toronto.
Anonymous (four interviewees), CBC, Winnipeg.

Party Strategists

United States
Bernley, Wendy, Republican Senatorial Committee, Washington.
Greene, Karen, media consultant, Washington.
Terzano, Jenny, Democratic National Committee, Washington.
Thomson, Randy, media consultant, Washington.
Anonymous (four interviewees), Washington.

Canada
Balagus, M., communications director, NDP.
Caplan, Gerald, Toronto NDP.

Fox, Bill, media consultant, Progressive Conservative party.
Hill, Ron, communications director, Reform Party.
Marvetti, J., provincial secretary, Ontario NDP.
O'Grady, Terry, media consultant, NDP.
O'Leary, Terry, director of organization for Paul Martin, Liberal party.
Segal, Hugh, media consultant, Progressive Conservative party.
Stayson, John, Libertarian party.
Vézina, Greg, Green Party of Canada.
Weaver, Sheila, Family Coalition party.
Anonymous (two interviewees), media consultant, Liberal party.

BIBLIOGRAPHY

Allarcom Ltd. 1987. *Petition to the Governor in Council.* Edmonton, 21 December.

Allen, Glen. 1989. "News Around the Clock." *Maclean's,* 7 August, 40–41.

Alter, Jonathan. 1990a. "Prime-time Revolution." *Newsweek,* 8 January, 25.

————. 1990b. "Ted's Global Village." *Newsweek,* 11 June, 48–52.

Amiel, Barbara. 1988. "What Makes News at the CBC." *Maclean's,* 8 February, 7.

Atherton, Tony. 1989. "The All-news Channel." *Content* (April/May): 9–10.

Bain, George. 1987. "News, Influence and Propaganda." *Maclean's,* 21 September, 45.

Becker, Ted. 1981. "Teledemocracy." *The Futurist* 15 (December): 6–9.

Belkin, Lisa. 1987. "CBS and CNN Project Coverage for Election." *New York Times,* 24 April, C30.

Bethke-Elshtain, Jean. 1982. "Democracy and the QUBE Tube." *Nation* (7–14 August): 108–10.

Blume, Keith. 1985. *The Presidential Election Show: Campaign '84 and Beyond on the Nightly News.* South Hadley: Bergin and Garvey.

Boone, Mike. 1990. "In First Year, All-news Channel Won Spurs." *Gazette* (Montreal), 25 July, B6.

Broadcasting. 1979. "CNN: Bringing the Blue Sky Down to Earth." 3 December, 44–47.

————. 1980a. "The Cable News Network: Poised for the Unknown." 5 May, 72–77.

————. 1980b. "Star-spangled Start for CNN." 9 June, 48–52.

———. 1982. "CNN: Schonfeld Quits." 24 May, 62–63.

Business Week. 1981. "Cable News Team Wants Equal Rights."
25 May, 44–45.

———. 1984. "No One Is Laughing at Ted Turner Now." 16 April, 141.

———. 1990. "Turner's Gutsy New News Service." 11 January, 42–46.

Calgary Herald. 1989. "News Is Good for CBC Bosses." 3 November, C5.

Canada. Task Force on Broadcasting Policy. 1986. *Report.* Ottawa: Minister of
Supply and Services Canada.

Canadian Broadcasting Corporation (CBC). 1985. *Regulations Governing Party
Political Broadcasts.* Ottawa, March.

———. 1987. *Before the CRTC: A Proposal for an All-Canadian News Channel.*
Ottawa, 30 April.

———. 1988. *Comments of the CBC on the CRTC Licensing of a Canadian News
Channel and the Petition of Allarcom Ltd. to the Governor in Council for the
Setting Aside of the Decision.* Ottawa, January.

———. 1990. Submission to the Royal Commission on Electoral Reform and
Party Financing. Ottawa, May.

Canadian Radio-television and Telecommunications Commission (CRTC).
1987a. *Television Broadcasting Regulations.* Ottawa, 9 January.

———. 1987b. *Speciality Programming Public Hearings,* Vol. 8, 29 July. Ottawa.

———. 1987c. *Canadian Broadcasting Corporation.* Decision CRTC 87-904.
Ottawa, 30 November.

———. 1989a. *Canadian Broadcasting Corporation.* Decision CRTC 89-599.
Ottawa, 25 August.

———. 1989b. *Canadian Broadcasting Corporation.* Decision CRTC 89-831.
Ottawa, 8 November.

———. 1990. *Canadian Broadcasting Corporation.* Decision CRTC 90-504.
Ottawa, 1 June.

Caplan, Gerald. 1988. "Ugly Chapter in Broadcasting History." *Toronto Star,*
19 October, F1.

Cappuzi, Cecillia. 1987. "CNN." *Channels of Communication* 7 (October):
44–45.

Careless, James. 1988. "Questionable Sources." *Maclean's,* 15 February, 53.

Cinema Canada. 1988. "All-news Station Good Move." (January): 37.

Content. 1989. "Quest for French-Language Newsworld Continues."
(November/December): 5–6.

Corelli, Rae. 1989. "The CBC's Future." *Maclean's*, 7 August, 34–39.

Corry, John. 1988. "C-SPAN: Electronic Sunshine." *New York Times*, 21 February.

Crain, W. Mark, and Brian L. Goff. 1985. *Televised Legislatures*. Annapolis: Kluwer Academy Publishing Group.

Cuff, John Haslett. 1990. "Newsworld Flawed but Worth Preserving." *Globe and Mail*, 21 July, C3.

Fineman, Howard. 1982. "The Technology of Politics." *Newsweek*, 25 October, 29.

Fischer, Raymond T. 1980. "Ted Turner's Cable News Network – An Impossible Dream?" *USA Today*, 14 November, 60–62.

Fletcher, Frederick. 1981. "Playing the Game: The Mass Media and the 1979 Campaign." In *Canada at the Polls*, ed. H. Penniman. Washington, DC: American Enterprise Institute for Public Policy Research.

———. 1985. "The Media and the 1984 Landslide." In *Canada at the Polls, 1984*, ed. H. Penniman. Washington, DC: American Enterprise Institute for Public Policy Research.

Fletcher, Frederick, and Bob Everett. 1989. "An Unusual Campaign." *Content* (January/February): 5–7.

Fotheringham, Allan. 1984. "A House of Illusion." *Maclean's*, 20 April, 68.

Fulford, Robert. 1988. "Newsworld Betrayal." *Financial Times*, 21 March, 42.

Gazette (Montreal). 1987. "CBC Needs More Reporters for All-news Channel, Union Says." 2 December, B1.

———. 1988a. "All-news Channel to Go on the Air February 15." 6 December, B7.

———. 1988b. "CBC Slams Critics of All-news Channel." 8 January, B1.

———. 1988c. "Legal Quirk Could Delay Cabinet Challenge to All-News Channel." 12 January, B1.

———. 1989a. "CBC All-news License Suddenly in Jeopardy." 11 January, C8.

———. 1989b. "Let English News Station Subsidize French: CBC." 17 May, A17.

———. 1990a. "Fast Reliable Reporting Has Made CNN News Junkie's Best Friend." 3 June, F2.

———. 1990b. "Why Presidents and Princes Watch CNN." 4 February, A1.

Gerard, Jeremy. 1988. "Networks Changing Coverage of Conventions." *New York Times*, 16 July, 9.

Gilsdorf, William. 1981a. "The Communication Strategy of the Federal Liberal Party in the 1979 and 1980 Canadian Federal Elections." In *Communication Studies in Canada*, ed. L. Salter. Toronto: Butterworths.

———. 1981b. " 'Mediated Politics': Thoughts on the Relationship of Media to the Political Communication Process in Canada." Paper presented in June to the Canadian Communication Association.

———. 1990. "The Organizing Processes of the CBC-TV National Election Unit in the 1988 Canadian Federal Election." Paper presented in June to the Canadian Communication Association.

Globe and Mail. 1987a. "All-news Rivals Take Shots at One Another." 4 August, B5.

———. 1987b. "CBC Makes Strident Bid for All-news TV Channel." 30 July, B3.

———. 1987c. "CBC Wins Nod to Offer News 24 Hours a Day." 1 December, A1.

———. 1988a. "A Job for the CBC." 20 January, A6.

———. 1988b. "All-news Channel Is More than Just News." 20 October, C7.

———. 1988c. "All-news Is Bad News." 16 January, B1.

———. 1988d. "CBC All-news Service Looks to Private Sector." 18 October, B7.

———. 1988e. "CBC All-news TV Service Gets Cabinet Informal Go-ahead." 18 October, A1.

———. 1988f. "CBC at Bitter Impasse with Private Affiliated TV Stations." 25 May, B12.

———. 1988g. "CBC Awaits Decision on All-news Channel." 1 September, A10.

———. 1988h. "CBC Cabinet Decision May Be Delayed." 12 January, A9.

———. 1988i. "CBC President Fires Back in Row over News Channel." 8 January, A3.

———. 1988j. "Heavy Spending Off CBC Agenda." 29 January, B7.

———. 1988k. "Lobby Group Attacks Interference in CBC." 29 January, A3.

———. 1988l. "She's Carrying the Ball for the CBC's News Channel." 26 February, C3.

———. 1988m. "Sin in Replacing Arm's Length with Hands on." 26 February, A7.

———. 1989a. "All-news Channel Moves Launch Date." 6 May, C8.

———. 1989b. "Brave News World." 29 July, C1.

————. 1989c. "CBC All-news Network Launch Put Off to August from February." 23 December, B2.

Goar, Carol. 1988. "All-news Television: Ottawa Plays for Time." *Toronto Star*, 29 January, A17.

Huey, John. 1980. "Cable TV News Link May Surprise Skeptics." *Wall Street Journal*, 30 May, 1.

Johnson, William. 1988. "Tory Blindness Could Scupper CBC Initiative." *Gazette* (Montreal), 14 January, B3.

Kaid, Lynda Lee, and Joe Fotte. 1985. "How Network Coverage of the President and Congress Compares." *Journalism Quarterly* 62 (Spring): 59–65.

Kaplan, Peter W. 1983. "Ted Turner, Station to Station." *Esquire* (February): 100.

Kinsley, Michael. 1990. "Democracy Theater." *The New Republic*, 1 January, 4.

Lacey, Liam. 1989. "Ask All the Right Questions that Need to Be Asked." *Globe and Mail*, 29 July, C1.

Lamb, Brian. 1988. *America's Town Hall.* Acropolis: Acropolis Press.

Maines, P., ed. 1984. *CNN Versus the Networks: Is More News Better News?* Washington, DC: Media Institute.

Marketing. 1990. "CBC Newsworld – All News Is Good News." 1 January, 15.

McGillivray, Don. 1988. "PCs Manoeuvering on CBC Channel Is for Best." *Gazette* (Montreal), 28 January, A16.

McQueen, Trina. 1990. "How the CBC Covered Meech Lake." *Toronto Star*, 25 July, A27.

National Review. 1984. "Gutter Politics and the Global Village." 20 April, 30–34.

Negrine, Ralph. 1985. *Cable Television and the Future of Broadcasting.* London: Croom Helm.

The New Republic. 1984. "The Big Tune-out." 3 September, 5–8.

New York Times. 1984. "Cable's CNN Takes Up Gauntlet." 19 August, A1.

————. 1988. "Turner Pledges Full Convention Coverage." 20 March, C14.

The New Yorker. 1985. "Onward and Upward with the Arts." 3 June, 82–105.

Nikiforuk, Andrew. 1990. "How CBC Handed Mulroney the Mike." *Toronto Star*, 1 August, A21.

Nunes, Julia. 1990. "One Year Later Is Anybody Watching?" *Globe and Mail*, 21 July, C3.

O'Connor, John J. 1980. "CNN Provides Electronic Sunshine for Election." *New York Times*, 29 October, C7.

Ranney, Austin. 1983. *Channels of Power: The Impact of Television on American Politics*. New York: Basic Books.

Rather, Dan. 1988. "A Window on Democracy." *Newsweek*, 22 August, 6.

Reagan, Joey. 1984. "Effects of Cable Television on News Use." *Journalism Quarterly* (Summer): 317–24.

Roman, James. 1983. *Cablemania: The Cable Television Sourcebook*. Englewood Cliffs: Prentice-Hall.

Saldich, Anne Rawley. 1979. *Electronic Democracy: Television's Impact on the American Political Process*. New York: Praeger.

Stevens, Geoffrey. 1990. "All-news TV Channel Becomes Player in Game of Politics." *Gazette* (Montreal), 2 July, B3.

Ticer, Scott. 1989. "From Chicken Noodle Network to Global Powerhouse." *Business Week*, 17 July, 106.

Time. 1990. "The Bombshell from Moscow." 12 February, 53.

Toronto Star. 1988a. "Outsiders to Have Voice in Newsworld." 18 October, B1.

———. 1988b. "Poll Finds 43% Back CBC Bid." 1 February, A1.

———. 1989. "Newsworld Shows More of Canada, Official Says." 18 October, A9.

Turbide, Diane. 1989. "Newsworld's U.S. Model." *Maclean's*, 7 August, 42.

Tyler, Gus. 1984. "Democracy vs. Mediacracy." *New Leader*, 28 May, 10–12.

US News and World Report. 1990. "Instant Messengers of the Global Village." 12 February, 16–17.

Vancouver Sun. 1989. "Newsworld Lacks Financial Staying Power." 6 November, C8.

Van Dusen, Julie. 1982. "Politicking via Cable TV." *Maclean's*, 2 August, 48.

Vanhorne, H. 1980. "Night and Day, Play by Play – It's the News." *Television Quarterly* 17(2): 19–21.

Verzuh, Ron. 1989. "Working on Labor's Image." *Content* (November/December): 30–31.

Waters, David. 1988. "All-news TV ... Almost." *Content* (January/February): 3–6.

Waters, Harry F., and Neal Karlen. 1982. "News while You Snooze." *Newsweek*, 18 October, 65.

Whitfield, Scott. 1990. "Networks Challenge CRTC Rule." *Content* (March/April): 5.

Whittemore, Hank. 1990. *CNN: The Inside Story*. Boston: Little, Brown.

Williams, Raymond. 1983. *Towards 2000*. London: Chatto and Windus.

Winnipeg Free Press. 1988. "Calgary to Act as Western Base for CBC News Channel." 9 January, 18.

————. 1989. "Newsworld Marks End, Beginning of Era." 1 August, B1.

Winsor, Hugh. 1988. "Fuss over CBC's News Service Masks More Important Issue." *Globe and Mail*, 1 February, A2.

Womack, David L. 1989. *Live Interviews Conducted at the 1988 GOP Convention by ABC, CBS, NBC and CNN*. Philadelphia: Temple University, Department of Journalism.

Young, Pamela. 1989. "A Promising Start." *Maclean's*, 7 August, 52.

Zerbisias, Antonia. 1990. "Newsworld's No Beauty but It Runs." *Toronto Star*, 29 July, C1.

Zuckerman, Laurence. 1982. "Cable News Hits the Small Time." *Columbia Journalism Review* 21(3): 35–38.

————. 1988. "A New Member Joins the Club." *Time*, 22 February, 60.

4

CABLE TELEVISION AND FEDERAL ELECTION CAMPAIGNS IN CANADA

Peter Desbarats

THE FIRST COAXIAL cable system to distribute television to Canadian homes was established in 1951 in London, Ontario (Canada, Task Force 1986, 551). Because of strong domestic demand for imported U.S. programming, particularly in English-speaking Canada, cable TV expanded rapidly in Canada, growing from about 500 000 subscribers in 1967 to 5.5 million in 1985. By that time, according to the 1986 *Report* of the Task Force on Broadcasting Policy, 62 percent of Canadian households subscribed to cable TV, making Canada "after Belgium, ... the second most cabled country in the world" (ibid.). This household penetration rate had risen to 70.8 percent by 1989 (Canada, Statistics Canada 1990, xv).

Almost from the outset, cable TV presented unique and complex problems to government regulators of communications systems. It was the first of the new electronic media to blur the traditional distinction between print and electronic media that had provided a guiding principle for regulatory agencies up to that time. Application of this principle meant that print media in North America, protected by constitutional and traditional guarantees of press freedom, were exempt from government regulation; electronic media, on the other hand, were regulated by agencies which allocated to them portions of a scarce public resource – radio frequencies and television channels.

By vastly increasing the number of channels available to the average subscriber – up to more than 50 at the moment – cable TV invalidated the scarcity rationale for government regulation. In this sense, cable TV seemed to be akin to print media. At the same time, however, the practice of granting a limited number of franchises for local monopolies to cable TV operators created a new basis for regulation. In this respect, cable TV resembled broadcast media. Because it appears to share characteristics of both print and electronic media, cable TV has appeared to regulators to be a hybrid medium that is difficult to classify and control. The regulatory dilemmas posed by cable TV will increase as new technologies, particularly fibre optics and satellites, continue to multiply the number of video, audio and data channels available to Canadians.

In the United States, cable TV expanded more slowly than in English-speaking Canada. Only in the past decade did the availability of specialty channels transmitted to cable systems by satellite, offering programs exclusive to cable TV, sharply increase the market. By the end of the 1980s about half of U.S. homes were wired for cable (*Broadcasting* 1988, 67).

As a result of this, cable TV has quickly become a measurable, significant and growing factor in U.S. politics. In the 1984 presidential election, political advertising on cable was too small to register; in 1988, the Bush campaign spent about 5 percent of its national television advertising budget on cable, and cable TV was described as being a "pivotal player" in many state and local elections that year (Abramson et al. 1988, xii).

In Canada, unlike the United States, cable TV operators are not permitted to accept paid political advertising. In fact, their ability to accept any advertising at all is extremely limited, compared with conventional television broadcasters. At the moment, there is no demand from the cable industry in Canada to alter this, and television broadcasters have clearly stated their opposition to meaningful advertising competition from cable. But any study of the political role of cable TV in Canada should examine the pros and cons of paid political advertising on cable TV, particularly in the light of U.S. experience.

In the coverage of political news and current events and in the provision of free time to political parties and various public interest groups, cable TV has already become an important medium of political communication in Canada. Its role will increase with the growing sophistication of politicians in the use of television and with the appearance of specialty channels devoted to news and current affairs. Questions about the availability and allocation of free time are central to a study of cable TV and election campaigns in Canada.

This study opens with a brief history of the development of cable TV systems in Canada. It surveys the Canadian experience with the political/electoral uses of cable TV and refers to parallel experience in the United States. There is an attempt to summarize current thinking about future development of cable TV systems. A brief reference to

Canada's special contribution to the concept of public access to cable TV precedes a description of the regulatory framework governing free and paid election broadcasting on cable TV. The study ends by suggesting principles for regulation based on past experience and anticipated developments, and by offering the Royal Commission some suggestions on policy.

The working definition of cable television employed in the study includes all channels or services provided exclusively on cable. This excludes the over-the-air stations which also happen to be carried on cable systems, but includes community channels and specialty channels, particularly the specialty channels such as the House of Commons service and Newsworld that function as increasingly important carriers of political information.

HISTORY AND DEVELOPMENT OF CABLE TV SYSTEMS

Community Channels

The usefulness of any kind of television transmission system in furthering the democratic process depends largely on its availability to voters. Only in recent years have cable systems fed by satellite transmission come close to the potential of over-the-air radio and TV broadcasting to reach the whole electorate.

Cable TV started in Canada almost 40 years ago, as stated earlier, just before CBC television stations in Toronto and Montreal started to broadcast. At first, development was relatively gradual. As late as 1967 there were only about 500 000 Canadian cable subscribers, but by 1985 this figure had reached 5.5 million. Statistics Canada reported in 1989 (Canada, Statistics Canada 1990, xv) that 70.8 percent of Canadian households subscribed to cable TV (98.7 percent were equipped with at least one TV set).

Cable grew initially because of Canadians' appetite for U.S. TV programming. More recently, growth has been stimulated, particularly in French-speaking Canada, by the availability of specialty cable channels carrying programs not distributed by conventional over-the-air broadcasters. These specialty channels came into existence when satellites provided a reliable and relatively cheap means of transmitting their programs to local cable TV systems. Satellites also made it feasible to install cable in communities that previously would have been considered too small or remote. Communities with as few as 50 households now have cable systems.

Another measure of penetration, indicative of the popularity of cable, is the percentage of households passed by cable that actually subscribe. More than 75 percent of Canadian households passed by cable subscribed in 1989 (Canada, Statistics Canada 1990).

Both types of measurement indicate that cable penetration varies considerably from region to region. The following table, derived from StatsCan data, gives households with cable as a percentage of all households:

Canada	70.8
Newfoundland	73.7
Prince Edward Island	45.5
Nova Scotia	71.5
New Brunswick	66.5
Quebec	62.5
Ontario	75.8
Manitoba	66.0
Saskatchewan	47.8
Alberta	70.4
British Columbia	84.0

The low penetration in Saskatchewan, whose population remains heavily rural, shows the difficulty of extending cable where houses are far apart. Similarly the farming country of Prince Edward Island does not lend itself to cabling. In Quebec, cable lagged behind popularity levels in other provinces for many years because all the French-language stations were available over the air to nearly all owners of TV sets. Quebec penetration levels have been catching up as the number of services in French that are available only on cable has increased. In the Prairie region, improvement in the quality and quantity of services supplied by satellite appears to be bringing penetration levels closer to those of Ontario and British Columbia.

Penetration also varies considerably within regions. Some urban areas have virtually 100 percent cable availability. Within cabled areas, income levels often determine whether a household subscribes to cable. Outside cabled areas, viewers must purchase expensive dish antennas to receive the variety of channels available to cable subscribers.

The average cable system can now carry up to 52 channels. New television sets equipped with converters typically can display about 60 channels.

All but the smallest cable systems have a community channel to carry programming provided by the cable company or by various contributors in the community, including elected politicians, political candidates and public interest groups. Some may not carry it as part of the "basic basic" service, available to subscribers who have older television sets not equipped with converters. If the community channel is above channel 13, a converter is needed to receive it. But all cable operators include the community channel as part of the "basic" package of programming received by subscribers who pay the minimum monthly fee.

In its *Report*, the Task Force on Broadcasting Policy stated that "community broadcasting, complementing the private and public sectors, must be seen as an essential third sector of broadcasting" (Canada, Task Force 1986, 491). It reported that 21 community radio stations were operating in Quebec at the end of 1985, with six more being organized. In English-speaking Canada, apart from stations in remote communities and on university campuses, there were only two community radio stations, one in Kitchener and the other in Vancouver. There were 19 student radio stations (ibid., 494–95).

Community television is also highly developed in Quebec where the Task Force discovered, at the beginning of 1986, that 33 community television associations were in operation, each one producing an average of 16 hours a week of programming. In English-speaking Canada, cable companies play a larger role in programming community channels, often with the involvement of local groups.

To avoid confusion, it is necessary to distinguish here between two types of programming on community channels. The first type is programming organized by the operators of cable systems, produced either by themselves or by various local organizations. The second type occurs where operators of cable systems allot a significant amount of time on community channels to programming produced by a community television association. It is this second type that is more prevalent in Quebec than elsewhere in Canada. As the Task Force (1986, 503) stated: "In many parts of Canada, the cable system operators themselves provide all or part of the programming on the community channel." The distinction between "community broadcasters" operating within a community television association and "community channels" is important because the former often enjoy and utilize a greater degree of editorial autonomy. The new *Broadcasting Act* (Bill C-40) also contains provisions relevant to this study, stating in various places that "the programming provided by the Canadian broadcasting system should ... include educational and community programs" (section 3(1)(*i*)(iii)); that it "provide a reasonable opportunity for the public to be exposed to the expression of differing views on matters of public concern" (section 3(1)(*i*)(iv)); and that "the programming provided by alternative television programming services should ... be innovative and be complementary to the programming provided for mass audiences" (section 3(1)(*r*)(i)) and "as far as possible, be acquired rather than produced by those services" (section 3(1)(*r*)(iv)).

By whatever measure one uses, current levels of cable penetration indicate that a majority of the electorate – a large majority in those parts of the country where most Canadians live – now receives television channels that are available only on cable, whether they are channels carrying distant television stations, specialty channels provided via satellite or community channels.

Despite the high level of penetration, it should be acknowledged that the ability of cable to deliver political broadcasts varies between provinces and regions, and between rural or remote areas and built-up areas. It also depends on the availability of community channels and specialty channels on certain cable systems. Even where full cable service is available, some potential subscribers choose not to take it either because they can't afford it or because they can't abide it. As Charles Dalfen, a former vice-chairman of the CRTC who served two terms as broadcasting arbitrator for the chief electoral officer, observed in an interview for this study: "There are now cable penetration levels of 70, 80 and 90 percent. But that also means that 10, 20 or 30 percent don't get it. Some can't afford it. So in that sense, over-the-air is a more universal medium for political coverage and advertising."

Specialty Channels

Satellite-to-cable specialty channels have multiplied in North America since 1976 when Home Box Office started to deliver programming to U.S. subscribers. A partial catalogue of U.S. specialty channels listed by the Task Force included channels devoted to sports, news, various kinds of music, religious denominations, children's interests, health, the U.S. Congress and public affairs, financial news and information, Black Americans, the arts and Spanish-language programming (1986, 476). The Task Force cited 1985 statistics to show that pay services on cable accounted for 12 percent of television viewing in the United States at that time, while advertiser-supported specialty channels on cable accounted for 15 percent (ibid.).

In Canada, the CRTC delayed the introduction of pay-TV until 1982 because of concerns about the economic viability of these services. Despite this caution, "the launch of pay-TV was a disaster," in the words of the Task Force (1986, 479). Competing services failed and merged in the first two years; an ambitious attempt to launch an arts-and-culture service, C-Channel, miscarried within a short time.

In 1983, the CRTC received 40 applications for the first specialty channels to be funded by a combination of subscriber fees, advertising and, in some cases, institutional support. Eventually 15 applications were heard and two services were licensed: a music channel (MuchMusic) operated by CHUM Ltd. and The Sports Network (TSN), owned by Labatt's Breweries. By 1985, each service had about 800 000 subscribers (Canada, Task Force 1986, 483).

The Task Force reported that less than 3 percent of English-language television viewing in Canada was attributed to pay and specialty services, and even less of French-language TV viewing (1986, 475). With the inclusion of several specialty services in basic cable service in recent years, some of these channels are now reaching millions of viewers. English-language specialty services that can be watched by more than 5 million cable subscribers as part of their basic service include The Sports Network (TSN), The Weather Network, MuchMusic, CBC Newsworld, Youth TV (YTV) and Vision (a religious channel). French-language specialty services available on a similar basis to more than 1.5 million cable subscribers include Canal Famille, Réseau des Sports (RDS), Météomedia and MusiquePlus.

Specialty channels now available in Canada that might be attractive to political advertisers include Canal Famille (based in Montreal); CBC Newsworld (Toronto); Chinavision (Toronto); MuchMusic (Toronto); MusiquePlus (Montreal); RDS (Montreal); TSN (Toronto); Telelatino (Toronto); TV5 (French-language programming, Montreal); Vision (Toronto); The Weather Network; and YTV (Toronto).

According to Bureau of Broadcast Measurement statistics for three metropolitan areas (Montreal, Toronto and Vancouver) from 22 February to 31 March 1990, the more popular channels among the specialty services were TSN in Toronto and Vancouver, and its French-language counterpart, RDS, in Montreal; Canal Famille, which outdrew RDS in Montreal; YTV (more narrowly focused than Canal Famille on the youth audience), which did less than half as well as TSN in Toronto and Vancouver but better than MuchMusic in those two centres; and MuchMusic.

CBC Newsworld, launched in 1989 and expected to become a major vehicle for election campaign coverage in future, ranked behind MuchMusic in Toronto but ahead of it in Vancouver and is steadily building up its audience for public affairs programming. Another specialty channel that might be expected to give serious attention to aspects of election campaigns is Vision.

CBC Newsworld is the subject of a separate research project for the Royal Commission. It will obviously be an important source of campaign news for an influential segment of the Canadian television audience as well as a prime conduit for political advertising.

In an interview for this study, Terry Hargreaves, senior adviser to the president of the CBC, stated that the CBC intends to offer free and paid time on Newsworld to political parties in the same way it does on its main networks and stations. Newsworld will also provide extensive campaign coverage.

Hargreaves noted that the CBC regards equitable treatment in news, public affairs, advertising and other political broadcasting as its responsibility, not a responsibility of the CRTC. He anticipated that the political parties would probably gear their campaigns to Newsworld to some extent, but warned there would be a serious imbalance of service between English and French electorates if Newsworld continues to lack a French-language counterpart.

Newsworld is still below full potential cable coverage because it is optional for cable outlets to include it in their basic service. However, most cable companies now provide it.

In the last federal election, Elections Canada was advised by its media counsellors to consider placing part of its video information service on MuchMusic in order to reach a younger audience. A decision on this was postponed while Elections Canada experimented with the use of the House of Commons channel in the 1988 election.

House of Commons Channel

The House of Commons broadcasting service, although paid for by Parliament and the CBC, can also be classified as a specialty service available as part of the basic cable service. It was inaugurated in 1977; in 1979, the CBC was granted the first licences by the CRTC for national distribution of this service (Canada, House of Commons 1989, 31).

In 1988, the House of Commons channel carried election campaign broadcasting for the first time. The former Chief Electoral Officer of Canada, Jean-Marc Hamel, arranged to use it for the Voter Information Program of Elections Canada. (This and following information on the Voter Information Program is taken from a memorandum on the project prepared by the Communications Branch of Elections Canada and dated 14 March 1989.)

When the use of the House of Commons channel for election information was first broached, Carder Gray, the advertising agency that had won the contract to do English-language advertising for Elections Canada, proposed using the channel for a series of programs to be hosted by Pierre Berton and a French-speaking counterpart. This proposal was regarded as too expensive. After reviewing the Voter Information Program with its public relations agency, Heather Reid and Associates of Toronto, Elections Canada decided to request the use of the House of Commons channel for a more modest presentation.

Following approval by the Speaker of the House, Elections Canada obtained a special broadcast licence from the CRTC to enable it to broadcast election information over the House of Commons channel during a 48-day period. (The House of Commons channel normally was in use only when Parliament was in session.) The Canadian Cable Television Association subsequently asked all cable services to cooperate.

Jean-Marc Hamel launched "Countdown to Election 88" at a press conference in the theatre of the National Press Building in Ottawa on 5 October 1988. As his presentation concluded, the first script began to roll on television screens across Canada.

Production personnel from the CBC and a writer from private broadcasting collaborated with Elections Canada in preparing programming for the "Countdown." To keep costs low, scrolled text was used rather than a studio announcer. Six scripts were prepared every week – one for each weekday and a weekend script. Scripts were written in English, translated into French, transcribed on videotape and provided with background music. English and French tapes were transmitted to cable services by satellite.

Scripts rolled upward on the screen at a comfortable reading speed. Each one lasted about 25 minutes and was repeated about 25 to 30 times a day. It consisted of an election news digest, election facts, trivia questions and answers, and information directed specifically at voters, the media, candidates and their official agents. Telephone numbers of election information centres throughout the country appeared at the end of each scroll.

The election news digest contained headlines and stories about such matters as enumeration, revision, deadline for getting on the voters list and arrangements for voting day. It included information about voting assistance for the blind and physically disabled, and special voting arrangements for Canadian diplomats and public servants in other countries. It carried news stories about the record numbers of candidates, new cardboard ballot boxes and the weather expected on election day. Many items explained how to get on the voters list, how to mark a ballot and what to expect at the polling station. Others told about court decisions on federal judges' right to vote and the electoral status of the mentally disabled. Each daily news digest ended with a human interest story, often supplied by returning officers or enumerators.

Two trivia questions were broadcast daily, with answers supplied later in the broadcast.

Information for viewers, the media and candidates included key dates in the electoral process, and details about election-expense seminars given locally by officials of Elections Canada.

Elections Canada also produced videos explaining enumeration, revision of voters lists and voting procedure. Another video dealt with the election expenses law. These videos also were transmitted on the House of Commons channel as part of the "Countdown" programming.

In its memorandum of March 1989, Elections Canada noted: "The written material was kept strictly non-partisan. The names of any 1988 candidates were rarely mentioned and certainly not in any partisan way. One of the rare items that included any candidates' names was a list of Canada's prime ministers. Another rule Elections Canada imposed upon itself was never to broadcast the name of just one political party. If one or two were to appear, the names of all 12 official parties had to appear together. Several stories mentioned the televised debates. [They referred to] the debates 'between the leaders of the three federal parties.'"

Elections Canada received 120 letters about the program. Only five were critical. There were isolated complaints that the program was not available in some areas in both French and English, or not available at all because some cable systems used the House channel for other purposes when the House was not sitting. Language restrictions applied because most cable systems allotted only one channel to the House. In some cases, they alternated English and French "Countdown" programming or ran 12 hours in French followed by 12 hours in English.

The total cost of using the House channel in this way during the election period was about $50 000, including text preparation, translation, CBC production, internal coordination and support services, live transmission of the chief electoral officer's initial press conference and the production of videos in both languages.

A Gallup survey after the election found that of 67 percent of respondents who said that they had access to cable TV, 37 percent were aware that election information was running on the House of Commons channel. Of that group, 7 percent said that they watched the program regularly, while 28 percent said that they watched it occasionally.

In its memorandum of March 1989, Elections Canada stated that this response was "very significant ... given that we did not promote the channel in any consistent manner" and that "Elections Canada is very optimistic about arranging to use the House of Commons channel in future elections."

The House of Commons channels, English and French, are now operated by the CBC under a short-term renewal (CRTC 1990c) valid until 31 August 1991. In granting this, the Commission noted that it already had given three short-term renewals to this service, in 1987, 1988 and 1989, "to allow the Corporation to consult with representatives of the Canadian television industry and with the Office of the Speaker of the House of Commons on proposed enhancements to this service." In its last short-term renewal, the Commission called on the CBC to submit "a complete application for a new, enhanced service or a complete renewal application" by 24 February 1991.

Canadian Parliamentary Channel

In recent years the CRTC has granted short-term renewals to the CBC's House of Commons service because of uncertainty about its long-range future. In 1989, a proposal to replace the House of Commons service on its dedicated channel with a more elaborate public affairs channel, operated as a non-profit joint venture by the CBC and the Canadian cable television industry, was endorsed by the House of Commons' Standing Committee on Elections, Privileges, Procedure and Private Members' Business. Since then, the decision by the CBC at the end of 1990 to abandon the House of Commons service, as part of its own budget-reduction exercise, has cast uncertainty over the future of the proposed Canadian Parliamentary Channel (CPaC).

Under the scheme endorsed by the Committee, CPaC would be funded by a monthly charge of eight cents (rising to 10 cents in the fifth year) added to the basic cable fee to cover the cost of CPaC programming over and above the parliamentary proceedings. The CBC would continue to provide $3.7 million to pay for broadcast facilities and personnel while the House of Commons would still be responsible for the costs of televising its proceedings ($1.5 million annually).

The CPaC plan approved by the Committee was strongly influenced by the success of C-SPAN, a non-profit public affairs channel that the U.S. cable television industry has operated since 1979. The CPaC proposal provided for five categories of programming:

- Parliament and parliamentary institutions;
- national political party activities;
- public discussion and participation;
- provincial affairs;
- other public events of national significance.

The CPaC proposal approved by the Committee made no mention of programming that CPaC, with both English and French channels, would carry during federal election campaigns. Nor did the Committee's report refer to the question of campaign use of the channel. Still, the CPaC proposal is indicative of the type of campaign broadcasting that might be carried.

One of the categories – *national political party activities* – is described in such a way as to lend itself to election-campaign broadcasting. The description of two other categories – *public discussion and participation,* and *other public events of national significance* – could be extended to include campaign broadcasting.

Under *national political party activities,* CPaC proposed to "provide the national political parties with a regularly scheduled opportunity to outline in greater detail their views on current public affairs issues, subject to an all-party agreement with respect to a formula for sharing the time available and an agreement with respect to the type of programming material which may be delivered" (Canada, House of Commons 1989, 34).

Under *public discussion and participation,* CPaC proposed to "offer open line programming which will focus on issues currently being considered in Parliament or by one of the institutions which are related to Parliament" (Canada, House of Commons 1989, 35). The main vehicle would be a national open-line program following CPaC's early evening repeat of Question Period. It would feature "representatives of major points of view from government and opposition parties, or from appropriate interest groups" and "a neutral moderator who would ensure an appropriate regional and political balance in the calls taken" (ibid., 45). The scheduling of this program after Question Period would indicate that it might not be broadcast when the House was not sitting.

Finally, *other public events of national significance* would "provide exposure for the diverse views which are held on public affairs by Canadians who are not generally seen as practicing politicians" (Canada, House of Commons 1989, 35). CPaC suggested that such events might include church conferences, conferences devoted to such subjects as AIDS, native land-claim inquiries, and other activities with strong political relevance. This category of programming would also include a format that would use "a documentary program on a current or controversial issue to stimulate public discussion in a national Sunday evening phone-in" (ibid., 47).

Other categories of programming cited in the CPaC proposal, particularly *provincial affairs,* might often have a direct bearing on issues under discussion in a federal election campaign.

The broad categories of programming described in the CPaC proposal make it clear that this channel could play a major role as a conduit of information and opinion about a federal election campaign from a variety of sources. Even if CPaC is not implemented in the form approved by the Committee, it seems evident that a major restructuring of the current parliamentary channel is about to occur and that this will move the channel toward a less restricted public-affairs model.

POLITICAL/ELECTORAL USES OF CABLE TV – THE CANADIAN EXPERIENCE

Public Affairs Programming on Community Channels

Public affairs is the leading program category on cable TV's community channels, according to a survey conducted in March 1990 by the Canadian Cable Television Association (CCTA). Respondents (125 of 225 member companies representing 5.2 million of a total of 6.3 million subscribers served by CCTA members) said that public affairs accounted for 29.4 percent of their original programming hours. Main categories of public affairs programming were coverage of municipal councils, news and information programs of various kinds and programs contributed by elected politicians.

Public affairs programming accounted for twice as much time as educational programming (15.3 percent of original programming hours). Other categories mentioned by the survey respondents were sports (10 percent), other programming including programs for children (9.5 percent) and religious programs (9.4 percent).

Thirty-two percent of the reported programming was original programming aired for the first time. Repeat use of previously aired programming represented 50 percent of the total. Producers outside the cable company itself contributed 18 percent.

(At the time of the survey, A.C. Nielsen Company of Canada Ltd. reported that 712 000 households tuned to community channels on cable TV at least once a week.)

During nonelection periods, much of the contributed public affairs programming on community channels is provided by members of Parliament. Representatives of all three major federal parties interviewed for this study indicated that most MPs regard this type of programming as an essential part of their constituency work. These video "reports" have become the electronic equivalent of the written columns from local MPs printed by many weekly newspapers, and the tabloid "householders" that MPs can send to constituents quarterly with production and postage paid by Parliament. Many MPs refer to them as "video householders." Programs usually consist of a talk by the MP delivered straight to camera or an interview. They are 15, 30 or 60 minutes long.

Brian McInnis, director of the Radio and TV Bureau of the Progressive Conservative party, estimated that about half the members of the Conservative caucus make video programs for their local community channels. He thought that "probably 40 of our 48 Ontario MPs have done a cable show at one time or another."

McInnis said that he strongly advises the use of cable TV because of studies showing that MPs who use all means of communication with their constituents, including cable, are most likely to be re-elected.

He also urges MPs to advertise their appearances on cable because relatively few people watch community channels regularly, or are aware of program schedules on these channels. The video appearances can be publicized in the MP's newspaper columns and newsletters, in newspaper advertisements and in paid advertisements appearing on the alphanumeric (print on the TV screen) services of cable TV. These alphanumeric channels, which may combine time and weather information with a rotating series of advertisements using print and static graphics, carry the only paid advertising currently permitted cable companies.

André Tessier, director of communications for the Liberal party, said that MPs never have trouble getting community channels to accept their programs. He felt that the impact of cable TV was strongest in smaller communities. "There is a real neighbourly feeling about the community channel."

Tessier said that he had no idea how many people watch community channels, "but if a program is well promoted, you get people." He observed that production quality on community channels has steadily improved: "Often you get very high quality production – as good as the over-the-air stations."

Nelson Riis, House Leader of the New Democratic Party, said that he and a number of his colleagues do regular programs on their local community channels between elections.

"I try to do a half-hour program every week, and it is repeated two or three times," said Riis, who represents the British Columbia riding of Kamloops. "I promote the program in my householder (newsletter), saying that if you would like to hear from me more regularly, tune in to the program. I also advertise it on the alphanumeric channel."

"I'm a professor by profession, so I like teaching," Riis added. "I use a blackboard, flip charts, pictures and so on to make the program interesting and get my points across."

MPs often use the production facilities of local cable companies to produce their video messages. These are provided without cost as part of the company's community programming service. The popularity of "video householders" among MPs persuaded Rogers Communications Inc., Canada's largest cable licensee, to offer MPs centralized production facilities in Ottawa in the early 1980s. Colette Watson, bureau chief of Rogers Ottawa, said that the facilities had operated for two years at that time, were closed for a period when cable company revenues were affected by anti-inflation guidelines, but were re-opened in 1986.

The Rogers Ottawa Bureau has an office in the National Press Building across Wellington Street from Parliament Hill. It rents studio space in the evening from Global Television, in the same building, and uses Rogers production staff. These facilities are available without charge to all MPs, whether or not they come from an area served by Rogers Cable. MPs are asked only to pay for the tapes and to be responsible for sending them to local cable companies.

"An MP calls and asks to be booked for a show, or a holiday message to constituents, or whatever," explained Watson, an administrator with a background in cable production who formerly worked for the CCTA. "We tape between 7:30 PM and 10 PM Monday through Thursday – most MPs travel on Friday. Within 24 hours of taping, we give the MPs a cassette and they send it to the community channel in their riding."

The service is available only when the House is in session; it is suspended as soon as an election is called. Watson estimated that providing the service costs Rogers about $250 000 annually. "We do it because we need the programming for the community channels," she said. "Rogers wants this type of programming on all its community channels. The Ottawa Bureau is an initiative to generate programming for those channels."

Nelson Riis explained that some MPs, including himself, do not use the Rogers facilities because they believe this would involve a conflict of interest. By using the facilities, according to Riis, MPs are accepting a benefit from a cable company that also lobbies MPs and seeks to influence their decisions on broadcasting policies. Brian McInnis of the Conservative party, quoted earlier, disputes this, claiming that Rogers' Ottawa Bureau is simply a business operation on the part of the company to get program content for its community channels.

McInnis favours a current proposal by Rogers to lease an unused production studio from the House of Commons television service in order to provide MPs with an extended production schedule (the leased Global facilities are available only in the evening). Riis of the NDP opposes this.

Apart from programming provided by MPs, cable systems may originate their own public affairs programming dealing with federal issues. Local cable companies, for instance, covered the series of regional debates among candidates for the Liberal leadership in 1990. CBC Newsworld at times has used this type of material produced by cable companies. The Liberal leadership convention was recorded and aired by a local Calgary cable company. (At this level, conflicts of interest are sometimes tolerated that would be unacceptable in larger broadcast organizations. Gérald Lavallée, vice-president for regulatory affairs of the CCTA, said in an interview that he had acted as the executive producer of the Calgary cable company's coverage of the Liberal leadership convention while being a registered delegate to the convention.)

Community Channels and Federal Election Campaigns

At the request of the Royal Commission, the CCTA asked its members in March 1990 to reply to a questionnaire on community channel coverage of the 1988 federal election. Responses were received from 82 licensees with about 3.3 million subscribers, almost half the total number of subscribers served by CCTA members.

Seventy-one respondents (86.5 percent) reported that they had offered free time on the community channel to all accredited parties. Fifty-seven respondents (69.5 percent) divided the time equally among all parties while 14 respondents (17 percent) distributed it on an equitable basis in accordance with the *Canada Elections Act*. (Regulations governing the use of community channels during election campaigns will be discussed later.)

The following table shows the number of respondents who allocated time to a particular party and the average number of minutes allocated to it:

Respondents		Party	Average minutes
66	(80.4%)	Conservative	30.1
65	(79.3%)	Liberal	30.4
65	(79.3%)	New Democrats	30.2
8	(9.7%)	Rhino	39.7
14	(17.7%)	Christian Heritage	38.5
15	(18.3%)	Green	28.2
12	(14.6%)	Libertarian	19.8
4	(4.8%)	Confederation of Regions	19.5
2	(2.4%)	Social Credit	17.5
12	(14.6%)	Independent	16.8
14	(17.1%)	Communist	16.1
17	(20.7%)	Reform	15.1
3	(3.6%)	Others	17.5

Thirty-eight respondents (46.3 percent) initiated and produced all-candidate debates while 41 (50 percent) covered locally organized all-candidate debates. The respondents indicated that, on average, they covered or produced more than two all-candidate debates. The average debate lasted about 95 minutes. Fifty-four respondents (65.9

percent) repeated the all-candidate debates at different times leading up to the election. The repeat factor averaged 2.66.

Only 16 respondents (19.5 percent) stated that political parties had paid for advertising time on alphanumeric channels.

Commenting on the survey, Gérald Lavallée, CCTA vice-president for regulatory affairs, noted that community channels are required to keep their logs for only a year. Many respondents had to rely on memory in completing the survey.

Lavallée said the survey indicated the tendency of cable operators to interpret "equitable time" as "equal time." He said that complaints about time allocation would be referred to the CRTC, but that these had been rare in 1988.

The survey also indicated that community channels provide time to fringe parties that are rarely covered by over-the-air television stations. "The community channel has often been the vehicle for fringe parties," Lavallée stated.

Community channels also provided gavel-to-gavel coverage of local candidates' debates. People who missed the live coverage were often able to see repeat broadcasts. "Campaign coverage on the community channel gives more opportunity for participation in the political process to shut-ins and people who don't go to meetings," Lavallée stated.

Because community channels are not permitted to accept paid advertising, apart from messages on the alphanumeric channel, no political advertising is carried on the community channels. Neither the CCTA nor its members, according to Lavallée, has ever sought the right to carry paid advertising on the community channel.

"Our mission on the community channel is to provide free access," he said. "We view it as participatory TV – putting television production into people's hands."

The absence of paid advertising on community channels differentiates the roles of cable television in Canadian and U.S. election campaigns.

POLITICAL/ELECTORAL USES OF CABLE TV – THE U.S. EXPERIENCE

No one seriously doubts the effectiveness of using television advertising to influence voters. A number of academic studies in the United States have confirmed a popular assumption that there is "a strong positive relationship between broadcasting advertising effort and the proportion of the vote won" (Nowlan and Moutray 1984, 361). In congressional elections in the United States, spending on television advertising vastly outstrips amounts spent on all other media combined and amounted in 1990 to an estimated total of $230 500 000, an increase of $68 856 700 or 42.8 percent since the 1986 congressional election year (Holder 1990). The Markle Commission on the Media and the Electorate, in its 1990 report, found that in the 1988 presidential campaign, "the public got most of its information about the candidates from the Bush campaign's paid advertising" (Markle Commission 1990, 13).

As cable television has become more important in the United States as a source of television viewing and as an advertising medium, political advertising on cable TV has grown in volume and significance. This has accompanied a parallel growth in campaign news coverage on cable TV, both at the local level and on such cable network services as the 24-hour news channel (Cable News Network) and the cable TV industry's public affairs channel (C-SPAN). These two cable networks, according to a 1988 article in *Broadcasting*, "are providing more – and more in-depth – coverage, while the traditional over-the-air networks are providing less, and much of that pegged too often to polls" (*Broadcasting* 1988, 67).

The same issue of *Broadcasting* quoted William Headline, vice-president and Washington bureau chief of Cable News Network (CNN), as stating that "there has been a dramatic change" in the relative impact of broadcast and cable journalism. He quoted an anonymous member of the Bush campaign to support his own contention that CNN had become "the pre-eminent network" in campaign coverage, and forecast that the major television networks would increasingly transfer responsibility for heavy day-by-day campaign coverage to CNN and C-SPAN.

Washington political consultant Bob Beckel was also quoted in the same *Broadcasting* article as saying that cable TV has become a major element of presidential campaign coverage as network television reporting "has deteriorated to a series of news bites, a series of polls, no serious analysis and very little view of the candidates." Mr. Beckel's critical view of network coverage was confirmed statistically in 1990 when a Harvard sociologist reported that average length of "sound bites" taken from the statements of presidential candidates and broadcast as part of network news reports on television had shrunk from 42.3 seconds in 1968 to 9.8 seconds in 1988 (Rothenberg 1990, E4). Beckel also predicted that cable TV "will singlehandedly revolutionize local politics from here on out." He stated that he had never seen "a better opportunity for a state legislature candidate to buy cable time in a highly targeted way, and at a lower price" than in the 1988 election year.

According to a February 1988 issue of *Channels*, another U.S. trade publication for the television industry, "cable TV is making its strongest pitch ever for political advertising, and reinforcing its pursuit with increased coverage of the '88 campaign" (Vitale 1988, 92). It reported that CNN had launched a weeknightly half-hour program on the presidential campaign in the fall of 1987, supplementing this early in 1988 with a weekend show featuring political journalists analysing the campaign. C-SPAN was broadcasting a weekly 90-minute program entitled *Road to the White House,* offering "an unvarnished look at the front-runner candidates."

The same issue of *Channels* stated that "industry advocates argue that cable allows candidates to target their spot buys in ways they cannot on broadcast television." It permits candidates "to buy time on systems that more closely adhere to their districts." It quoted Lloyd Trufelman, a spokesman for the Cable Television Advertising Bureau, as saying that "cable has two things political consultants love – the impact of television and direct mail." Cable services such as CNN and C-SPAN also are seen to attract "politically active viewers" who may be influential in affecting the voting decisions of other people.

In a 1990 preface to a new edition of their 1988 study of "the impact of new media technologies on democratic politics," scholars at Harvard University's Institute of Politics identified two related major developments in the 1988 presidential campaign. The first was "the leading role televised political advertisements played in defining the agenda of public debate." Polling enabled television ads to be more timely and "data-driven" than before, encouraging the use of negative advertising, and creating a campaign in which "the real 'debate' between the candidates in 1988 was conducted through thirty-second television spots, with attack quickly provoking counterattack." The second major development was "the breakthrough made by cable and satellite television services" (Abramson et al. 1990, xi–xii).

The authors of the Harvard study cited the following examples of cable's influence:

- In the 1984 presidential election, political advertising on cable was too small to register. In 1988, the Bush campaign spent about 5 percent of its national television advertising budget on cable. The Dukakis camp followed, with about 3 percent of its budget devoted to cable.
- Cable was also a pivotal player in many state and local elections in 1988. One among many examples comes from California, where a single cable advertising company reports placing nearly $400 000 worth of ads regarding various initiatives on the California ballot.
- One cable ad in particular became a news item on its own. In September, an independent political action committee aired

exclusively on cable an ad featuring a police mug shot of Willie Horton – the Massachusetts prisoner whose criminal rampage following his failure to return to prison from a weekend furlough was the subject of the Bush campaign's own ads on broadcast television. The Bush campaign carefully avoided advertising that Horton was a black man but the independent ad broke this taboo. The media consultant who placed the ad has described how he carefully selected the cable networks on which the ad ran, targeting women and southern audiences in particular as groups likely to be responsive to the Horton ad.

- 1988 was a year for candidate-controlled satellite feeds. When George Bush officially announced his run for the presidency, he used a private satellite service to beam the announcement to local television stations around the country. In the primaries, Dukakis purchased satellite time to transmit a program on elderly affairs to a onetime network of midwestern cable stations. During the general election, both Bush and Dukakis frequently made themselves available for live interviews on local newscasts via satellite. (Abramson et al. 1990, xii–xiii)

Another indication of cable's growing importance in U.S. elections appeared in the report of a 1990 U.S. Senate task force on campaign reform that approved a proposal to require each television station and cable network to provide four hours of free time to Republican and Democratic parties during congressional elections (Rothenberg 1990, E4).

Because of the rapid growth of cable TV in the United States, and the ranking of Canada as the second most cabled country in the world, North America has provided a unique experience in the use of cable TV as a medium of political communication. Because of a decentralized regulatory system that permits paid advertising on many community channels operated by cable companies, the United States has acquired the only significant experience in the use of paid political advertising on cable TV.

While it has been outside the scope of this study to survey the use of cable TV as a medium of political communication in other countries, experience in other countries has probably been too limited to be of value to Canadians. The 1988 Harvard study cited above dealt with political communication by over-the-air television broadcasters in the United Kingdom and the Netherlands, for example, but made only fleeting references to cable.

Direct broadcast satellite services which can bypass cable systems by beaming television programs from satellite to small home receivers have not reached the stage in 1990 where they are significant channels of political communication.

FUTURE DEVELOPMENT OF CABLE SYSTEMS

Although this study deals mainly with existing cable TV facilities and their use in federal election campaigns currently and in the foreseeable future, it would not be complete without a glance at future possibilities and problems.

The installation of cable systems offering more than 50 channels, with the promise of more to come, was accompanied by efforts to use this capacity to create interactive systems which would not only transmit signals to viewers but carry signals *from* viewers, usually to a central computer. Prototype versions of these systems were developed in the 1970s by both cable and telephone companies as each sought to stake out territory in the new technology.

Despite a great deal of excited anticipation in the late 1970s, development of these videotex systems has been slower than many experts anticipated, particularly in North America. In Europe, strong government support has fostered more rapid growth; in France, for example, millions of small videotex terminals have been installed by the state telephone monopoly to replace telephone directories and to provide other types of information.

In the 1970s, when a videotex system called Telidon was developed by the federal Department of Communications, it appeared for a time that Canada might follow the European route (Desbarats 1981). Federal funds were used to create prototype videotex systems in most provinces, in particular the "Grassroots" system designed to provide information and interactive services to farmers in the Prairie provinces.

At the same time, media corporations in the United States sponsored extensive videotex trials, particularly in affluent areas of Florida and California. All of these ended in the 1980s when it became evident that the information and services provided by videotex did not justify the costs of acquiring and using videotex equipment and services.

It was about the same time that the CBC experimented with another system, entitled teletext, that used conventional television signals to carry data to storage and retrieval devices in home TV sets. Teletext created the illusion of an interactive service when a viewer at home used a hand-held keypad to access information received and stored by the device in the TV set. The information, constantly updated, is displayed in printed or graphic form on the TV screen. Like videotex, teletext was developed more rapidly in Europe than in North America. The CBC experiment ended in the early 1980s.

Despite these setbacks, development of videotex continues in North America, with both telephone and cable companies jockeying for starting positions in the race to exploit a potentially vast market for interactive services. Computers and high-volume communications facilities such as satellites and fibre optics are the basic building blocks of these new services.

A recent U.S. study attempted to compile a comprehensive list of "new media" as opposed to such "old media" as broadcast television, radio, newspapers, magazines, telephone and telegraph. The "new media" were:

Computers
Satellites
Cable Television
Videocassette Recorders
Direct Broadcast Satellite
Multipoint Distribution Service
Satellite Master Antennae Television
Subscription Television
Low-Power Television
VHF Drop-in Television
Videotex
Teletext
Lasers
Fiber optics. (Abramson et al. 1988, 5)

The common characteristic of almost all these systems, individually and collectively, is that they increase the range of choice for the user. At the lower end of the scale, contemporary cable TV systems already provide the user with an almost bewildering number of choices among programmed television channels. At the upper end of the scale, interactive videotex systems or pay-per-view subscription television services enable users in effect to program their own systems from a seemingly infinite variety of options.

All these new systems can be used, and already have been used in some cases, to convey political information during election campaigns. Questions of balance and fairness in providing political information to the electorate exist in an entirely new and perplexing dimension in a world of infinite choices – or they may not exist at all.

Dealing with this paradox will be easier in the light of principles for electoral communication that will be formulated later in this study.

PUBLIC ACCESS TO CABLE TV – CANADA'S SPECIAL CONTRIBUTION

In its *Report*, the federal Task Force on Broadcasting Policy stated that "community broadcasting, complementing the public and private sectors, must be seen as an essential third sector of broadcasting if we are to realize the objective of reasonable access to the system that is the central theme of this *Report*" (1986, 491). To implement the Task Force's desire that "the community sector of broadcasting should play an increasingly important role as a forum of community expression," it recommended that community television associations should be licensed, that the CRTC should regulate relations between licensed community television broadcasters and cable companies, and that the licences of community broadcasters "should recognize the need of fair access for various ethnic, cultural, interest and opinion groups" (ibid., 504).

In formulating these objectives, the Task Force referred to a 1975 CRTC policy which stated that "the community channel must become a primary social commitment of the cable television licensee." But the principle of public access to television in Canada was strongly formulated long before that. In fact, it represents a special and influential Canadian contribution to the development of television in North America and, to some extent, internationally.

It is significant that a recent U.S. study of "The Origins of Public Access Cable Television" by Ralph Engelman (1990), chair of the Journalism Department at the Brooklyn Campus of Long Island University, devotes almost as much attention to the Canadian as to the U.S. experience.

Engelman describes the *Challenge for Change/Société Nouvelle* project of the National Film Board (NFB) in the 1960s as North America's most viable and influential model for community television. This series of film programs, which drew on the tradition of the social documentary pioneered in the 1940s by John Grierson, founder of the NFB, involved making films *with* rather than *about* people. Among the most renowned programs of this series were those on the people of Fogo Island off Newfoundland where, according to Engelman, "the process by which the films were made and screened was central to their impact on the lives of the islanders" (Engelman 1990, 9).

The introduction by Sony of a portable video camera and recording unit in 1968 expanded the scope of *Challenge for Change* as NFB producers took the new "portapaks" into mining areas of Alberta and the slums of Montreal.

By 1968, before cable had gained a foothold in the United States, about 25 percent of Canadian households were receiving cable TV. In

Thunder Bay, Ontario, personnel from *Challenge for Change* collaborated with a community group in 1970 to produce community programming on the local cable system using videotapes, live studio segments and phone-ins. Another early community access project was at Normandin in the Lac Saint-Jean area of Quebec.

Drawing on these experiments, the CRTC held public hearings on the future of public access, leading to a policy statement on 16 July 1971, that access channels be an integral part of the development of cable television. After 1971, according to Engelman, "the concept of community television became institutionalized in Canada" (Engelman 1990, 16).

The Canadian experience contributed directly to the development of community television in the United States. American filmmaker George Stoney, after acting as guest executive producer of *Challenge for Change* for two years, returned to the U.S. in 1971 to found the Alternate Media Center at New York University, taking with him a Canadian documentary filmmaker trained at the NFB, Red Barber. In the subsequent five years, the Alternate Media Center became "the focal point of the community television movement in the United States," according to Engelman; Stoney and Barber "were instrumental in the creation of federal requirements for access channels in 1972" (Engelman 1990, 19–20).

Canadian media theorist Marshall McLuhan also became a major influence on the radical video collectives that emerged in the United States in the late 1960s and early 1970s (Engelman 1990, 29–31).

Although community television in the United States faced major challenges in the late 1970s and early 1980s as the political climate became more conservative – including a Supreme Court decision in 1979 (*FCC v. Midwest Video Corporation*) that the Federal Communications Commission did not have the statutory authority to require public access – "the community television movement has continued to grow" (Engelman 1990, 42).

The history of community access television in North America indicates that the Canadian experience has been innovative, distinctive and influential. This special contribution to the development of television should be reflected in future patterns of political communication on Canadian cable TV.

CURRENT REGULATORY FRAMEWORK GOVERNING ELECTION BROADCASTING ON CABLE TV

Introduction

Regulations governing the use of cable TV for journalistic coverage, free time political broadcasts and paid political advertising during election campaigns are derived from the *Canada Elections Act* and the *Broadcasting Act*.

The *Canada Elections Act* does not require cable licensees to provide mandatory free and paid political time during federal election periods, as it does holders of over-the-air broadcast licences. Nor does it prohibit cable licensees from voluntarily providing free time to political parties. But it does require community channels to observe *Canada Elections Act* rules for the duration of the election period. The Act defines the election period as (section 307(1)) "the period beginning on Sunday, the twenty-ninth day before polling day at a general election and ending on the second day before polling day." (This is considerably shorter than the "election period" prescribed in CRTC regulations which lasts from the day of the announcement of the election to election day.)

The general authority for CRTC regulation of political broadcasting is section 3(*d*) of the *Broadcasting Act*, declaring that "the programming provided by the Canadian broadcasting system should be ... varied and comprehensive and should provide reasonable, balanced opportunity for the expression of differing views on matters of public concern."

The proposed new *Broadcasting Act*, Bill C-40, would retain a similar provision in section 3(1)(*i*):

> [T]he programming provided by the Canadian broadcasting system should
>
> (i) be varied and comprehensive, providing a balance of information, enlightenment and entertainment for men, women and children of all ages, interests and tastes,
>
> (ii) be drawn from local, regional, national and international sources,
>
> (iii) include educational and community programs,
>
> (iv) provide a reasonable opportunity for the public to be exposed to the expression of differing views on matters of public concern, and
>
> (v) include a significant contribution from the Canadian independent production sector.

The *Canada Elections Act* requires the CRTC to prepare guidelines before every federal election on the applicability of the *Broadcasting Act* and CRTC regulations to the conduct of broadcasters in relation to a general election. These guidelines are submitted to the broadcasting arbitrator, appointed by the chief electoral officer after consultation with the parties, who supervises the allocation of free and paid political time on over-the-air radio and television stations during federal election campaigns.

The CRTC publishes the guidelines in circulars. The latest circulars – nos. 372 and 373 of 13 August 1990 – were issued for the Ontario and Manitoba elections and are identical with one another except for a few specific provincial references. They are also almost the same as Circular no. 351 of 4 October 1988, issued for the last federal election. Information used in this study is taken primarily from the 1990 Manitoba circular; for a few matters specific to federal elections, the 1988 circular is mentioned as the source.

Equitable Treatment

The CRTC requires over-the-air broadcasters to allocate time "on an equitable basis" to each recognized party for partisan programs, advertisements or announcements during the election period as defined by the CRTC (from the announcement of the election until election day). Channels available only on cable TV are governed generally by the same provision.

Neither the CRTC regulations nor the *Canada Elections Act* requires community channels or specialty channels to allocate time to political parties during federal election campaigns. But the CRTC's 1990 *Specialty Service Regulations* (section 6) state: "Where a licensee provides time on its service during an election period for the distribution of programs, advertisements or announcements of a partisan political character, the licensee shall allocate the time on an equitable basis to all accredited political parties and rival candidates represented in the election or referendum."

Earlier, the 1986 *Cable Television Regulations* (section 15) had made similar provisions for community channels on cable: "Where a licensee provides time on its community channel during an election period for the distribution of programming of a partisan political character, the licensee shall allocate that time on an equitable basis to all accredited political parties and rival candidates."

The 1990 Manitoba circular notes that, since broadcasting regulation began, broadcasters have been required as part of their service to the public to cover elections and, if they allocate paid or free political time, to allocate it equitably to all political parties and rival candidates. The circular continues: "The purpose of these requirements is to ensure the public's right to be informed of the issues involved so that it has sufficient knowledge to make an informed choice from among the various parties and candidates. This right is a quintessential one for the effective functioning of a democracy, particularly at election time. The broadcaster's obligation as a trustee of the public airwaves is seldom greater than it is in respect to this exercise of the most fundamental democratic freedom."

The CRTC has also stated (Circular no. 334 issued 4 June 1987): "It is the broadcaster's duty to ensure that the public has adequate knowledge of the issues surrounding an election and the position of the parties and candidates. The broadcaster does not enjoy the position of a benevolent censor who is able to give the public only what it 'should' know. Nor is it the broadcaster's role to decide in advance which candidates are 'worthy' of broadcast time." From the obligation to inform the electorate flows the obligation to provide what the CRTC terms "equitable – fair and just – treatment of issues, candidates and parties." It states that "equitable does not necessarily mean equal" but it does mean that "generally, all candidates and parties are entitled to some coverage that will give them the opportunity to expose their ideas to the public." Equitable treatment is given broad application by the CRTC: "The question of equitable treatment applies to parties and to candidates; to programs, advertisements and announcements; to federal, provincial and municipal elections, as well as to referenda. Equity also applies to the duration of broadcasts, to scheduling, to potential audience, to the choice of which electoral districts and offices to cover, to language of broadcast, to issue coverage and approach, to conditions under which an appearance may be made, and – in the case of paid-time programming – to price." The equitable treatment rule applies to all four categories of political campaign broadcasting identified by the CRTC: paid time, free time, news and current affairs. If one party or candidate receives free time, all must be offered "equitable time." If paid time is sold to one party or candidate, rivals must have access "on an equitable basis."

In news broadcasting, the editorial judgement of broadcasters should generally be respected but, under section 3 of the *Broadcasting Act*, broadcasters have an obligation to see that their audiences are "informed of the main issues and of the positions of all candidates and registered parties on those issues." Section 3 must also be applied when presenting public affairs programs such as party or candidate profiles, features on campaign issues or panel discussions. For example: "In the case of so-called 'debates,' it may be impractical to include all rival parties or candidates in one program. However, if this type of broadcast takes place, all parties and candidates should be accommodated, even if doing so requires that more than one program be broadcast." The CRTC specifically regards it as inequitable for an on-air personality who is running for office to remain on air during a campaign.

Community Channels

Political Programming in General

Political programming on community channels generally is limited by the definition of community programming as stated in the 1986 *Cable Television Regulations:*

> "[C]ommunity programming" means, in relation to an undertaking, programming that is produced
> (a) by the licensee of that undertaking or by members of the community served by that undertaking,
> (b) by the licensee of another undertaking or by the members of the community served by that other undertaking and that is relevant and of particular interest to the community referred to in paragraph (a), or
> (c) by a network operator licensed to provide programming to a licensee for distribution on a community channel.

This appears to mean that program content on community channels must be strongly oriented to local interests even if the program is produced elsewhere. In a federal election, this would make the community channel unavailable for national party coverage but available for programming involving local candidates and local aspects of national concerns.

Paid Advertising

Under current regulations, only the most limited form of advertising is allowed on cable's alphanumeric channels. Presumably this could be purchased to advertise partisan campaign events or to carry partisan messages provided that this facility is made available to all parties and candidates on an equitable basis.

The Canadian Association of Broadcasters (CAB), representing over-the-air broadcasters, is strongly opposed to any extension of advertising on cable. In its 1989 "television strategic plan," the CAB stated: "Local advertising should continue to be available only when local service is provided. Over-the-air broadcasters should have sole access to local advertising since they have to fulfill public obligations befitting their foundation role" (Canadian Association of Broadcasters 1989, 12). In an interview for this study, Tony Scapillati, legal counsel for the CAB, said that the Association believes that community channels should continue to be free of advertising, and that political advertising should be treated in the same way as other advertising in this regard. "This has been a carefully guarded market for the local broadcaster," he stated.

Unless cable companies are granted much wider powers to compete for all types of advertising with over-the-air broadcasters, the question of paid political advertising on community channels probably will not become a major issue in Canada.

It is possible that copyright fees on distant programming levied on cable companies at the end of 1989 may stimulate their desire for greater access to advertising.

Free Time

The CRTC notes that "no cable operator is obliged to engage in political programming" but, for those that do, it sets out criteria for what it calls "free access" programs (produced by an outside source such as a candidate or political party) and "licensee-controlled" programming produced by the cable company.

In "free access" programming, the licensee has ultimate responsibility for content but "the candidate or party is afforded the widest possible latitude and control." In Circular no. 351 issued for the 1988 federal election, the CRTC stated:

> Insofar as local candidates are concerned, since this type of programming is so closely related to political advertising, the Commission advises that it should be permitted only during the period which is allowed for radio and television advertising under the Canada Elections Act.
>
> During this period, a licensee who decides to make time available to candidates, should do so on an equitable basis and should inform concerned candidates of the availability of such time.
>
> If this type of free access programming is currently being carried by the licensee, *it should stop immediately upon issuance of the writs* for the election and resume only during the prescribed campaign period or after the election.

In "licensee-controlled" programming, where the cable operator decides on subject, format and participants, Circular no. 351 stated: "These programs can be likened to public affairs programs and as such *are not restricted at any time* before, during or after the elections. Again, such programming *must be done on an equitable basis for all political parties and rival candidates* and must conform to the Commission's regulations and policies respecting community programming."

Specialty Channels

Paid Time

Specialty channels wishing to sell advertising time to parties or candidates during an election campaign are required by CRTC regulations, cited immediately below, to offer it to all parties and candidates on an equitable basis.

Specialty channels in Canada have not yet been used for political advertising, but interviews for this study indicate that their use is under consideration by the political parties and their media advisers. André Tessier, director of communications for the Liberal party, stated that The Sports Network (TSN) and MuchMusic, and their French-language counterparts, might be useful to target messages to particular audiences. He said that the Liberal party also was looking into the production of "infomercials," party commercials featuring public-affairs-type examination and discussion of leading issues, that might be suitable for use on specialty channels.

CBC Newsworld, which appeared on cable in 1989, intends to offer both free and paid time to political parties in the next federal election in the same way that it does on its main networks and stations, according to Terry Hargreaves, senior adviser to the president of the CBC.

Free Time

Neither CRTC regulations nor the *Canada Elections Act* requires specialty channels to allocate free time to parties or candidates. But the CRTC's 1990 *Specialty Service Regulations* (section 6) state: "Where a licensee provides time on its service during an election period for the distribution of programs, advertisements or announcements of a partisan political character, the licensee shall allocate the time on an equitable basis to all accredited political parties and rival candidates represented in the election or referendum."

Publication of Election Results on Cable TV

The CRTC notes that the *Canada Elections Act* forbids publication before closing of the polls of results from polls in earlier time zones. Cable operators are responsible for seeing that they do not bring in distant signals giving such results. This will create problems for specialty channels, particularly news channels, that are not normally delayed to suit local schedules. Resolution of this problem will have to be made in the broader context of regulations governing release of electoral results in all media. Pending that, the current prohibition against premature release of election results on cable TV is reasonable.

PRINCIPLES AND CONCLUSIONS

Modern democracy is based on the belief that the best guarantee of democracy is an informed citizenry, and that information is the basis of citizen participation in government. According to this belief, societies that have the most efficient systems or methods of transmitting information to citizens should be the most democratic.

In our own era, Western societies do not always appear to conform to this model. In particular, the United States presents us with an apparent paradox – a society that has the most highly developed information systems in the world, operating relatively free of official restraint, and an electorate that appears to be increasingly passive if not actually alienated from the processes of government.

This was the paradox investigated recently in the United States by the Markle Commission on the Media and the Electorate, sponsored by the Markle Foundation. Working on the principle that voters in a functioning democracy must be both capable (possessing the right to vote) and competent (possessing sufficient information to make reasoned judgements), the Commission identified "citizen abdication of the electoral process" as its most disturbing finding. It stated that voter disaffection, evident in a voter turnout of 50.1 percent in 1988, the lowest presidential election percentage in 64 years, had been abetted by both candidates and news media. It characterized news media reporting of politics in the United States as generally superficial, sensational and prone to manipulation by the professional managers or "handlers" of political candidates. This had contributed to a conviction among voters that "politics is a cynical, unsavory business" (Markle Commission 1990, 1–23).

While voter turnout in Canadian federal elections remains relatively strong, compared with the United States, there are many signs of disaffection. Particularly in recent years, public opinion polls have revealed a high degree of cynicism about the political process. Many observers have related this to an apparent loss of faith among many Canadians in the ability of politicians to resolve the problems that confront the federation and even to maintain the unity of the federation.

Content is all-important in information systems. If our highly developed systems of print and electronic information are not producing an informed and active electorate, the problem must lie in the content of these systems.

One of the principal characteristics of the content of modern media systems, and the one most relevant to this study, is *uniformity*. Many media scholars and critics have testified to this. While media systems have become increasingly sophisticated, the content of these systems has become increasingly homogeneous.

In the 19th century and the early decades of this century, political information reached voters mainly through highly partisan newspapers. Canadians in those days were remarkably literate and involved in public affairs. In our own time, newspaper reading has decreased, particularly among younger people, while electronic channels of information have proliferated. At the same time, uniformity of content and reliance on "official" information controlled by those at the centre of power has contributed to an absence of meaningful debate on political issues (Wolfe 1990).

Many reasons for this have been suggested, including changes in society itself, the limitations of television as a medium of information, growing information expertise in government, increasing affluence and professionalism of journalists, concentration of media ownership, and so forth. The purpose of this study is not to analyse this phenomenon – uniformity of media content – but to identify it as a problem and to relate it to the development of cable TV as a channel of political information.

Despite a great deal of discussion in recent years about uniformity of media content and its effects on political activity, particularly in the 1981 report of the Royal Commission on Newspapers, *established media systems seem unable to diversify content*. In fact, under competitive pressure, the tendency has been to lower rather than raise the quality of content. Everywhere in Canada in the past several decades, so-called "quality newspapers" have struggled while tabloids have prospered. In the United States, major U.S. networks have experimented increasingly with tabloid-style journalism in an effort to maintain audience levels in a fragmented market.

Attempts to diversify media content should focus on new media systems. The very fragmentation of the television audience that is creating downward pressure on the content of network television creates opportunities for diversified content as the television audience breaks up into smaller and more specialized groups and technology provides the many channels needed to communicate with these groups. *As the current major technology of television diversification, cable television offers the most promising means of increasing access to political communication, enhancing diversity of media content and encouraging informed citizen participation in the political process.* As indicated earlier in this study, cable TV also has a history of public access which can serve as a foundation for this development, particularly in Canada. Canada also has relatively strong traditions of state regulation and public ownership of information media which should encourage and facilitate efforts to shape the development of cable TV in the public interest.

"Used wisely, mass communications is a powerful antidote to the democratic ills of group faction and personal isolation," according to the U.S. study of *The Electronic Commonwealth* cited earlier in this study. "Across obstacles of time and distance, the mass media make it possible to expand participation in the debates and deliberations, the meetings and assemblies that are the hallmark of democratic politics. Used unwisely, the mass media are themselves the disease. They turn active citizens into passive spectators, lulled by bland and homogeneous messages" (Abramson et al. 1990, xvi).

POLICY SUGGESTIONS

1. Current general restrictions on advertising on cable TV should continue to include a ban on most types of political advertising (with the exception of brief information messages on alphanumeric channels). If and when the current restrictions are eased, the question of political advertising on cable TV can be re-examined. A re-examination of the issue should be based on the principle that wide access to cable TV for political communication should not be compromised in any way by political advertising on cable TV.

2. Community channels should be required to provide free time to local candidates and interest groups during election campaigns. The definition of eligible candidate and interest group should be as inclusive as possible. The possibility of devoting a special community channel to political communication during election campaigns should be explored in an effort to provide as much time as possible to as many groups as possible. (This special channel could be assigned to community television associations for administration if the CRTC should decide in future to license these associations as recommended in 1986 by the Task Force on Broadcasting Policy.) The campaign period for cable TV should be defined by the CRTC, as it is for over-the-air television; the shorter campaign period taken from the *Canada Elections Act* should not be applied to community channels.

3. Specialty channels on cable TV should be required to provide free and paid time to parties during federal campaigns on an equitable basis, as are over-the-air networks and stations, provided that the nature of the channel makes it a suitable vehicle for political communication. If the current House of Commons channel continues in operation, it should continue to be available for Elections Canada information during campaign periods. If the House of Commons channel is replaced by CPaC or a similar public affairs

channel, the new channel should be available during federal campaigns for Elections Canada information and free time political broadcasts of national parties on an equitable basis.

4. All paid and free time political communication on cable TV channels should come under the broadcasting arbitrator.

5. The cable industry should consider creating a mechanism of public accountability, perhaps similar to the Broadcast Standards Councils currently being created by the Canadian Association of Broadcasters (CAB). An increase in the use of cable TV channels for political communication will increase the need for such a body. Disputes about fair political representation on cable TV programming should not be settled by the CRTC, except as a last resort. The broadcasting arbitrator, useful as a means of allocating time prior to an election period, does not provide a suitable forum for the kind of public discussion of equitable treatment that would be helpful as the electoral role of cable TV grows.

6. A minimum of regulation should govern political communication on future interactive systems where the user, in effect, controls the program, except to ensure that central databases or depots of video material contain information from the widest possible variety of sources and that all of it is equally accessible to users of these systems.

ACKNOWLEDGEMENTS

The author of this study is grateful for the assistance of Tim Creery, who acted as consultant. The author is solely responsible for conclusions and policy suggestions.

ABBREVIATIONS

c.	chapter
R.S.C.	Revised Statutes of Canada
S.C.	Statutes of Canada
SOR	Statutory Order and Regulation Number
s(s).	section(s)

INTERVIEWS

Charlebois, Marcel, Complaints and Audits Co-ordinator, Office of the Commissioner of Official Languages.

Charman, Wayne, Acting Director, Policy, Pay and Specialty Services, CRTC.

Dalfen, Charles, Former broadcasting arbitrator for Elections Canada.

Gorman, Brent, Assistant to Chuck Cook, MP, Chairman of the House of Commons Standing Committee on Elections, Privileges, Procedure and Private Members' Business.

Gorman, Tom, Services Division, Statistics Canada.

Hargreaves, Terry, Senior Adviser to the President, CBC.

Helm, Michael, Director General, Broadcasting and Cultural Industries, Department of Communications.

Howard, Bill, Legal Counsel, CRTC.

Jackson, Christine, Director of Communications, Elections Canada.

Lavallée, Gérald, Vice-President for Regulatory Affairs, Canadian Cable Television Association.

McInnis, Brian, Director, Radio and TV Bureau, Progressive Conservative Party of Canada.

O'Grady, Terry, Director of Communications, New Democratic Party of Canada.

Riis, Nelson, House Leader, New Democratic Party of Canada.

Scapillati, Tony, Legal Counsel, Canadian Association of Broadcasters.

Tessier, André, Director of Communications, Liberal Party of Canada.

Walker, Michael, Industry Statistics, Statistics Canada.

Warren, John, Host, House of Commons Channel.

REFERENCES

This study was completed in December 1990.

Abramson, Jeffrey B., F. Christopher Arterton and Gary R. Orren. 1988. *The Electronic Commonwealth.* New York: Basic Books.

———. 1990. *The Electronic Commonwealth.* 2d ed. New York: Basic Books.

Broadcasting. 1988. "The Cabling of Campaign Coverage." 25 April, 67–68.

Canada. Bill C-40, s. 3. *Broadcasting Act* [now S.C. 1991, c. 11; proclaimed in force 4 June 1991].

———. *Broadcasting Act,* R.S.C. 1985, c. B-9, s. 3.

———. *Cable Television Regulations, 1986,* SOR/86-831, s. 15.

———. *Canada Elections Act,* R.S.C. 1985, c. E-2, s. 307.

———. *Specialty Service Regulations, 1990,* SOR/90-106, s. 6.

Canada. Commissioner of Official Languages. 1990. *Annual Report 1989.* Ottawa: Minister of Supply and Services Canada.

Canada. Elections Canada. 1989. *Countdown to Election 88, Elections Canada. Information Program Broadcast on the House of Commons Television Channel from October 5 to November 21, 1988, Canada's 34th General Election.* Ottawa.

Canada. House of Commons. Standing Committee on Elections, Privileges, Procedure and Private Members' Business. 1989. *Watching the House at Work.* Ottawa: Queen's Printer.

Canada. Royal Commission on Newspapers. 1981. *Report.* Ottawa: Minister of Supply and Services Canada.

Canada. Statistics Canada. 1990. *Cable Television 1989.* Cat. no. 56-205. Ottawa: Minister of Supply and Services Canada.

Canada. Task Force on Broadcasting Policy. 1986. *Report.* Ottawa: Minister of Supply and Services Canada.

Canadian Association of Broadcasters. 1989. *Taking the Lead.* Ottawa: CAB.

Canadian Cable Television Association. 1990. "Community Channel Survey Results." Ottawa: CCTA.

Canadian Radio-television and Telecommunications Commission (CRTC). 1987a. *Election Campaign Broadcasting.* Public Notice CRTC 1987-209. Ottawa: CRTC.

———. 1987b. *Political Broadcasting – Complaints re: Free Time and Editorial Time Allocations.* Circular no. 334. Ottawa: CRTC.

———. 1988a. *Federal General Election.* Circular no. 351. Ottawa: CRTC.

———. 1988b. *A Policy with Respect to Election Campaign Broadcasting.* Public Notice CRTC 1988-142. Ottawa: CRTC.

———. 1990a. *To All Licensees of Broadcasting Undertakings Serving the Province of Manitoba.* Circular no. 373. Ottawa: CRTC.

———. 1990b. *To All Licensees of Broadcasting Undertakings Serving the Province of Ontario.* Circular no. 372. Ottawa: CRTC.

———. 1990c. *Short-term Renewal of the CBC's Television Network Licences for the Distribution of the House of Commons Proceedings.* Decision CRTC 90-807. Ottawa: CRTC.

Desbarats, Peter. 1981. *Newspapers and Computers – An Industry in Transition.* Vol. 8 of the research studies of the Royal Commission on Newspapers. Ottawa: Minister of Supply and Services Canada.

Engelman, Ralph. 1990. "The Origins of Public Access Cable Television." *Journalism Monographs* 123:1–47.

Holder, Dennis. 1990. "Political Payoff." *Channels,* 7 May, 28–30.

Markle Commission. 1990. *Markle Commission on the Media and the Electorate: Summary of Key Findings.* New York: Markle Foundation.

Nowlan, J.D., and Mary Jo Moutray. 1984. "Broadcast Advertising and Party Endorsement in a Statewide Primary." *Journal of Broadcasting* 28 (3): 361–63.

Rothenberg, Randall. 1990. "Politics on TV: Too Fast, Too Loose?" *New York Times,* 15 July, E1–E4.

Vitale, Joseph. 1988. "Chasing the Political Ad Dollar on TV." *Channels* (February): 91–92.

Wolfe, Morris. 1990. "News Media Has Unhealthy Alliances with Official Sources." *Globe and Mail,* 3 January, C1.

5

POLITICAL BROADCAST ADVERTISING IN CANADA

Stephen Kline
Rovin Deodat
Arlene Shwetz
William Leiss

THE HISTORICAL CONTEXT OF POLITICAL ADVERTISING

AN HISTORICAL OVERVIEW of political advertising reveals the subtle process of adoption of advertising design and practices by political strategists in response to the emerging media of the day. While the print media – newspapers, pamphlets and posters – were major parts of political campaigns in the 18th and 19th centuries, the 20th century saw the rise of the electronic media; first radio, then television. The advertising opportunities brought about by broadcasting channels – the potential to address the electorate directly through electronic media – became more desirable to campaign managers as they learned how to manage broadcast communications. The trends in election expenditure (see appendices A–D) reveal that increasing proportions of campaign resources were devoted to broadcast advertising. And while the journalistic media continued to provide extensive campaign coverage, broadcast advertising came to be seen by the major political parties as a form of communication that bypassed the news media, thereby maximizing central party control over the campaign message. It was this ability to communicate directly with the electorate on a national as well as regional basis that justified the increasing use of commercial advertising techniques and tactics and necessitated the recruitment of advertising specialists into campaign teams.

Gradually, the experience gained through the practical application of various advertising communication techniques to campaigns has contributed to a more sophisticated array of campaign options, including targeted media buying, coordinated research management and research-based message design. There can be little doubt that these advertising approaches have had a considerable impact on election campaigning over the last 50 years.

The Role of the Advertising Agency in Political Campaigns

By the opening decades of the 20th century, advertising agencies had fully defined their organizational niche by mediating between the manufacturer with goods to sell and the burgeoning commercial media (Leiss et al. 1990). Their familiarity with all aspects of the media led them to offer a wider scope of services to clients, including research, the development of campaign strategies and the preparation of advertising materials.

As early as 1917, advertising agency services were being used by governments, particularly in the sale of government bonds and in military recruitment. The apparent success of advertising in explaining conscription to the public led the Union government of Sir Robert Borden to hire an advertising agency for the election campaign of 1917 (Whitaker 1977, 221). By the 1930s, the role of advertising agencies in political campaigns was fairly well established.

Agency skills and understanding of media were particularly important as radio came to be the pre-eminent medium for public communication. In the 1930s, Cockfield, Brown placed national radio advertisements for the Liberal party and also helped in organizing special party events like a commemorative dinner for Mackenzie King (Simpson 1988, 143). New advertising-oriented approaches to communication design were evidenced in the highly controversial "Mr. Sage" radio series during the 1935 election, which was aired over a network of private stations. The series consisted of conversations between Mr. Sage and a politically concerned citizen called Bill (Bird 1988, 133). As Bird indicates, it was written by a Toronto advertising firm for the Conservative party, but early episodes failed to identify the Conservative party as the sponsor. An excerpt from the series ran as follows:

> [Sage returns to talk with Bill after completing a phone call with his niece, Mary]
>
> *Sage:*   … Mary's a fine girl. Seemed kind of frightened tonight though. Didn't like that – much.
>
> *Bill:*   (concerned) Why, anything the matter?

Sage: ... She's been hearing about Mackenzie King's war speech –

Bill: War – what war? ... We don't want war days back again in Canada.

Sage: We do not, my boy. And that's why I hate this attempt to stir up old war wounds ... It looks to me like a deliberate attempt [by Mackenzie King] to frighten people – women and the younger –

Bill: (interrupting) Surely King wouldn't stoop to that –

Sage: No? He did it before – in 1930 – and there was no world crisis then like there is to-day ... Mr. King's henchmen [in Quebec] used to call up the farmers – and their wives – in the early hours of the morning and tell them their sons would be conscripted for war if they voted against King –

Bill: Gosh, that's kind of low-down stuff – I didn't think King would do a thing like that.

Sage: Well, he said the same thing in his speeches down there. And he said practically the same thing last month.

Bill: (reflectively) I don't wonder Mary got frightened, poor girl. I can't see why King has to bring that up.

(Bird 1988, 136–37)

It was the success of these early initiatives that led the major parties to turn to advertising agency personnel and approaches in their election campaigns to help to articulate and manage the communicative dimensions of electioneering. For example, King's Liberals invested heavily in media advertising for the election of 1940. Using the services of Cockfield, Brown, the largest Canadian advertising agency, King commissioned an orchestrated series of radio broadcasts, billboards, and newspaper and farm paper advertisements. These proved to be highly effective, in part because the opposition lacked the funds needed to compete.

While radio quickly became the primary advertising tool in the campaign strategy of the major political parties in Canada over the next decade, television was added to their arsenal in the 1953 election. However, as only a limited set of free time broadcasts was offered by the CBC, television advertising remained a minor factor in the overall campaign. This was true despite the fact that technical and studio facilities were provided free of charge to all recognized political parties.

Between 1956 and 1957, with another election on the horizon, the Liberal communications committee was expanded to include the staff of Cockfield, Brown in the planning of the party's campaign strategy. Likewise, the Conservative party began to engage a number of advertising agency personnel, including Allister Grosart, Art Burns, Mickey O'Brien and Dalton Camp. The obvious potential of television's dramatic impact for political campaigns had further encouraged the inclusion of advertising skills and personnel in the campaign team. This meant there was jostling in the back rooms as the political hierarchy had to accommodate "young men with arrogant manners, full of self-assurance and incomprehensible jargon, demanding large sums from party campaign funds for doubtful enterprises in publicity" (Camp 1970, 280). Campaigning increasingly demanded a staff of experienced media handlers to help to navigate the campaign trail, as well as to develop advertising strategies.

The exigencies of television campaigning contributed to an increasing emphasis on skilful public presentation of the party leader. Thus, in addition to traditional political skills and a commitment to tireless campaigning, politicians – especially party leaders – had to learn to project a "stage presence" appropriate to television (Shwartz 1973; Soderlund et al. 1984, 129).

Of the two major figures in the 1957 election, John Diefenbaker was comfortable with television, while Louis St. Laurent was not. St. Laurent disliked the new medium and felt that the teleprompted broadcasts were too contrived. He objected to make-up and never managed to feel at ease in front of the television camera (Meisel 1962, 163).

Diefenbaker's landslide victory in 1958 was a lesson about the changing role of the leader in media-age politics that was taken to heart by many observers and was confirmed during the 1960 American presidential election with the victory of John F. Kennedy. For their 1965 campaign, even the CCF/NDP, who had hitherto relied on the more traditional tactics of mass rallies and constituency organizations, shocked many adherents by deciding to use a limited amount of national advertising and a federal leader's tour as central features of the campaign. National party secretary Terry Grier retained a small Montreal advertising agency headed by Manny Dunsky, who put together a low-budget campaign designed to present a few carefully chosen messages. The slogan "Let's give the two old parties a well deserved rest – this country needs it" was often repeated throughout the campaign (Morton 1986, 62).

The use of polling in campaign scripting, like its use in marketing, has also had an enormous impact on political communication. At the outset, the results of polls were used merely to focus the campaign on a few often-repeated themes that could anchor the leader's speeches and the party's advertising on a firm foundation of public acceptance and popularity. This approach to campaign management proved effective in the Liberals' 1962 campaign strategy against the Progressive Conservatives' attempt to revive the "mystic bond" between Diefenbaker and the "ordinary Canadian" (Newman 1973, 383).

Liberal Keith Davey, familiar with the growing American political literature on the integrated use of research and advertising in television campaigning, helped to get Lou Harris, President Kennedy's pollster, hired as an adviser to the party for the 1963 general election (McCall-Newman 1982, 41). Throughout the 1960s, opinion research became ever more important in Canada because it made it possible to target swing ridings through selective media buys and to identify effective campaign themes. The pollster was elevated to a position between the populace and the leader previously occupied by the party machine, thereby making advice on the interpretation of the public mood a central part of campaign strategy, one that communications designers understand well (Lee 1989, 34). This organizational innovation also linked polling to the centralized development, scripting and design of all party communication, including advertising. Davey was instrumental in a restructuring of the national Liberal campaign organization to take maximum advantage of the opportunities offered by these new techniques, but he was also concerned not to let the advertising professionals drive the campaign (Davey 1986, 165).

The importance of integrated campaign management took on new dimensions in the 1968 election, which saw Pierre Trudeau come to power in a wave of media excitement orchestrated by the Liberals. In contrast, the Conservatives had planned the election campaign poorly and were unprepared, with no centralized budget, no polling and no goals for Stanfield's tour. Print advertisements, radio commercials and pamphlets had been produced without reference to each other, and the media handlers proved ineffective in managing the journalists who swarmed around the campaign. But by 1970, a Conservative campaign planning committee had produced a working document that outlined the integration of polling, advertising, touring and media exposure as essential to efficient campaign management (Graham 1985, 22).

The reimbursement of some advertising expenditures allowed by the *Election Expenses Act*, the growing sophistication of party aides and strategists and the increasing size of television audiences jointly contributed to making the 1979 general election a "full-force" television campaign (Gilsdorf 1981, 62). A majority of voters – 52 percent – reported getting most of their campaign information from television, 30 percent mentioned newspapers and 11 percent indicated radio (Fletcher 1981, 285). The use of broadcast media, the tendency to focus on party leaders, the concern with image and style, the obsession with polls, and the use of media consultants were even more evident in 1979 than in earlier campaigns (ibid., 281). The 1979 election was also marked by an increase in party spending on advertising, specifically on television. The Conservatives spent 56 percent of their advertising budget on television advertising, the Liberals 53 percent and the NDP 58 percent (ibid., 289). Such statistics demonstrate the growing dependency of all the major political parties on television advertising to reach voters.

In the 1980 election, the parties mobilized their advertising teams for the election battle once again, focusing primarily on leadership issues. The Tory campaign reiterated its 1979 theme, stressing the unpopularity of Trudeau. One advertisement showed him surrounded by former Liberal cabinet ministers whose pictures disappeared, one by one. An announcer said, "Let's face it. If you vote Liberal, you're getting Trudeau and nothing else" (Irvine 1981, 369). Liberal advertising was equally critical, attacking Clark's policy flip-flops and taking issue with his budget. The NDP campaign criticized both major parties while keeping its primary focus on Broadbent, who spoke in very common-sense terms about particular economic and energy issues.

In the 1984 election, the advertising of the three parties again focused on their leaders. Also, innovations in the use of polling and the regional targeting of party messages were increasingly in evidence (Fletcher 1988, 165). The conscious adoption of advertising strategies in the campaigns of the major parties led one commentator to the observation that "increasingly elections are being seen as contests between leaders rather than as confrontations between policy stands or ideological positions. This reflects the reality of the increasing power of leaders in their own parties and of changes in campaign strategy" (Frizzell and Westell 1985, 97).

Television advertising continued to be a major feature of campaign activity in the election of 1988. The strategies and expenditure patterns were similar to those employed in 1984. The Conservatives devoted nearly $4 million to broadcast advertising in 1988, while the Liberals and NDP spent about $3 million each (see appendix B1 and appendix D). However, the 1988 campaign featured the first significant use in a Canadian federal election of sophisticated direct mail techniques to mobilize voter support (Lee 1989, 260–65). This new approach to political marketing may become increasingly important and could result in shifts in expenditure patterns and strategies.

The introduction of new advertising techniques to the political campaign was simply an elaboration of traditional marketing approaches, combined with the public relations lessons learned in managing broadcast journalism. These techniques produced advertising campaigns that were:

1. *Targeted*   Thinking about the audience in segments made the parties become more concerned with timing and audience composition in their media buying.
2. *Value based*   Advertising personnel familiar with the use of attitudinal and polling research contributed to developing new approaches to political mobilization based on the communication of party positions on policy within the basic predispositions of the audience's values or attitudes.
3. *Impression managed*   What is often called "image politics" refers to the application of basic advertising and public relations principles to election campaigns. In particular, this involves:
   a. *Personalization*   Credibility with an audience depends upon establishing a public persona that is liked, respected and trusted. Therefore, the presentation of a leader must be crafted in terms of predicted audience response.
   b. *Impact*   Grab attention and emotionally engage the audience whenever possible. It is not what is said but how it makes the audience feel that counts.
   c. *Condensation*   Audiences' limited attention and interest mean that simpler ideas and communication formats are most likely to be effective.

Summary and Implications

As has been shown above, the practice of political advertising is not new, but it has been significantly transformed by the application of modern marketing techniques. Advertising strategists have guided campaign managers in an exploration of the many ways in which electronic media present opportunities for more effective campaigns. The reasons for the increasing use of broadcast advertising can accordingly be summarized in terms of four key advantages:

1. *Cost effectiveness*   Broadcasting's advantages as a delivery system are the national scope of the potential audience and the low cost per voter reached.
2. *Dramatic presentation*   Television allows the benefit of visual images and emotional appeals that could increase impact and strengthen impressions.
3. *Creative design*   The advertising agencies' effective use of modern commercial art and marketing techniques can be translated into the political arena.
4. *Integrated management techniques*   An integrated approach to the campaign attempts to manage public relations, advertising and the press in terms of common objectives.

In light of these advantages, it is not surprising that our review of expenditures in recent campaigns revealed increasing emphasis on and allocations to broadcast advertising. It remains the major campaign investment for the larger parties and has brought about important changes in the nature of campaign communication.

Opportunities for partisan political communication through the broadcast media (employing both news management and advertising) have made access to the public through the media the primary activity of campaigning. The emphasis placed on the electronic media by the parties demands that limited resources be increasingly siphoned away from traditional campaign techniques, such as candidate rallies, and instead be redirected to broadcast advertising.

Party strategists are concerned about controlling the message. However, their inability to control the message within general news coverage encourages them to supplement attempts at news management with advertising, where their ability to shape the ideas, issues and impressions communicated is considerable. Strategists complain about media bias but want greater freedom to use advertising in ways they see fit.

Increasingly, television has become the dominant campaign medium. Declining print media readership and the relative credibility and perceived impact of television have made it the preferred channel for waging national campaigns. Party strategists prefer television to other media, not only because of its audience size, but also because of its greater emotional impact and ability to persuade.

THE CANADIAN REGULATORY SYSTEM AND POLITICAL BROADCASTING

As political broadcasting in Canada has shown itself to be an important means of political influence on the electorate, legislative bodies have tried to ensure that political campaigning through radio and television broadcasting is conducted in a "fair and equitable" manner. The electoral system in Canada is not, however, regulated by a single statute. The most direct references to political advertising are in the *Canada Elections Act*. Most of its current provisions deal with the allocation of paid and free political broadcast time[1] among the registered parties during the electoral advertising period (Canada, *Canada Elections Act* 1985, ss. 310–19). Although there is no detailed specification of what distinguishes "political" advertisements from other forms of commercial and political speech (such as institutional, advocacy, government advertising, social marketing, public service announcements and product advertising), the Act implicitly defines political advertising narrowly through its restrictions on those permitted to spend money on advertisements for the purposes of promoting and opposing parties and candidates. The primary regulatory concern in this Act is with the issue of fairness and equity in party access to broadcast time. In keeping with these objectives, the Act ensures that there is an arbitrator for the allocation process so that media buying proceeds fairly and in the public interest (ibid., s. 308(1)).

To further the goals of fair and equitable campaigns the *Canada Elections Act* requires each broadcaster to make available 6 1/2 hours of paid time (Canada, *Canada Elections Act* 1985, s. 307(1)). The Act sets out allocation rules based on several factors – percentage of seats, percentage of popular vote and number of candidates endorsed in the previous election – and specifies that no party may be allocated more than half of the total time (ibid., s. 310(1–4)). The Act also specifies the manner in which parties negotiate their broadcast spots with broadcasters, ensuring that scheduling is done fairly throughout prime time. The Act specifies further that the broadcasting arbitrator should ensure that parties have the freedom and flexibility to pursue their preferred strategies in their media buys. In addition, the Act requires broadcasters to charge all registered parties the lowest rate it would charge a commercial advertiser for equivalent time (ibid., s. 321).

Criteria for free time political broadcasts are also outlined (Canada, *Canada Elections Act* 1985, s. 316). Network operators are required to make available the equivalent of their free time allocation during the last pre-election period, with two minutes for each registered party, and to assign the remainder in proportion to the allocation formula for paid time (ibid., s. 316(2)). The allocations of free time are not considered election expenses (ibid., s. 316(3)) or donations to the parties. The Act ensures that paid spots are considered election expenses and allows refunds for certified claims of 22.5 percent of total election expenses (ibid., s. 322).

The *Canada Elections Act* provisions must be understood within the general framework of broadcast regulation by the Canadian Radio-television and Telecommunications Commission (CRTC) under the *Broadcasting Act*. The CRTC issues guidelines to broadcasters for coverage of all elections held in Canada, informing broadcasters of CRTC regulations and guidelines as well as provisions of the relevant election legislation (federal or provincial). The guidelines are based on traditions developed over the years since broadcast regulation began in the 1930s and on the general principles of the *Broadcasting Act*. The central principle in the Act has been retained through various revisions: "The programming provided by the Canadian broadcasting system should ... provide a reasonable opportunity for the public to be exposed to the expression of differing views on matters of public concern" (Canada, *Broadcasting Act* 1991, s. 3(1)(*i*)(iv)) in furtherance of the general objectives for the broadcasting system set out in the Act. These objectives stipulate, for example, that programming should:

> safeguard, enrich and strengthen the cultural, political, social and economic fabric of Canada; (s. 3(1)(*d*)(i))

> be varied and comprehensive, providing a balance of information, enlightenment and entertainment ... ; (s. 3(1)(*i*)(i))

> reflect the circumstances and aspirations of Canadian men, women and children, including equal rights, the linguistic duality and multicultural and multiracial nature of Canadian society and the special place of aboriginal peoples within that society. (s. 3(1)(*d*)(iii))

These provisions, as well as others in the Act, require the CRTC to deal with the content of programming, including that of news and public affairs, political broadcasts and advertising (including campaign advertising). In addition, in section 10(1)(*e*), the CRTC is authorized to make regulations "respecting the proportion of time that may be devoted to the broadcasting of programs, including advertisements or announcements, of a partisan political character and the assignment of that time on an equitable basis to political parties and candidates." The CRTC reconsidered its election campaign guidelines in 1987, requesting public input, and issued a revised version in 1988. The substance of the current guidelines is discussed below.

In addition, the *Income Tax Act* has some relevance to campaign advertising because it encourages contributions to registered parties through tax credits (Seidle and Paltiel 1981, 235) and, more importantly, because it permits corporations to declare the costs of advocacy advertising as a business expense (Winter 1990, 4).

Overall, there is a mishmash of regulations, many of which are confusing to participants, and some overlapping between the two primary statutes. Some areas of campaign advertising, such as the content of political broadcasts, remain essentially unregulated, unlike commercial advertising.

Evolution of the Canadian Regulatory System and Political Broadcasting
In 1929, ten years after radio was introduced in Canada, the Royal Commission on Radio Broadcasting (Aird Commission) released its report. Baum states that the Aird Commission did not want to encourage political programs but, rather, to "discourage them without imposing an absolute prohibition" (Baum 1970, 160). Because of the positive response

to Franklin D. Roosevelt's "fireside chats" in the United States and to the
oratorical success of William Aberhart in Alberta, the Commission
emphasized the fear of political propagandizing (LaCalamita 1984, 545).
In essence, the Commission expressed a common fear among intellec-
tuals of the period that radio could become a powerful tool of political
propaganda. The proposals of the Aird Commission led to a call for
public control over public and privately owned stations. The passage
of the 1932 *Canadian Radio Broadcasting Act* created the Canadian Radio
Broadcasting Commission (CRBC, later the CBC), which had the dual role
of broadcaster and regulator. As LaCalamita indicates, the question of
free access to the public airwaves was brought up often in the House
of Commons. Policy considerations in 1934, which would shape the
extent and content of political broadcasting regulations, were voiced by
Mackenzie King: "Each political party which has a representative
following should be entitled to have broadcast at the expense of the
state, one or two addresses, which would set forth its platform or policies before the people" (LaCalamita 1984, 546).

In 1936, a Special Committee was appointed to inquire into the
operations of the CRBC and its administration of the *Canadian Radio
Broadcasting Act* of 1932, in order to recommend changes in the broadcast system and to investigate whether there had been any abuse of
broadcast privileges for either political or advertising purposes (Boyer
1983, 327). The Committee reported that, during the 1935 federal election, there had been abuses, such as the "Mr. Sage" broadcast, which
utilized drama to carry its politically partisan message without identifying its sponsor. Such complaints served to exacerbate the general
dissatisfaction with the performance of the CRBC.

As a result, the Committee recommended that "dramatized political broadcasts be prohibited, that full sponsorship be required, that
the proposed new CBC ensure that time be allocated on an equitable
basis among all parties and that no political broadcasts be allowed on
election day or during the two days immediately preceding election
day" (Boyer 1983, 327–28). The 1936 Committee further recommended
that the CBC exercise regulatory authority over all programming and
advertising broadcast by private stations and networks (Canada,
Committee 1966, 363).

In 1939, a committee consisting of representatives of the CBC and
the political parties was established to study the unresolved issue of
equitable allocation of radio time among the parties. The Corporation's
white paper stated in section 22 that "political broadcasts during a
general election [are] to be on a sustaining or free basis ... Privately
owned stations affiliated to the network are required to carry these

broadcasts; and other private stations are *invited* to do so" (Canada, Committee 1966, 365). Furthermore, time was allocated among existing parties in the House of Commons, and a special provision was made for new political parties, which were defined as having a recognized leader, a nationwide organization and nominations in at least one-quarter of the constituencies (Boyer 1983, 441).

The white paper was revised in 1944 to include a provision of "network time free of charge to recognized political parties during ... elections" (CBC 1944, reprinted in Bird 1988, 184). Provisions were also made for the purchase of time on privately owned stations. With regard to political advertising, section 22 (paragraphs 3, 4 and 5) of the 1936 *Canadian Broadcasting Act* set out the following rules:

> Dramatized political broadcasts are prohibited.

> The names of the sponsor or sponsors and the political party, if any, upon whose behalf any political speech or address is broadcast shall be announced immediately preceding and immediately after such broadcast.

> Political broadcasts on any dominion, provincial or municipal election day and on the two days immediately preceding any such election day are prohibited. (CBC 1944, reprinted in Bird 1988, 184–85)

Political broadcasts presented in a dramatic manner included "Question and Answer" programs in the form of a dialogue, and dramatic skits or plays presented as a complete broadcast or part of a broadcast (Bird 1988, 185). The election of 1945 was the first in which political parties were allocated free time in which to broadcast their messages, albeit within stringent restrictions.

Between 1944 and 1958, despite dramatic changes in broadcasting, no significant changes in election broadcasting legislation took place. The CBC performed the dual role of broadcaster and regulator as the number of private radio stations grew. By 1930, over 60 radio stations were in operation in Canada, and one-third of Canadians had radios; by 1940, three-quarters of all Canadian homes had radios, and by 1950, almost everyone possessed a set (Vipond 1989, 38–39). During the 1950s, television viewing increased substantially in Canada, thanks to access to American network programming in Canadian border cities. The growing strength of the association of private stations – the Canadian Association of Broadcasters (CAB) formed in 1926 – and the recommendations made by the 1957 Royal Commission on Broadcasting (Fowler Commission) led to structural changes. In the 1958 *Broadcasting Act*, the regulatory responsibilities of the CBC were transferred to the newly created Board of Broadcast Governors (BBG) (Canada, Task Force on Broadcasting Policy 1986, 9–11). This was done despite strong recommendations by the Massey Commission in 1951 that the CBC continue as both regulator and broadcaster.

The cautious attitude of Parliament in 1936 toward political programming was still visible in the 1958 *Broadcasting Act*. The regulations pertaining to the ban on dramatized political broadcasts, blackout periods for advertising prior to and on election day, and identification of the sponsors of political broadcasts were retained in chapter 22, section 17. The BBG was given the authority to make regulations concerning the compulsory provision and equitable allocation of time, and the monitoring of partisan broadcasts (Canada, *Broadcasting Act* 1958, s. 11(1)(*f*) and (*i*)). In practice, however, the BBG laid down general guidelines for free time broadcasts and left it to the parties and the broadcasters to agree on the details (LaCalamita 1984, 547).

In the 1960s, in response to the growing concern about political advertising on television, a process of legislative reform began to take place in Canada, starting with the Barbeau Committee (1963–66) and continuing with the *Election Expenses Act* (1974) and amendments in 1979 and 1983, Bill C-79 (1986–87), *An Act to amend the Canada Elections Act*, and culminating in the work of the present Commission. All of these efforts have attempted to refine and elaborate what is meant by fairness and equity in election campaigns in the face of dramatically changing campaign practices.

It was not until the beginning of the 1960s, however, that the issue of political broadcasting became pre-eminent. In response, the BBG issued a document entitled "Political and Controversial Broadcasting Policies" (BBG 1961) which outlined the procedures to be followed during election campaigns. The BBG's policy for dramatized political broadcasts permitted the following:

(a) Multiple speaker, discussion and question and answer presentation may be used provided that the sponsoring party takes responsibility for those taking part and for what they say and what they do, and that they appear in their own identity ...

(b) To illustrate verbal presentations, visual materials will be permitted as follows: Charts, graphics and maps, providing the sponsoring party furnishes all such material and takes full responsibility for the nature of the material and the use made thereof.

(c) Provided the material depicts real events, including the normal activities of a candidate engaged in an election, film and video tape clips, disks, slides, animation and still photographs may be used. (BBG 1961, s. III.1)

In 1962 the BBG responded to inquiries asking for a definition of the term "unnecessarily theatrical" in its restrictions on dramatization by providing the following rules:

1. Political cartoons, still or animated, are not permissible.
2. Background music inserted into a studio presentation is not permitted ...
3. Jingles on political broadcasts are not allowed.
4. Speakers cannot arrange dialogues in the studio between themselves and imaginary opponents.
5. "Role playing" is not permitted ...
6. Parties may not introduce film footage of political opponents ... (BBG 1962b)

The 1961 Circular also presented guidelines for the allocation of free time in section IV:

> Any free time network broadcasts over a Canadian network will be arranged by agreement between the network operator and representatives of interested political parties. In the event that agreement cannot be reached for such free time broadcasts, the Board will, upon the matter being referred to it by either the network operator or the representatives of the party concerned, allocate the available time in such fair and reasonable manner as it deems necessary. Nothing herein shall be construed as placing upon a network operator an obligation to allocate free time for political broadcasting. (BBG 1961)

The 1960s saw a new type of election campaign with an emphasis on expensive television spots created by advertising agencies. The agencies knew how to use television. Their market research (public opinion polling) and knowledge of television techniques led to a new emphasis on image-oriented spot broadcasts. The single most important consequence was a sharp rise in the cost of election campaigns, particularly in the share of the parties' election budgets spent on media advertising (Seidle 1985, 114). The increased cost of using television in political campaigns strained party resources. In fact, the escalation of expenses required to finance four election campaigns in six years (1957, 1958, 1962, 1963) led to serious consideration of ways to limit election expenses and to provide disclosure of political contributions.

In 1963 the Liberal government established the Advisory Committee to Study Curtailment of Election Expenses, which became known as the Barbeau Committee (Canada, Committee 1966). The Committee's principal recommendations were:

- legal recognition and registration of political parties, which should then be held legally responsible for their financial activities;
- reimbursement of a portion of the parties' advertising expenses and the provision of free time to all registered parties;
- election advertising to be permitted only during the last four weeks prior to an election in order to restrict expenses;
- disclosure of the income and expenditures of parties and candidates; and
- tax concessions for financial donors to political parties.

For several years, little was heard of these recommendations, but they were given more attention in the early 1970s.

Between 1957 and 1968, the broadcasting industry expanded to include large private stations serving major urban markets, and the BBG licensed the private English-language CTV network in 1961. The *Broadcasting Act* was revised in 1968. Regulatory authority was expanded and a new agency replaced the BBG, the Canadian Radio-Television Commission, later renamed the Canadian Radio-television and Telecommunications Commission (CRTC).

In addition to its powers under the *Broadcasting Act*, the CRTC was given authority in the 1974 amendments to the *Canada Elections Act* to allocate paid and free time among the registered political parties (Canada, *Canada Elections Act* 1985, ss. 307(1) and 316). Under these amendments, parties were required for the first time to register (ibid., ss. 24–32). The CRTC continued to be responsible for ensuring that time for party political broadcasts was allocated on an equitable basis and for ensuring that party advertisements were not excessively theatrical. However, it left the latter responsibility to the parties themselves, responding only to complaints (Boyer 1983, 370).

The 1968 *Broadcasting Act* also retained, in section 19, the regulations that the sponsor and the political party be identified in political broadcasts. (The sponsor identification provision was dropped in the 1991 revision.)

Subsequent to the Act and in preparation for the June 1968 election, the CRTC defined political broadcasts of two minutes or less as commercial content. In June 1971, the House of Commons Special Committee on Election Expenses recommended a series of amendments to the *Canada Elections Act* which followed the general pattern of the proposals made by the 1966 Barbeau Committee. In June 1973, Bill C-203 (eventually the *Election Expenses Act*) was introduced, proposing changes to three statutes – the *Canada Elections Act*, the *Income Tax Act* and the *Broadcasting Act* (Seidle 1985, 116). The intention of the reforms – the principal purpose of the *Election Expenses Act* – was to control election spending by both parties and candidates.

Seidle classifies these changes under four broad headings:

1. *Party recognition and agency* ... All registered parties must appoint a chief agent who is to ensure the spending limit is not exceeded during an election ...

2. *Spending restrictions.* Parties and candidates are subject to statutory spending limits ... must file a return of expenses ... and ... must submit a return of expenses and contributions ... Parties and candidates are prohibited from advertising on the broadcast media or in any publication other than during a four-week period ending on midnight of the day before polling day.

3. *Reimbursements.* All candidates who receive 15 per cent of the votes cast in an electoral district are entitled to a reimbursement outlined in a formula in the *Act*. Registered parties were reimbursed for up to 50 per cent of the expenses they incurred on radio and television advertising. [This was changed in 1983 to a general reimbursement of a portion of all campaign expenses.]

4. *Tax credits.* Taxpayers may subtract from their federal income tax an amount based on a sliding scale that favours relatively small donations. (Seidle 1985, 118)

The 1974 amendments to the *Canada Elections Act* also affected broadcasting in other respects. Sections 13.7 and 61.2 limited the length of the electoral campaign for the candidate and parties; section 70.1 restricted the right to advertise during a campaign to registered candidates and parties; and section 99.1 dealt with the central issue of political broadcasting (LaCalamita 1984, 549). Section 99.1 required that each broadcaster make 6 1/2 hours of air time available for purchase by registered parties, each of which was allocated a maximum that it could purchase from any one broadcaster (a figure based on its success in the previous election). Parties were allowed to purchase as much of their advertising allocation as they wished within the overall campaign spending limits (Fletcher 1988, 162).

The Act provided for fines of up to $25 000 for any broadcaster or network operator who failed to provide the required 6 1/2 hours, who failed to comply with a binding allocation of time, or who gave one party extra time without offering the same to other parties (Boyer 1983, 455). What section 99.1(16) did, in effect, was to compel the broadcaster

.to provide broadcast time to all registered parties and to make time for political advertising, even if corporate advertisers had time booked prior to the election.

The role of arbitrator was assigned to the CRTC, which was to step in when parties and broadcasters could not agree on matters such as the time allocations, scheduling of paid and free time, and rates for paid time. The new rules restricted paid advertising to the final half of the eight-week campaign, regulated the allocation of paid and free time, and provided for reimbursement from the federal treasury of one-half the cost of radio and television commercials purchased by registered parties (LaCalamita 1984, 559). These new election expenses and election advertising rules were first applied in the 1979 election.

Amendments to the *Canada Elections Act* in November 1983, contained in Bill C-169, changed the former subsidy of radio and television time costs for registered parties into a refund of a portion of registered party expenses (Paltiel 1988, 142; Fletcher 1988, 163). The print media had lobbied for the change to the reimbursement formula, citing discrimination. The repayment for registered parties was transformed from a reimbursement of broadcast costs into a general refund of up to 22.5 percent of election expenses for any registered party, provided it spent at least 10 percent of the party's allowed limit. The changes also linked the expenditure ceilings to variations in the Consumer Price Index (Canada, *Canada Elections Act* 1985, ss. 322(1), 39(3)). In 1983, section 99 of the Act was amended, defining prime time as 6:00 PM to midnight, rather than the previous 7:00 PM to 11:00 PM. This redefinition allowed broadcasters extra time in which to place the required political paid time.

In the 1985 *Canada Elections Act*, section 304(4) made provisions for an independent broadcasting arbitrator to be selected by the parties themselves, providing the choice was unanimous. Section 304(5) states that where the parties are unable to reach a unanimous decision, the arbitrator shall be appointed by the chief electoral officer. If the parties cannot reach a satisfactory agreement on allocation of paid and free time, the broadcasting arbitrator is empowered to make the allocations, applying a formula set out in the Act (s. 310). However, no registered party may be allocated more than 50 percent of the aggregate broadcast time available.

Spending on election advertising has increased steadily since the passage of the *Election Expenses Act* of 1974. The 1984 campaign saw a sharp rise in party spending. The three largest parties spent about $12 million on advertising, mostly for television, including production costs and air time, but not research. The latter category – polls and focus groups – is not covered under the spending limits. In 1984, for the first time, the spending limits were adjusted, not only for the growth of the electorate but also for inflation (as measured by the Consumer Price Index). The upper limit for a registered party with a full slate of candidates was increased to $6 391 497, up 40 percent from that set in 1980 (Paltiel 1988, 151–52).

Fairness and Equity

The regulatory response to the rise of broadcast political advertising in Canada rests on the fundamental principles of fairness and equity. These principles have been elaborated primarily in terms of access to the broadcast media and the reimbursement of election expenses. The elements reflected in free time broadcasts (appendix C), paid time advertising (appendix D) and partial reimbursement of election costs have been concerned with the following questions: Should registered political parties receive free time and paid time and in what amounts? Should parties receive reimbursement of election expenses and in what amounts?

In 1974, the equitable allocation principles of the reforms became "legally anchored" in the *Broadcasting Act* and the *Canada Elections Act* (LaCalamita 1984, 556–57). LaCalamita calls the Canadian political broadcasting regulations a "careful restriction as a means of protecting and controlling the political process," noting that the regulations have sought "the facilitation of free speech while maintaining fair and equitable exposure in the face of potentially overwhelming partisan spending" (ibid., 543). Since 1936, regulatory bodies have consciously attempted to limit inequality in the amount of broadcast time made available to political parties. With the introduction of Bill C-203, which eventually became the *Election Expenses Act*, regulation further attempted to reduce the imbalance between parties with respect to funds and time. The main purpose of the *Election Expenses Act* was to "control election spending by both parties and candidates ... It was also argued at the time that the spending limits and reimbursements would help to equalize chances among parties and candidates" (Seidle 1985, 117). However, communication issues also had to be addressed: which registered political parties were financially able to produce free time or paid advertisements and to purchase broadcast time (see appendix E), and which registered political parties could realistically expect reimbursements (see appendix D).

CRTC Public Notice No. 1988–142 sets out guidelines for election campaign broadcasting. It states that "throughout the history of broadcasting in Canada, licensees, as part of their service to the public, have been required to cover elections. Moreover, where licensees have allocated paid or free campaign time, they have been required to do so in a manner that is equitable to all political parties and rival candidates. The purpose of these requirements is to ensure the public's right to be informed of the issues involved so that it has sufficient knowledge to make an informed choice from among the various parties and candidates" (CRTC 1988b, 7–8). The CRTC defines "equitable" as "fair and just," noting that equitable does not necessarily mean equal, but that candidates and parties are entitled to some coverage that will give them the opportunity to present their ideas to the public (ibid., 8). These guidelines apply to election broadcasting at all levels of government.

Although the existing system offers the "opportunity" for registered political parties to participate in elections, the reality is that few smaller registered political parties can afford to do so in any meaningful way. It seems clear that the present system of reimbursement and broadcast time allocation favours the larger political parties. The smaller parties rarely receive reimbursements under the current formula and are allocated only minimal amounts of free and paid time. Even a wealthy party could not run an effective broadcast campaign if it had not been at least moderately successful in the previous election and had accordingly qualified for time.

Information on the free and paid time actually used by all parties was not available for this study. What is known is the amount of paid time that the parties were permitted to purchase under the formula. It appears that even the larger parties were able to purchase only some of the time made available to them. Smaller parties are rarely able to afford the cost of the air time, let alone the production costs for television spots.

For the 1988 election, the Progressive Conservative party was allocated 48 percent of the available paid time, the Liberal party 22 percent and the New Democratic Party 16.5 percent. In contrast, the Reform Party of Canada and the Communist Party of Canada each received 0.7 percent of the available time. The Green Party of Canada and the Parti Rhinocéros fared better than the Reform or Communist parties, receiving 1 percent and 2 percent, respectively (see appendix D).

The allocation of free time was similar, favouring parties that held seats in the House of Commons. In 1988, the Progressive Conservative, Liberal and New Democratic parties were allocated 47, 21 and 16 percent of the time available, respectively. The smallest share – 0.9 percent – went to the Communist, Green and Confederation of Regions Western parties (see appendix C).

It is clear that one of the barriers to the purchase of advertising time by minor parties is the cost involved in all phases of researching and executing an advertising strategy. When the total election spending of minor parties is reviewed, it is also clear that they cannot realistically hope to compete effectively in national campaigns. For example, the cost of purchasing one 30-second television advertisement on the CTV network in November 1988 was $12 279.[2] The total campaign spending for the Confederation of Regions Western Party, for example, was $6 868. More established minor parties, such as the Communist Party, reported campaign spending totalling $37 001. Neither party could afford to purchase significant television advertising time.

As the figures for expenses and advertising time illustrate, the *Canada Elections Act* does not provide a "true" opportunity for all registered political parties to participate on an equal basis. The parties with seats in the House have a distinct advantage over other registered political parties because they have more campaign funds. Yet, based on the formulae in place, they also receive more free broadcast time, have the right to buy more paid time and receive reimbursement for campaign expenditures. Indeed, the goal of an electoral structure that is equitable to minor registered political parties and to nonpartisan interest groups remains elusive.

In fact, during the 1988 election, independent spending, i.e., spending unauthorized by any registered party, was much more significant than expenditures of smaller parties. The Canadian Alliance for Trade and Job Opportunities, a coalition of business organizations, spent $2 million promoting free trade. As Janet Hiebert indicates, "The coalition ran a series of four-page newspaper advertisements entitled 'Straight Talk on Free Trade,' which appeared many times in Toronto and at least twice in forty other cities across the country" (Hiebert 1989–90, 80). Further, the National Citizens' Coalition spent $720 000, mostly to promote free trade, and the Alberta government ran an extensive pro–free trade campaign within the province. The principal anti–free trade group was the Pro-Canada Network, which estimated its spending at $750 000 (Hiebert 1989–90). Many of the advertisements run by these interest groups named candidates and parties, a clear violation of the 1983 amendments to the *Canada Elections Act*.

Policy Considerations

Critical analysis of the development of political advertising in Canada has not been extensive. It must be recognized that the ability to gather information relevant to policy research in this area or to evaluate the impact of changing practices is hampered by the fact that much of the information is proprietary or not reported (for example, each party's expenditures by media, by region and by week of the campaign are not readily available). Yet it is clear to most observers that political advertising involves a number of very important policy issues, including:

1. *Fairness*

   a. Is access to media channels broad enough to include all legitimate political voices?
   b. How should the process of access be structured so as not to constitute a bias in favour of any party?
   c. How are we to deal with nonparty voices who wish to use broadcast advertising to address issues of public importance during the election?

2. *Equity*

   a. What model or definition of equity is appropriate to assure balance in political debates through the media?
   b. Is the current model open to exploitation by parties and/or broadcasters?
   c. Do the high costs of election campaigns constitute an entrance barrier to new parties?
   d. Should there be public "subsidization" or refunds for political advertising, if this subsidization is not in the interest of equity?

3. *Ethics*

   a. Can "reasonable grounds" for restricting political speech be defined and harm found that might sustain a constitutional challenge?
   b. Is negative advertising likely to disturb the decorum of Canadian politics and create unfair advantages for strategists willing to use it?
   c. How should the responsibility for libel, misleading or controversial statements made in political advertising be allocated among broadcasters, regulatory authorities and sponsors?
   d. Should candidates or parties have the right of response to statements made about them in the broadcast media?
   e. What role of monitoring, researching, informing and educating the public about political advertising and its regulation should the chief electoral officer have?

It is impossible to examine these issues in great detail in this study. However, we hope that the background material and analysis provided here will sharpen the focus of the debate and suggest directions for reform.

PRINT MEDIA DEBATES ON POLITICAL ADVERTISING

In this section of the study we examine print media coverage of the issues surrounding campaign advertising. This examination has three purposes. The first is to refine our list of central issues by comparing it to the issues identified by journalists assessing specific campaigns. The second is to assess the quality of the print media's scrutiny of campaign advertising practices. The third objective is to consider the potential of the print media as an alternative to self-policing by parties or formal regulation. In order to analyse the press debates on political advertising, 103 print media stories and feature articles were selected for study in the period 1977–90. These were drawn mainly from the *Canadian Business and Current Affairs Index*, which contains articles that appeared in "500 Canadian journals and newspapers" between the years 1982 and 1990. A search was also made of the *Canadian Newspaper Index* and the *Canadian Periodical Index* for relevant entries between 1977 and 1981 to incorporate into our database. The timeframe of 1977–90 allowed us to sample stories that surrounded four national elections as well as those appearing in the years prior to and after these elections.

It is significant to note that the comprehensive *Canadian Business and Current Affairs Index* revealed 67 stories on the subject of "Elections Advertising" and an additional 20 stories on "Political Advertising" (one of these was also included in the category of "Elections Advertising"), giving a total of 86 stories for the 9-year period covered by this index. When this total is set against the 14 338 stories listed by this index under "Elections" or the 9 804 shown for "Advertising" for this same period, political advertising received minimal attention in purely numerical terms. Our intention is, however, to focus not on the numbers, but on the scope and depth of the coverage by the press. Public scrutiny is an important constraint on unethical campaign behaviour, and public debate on campaign tactics is desirable in a democracy.

Preference for Event over Process

The overall analysis of the news stories reveals, not surprisingly, an overwhelming bias toward coverage of events occasioned by political advertising rather than the process involved or the issues arising from its marked growth over the past two decades in Canadian political practice. While the legislative debates, initiatives and actions taken have been in reaction to the more controversial aspects of political advertising, the print media debates and coverage have barely kept pace with the variety and depth of arguments that have emerged.

For example, there was a remarkable silence in the print media concerning the adoption of Bill C-169 in 1983, which updated and amended the long-awaited Bill C-58. The event was reported, but there was no evidence of a deep reflection upon, or even a full appreciation of, the implications for so-called "third party" involvement in election advertising in the 1983 legislation. When the issue burst upon the public scene in the 1984 National Citizens' Coalition (NCC) Alberta court case, there was, again, reporting of the event without discussion of the far-reaching effect of the ruling as it related to the provisions of the *Canada Elections Act* or to freedom of expression. This seems particularly ironic when one notes that the NCC, which brought the action against the 1983 legislation, claimed support from the Canadian Daily Newspaper Publishers Association among other groups in Canada.

Our examination of the news stories covering the period in question identifies issues that predominated in the popular press as well as important areas that received little or no coverage. Our conclusion points to some of the major limitations and obstacles that explain the lapses in the print media's coverage; some of these are partially implicit in the way the press is organized and functions in North America, but others are fostered by party politics and the election environment in Canada.

THEMES IN PRINT MEDIA COVERAGE OF POLITICAL ADVERTISING
The issues covered in the print media deal with five main themes, each with its own subthemes:

1. leader image manipulation;
2. polling and marketing strategies;
3. the regulatory process;
4. freedom of expression; and
5. structural/economic issues.

Leader Image Manipulation, Advertising and Marketing Strategies
News reports that stressed leader image manipulation often emphasized subthemes such as leader-centredness, personality rather than issues, image politics, the use of advertising agencies and advertising strategies, politicians as marketable products, and the backroom manipulation of politicians and the public to secure election victories. These subthemes appeared in the majority of the stories on political advertising.

They took one of two forms, being either straightforward reports on the content of political advertising used by one party or another or commentaries on political advertising as a whole. Fifty-four of the 103 articles in our database dealt with image manipulation.

A review of articles from two of Canada's leading publications illuminates the history of the leader-as-marketable-product reading of political advertising.

In April 1962 Richard Gwyn, in an article in the *Financial Post* entitled "Admen and Scientists Run This Election," sounds the alarm to herald a new era in Canadian politics. "The 20th century and Canadian politics come to terms this year. The nation will have its first scientific election. For the first time the skills of sociologists, statisticians, advertising experts, pollsters and mass communications experts may be as decisive as the age-old talents of politicians. Two completely new weapons are being brought into the fray: Intensive, privately hired public opinion surveys and sophisticated, probing statistical analysis. To these are added the latest techniques of advertising and mass communications" (Gwyn 1962, 25).

Later in the article Gwyn proceeds to spell out what he sees as the natural outcome of this new tendency in political affairs: "Criticisms have often been made that political parties are being sold to the public like soap or toothpaste. This is exactly what is happening. The criticism is interesting mainly because it implies there is some other way by which a political party can win these days. There may be some other way but no party is willing to take the risk of trying it" (Gwyn 1962, 26). He concludes darkly: "Democracy, if that word is taken to mean government by conscious approval of a majority of the people, may have to be re-examined. So also is any concept of an election as representing the considered judgement of the public on the real merits of rival parties." Gwyn, in this early analysis of image politics, identifies the nodes of the debate that is still taking place.

But even at this early juncture, others were already beginning to question the power of the "back-room conspiracy" theory. Writer Barbara Moon's feature article in *Maclean's* was illustrated by a drawing of six strategists representing the four political parties in the 1962 federal election (the Liberals, the NDP, Social Credit and the Progressive Conservatives) moving, as in a game of chess, doll figures of the four party leaders (pawns?). The strategists simultaneously read polls and arranged camera angles for their individual leaders. Looming over the strategists themselves are two huge, disembodied hands with strings attached to each finger, the strings dissolving into the pictures of the strategists (Moon 1962).

In her investigation for the article, Moon attempted to track down the real power behind the strategists in the major political parties, but failed to find conclusive evidence. A grand manipulator was hard to find, although many lesser figures admitted to having a role in plotting election strategies. It was generally conceded, however, that there was "almost universal usage in Ottawa, during the campaign, for *The Making of the President, 1960* by Theodore White. The Book's message [it was referred to simply as 'The Book'] for campaign planners is that if you pinpoint the pivotal electoral districts, psychoanalyze the voters, come across well on TV, are tactful to lesser politicians who have influence and tough with the rest, have enough money, troops and kinfolk – and if the wind is right – you can get elected" (Moon 1962, 42).

Moon completes her assignment without finding much evidence to support the grand conspiracy or manipulation theory and suggests that, given the volatility of voters, luck plays just as big a part as strategy. Her article, far from contradicting Gwyn's, however, adds another point of view and illustrates how quickly image politics, supported by astute packaging and marketing of political "products," was coming to be taken for granted. The question, then, was whether it worked or not.

It seems like a throwback to the sixties to read a story entitled "$6 Million Worth of Spit and Polish," an article written by Carol Goar in 1980 for the *Winnipeg Free Press*. Goar describes not only a "strange new world" of plastic, but a secretive and even sinister one as well, where the advertising experts are totally in charge. They are the high priests of this world, and television is the sacred altar. As Goar notes: "A strange new plastic structure is springing up on the election horizon to replace the smoky train stations of yesteryear. Enter, if you will, this airtight television cocoon in which Joe Clark never stumbles, Ed Broadbent never sounds shrill and Pierre Trudeau oozes humble sincerity. Visitors may proceed into the vestibule, but no further. The private offices of the three high-priced Toronto admen who are now working 18 hours a day to polish and package the country's political leaders are a sanctum so closed that few party insiders – let alone ordinary voters – ever get past the door" (Goar 1980, 97). Goar may have overdramatized the situation, but she has nonetheless captured the suspicion of, and fascination with, the power of broadcasting – television in particular – to influence elections in Canada. There is no doubt that political advertising, in the eyes of the press, had by this time emerged as a major player in election campaigns, but was not seen as an altogether welcome or even legitimate player. In addition, Goar amply illustrates the development of this particular trend in electioneering and the print media's continuing concern with and focus on the subthemes already identified.

Here is a 1988 version of the same type of commentary, taken from the Montreal *Gazette*, a front-page article written by Jennifer Robinson, entitled "Slick Television Ad Campaign Under Way to Sell Parties to Canadians":

> Ketchup, Mulroney, Turner or oatmeal: When it comes to selling a product, there's not much difference between methods used in peddling a political party or a consumer product ...
>
> "The only thing that changes are the words – it's all image," said Margaret Buhlman, vice-president of the Toronto-based polling and market-research firm Decima Research ...
>
> The political advertising that began yesterday is the product of sophisticated polling and market research – you figure out what voters or consumers want and mould your message accordingly ...
>
> "It's how you package a given product – a bottle of ketchup for example – so that it corresponds to the market that you're trying to go after," Buhlman said. (Robinson 1988, A1)

Among the subthemes within this group of stories, Goar and Robinson focus on the most popular one, the leader-centred package, and in some instances on the battle that occurs around that image among contending parties in the form of negative advertising, a topic that will be dealt with later. Thirty-three of the 54 articles identified under the theme of "leader image manipulation" touch upon the issue of the leader-centred story. The examples below show the variety of ways in which this is done.

A front-page article in *Marketing* (Smyka 1979) entitled "This Time the 'Products' Are Political Leaders" used the old image of a horse race among political rivals to develop its story on the role of advertising and advertising agencies in the national election of 22 May. Although the leaders are the focal point, they are still seen as leading a team.

The 1980 election campaign generated stories that supported this trend in a general way, but the leaders were reported to have been positioned either in the foreground or the background, depending on where they were being "sold" or on who was doing the "selling." This is one of the points made by Hubert Bauch in the Montreal *Gazette*:

> In the rest of Canada the Liberals will be stressing the Liberal team. There Pierre Trudeau is their greatest liability, just as Clark is their best friend. In the national media campaign, says [Gordon] Ashworth [the Liberal campaign director], Trudeau will be in "some" of the spots.

In Quebec, on the other hand, where he is the most popular politician in the province, Trudeau will be in all the spots. Here the slant is to present Trudeau as the senior statesman; a sort of parental figure who speaks to people in their living rooms from his living room.

The Liberal ads don't even bother to attack Joe Clark. But then most people in Quebec tend to know the Prime Minister as "Joe Binne" – "binne" being slang for bean and a play on the Clark company that cans beans. So the hatchet job here is largely done. (Bauch 1980, 10)

A leader-centred campaign strategy is compatible with both negative and positive advertisements. The increasing sophistication of media buying permits spots to be targeted at segments of the electorate most likely to be influenced by a particular type of advertisement, positive or negative.

In the 1984 national elections, the news stories were firmly fixed on this aspect of political advertising. In *Marketing*, the article "Turner Is the Product That Liberal Ads Will Sell" appeared on the front page in August, and an editorial by Colin Muncie in September was even more forthright. Entitled "The Selling of Brian, John and Ed," it was extremely critical of the "selling" approach of campaigns and summed up a number of the key arguments:

Having just gone through several weeks of advertising hype and media manipulation by the image-makers behind John Turner, Brian Mulroney and Ed Broadbent, the most charitable comment we have about Canada's method of picking a new government and a new prime minister is that it's at least preferable to the way they do it in Russia.

We suspect we are not alone in feeling that we were ... deceived by the Progressive Conservatives, deceived by the Liberals, deceived by the New Democrats.

Most of us voted for one of three party leaders in this election rather than the local candidate best qualified to serve our riding, which is what we should do ...

What they served up, especially on TV, was a bum-patting Turner who betrays his nervousness of the TV camera by braying like a jackass; Mulroney, a man with a zip-on smile and all the glib smarm of a TV game-show host; and Broadbent, a man who gets so excited during a speech that his voice reaches such a shrill pitch he sounds like he's just been "goosed" ...

As a result of the work of the image-makers, the best they [voters of Canada] can hope for is that the man who will lead them for the next four or five years is nothing like the one they saw on TV in this election. (Muncie 1984, 4)

This is a colourful argument against leader-centred political advertising and politics. But the *Toronto Star* (1984) was not as convinced in its examination entitled: "The Selling of a Leader: Do TV Ads Work? – Experts Doubt They Do Much to Change Anyone's Mind."

Hugh Winsor's analysis in the *Globe and Mail* focused on Norman Atkins, chief strategist of the Conservatives. The article opens with this recipe: "Take a candidate who's something of a quick study, add nine months of meticulous preparation and unlimited funds, marry them to the latest technology and stir. That was the recipe for the Conservative landslide last week, according to the man [Atkins] who did a lot of the stirring" (Winsor 1984, 7). By the end of the article it is made clear that Mulroney defeated Turner in a one-on-one strategy struggle. The Progressive Conservatives were elected to replace the Liberal government not because of issues, but because of the image of the leader. During campaigns, parties seem almost redundant. For example, when the Liberals' commercial asking "Who would you trust to run the country?" hit the airwaves, Atkins notes, "our research was showing us that by that time Brian was running ahead on trust" (ibid.).

The battle of leader images is picked up by the print media again in the 1988 elections. Patricia Poirier's report in the *Globe and Mail*, "Parties Blanket Francophones with $4 Million in Election Ads," gives the following details:

> The ads, which were unveiled yesterday in Montreal and began to be broadcast last night, are surprising only for what they fail to high-light.
>
> The Progressive Conservative ads feature a statesman-like Brian Mulroney, speaking in soothing tones about the economy, the environment and new federal-provincial co-operation.
>
> There is not one word about the Tory team in Quebec.
>
> Liberal ads focus on issues, such as the environment, free trade and job creation, and the message is delivered by an anonymous, off-camera voice.
>
> There is not one reference to Liberal Leader John Turner or his team.
>
> NDP ads also focus on the issues, the plight of the elderly, the environment and fair taxation. Although party leader Edward Broadbent appears in only one television commercial, his name is mentioned four or five times in the other ads to reinforce his personal popularity. (Poirier 1988, A11)

As each party attempts to capitalize on the image of the leader, its rivals are openly attacking that image. On that same day, a front-page article in the *Toronto Star* reported that the "Liberals have launched an advertising blitz on French television depicting Prime Minister Brian Mulroney as a liar, surrounded by scandals, who has sold out to big business and the Americans" (McKenzie 1988, 1).

On 2 November, the *Toronto Star* published Val Sears' article entitled, "Tories Plan to Step Up 'Liar' Ads on Turner." Many commentators view such advertisements as politics at its worst and a trend inspired by American practices. According to Sears, "the success of 'black' or negative advertising in the Republican national campaign for George Bush has been an inspiration for all three parties in Canada, although the Tories have been using the toughest language. One commercial has a voice saying: 'John Turner is lying. John Turner is trying to mislead Canadians. Canadians deserve better' " (Sears 1988).

Even the NDP leader could not escape criticism. The Montreal *Gazette* reported that " 'Humorous' Ads Compare Broadbent to Marx, Ayatollah" in its issue of 25 October (Barrett 1988). The twist here is that the advertising volleys aimed at the NDP leader were not fired by another registered political party, but by an interest group, the National Citizens' Coalition.

The press coverage of leader-centred political advertising thus also captured the upsurge of negative advertising. In the process, it also demonstrated the paramountcy that advertising and advertising agencies have achieved in political campaigns.

In the 1979 election, there was more explicit discussion of the link between the role of advertising agencies in the campaign and the politician-as-product approach to political marketing. *Marketing* magazine reported that Liberals would once again be using a special-purpose agency – Red Leaf Communications – headed by Jerry Grafstein and staffed by top professionals from a number of agencies. The Conservatives employed Media Buying Services, whose top man, Peter Swain, "beefed up his agency with outside help" (Smyka 1979, 1).

By 1984, according to a list provided by *Marketing* (1984, 1), "outside help" for the Liberal campaign included the presidents or chief executive officers of at least seven major advertising agencies. In its issue of 16 July, *Marketing* had already given some indication of the strength of the Progressive Conservatives' media team. In Quebec alone, the team included five presidents or vice-presidents of noted media agencies.

The media teams were not only high powered, but large and possessed of considerable talent. Yet it is interesting to note that apart from *Marketing*, none of the major publications in Canada seemed up to this point to have reported on the increasing influence of the publicity teams. By the 1988 election, however, high-profile advertising agencies, along with their sophisticated election advertising campaigns, particularly geared for television, were taken for granted. As Murray Campbell noted in the *Globe and Mail*:

> You could call it the "boob-tube election," except that the label ignores a complex interplay of many factors that political scientists say have made the current and 1984 election campaigns dramatically different from those that Pierre Trudeau waged for the Liberals from 1968 to 1980.
>
> Fifteen years ago, newspaper reporters used to rail against politicians trying to tailor their campaigns to TV. Now, even the surliest of print reporters accepts with a shrug the need to get videotape for the evening news and the fact that all political campaigns are geared to TV.
>
> But the increased prominence of television, with its ability to convey images and emotions, is only part of the story. The sharp rise of public opinion polls, along with the widespread acceptance that it is the character of party leaders that should determine how a vote is cast, have contributed to a consistently high degree of voter volatility in recent years. (Campbell 1988, 1)

Regulatory Process Issues

The question of standards and/or controls for election advertising has not been addressed in any meaningful way by the popular press in Canada. Despite the undoubted influence of media teams in shaping the agenda of recent campaigns, critical analysis of the process has been slight. The major dailies have picked up very little of this discussion, although *Marketing* carried two stories during the 1984 election campaign, hinting at such an influence. Discussion has focused instead on criticizing the packaging of the leaders.

Prior to the advent of radio and television, politicians were obliged to meet their constituents face to face in a public forum. Promises and sales pitches from politicians could be met with direct questions and open challenges by interested persons in public exchanges. With the arrival of the electronic media, however, politicians could enter a voter's home, uninvited, to peddle their wares. Through radio and television advertising, politicians are able to make promises and claims without fear of immediate challenge. Politicians are allowed to use the latest advertising gimmicks produced by high-powered media teams targeted to specific audiences. Apart from general legal constraints, the standards and limitations that govern other types of advertising do not apply to political advertising. Competing messages and/or images produced by other parties often escalate into negative campaigning on both sides. Voters are thus frequently left confused, frustrated and angry, and finally, understandably, grow apathetic.

Only *Marketing*, a magazine for the advertising industry, has had much to say about the regulatory issues raised by party campaign advertising practices. In 1984, for example, Rob Wilson presented in *Marketing* a catalogue of the "sins" that political advertising can commit with impunity:

> Despite the fact that much advertising is heavily controlled, either by the industry itself or by direct legislation (such as beverage alcohol), election ads seem to be immune to normal standards of good taste or false claims.
>
> There will be all sorts of promises, for example. None of them will be kept, and very few will be intended to be kept.
>
> There will be all sorts of criticisms of the other guy. Much of it will be true. That, however, doesn't mean that the critic would do anything differently, or intends to change things.
>
> Much of the criticism will be false. Perhaps not blatantly – the truth being squeezed just enough to make the intended political point.
>
> What would happen if a major department store such as Eaton's advertised that television sets were going to be sold for $200 all next week, but charged you $400 when you came to the store?
>
> Apart from having to handle the outrage of customers, the store would be charged and fined for false advertising quicker than you could say Timothy.
>
> Eaton's, or Sears, or any other merchant or manufacturer has to, under penalty of law, keep the advertising promises he makes.
>
> And, when it comes to comparative advertising, companies are enjoined to tread a careful line between saying their competitor's product is junk, and making a fair sales comparison.
>
> Any comparison, say on something like taste, has to be backed up by some form of research or survey. You can't just badmouth the other guy for the sake of making yourself look good.
>
> There will be much in the way of criticism and comparative advertising in the election to come ...
>
> And, I suppose the democratic process needs the freedom, denied to businesses, that allows them to make wild claims and promises, and belittle their competitors.
>
> I wouldn't blame businesses for being more than a little jealous. And I wouldn't blame them for feeling that their ads will become a little bit tainted because election ads have so few controls. (Wilson 1984, 12)

Wilson's provocative critique of party campaign advertising provides support for the argument that only some form of legislated guidelines or regulations will prevent abuses and ensure that election campaign advertising is socially responsible and informative for voters.

Also in 1984, Cautley Tatham, commenting in *Marketing* on campaign advertising, suggests that it reflects badly on the advertising industry and adds this observation:

> Commenting on the U.S primaries, the U.K. publication *Campaign* wrote: "Despite the supposed expertise of those involved, political advertising is easily the most obviously manipulative of all ad categories. Legally, there are no restrictions on content (unlike other categories), so campaigners can, and do, say what they like. Political advertising tends to talk down to people. It is patronising and boring; it is unimaginative, badly produced and predictable; and it lies. Worse still, in campaigner's eyes, it gets found out."
>
> Canada, as always, is not far behind. "Selling politicians like soap?" queries one marketer, "I wish that were still true." (Tatham 1984, 13)

The primary concern for *Marketing* and its readers has been, of course, the possible negative effects of campaign advertising on the credibility of commercial advertising, not the implications for Canadian democratic discourse. These implications would appear to fall within the traditional mandate of the popular press but the major daily newspapers did not provide their readers with a parallel discussion of these issues during the period studied. We found little examination of questions of standards in campaign advertising, nor of approaches to regulation or self-policing by parties or the advertising industry.

It appears from our overview of the evolution of political marketing that competition among the parties is not by itself sufficient to ensure that campaign advertising plays a positive role in democratic discourse. Media scrutiny of the techniques of political marketing employed in Canadian elections would undoubtedly help to deter abuses and stimulate public debate.

Freedom of Expression Issues

Newspaper and magazine items written about freedom of expression and political advertising have focused primarily on issues involving advocacy advertising by third parties. Such interest-group election advertising became an issue after an Alberta court ruled in 1984 (*National Citizens' Coalition Inc./Coalition nationale des citoyens inc. v. Canada (Attorney General)*) that advertising restrictions during elections, added to the

Canada Elections Act in 1983, were a violation of the *Canadian Charter of Rights and Freedoms*. (For further discussion of this case, see the section "A Framework for Regulating Political Advertising," below.) Apart from the coverage of the court's decision, the press did not mention this matter during the 1984 election. The case came to the fore in 1988, however, when various special-interest and lobby groups spent millions of dollars on both sides of the free trade debate.

Most coverage of campaign advertising by advocacy groups took the form of straight reporting on expenditures by various groups or commentary on the possible impact of independent spending on the principle of election spending limits. Parties and candidates pointed out that they were fettered while third parties were not. There was also some concern expressed that advocacy groups could ignore the blackout rules that restrict party and candidate advertising to a four-week period beginning in mid-campaign and ending 48 hours before the close of polls on election day.

While the dailies produced most of the "event" reports on independent campaign spending, *Marketing* published a few editorials on their implications, especially after George Allen, the elections commissioner, spoke out strongly against the growing trend. *Marketing*'s first article covered the commissioner's observations and included a review of the Alberta court case. The first three paragraphs give the general tenor of the story:

> The unprecedented deluge of third-party ads supporting the Free Trade Agreement that led up to the federal vote has revealed a huge flaw in the rules governing election advertising, says the commissioner of elections.
>
> A 1984 court ruling allowing non-party groups to run advocacy ads during elections is skewing the principle of controlling party spending that was designed to keep "people with money or power" from buying their way into Parliament, said George Allen, commissioner in charge of ensuring that the Canada Elections Act is enforced.
>
> Allen described the situation as "patently unfair" to candidates bound by spending restrictions and blackout rules. At the very least, he said, third-party advertisers should be subject to the same blackout regulations and be required to state publicly where their funding comes from. (*Marketing* 1988a, 20)

Allen reluctantly suggested this alternative: "There's another way to go, of course, and that is just to take the restraints off the candidates and the parties. However, to do that you have to drop this idea that somehow you're going to try to create this level playing field" (ibid.).

On 29 November 1988, the *Toronto Star,* in a feature article entitled "Are Ad Blitzes Eroding Democracy?" (1988a), also based a story on the remarks of Commissioner Allen, but gave more details on the various groups that were involved in major third-party advertising. Both the *Marketing* and *Toronto Star* items appeared after the election.

In a subsequent article in *Marketing,* entitled "Elections: Violating the Spirit of Fair Play – Third-Party Advertising Unfair," Stan Sutter renews the argument raised by Commissioner Allen in 1988 for an official examination of the issue of third-party advertising:

> One generally overlooked item in the April 3 Speech from the Throne was the Mulroney government's commitment to "appoint a commission of inquiry to make recommendations for needed changes and reforms to the electoral laws." Now, with any luck, there will be some new campaigning rules in place, particularly regarding advertising, by the time the next federal election rolls around.
>
> Last fall, federal commissioner of elections George Allen told *Marketing* ... that the unprecedented intervention by business groups and other third-party organizations into the campaign was "patently unfair" and a violation of the spirit of political fair play.
>
> The cover story for the March/April issue of *This Magazine,* indelicately titled "The Big Oink: How Business Swallowed Politics," pretty well sums up an emerging consensus that the 1988 election was "bought" with advertising. And there is ample evidence that that conclusion is more than simply sour grapes from the losers in the free-trade debate.
>
> The *This Magazine* piece, written by Nick Fillmore, quotes Don Murphy, senior vice-president and creative director, at Vickers and Benson Advertising, one of the Toronto shops that handled Liberal party work, as saying: "The business and Conservative ad blitz was the largest, most concentrated promotion campaign ever seen in Canada." (Sutter 1989, 4)

Except for these stories, the coverage and discussion of freedom of expression issues was nonexistent. The issue of access for minority groups without big purses was only hinted at. The question of the cost of campaigns as a factor limiting the diversity of political voices did not surface. Interestingly, one of the big-budget third-party spenders of the 1988 campaign earned a few inches of coverage in the *Globe and Mail* on the subject of the right to freedom of expression:

Special interest groups should have a free hand in spending to promote issues during elections, the leader of the National Citizens' Coalition told a royal commission yesterday.

Imposing spending limits would only curtail the freedom of Canadians, David Somerville told the commission on election reform and party financing reviewing the Elections Act.

Special interest groups, which offer opinions not always shared by political parties, played a major role in the last federal election, he told the five-member panel.

"The dynamic debate over the free-trade agreement in the 1988 election was an outstanding example of how we would like to see democracy function," said Mr. Somerville, whose 40 000-member group supports free trade. (Canadian Press 1990, A11)

If special-interest groups are seen to include business concerns, then perhaps Somerville is on the side of a majority of Canadians. The *Financial Times of Canada* reported that "56 Percent of Canadians Endorse the Use of Political Advertising by Business." According to a Financial Times/Decima Poll report, "most Canadians, it turns out, think political advertising by business can be more helpful than harmful. But a substantial minority fears that business could develop the habit of using its substantial financial strength to influence election outcomes" (*Financial Times* 1988, 5). Subsequent surveys revealed a more complex pattern of opinion: support for the right to advertise, along with support for some restrictions to ensure that the wealthy would not dominate the debate and a concern that independent spending not undermine the limits on party and candidate spending. (See Blais and Gidengil 1991, chap. 5.)

Structural/Economic Issues
Structural and economic issues include tax benefits, relationships between media and government through advertising, patronage and electoral spending on advertising, and ethical considerations concerning both the rising public costs of elections and unfair subsidies. There was fairly consistent coverage of the rising costs of election advertising, accompanied by occasional hints of government patronage for some media agencies, which had worked for that governing party during the election campaign. Other issues were not treated in any substantial way.

In 1988 the *Globe and Mail*, the *Toronto Star* and, in particular, *Marketing* mentioned the huge sums which were being spent on television advertising. The headlines focused on costs: "Coming at You Starting Sunday: $6 Million in TV Ads on Election" (*Toronto Star* 1988b);

"Last Ad Blitz Costing P.C.'s $2 Million" (*Globe and Mail* 1988b; see also *Marketing* 1988b). There were also concerns, as indicated above, regarding the amount spent in the last federal election by special-interest groups. It is clear that 1988 marked the year when election spending on advertising became a press "event."

On the other hand, only one story could be found that attempted to focus on tax benefits and subsidies attached to political advertising and election spending as a whole. This was a full-page article in the Montreal *Gazette* by Terrance Wills, entitled "Election Expected to Be the Costliest Ever: Taxpayers Will Help Finance a Record Spending Spree as Federal Parties Scramble for Voters' Favour" (Wills 1988). Wills discussed election spending, the spending limits of parties and candidates, spending by lobby groups or "one issue lobbies" as he called them, the eligibility of minor parties, and subsidies and tax benefits available to parties and individuals involved in election spending.

It is interesting to note that, while in 1980 one of the issues given most coverage dealt with the federal government's advertising during or just prior to national elections (10 of the 11 stories that focused on "government advertising" were from 1980), there was only one story on this subject in 1984. In 1988, the print media did not address this issue except as a secondary problem in provincial elections, particularly in Alberta and British Columbia. The following are a few examples of print media stories that dealt with this matter in 1980. In a feature article in the Montreal *Gazette* entitled "Feds Show They Are Masters of Subliminal Advertising," L. Ian MacDonald discussed the federal government's plans to spend $6 million on a multimedia campaign in support of the Liberal government's position in the upcoming constitutional talks (MacDonald 1980). A *Globe and Mail* editorial was more outspoken. Entitled "Call It Propaganda," it discussed the same issue raised by MacDonald and incorporated the objections of the opposition parties in Parliament. The *Globe and Mail* stated its own position very forcefully in the last three paragraphs:

> In an authoritarian country the government, being under no requirement to represent or be responsible to the people, uses the taxes it has collected from the people to run propaganda campaigns that will present the government's actions in the most attractive terms and defuse any opposition that might arise. No obligation to truth need be recognized.
>
> In a democracy the floor is supposed to be equally open to all debaters. The government presents its case in parliament; the opposition parties examine the government case for flaws and offer

alternatives. A majority government is almost always in a position to prevail, but it often alters its proposals to meet reasonable opposition objections. The ideal is to produce legislation that will serve the country.

This exceedingly precarious democratic balance can be completely overthrown if the Government uses massive amounts of public funds to sell the public on its proposals. Canada does not need a ministry of propaganda. (*Globe and Mail* 1980, 6)

Maclean's magazine carried a full-page feature by Murray Coolican entitled "Watch Those (Government) Ads: To Me the Memo Read Like the Outline for a Propaganda Campaign." The memo in question was leaked from the office of the director of communications of the Department of Energy and set out the strategy behind a series of government advertisements on energy. The government was roundly criticized and Coolican offered some thoughtful guidelines for government advertising: "What should be done? First, the government must correct the misleading and false information it has propagated [concerning Canadian Arctic energy resources]. Second, Parliament must change the law so that government admen have to play by the rules. Third, Parliament must establish more stringent guidelines of what is appropriate for government advertisements. Finally, the auditor-general must investigate this waste of government funds. Otherwise – the Canada goose in the constitution ads symbolizes something other than freedom" (Coolican 1980, 8).

The issue of government advertising seems to have almost disappeared from the coverage of the last two federal elections. It has, however, continued to be a heated point of debate in provincial politics. It may be possible to argue that the eradication of this "problem" from the federal scene is partly due to the outcries of the press in 1980. It seems clear to us that the quality of democratic discourse in Canadian election campaigns would be enhanced if the news media provided more coverage and commentary on campaign advertising issues, especially if the coverage probed the issues involved more deeply.

Discussion

Because the press has its own traditional and structural biases toward stories that are timely, generally concise and headline oriented, it is understandable that there would be a preference for events over process stories, and for stories that are leader-centred rather than about party representation and policy. Reporters are often more comfortable with events than analysis, especially with respect to issues where their conclusions may be subject to criticism. In such an environment, political advertising gets the predictable superficial treatment. The campaigns and the advertisements themselves are reported on, as well as the expenditures involved. The critical question is, therefore, "Can one expect the press to do much more than this?"

In 1984, just prior to the federal election, Michael Nolan, then an assistant professor of journalism at the University of Western Ontario, attempted to assess the role of the media in elections and formulated some thoughts on how they might become more effective:

> Now that Canadians are in the midst of their 33rd federal election, the question to be addressed is whether the media can serve any longer as an honest channel of communication between politicians and the people.
>
> If journalists are to be the filters and voters' eyes and ears, they will have to reassess some of their recently established practices. To avoid being merely captives of the political leaders and their skilled advisers, the media might have to consider adjustments in their style of reporting.
>
> First, campaign coverage that is less leader-oriented probably would allow for a more meaningful discussion of regional candidates and issues. Second, the media might also play more to their strengths, with TV focusing on breaking or "spot" news and newspapers providing almost exclusively the interpretation, commentary and independent analysis ...
>
> Since its inception some 30 years ago, TV has placed new demands on politicians and advertising agencies have moved front and centre on the campaign stage. During elections, the media have had to try to circumvent these strategists who have become adept at assisting politicians to control their campaign environment. (Nolan 1984, 7)

Similarly, the press could provide the interpretation, commentary and independent analysis necessary to extract political advertising from the strategist's domain. In each of the five broad areas dealt with in this section, the role of the press, as an aid to voters' understanding of the issues and processes, can be played by no other agency in a democracy.

Evaluation

Overall, we found that print media campaign coverage focused narrowly on campaign tactics. Political journalists made little attempt to report or analyse the strategic and regulatory context of campaigns. The coverage paid only minimal attention to the roles of the CRTC and the broadcasting arbitrator or to the evolution of advertising practices. The

event-based reporting meant that topics such as the overall policy framework, the legislative context and judicial challenges to it, and the agencies concerned with campaign advertising received minimal coverage.
For example, the release of the annual report of the chief electoral officer,
the House of Commons debate on Bill C-79, and the activities of the
broadcasting arbitrator received little coverage. Even the constitutional
challenge to the rules concerning political advertising by interest groups
in 1984 (*National Citizens' Coalition Inc./Coalition nationale des citoyens
inc. v. Canada (Attorney General)* was given limited coverage by the
popular press.

There are, of course, factors that make the reporting of campaign
strategy and election advertising difficult. First, few journalists are
acquainted with the tactical aspects of advertising. Second, strategists
do not like to talk about the objectives or intentions of their campaigns.
Third, the broadcasting arbitrator's report does not make public information that might stimulate stories or encourage close scrutiny (targeting
of swing ridings, for example, or differences between French- and
English-language campaigns). In other words, the process in which
fairness and equity are being adjudicated is not subject to adequate
public scrutiny and accountability.

Finally, the press has its own biases and preferences for stories that
are timely, leader-centred, and that favour events over processes.
Therefore, it has not provided extensive analysis or in-depth discussion of the legal, ethical, political and social issues raised by the new
party and nonparty strategies. The popular press has viewed political
advertising primarily within the framework of the "manipulation"
theory of advertising and, in so doing, has not fully informed the public
of the issues of balance, funding rebates, limits on participation, constitutional challenges, or the legislative process that is available for dealing
with them. The press has done a reasonably good job in alerting the
public to certain important changes in the ways campaigns are
conducted, but the "leader image" framework it tends to employ has
meant that the discussion of issues has been both less comprehensive
and less thoughtful than it could be.

A FRAMEWORK FOR REGULATING POLITICAL ADVERTISING

Several authors reviewing the provisions for maintaining fair and equitable election campaigns have identified concerns about Canadian
provisions for political advertising. In his detailed study of election
law, member of Parliament J. Patrick Boyer noted that a number of
statutes and provisions have been developed that apply to broadcast
election advertising campaigns, including the *Canada Elections Act*, the

Broadcasting Act, the CRTC regulations and guidelines and the *Income Tax Act*. In addition to the allocation and arbitration rules contained in the *Canada Elections Act*, Boyer lists a number of other important rules:

> 1. content restrictions, such as matters of privilege, copyright, libel and slander, untrue statements that reflect on a candidate's character and limitation on "theatrical" advertising;
> 2. source restrictions, such as advertising from outside Canada, third-party expenditures for the purposes of "promoting or opposing" a party or candidate, the Saskatchewan restriction on government advertising during elections, and sponsor identification rules;
> 3. language restrictions pertaining to the majority languages; and
> 4. election spending restrictions, such as spending ceilings and rebates.
> (Boyer 1983, 325)

As noted earlier, the allocation formula for both paid and free time works in favour of the major parties. If a wealthy but relatively new or regionally localized party came onto the scene (as may be the case in the next election), it would be eligible for very little broadcast time, because the allocation is based primarily on the results of the previous general election. Moreover, it is unlikely that smaller parties will be able to afford the media expertise essential for the planning, researching and execution of effective campaigns, even if more time is allocated to them. It is reasonable, therefore, to question whether or not the current allocation formula meets the test of equity. The reimbursement rules, which require a minimum expenditure by a party for eligibility, may also be considered to be tilted against emerging parties.

The allocations of paid and free time have been the subject of some complaints to the chief electoral officer (Canada, Elections Canada 1989). Several smaller parties have complained about inequalities in access to the media (Rose 1990; LaCalamita 1984). Other commentators, including the popular press, have also noted that the use of government advertising during the election period increases during the election year, thus constituting a de facto goodwill campaign for the incumbent party (Rose 1990; Boyer 1982; Strauss 1990). Boyer later returned to this idea: "Advertising by the government, a device relied upon by incumbent governments generally at the time of elections to foster a feeling of well-being and to remind the public of the scope of services and benefits that it provides to them gives an unfair advantage to the political party in power" (Boyer 1983, 387). The governing party's control over government advertising clearly constitutes an inequality in political communication not dealt with in current federal legislation.

From our historical overview, we conclude that the growth in political advertising stems largely from the opportunity it provides for
political parties to address Canadian voters directly, unmediated by
journalistic processes. It is this perceived need for direct communication to the voters that has justified the requirement that broadcasters
make available paid and free time to registered parties. Broadcasters
have traditionally accepted a responsibility for public education during
campaigns but have from time to time objected to being burdened
with legal obligations not placed on the print media. Two arguments
are usually presented in support of these special obligations. The first
is that broadcasters receive access to the public airwaves in return for
various services to the community (including obligations related to
election campaigns). The second is that the dominant role of the broadcast media in modern campaign discourse requires that parties have
access to those media within a framework designed to ensure equity
and fairness.

The regulations have been altered over the years to reduce the
burden on broadcasters and it may be that further modifications will
be required to adjust the rules to changes in technology and campaign
practices. For example, the definition of prime time was altered to make
it easier for broadcasters to place campaign advertisements in their
schedules. The proliferation of channels, which requires more advertising to reach the same number of voters, the entry of advocacy groups
into the process, and the advent of direct mail and other new means
for mobilizing voter support will likely produce changes in party strategies. In the short run, if advocacy group advertising is not limited, the
broadcast media may have difficulty meeting the demand for advertising
time – given the requirement that they provide a considerable amount
of time for purchase by registered parties – without extensive bumping
of advertisements placed by commercial clients. (The CRTC limits the
amount of time per broadcast hour that may be devoted to advertising
(permitting 12 minutes of advertising each hour for most television
broadcasters, for example).)

Concern has also been expressed regarding implicit subsidies for
advocacy group advertising in campaigns. In many cases, the costs can
be written off as a business expense or a charitable donation. The issue
of tax subsidies for advocacy advertising was a major issue in the implementation of the fairness doctrine in the United States (Meadow 1981;
Meeske 1974; Stridsberg 1977; Brennan 1989; *Congressional Digest* 1987a,
1987b). However, lack of reliable information makes it difficult to esti-
mate the scope of this practice. Direct and indirect subsidies for registered parties and candidates can be defended as serving the public

interest by ensuring that there is a degree of equity among participants in the electoral contest itself; the justification for subsidies to corporations and advocacy groups is less clear.

The current narrow scope of campaign accounting and the absence of public monitoring and accountability with respect to campaign advertising make it difficult to ensure that fairness and equity are being maintained in election campaigns. The broadcasting arbitrator and the CRTC have access to information regarding advertising purchases but no mandate to make them public. We have already noted that news coverage of campaign advertising generally lacks detailed information on these subjects and we found a reluctance on the part of both parties and the media to make them available to researchers. Indeed, the chief electoral officer has no explicit mandate to provide public information of any kind (Canada, Elections Canada 1989, 11), though reports to Parliament are required.

Another current problem is the possibility of a trend toward more negative advertising in Canadian campaigns (Romanow et al. 1991; Rose 1990) and toward other excesses of "rhetoric," which seem to be drifting into Canadian practices from the United States. John Coleman, president of the Canadian Advertising Foundation, stated that "we seem to be quick to emulate the excesses of the American approach to political advertising which is down and out dirty, by and large, and engages in rhetoric that is not acceptable in ordinary life" (Interview, Coleman, 1991). Although laws with general application (libel, slander, privilege), specific sections of the *Broadcasting Act* and guidelines circulated by the CRTC apply to political advertising, there are no express provisions for dealing with the content or style of broadcast advertising. Unlike the situation for commercial advertising, there are no guidelines for "comparative" statements and no industry-wide standards for "controversial" and advocacy advertising. There is also no complaints procedure or system of redress for false and misleading statements in advocacy advertising. Parties or other organizations who choose to address matters of public importance through noncommercial advertising, i.e., not related to the promotion of a product or service, are not subject to any form of systematic regulation. Moreover, since the provisions covering false and misleading advertising and comparative advertising are located in the *Competition Act* and the *Food and Drugs Act*, and the complaints procedures for advertising are administered by the Department of Consumer and Corporate Affairs, there is a great deal of regulatory ambiguity concerning partisan and general "political" advertising. However, Boyer, a leading legal commentator, does not believe that "the laws of general application regarding misleading advertising can be brought to bear on election advertisements. Efforts to do so are more likely to end in farce than enforcement" (Boyer 1983, 326).

It also remains unclear how the specifications in the *Broadcasting Act*, the directives of the CRTC, or network advertising codes, which prohibit certain kinds of advertising (for example, advertising of an "offensive and objectionable character," sex-role stereotyping, subliminal advertising), apply to political advertising (Boyer 1983, 441). Although the major networks do from time to time request changes in election campaign advertisements, broadcasters generally believe that they have no mandate to "censor" political content.

A useful guard against unethical advertising is to be found in the 1968 *Broadcasting Act*. Briefly, it states that "a licensee shall identify the sponsor and the political party, if any, on whose behalf a program, advertisement or announcement of a partisan character in relation to a referendum or an election ... is broadcast or received" (Canada, *Broadcasting Act* 1968, 19(2)). This section was inexplicably dropped from the 1991 *Broadcasting Act*. It seems self-evident that the principle of sponsor identification should apply to all political broadcast undertakings during an election period.

The most serious and troublesome aspect of the current provisions resides in the potential conflict between the restrictions on expenditures to "promote or oppose" a party or candidate and constitutional guarantees of freedom of speech (Hiebert 1989–90). The provision limiting such expenditures to registered political parties can be interpreted as restricting the political speech of groups outside the parties. As Seidle (1985, 126–28) notes, the 1983 amendments to the *Canada Elections Act* concerning independent expenditures also raised the secondary issue of whether third-party interest-group advertisements that neither promote nor oppose parties or candidates but advocate policies ("for the purpose of gaining support on an issue of public policy and done in good faith") are to be prohibited during the election period. In practice, the distinction between policy advocacy and the promotion of a party or candidate is not always clear. For example, support for the Free Trade Agreement with the United States during the 1988 campaign could be viewed as support for the Conservatives, the only large party supporting the deal.

While the 1983 amendments do restrict freedom of expression, they are deemed by many to be essential to protect the system of regulated competition among the registered parties established by the 1974 reforms. Parties and candidates feared that, faced with opposition from advocacy groups operating outside the advertising and spending limits, they would be unable to compete. In addition, parties and candidates could evade the limits by forming alliances with advocacy groups (or creating them). Even in the absence of alliances, the voices of those competing for public office could be drowned out by groups with specific ideologies or policy agendas. Nevertheless, it is clear that limiting the participation of advocacy groups in campaigns is a restriction on the public debate that is central to democratic elections.

These were the central issues in the 1984 Alberta court case of *National Citizens' Coalition Inc./Coalition nationale des citoyens inc. v. Canada (Attorney General)*, concerning interest-group advertisements in newspapers undertaken during the pre-election period by the NCC. Mr. Justice Medhurst reiterated the doctrine that "there should be actual demonstration of harm or a real likelihood of harm to a society value before a limitation [on freedom of expression] can be said to be justified" (*National Citizens' Coalition* 1984, 264). In this case, Mr. Justice Medhurst concluded, "it has not been established to the degree required that the fundamental freedom of expression need be limited. The limitation has not been shown to be reasonable or demonstrably justified in a free and democratic society" (ibid.). However, Hiebert comments in her examination of the implications of this particular judgement: "The ruling that regulations on interest-group spending are not justified and that freedom of expression during an election does not embrace qualitative considerations of access and opportunity has significant implications for the electoral process" (Hiebert 1989–90, 82). She notes in particular that without just such a regulatory framework, it is not only possible but highly likely that irreparable harm will be caused to the electoral system in Canada, which has been based on the principle that Canadians freely choose the government they want without undue influence from external forces such as advocacy advertisers. Echoing this concern, the report of the chief electoral officer states that there is good reason to be concerned that with "the lack of control, practically speaking, on advertising by third parties at election time ... the more the integrity of the electoral process is threatened" (Canada, Elections Canada 1989, 10).

Clearly, the matter of third-party advertising raises some very thorny issues, among which are the need to find a balance between the competing principles of freedom of political speech and a democratic electoral process. But the principal questions are whether organizations other than registered parties should be granted unfettered access to the purchase of broadcast time during the election period in order to address issues of public importance, and whether certain restrictions that apply to party advertising should similarly apply to third-party or advocacy advertising. The mainstream media, for the most part, focus their attention on party politics, often ignoring the legitimate concerns expressed by third-party interest groups on a number of important political, economic and social issues. How, then, are advocacy groups to convey their message to the Canadian public, other than through advertising, including broadcast advertising? Fair and equitable standards of practice and reasonable restrictions with respect to access and expenditures should apply to all forms of political advertising and to all those engaging in it. From the aforementioned arguments it is apparent that a genuine need for a regulatory framework exists, a regulatory framework for political speech in its broadest sense during election campaigns, ensuring that fairness and equity among all participants are maintained. To neglect to create such a framework would undermine a fundamental democratic cornerstone of Canadian political life.

Despite the inevitable restriction on freedom of expression, some regulatory framework is necessary. Peter Hogg, one of Canada's leading constitutional lawyers, states the case in these terms: "Restrictions on election expenditures are indirect restrictions on political speech ... However, there is a powerful reason for such restrictions, and that is to reduce the risk that the wealthy or well-financed candidate will have an unfair advantage by reason of his or her greater access to the media" (Hogg 1985, 717). Thus, protection of the spending limits and, by extension, preservation of a level playing field in campaign debate, requires some restriction on freedom of expression for all of the players in the campaign process.

Given the court's ruling in the NCC case, a new, more general framework for political speech during election campaigns must address the following five key issues concerning political advertising:

- the rising costs of campaigns and the justification for public subsidies to parties and candidates;
- the inequalities set up within the broadcast industry between competing broadcast enterprises (networks, stations, cable) in relationship to the commercial benefits and burdens of the allocation of free and paid time political broadcasts;
- the implicit privileging of party over nonparty access to political speech in the media;
- the potential of advocacy groups and large corporate interests with an interest in aspects of party platforms to use "advocacy" or "issue" advertising at election time to influence the policy debate and for special-interest groups to enjoy tax subsidization for such expenses; and
- the possibility of collusion between parties or candidates and advocacy groups to evade the advertising and expenditure limits now in force.

THE REGULATION OF COMMERCIAL ADVERTISING

Given recent advances in media technology and new approaches to political campaigning, it seems appropriate to consider whether the current arrangements for political advertising are capable of maintaining the fundamental goals of fairness and equity (Boyer 1983, 438). With these issues in mind, we reviewed the regulation of advertising in Canada in order to see whether regulatory models and rationales extant in this field offer guidance or alternatives to the present framework for the regulation of political advertising.

Recent commentary on advertising regulation and self-regulation itself reveals a loosely knit and confusing array of mechanisms, processes and rationales (Zarry and Wilson 1981; CRTC 1978a; Boyer 1983; Esbin 1979a, 1979b; Ginsberg 1979; American Academy of Advertising 1979; Leiss et al. 1990). The fabric of policy appears to be a web of confusion and legal uncertainty in this highly dynamic arena. New strategies for targeting, positioning, media buying and message design are constantly being developed, and cultural standards and communication mores are in flux. As Leiss et al. (1990, 356) stated in their examination of social communication in advertising: "The policy debates about advertising should now ... recognize that the increasing sophistication of marketing communication demands a new way of thinking about the consequences of the unique combination of economic and cultural forces at work in our society."

Yet there appears to be no preferred regulatory mechanism in the field of advertising regulation, in part because each of the mechanisms employed has evolved separately, in response to unique problems, with rationales developed specifically to deal with particular circumstances as they emerged. At first glance, the primary legislation pertaining to advertising appears to be the *Broadcasting Act* of 1968 that defined the powers of the CRTC to regulate licensees according to its guidelines for the "character of advertising and the amount of time that may be devoted to advertising; ... the proportion of time that may be devoted to the broadcasting of programs, advertisements or announcements of a partisan political character; and ... the use of dramatization in programs" (s. 6(1)(*b*)(ii) and (iv)). However, upon further review, the CRTC has increasingly preferred a self-regulatory approach (CRTC 1986; Swinton 1977), preferring to monitor and arbitrate policy. More direct, perhaps, are the provisions of the *Competition Act*, the *Food and Drugs Act*, and the procedures defined under the mandates of Consumer and Corporate Affairs Canada, Health and Welfare Canada, the Advertising Standards Council and the provincial liquor boards, which play a significant administrative role in preclearance, review and complaints concerning advertising. Additionally, the Canadian Association of Broadcasters, the Telecaster Committee, the CBC, the Canadian Advertising Advisory Board, the Better Business Bureau, and a variety of other self-regulatory and self-disciplinary bodies have had a role in establishing guidelines for advertising practices.

Given this array of overlapping jurisdictions and guidelines, there is no single definition of advertising and no legislated taxonomy that might help one to determine the authority and scope of these bodies in terms of either the source of the advertisements (government, party, corporate, advocacy or interest group, charitable organization) or their content (commercial, institutional, controversial, negative, issue, political). The industry itself accepts a broad definition, set out in the Canadian Code of Advertising Standards, which states: "Advertising [means] any paid message communicated by Canadian media with the intent to influence the choice, opinion or behaviour of those addressed by the commercial messages" (Canadian Advertising Foundation 1986, 2). This definition is helpful because it focuses on the "commercial transaction" aspect of advertising; that is, the fact that someone (a corporation, government, interest group or political party) buys time from a licensed broadcaster. Viewed in this way, advertising is the purchase of influence through the media, and there is no need to distinguish types of messages by source or content. The basic rules should apply to all such transactions.

There is a difficult and somewhat ill-defined grey area in the pressures upon broadcasters, who are dependent on the income from advertising and yet have obligations to maintain balance in their political programming, to contribute to the task of informing the public, and to maintain fairness in their treatment of matters of public importance. Indeed, the Canadian Code of Advertising Standards acknowledges:

> Public confidence exerts an important influence upon the effectiveness of advertising, just as it affects any other communication process in a democratic environment. So directing advertising practices toward meriting and enhancing such confidence is both socially responsible and an act of practical self-interest. (Canadian Advertising Foundation 1986, 7)

For these reasons, the provisions of broadcast advertising policy have been directed at three rather general areas of social concern, namely business, media and social relations. As Leiss et al. point out:

> Advertising impinges directly upon some very sensitive and important areas of life, and this forces policy makers to think very carefully

about its proper place within a democratic society. The uniqueness of advertising agencies, and the regulatory issues confronting them, is that they have emerged as the point of mediation between the industrial, cultural and communications sectors of society. Accordingly, advertising has encountered three different sets of social policy considerations – those connected with business, media and social relations. Each of these has its own mandate, organizational focus, and traditions of regulation. (Leiss et al. 1990, 357)

Fair Advertising Practices

As set out below, fair advertising practices are regulated by both public and private sectors in response to a number of specific concerns:

- prevention of competitive advantage to any firm willing to use deceptive, comparative or otherwise unfair advertising tactics;
- protection of the young, unwary or credulous consumer against false claims and other misleading advertising practices;
- restrictions on the advertising of risky or hazardous products (alcohol, tobacco) where public health and safety are concerned, and monitoring of the information provided about complex products (food and drugs, financial services) where the ability of all consumers to fully understand the nature of the claims is questioned.

In defining the legitimate limits of marketing practices, the *Competition Act* (1985) consolidates over 60 years of experience in regulating this complex field of communication. It goes to great lengths to specify what is considered a violation of fair advertising practice concerning "any representation to the public that is false or misleading in any material respect" (Canada, *Competition Act* 1985, s. 52(1)(*a*)). The criteria for misrepresentation are based "on the degree to which the purchaser is affected by the words" (Zarry and Wilson 1981, 373). The Crown does not, however, have to show that "someone was actually misled by the representation." These prohibitions apply to goods and services and include "representations by any and every means whatsoever" (Canada, Consumer and Corporate Affairs 1990a). The test for deception rests on the general impression created and not on the question as to whether the representation is technically or literally accurate. The intention to mislead or the lack of such intention is immaterial. An advertisement can be misleading because it "fails to reveal certain essential information; or because it is partially true and partially false; or the representation is capable of two meanings, one of which is false" (Zarry and Wilson 1981, 372).

The CBC considers advertising to be "deceptive or misleading ... whether it is caused by the omission of relevant information or by the arrangement of accurate information in such a way as to lead to a wrong conclusion" (CBC 1989, A1). The CBC considers such advertising unacceptable.

Similarly, according to the Canadian Code of Advertising Standards, "advertisements must not contain inaccurate or deceptive claims, statements, illustrations, or representations, either direct or implied, with regard to price, availability or performance of a product or service." In considering whether a message is misleading or not, the "focus is on the message as received or perceived, that is, the general impression conveyed by the advertisement." Additionally, advertisements "must not discredit or attack unfairly other products, services or advertisements or exaggerate the nature or importance of competitive differences" (Canadian Advertising Foundation 1986, 3, 4, 6).

Concern about medicinal advertising, one of the most controversial areas of commercial advertising, led to early calls from advertising and other media professionals for restraints on the excesses of "quacks." In our current *Food and Drugs Act*, certain drugs (narcotics, controlled drugs, etc.) may not be advertised to the "general public." Only drugs that are intended for those conditions which can be self-diagnosed and self-treated can be advertised to the general public. "Promotional material associated with a drug should describe both the positive aspects and the adverse effects associated with the use of a particular drug so that the consumer can make an informed decision regarding the drug use" (Canada, Health and Welfare 1990, 8).

To guard against false and misleading advertising, all advertisements for the purpose of promoting drugs must get preclearance from Health and Welfare Canada (CRTC 1986). Section 9.1 of the *Food and Drugs Act* additionally provides that "no person shall label, package, treat, process, sell or advertise any drug in a manner that is false, misleading or deceptive or is likely to create an erroneous impression regarding its character, value, quantity, composition, merit or safety." Health and Welfare Canada note that the "majority of objections raised about drug advertising are the result of the evaluation of visual and textual material" (Canada, Health and Welfare 1990, 16).

Health and Welfare Canada specify words, phrases and types of advertising appeals that are considered misleading; for example, quotations from media, testimonials and certificates of approval (Canada, Health and Welfare 1990, 17–18). The guidelines spell out a number of particularly problematic advertising practices. Among these, "competitive comparisons" are seen as the most troublesome (ibid., 19). According to Health and Welfare Canada, many competitive comparisons are misleading. They often exaggerate a product's competitive advantage, fail to disclose a difference of opinion among qualified experts or make incomplete comparisons of the qualities of one product over another (ibid.). The guidelines make particular note of some of the troublesome words found in comparative advertising. These include the terms "better," "richer" and "stronger." They advise against the use of such dangling comparatives (ibid.). The Health and Welfare Canada guidelines further stress that great care must be taken in the use of negative statements, scientific and technical terms, accepted opinion, questionnaires, qualifying statements, undue emphasis, misleading terminology, scare advertising and deceptive illustrations in comparative advertising (ibid., 20–30).

In addition to these provisions, the CBC, for example, has its own guidelines for comparison advertising, pertaining to all products and services, which state: "Comparison advertising should be positive, fair and meaningful in terms of benefits to the consumer and should avoid scenes or references derogatory to other products, services or industries. The emphasis must be on the advertiser's own goods or services and not on the disadvantages or shortcomings of competitors" (CBC 1989, A3).

The Telecaster Committee is an agency formed voluntarily by private television broadcasters, including networks, to assess television advertisements. Through a process called "preclearance," commercials are evaluated according to the Committee's guidelines of "general acceptability" (Telecaster Committee 1980). In this way, the staff of the Committee certify that an advertisement does not violate legislated standards and is in line with industry norms. The norms reflected in the Telecaster Committee standards are very similar to those set out in the Canadian Code of Advertising Standards. For example, "in order to avoid conveying information that misrepresents the truth," the Telecaster Committee urges advertisers to comply with the following guidelines:

1) The intent and connotation of the ad should be to inform and never to discredit or unfairly attack competitors, competing products or services.

2) When a competitive product is named, it should be one that exists in the marketplace as significant competition.

3) The competition should be fairly and properly identified but never in a manner or tone of voice that degrades the competitive product or service.

4) The advertising should compare related or similar properties or ingredients of the product, dimension to dimension, feature to feature.

5) The identification should be for honest comparison purposes and not simply to upgrade by association.
6) If a competitive test is conducted, it should be done by an objective testing source, preferably an independent one.
7) The advertising should never use partial results or stress insignificant differences to cause the consumer to draw an improper conclusion.
8) Comparatives delivered through the use of testimonials should not imply that the testimonial is more than one individual's thought unless that individual represents a sample of the majority viewpoint. (Telecaster Committee 1990, 10)

Fairness and Equity in Political Broadcasting

With regard to media policies for fairness, there are few limitations on the sale of advertising time to any agency or organization that chooses to buy it. The major restrictions on selling air time are the product of the CRTC's upper limit on the volume of advertising within a broadcast hour (12 minutes for most television broadcasters) and of the prohibition of advertisements within the first 10 minutes of a newscast (CRTC 1987a, 12). This specification does not differentiate between commercial, advocacy and political advertising and, therefore, during an election period, if the station has presold all its spots, bumping of commercial spots is often necessary under the terms of the *Canada Elections Act* and the CRTC limits on commercial programming in each hour (Canada, *Canada Elections Act* 1985, ss. 307–15; CRTC 1987a).

There are no mandatory guidelines that outline how broadcasters are to maintain fairness and equity in relation to the use of advertising for addressing controversial matters of public importance. Indeed, this is a very hazy area, in which it becomes difficult to differentiate the rights and obligations of broadcasters regarding programming, their obligation to maintain fairness, diversity and balance in political speech, and their obligation as channels of commercial speech. The CBC, aware of this problem, has tried to define a policy for "advocacy advertising," drawing an implicit distinction between it and commercial messages. Its stated concern is that "the airwaves must not come under the control of any individual or group who because of wealth, special position, etc., might be better able to influence listener or viewer attitudes" (CBC 1989, A2). The policy applies to corporate, institutional or public relations advertising from the private or government sectors, as well as any of the advertising often referred to as "societal." There has been energetic debate on this issue in the United States, particularly with regard to the recent elimination of the Fairness Doctrine (*Editorial Research Reports*

1987; *Broadcasting* 1990), and some criticism of the lack of fairness in the way Canadian broadcasters adjudicate "controversial" and "advocacy" advertising (Laxer 1976; Rose 1990).

The CBC operates under the stated belief that "discussion or comment on public issues should be confined to appropriate programming and tries to ensure that the principal points of view are presented fairly" (CBC 1989, A2). Defining a public issue as "a matter about which there is significant difference of opinion and which is or is likely to be the subject of public debate," the CBC does not sell or give away time to broadcast messages that advocate a point of view or course of action on a public issue (except for party political broadcasts and paid and free time during election campaigns). Moreover, "advertising from or on behalf of any group or organization, be it government-sponsored or private, which supports or advocates a point of view on the election, plebiscite or referendum issue, is unacceptable" (ibid., A6). Yet this does not preclude corporations and institutions from using "commercial messages that go beyond promotion of goods and services, e.g., institutional messages, to enhance the image of the advertiser," which "should be factual about the advertiser's projects and plans" (ibid., A2).

As stated, expenditures for advertising that pursue a "business interest" are recognized as tax-deductible expenses under the *Income Tax Act*, although certain kinds of public relations and advocacy activities may not be recognized as strictly pursuing a business interest. Curiously, the CBC guidelines will permit some such advertising, in that "commercial messages that do not promote tangible goods and services but rather urge the adoption of an attitude or course of action must include video or audio identification of the advertiser responsible for the message" (CBC 1989, A3).

These definitions have not been adopted industry-wide, however, so that the standards of what constitutes acceptable advocacy and interest-group advertising vary by networks and stations and may create regional disparities in the access of advocacy advertisers. The Telecaster Committee addresses "issue and opinion advertising" for its members, specifying that it will rule on the "acceptability of commercials from governments, corporations, associations, or individuals, when such advertising attempts to sway public opinion on an issue under public debate or of public controversy" (Telecaster Committee 1990, 12). The guidelines state that the "ability to purchase and pay for commercial time cannot be the only criteria in accepting announcements which advocate a particular point of view on an issue of public concern, or on government, political or social policy," and that each commercial will be judged "individually on its own merit" (ibid.).

Similarly, the Canadian Advertising Foundation states that "no adver-tisement shall be presented in a format which conceals its commercial intent. Advertising content should be clearly distinguished from edito-rial or program content" (Canadian Advertising Foundation 1986, 4). The Telecaster Committee offers a preclearance program, vetting these advertisements on the following three criteria: (1) the advertisement must not appear to be intentionally deceptive, erroneous or misleading; (2) the advertiser must be identified at the beginning and the views expressed must clearly be those of the advertiser; and (3) the message must meet all legal, regulatory and committee requirements (Telecaster Committee 1990, 12).

Taste and Community Standards in Advertising

With regard to social and cultural issues, the primary regulatory concerns are to prevent the abuse of specially vulnerable target groups and to uphold community moral and social standards in all communications, including the prevention of demeaning racial and/or gender repre-sentations. The CRTC holds that any decision about the good taste of a commercial is best made by the broadcast licensee, who is responsible for all material broadcast by his or her station. The CBC notes that although viewers exercise choice in programming, they do not have the same ability to choose the advertising they see within the "intimacy of the home in mixed company, and in family or social groups" (CBC 1989, A1). The Telecaster Committee specifies that "advertisers should bear in mind that all commercials must be of high standard and sensitive to matters of public opinion. Commercials containing elements of negative or degrading sex-role portrayal, negative racial or ethnic portrayal, sexualization of children, excessive violence, horror, or any other portrayals likely to be offensive to the majority of viewers will be rejected" (Telecaster Committee 1990, 13).

The CBC attempts to maintain its standards of taste in advertising with regard to "word, tone and scene." These standards specify that race and religion be "treated with dignity and decency. They must not be held up as subjects of ridicule" (CBC 1989, A1). Additionally, individuals or groups should not because of age, occupation, creed or sex be dispar-aged, exploited or unfairly represented and the CBC "encourages adver-tisers to present both sexes fairly in all types of occupational role" (ibid.). The guidelines also state that advertisements should not encourage any activity contrary to "widely held standards of behaviour" (ibid.). In this respect, advertising for beer, wine and cider is carefully monitored, and such commercials are not allowed to "promote the general use" of these products, nor be longer than 60 seconds. These advertisements must be precleared by the CRTC and the liquor boards and meet additional criteria, such as not encouraging nondrinkers to drink, not showing the act of consumption, not associating drinking with youth or status symbols and not showing the product as a necessity for the enjoyment of life or an escape from life's problems. Messages generally may not "use shock value of double entendre or by undue exploitation of sex, nudity or violence" (ibid., C2, A1). According to the BBG's "good taste" policy statement of 1965, which continues to influence the CRTC, " ... all advertising matter and commercial announcements should be of such a character that they can be freely introduced into a mixed company of adults and children as subjects of ordinary conversation" (Zarry and Wilson 1981, 380).

Modes of Regulation

The regulation of commercial advertising is fragmented, complex and multidimensional. It is also rich in terms of the administrative mechanisms of regulation employed. These vary from issue to issue but include legislated bans (for example, on harmful products like tobacco), official guidelines, monitoring and registration, review and certification, reporting, complaints procedures, standard-setting committees, professional codes of conduct, accreditation and self-censure. Indeed, one of the hallmarks of Canadian approaches to advertising regulation, in contrast with the cycles of regulation and deregulation in the United States, is the multidimensional use of all these mechanisms as an integral part of the policy infrastructure.

Outright bans on types of advertising design (like subliminal exposure), on advertising to vulnerable groups (such as children in Quebec) and on categories of products or services (tobacco and spirit alcohol, for example) have long been part of the Canadian regulatory tradition, but it must be noted that the most recent two attempts at bans have led to Supreme Court challenges. The judicial test for any absolute restriction on commercial speech will generally be that it must be a reasonable limitation in a democratic society and be based on demonstrated harm or threat. This is a stringent test, which is still being worked out in the courts as cases on advertising and commercial speech are heard. Some legal critics are, however, wary of having the judiciary substitute for the legislative process (LaCalamita 1984; Seidle 1985).

In addition to these bans, Canadian advertising regulation relies on a system of preclearance and CRTC logging and monitoring. Preclearance involves a process whereby committees of appropriate expertise or representativeness are assembled to consider matters of taste, scientific fact or violations of established standards. The preclearance agency varies according to the subject of the advertisement. Such review and monitoring procedures are now well tested in several different areas, most notably with regard to food and drugs, female hygiene, alcoholic beverages and children's advertising. The benefits of monitoring and preclearance procedures for policy formulation are clear. First, they establish media buying and advertising design within the public sphere, so that any concerns or disputes over media placements, trends in buying, or advertising design can be noted, researched and reported. Second, the committees generally are structured so that they include representatives of the various industries and groups interested in both the content and the administration of codes so that codes and standards can be adapted over time. Third, since competitive campaigns must be submitted to public scrutiny, there is little chance of competitive advantage being achieved by surprise tactics. It appears that the setting of standards and codes for advertising is a widely accepted means of regulating controversial communication without infringing upon the freedom of commercial speech.

Complaints procedures have also been a useful means of reducing the frequency of unacceptable advertising practice. Established within Consumer and Corporate Affairs Canada (CCAC) mainly to deal with infractions under the *Competition Act,* the Marketing Practices branch reports regularly on the complaints it receives (Canada, Consumer and Corporate Affairs 1990a, 1990b). These reports make the complaints public and analyse trends. By far the greatest number of complaints concern false and misleading advertising, but such complaints arise more as matters of competitive than consumer concern. It should be noted that there are relatively few complaints about those categories of offence that fall under the purview of monitoring and preclearance procedures (beer, food and drugs, female hygiene). Recent trends in complaints about advertising seem to indicate concerns based on changing social values, social representation and taste. It is not clear that the department is in a position to do anything about complaints about taste, sex-role stereotyping and general infractions of voluntary codes of conduct, each of which might also be made elsewhere (to the broadcaster, the Advertising Standards Council, the CRTC, etc.). The department does not investigate complaints about political or controversial advertising, and it is not clear where such complaints should be directed. Only the CRTC appears to have a mandate in this area.

All formal advertising organizations recognize that some restraints on commercial speech are necessary. Most advertisers acknowledge that their constitutional guarantees of free commercial speech must be accompanied by responsibilities to society and to the consumer. As Brian Philcox (1989), president of the Association of Canadian

Advertisers, wrote, "Commercial free speech simply means the right to inform the consumer of what is for sale. It is also the right of the consumer to be informed. At no time does an advertiser have license to misinform. Let's not forget that advertising, along with all other facets of marketing communication, is a deeply rooted part of our cultural heritage." Most advertisers recognize that the sometimes cumbersome system of restraints on commercial speech works in favour of maintaining fair and competitive business practice and of ensuring advertising that is a responsible, accepted and legitimate part of society (Esbin 1979a, 1979b). John Coleman, president of the Canadian Advertising Foundation, argues, therefore, that the monitoring, review and standards provisions for commercial advertising should be extended to include political advertising:

> There are clauses within the self-regulatory code of advertising stan-
> dards to which all responsible advertisers, agencies and media
> subscribe, as well as federal government provisions through Consumer
> and Corporate Affairs, which require strict adherence to truth in adver-
> tising. But ordinary advertising is different from political advertising
> which is not governed by those provisions. Ordinary advertisers know
> full well that if they breach the self-regulatory standards there are
> strict and severe penalties, but those rules don't apply to election
> advertising ... I agree entirely that there should be a compliance with
> basic normal standards for all forms of advertising, including elec-
> tion advertising ... Fair is fair for all within the ambit of existing regu-
> latory provisions ... [All] advertisers should play by the same rules
> and with no exceptions. (Interview, Coleman, 1991)

A system that has so many diverse and fragmented provisions and guidelines is not always considered fair to different categories of advertiser. For example, the CRTC is currently considering whe- ther to permit broadcast advertising for spirit alcohol. At present, only beer and wine products can be advertised on radio or television. Where special provisions are made, convincing rationales have been developed to answer questions as to why the same criteria and standards are not applied to all categories of products (risky, medicinal) or consumers (vulnerable groups like children). We would also note that the current system distinguishes broadcast advertis- ing from that in newspapers and magazines on the grounds that the former has special obligations as a public service under the *Broadcasting Act*. On the other hand, the differential treatment of cable distribution has long been a contested area of advertising law (Swinton 1977), leading to anomalous situations where children's advertisements that do not meet Canadian standards can be viewed on signals redistributed on cable from outside Canada (Kline 1988). There has been, however, no persuasive argument for the differential treatment of party political advertising and advocacy and institutional advertising.

We can see no problem in applying the standards for false and deceptive advertising and comparative advertising to political advertising in its broadest sense. The difficulties in applying Canada's approach to the regulation of commercial advertising to political advertising arise mainly from the failure to develop criteria for the application of general principles that should apply to all advertising in this subject area. Without a broad policy for political advertising (including standard setting, monitoring, review and tax status), a policy that applies to all forms of public service announcements, interest-group, advocacy, party, government and corporate advertising, charges of unfairness in political advertising are likely to increase.

CONCLUSIONS AND RECOMMENDATIONS

A healthy democracy presumes the existence of an informed and involved electorate. The increasing expenditures of the major political parties on broadcast advertising are not, however, a result of their pursuit of this goal. Broadcast advertising is currently the preferred means of exerting political influence for quite pragmatic reasons. By adopting strategies analogous to those employed in commercial advertising, political parties use broadcast advertising as the most effective direct channel available to them for exerting influence on the electorate. Political advertising is thought of as a form of social communication, which can consolidate party image and loyalty, introduce new leaders and policies to the public, shift a party's "market share" and help to influence swing voters. Because broadcast advertising is the most cost-effective and strategically valuable vehicle of political communication, it is therefore likely that its use will continue to grow among the major parties, the minor parties and special-interest groups.

It is for these reasons that we recommend a systemic approach to political communications at election time and, indeed, throughout the year to ensure a fair and diverse political debate and maintain a politically informed electorate, as well as to monitor, adjudicate and report on the maintenance of fairness and equity in the communication process.

To achieve these objectives, the expansion of the role of free broadcast advertising is becoming increasingly urgent, in order to provide greater direct access to the electorate for all legitimate political parties, irrespective of past performance and current popularity. More specifically, we believe that the most effective way to provide a more equitable and diverse allocation of direct access for all registered political parties to the public through broadcast media channels would be to institute a system of free time programming of two-minute units, both throughout the year and at election time.

The broadcast industry, including cable companies, has a special responsibility to contribute to the information of the electorate. The proposed system of free advertising time would address the problem of unfair competitive advantage currently held by the private broadcasters, who do not provide the same opportunities for party access to the public as does the CBC. Free time party programming in prime time should be required by the CRTC of all broadcast licensees and cable companies throughout the year, with a set allocation for each broadcast organization and special obligations during election campaigns. The performance of this obligation by broadcasters must be monitored and reported to the CRTC. Full compliance and evidence of fairness and equity in its performance should be required.

Free time programming is an important means of broadening the scope of political discussion in Canada and of encouraging fair partisan debate to take place throughout the year. The general approach to this category of political programming should follow the studio format of the "Nation's Business," so that it enables all registered parties equally to articulate their policies to the nation, without having journalists act as intermediaries. Programming of this sort should be regarded as "free time advertising" and should be equally available to all registered parties. That is, if there are 50 broadcast periods available and 10 registered political parties, each party would receive 5 broadcast periods. New political parties would also be eligible for time, based on the present criteria defining a registered political party. Free time broadcasts organized in this way would ensure that smaller parties without the resources to mount major campaigns in the broadcast media would have access to the public.

We further recommend that the government seek to replace the election "ban" on nonparty voices with a revised set of allocation, arbitration and monitoring procedures that recognize that both party and nonparty voices will want direct access to audiences for the purpose of expressing views on important public matters. To achieve this end and further guarantee fairness and equity in paid and free political advertising without impinging upon freedoms of political speech, new legislation should be enacted to expand the role and scope of the work performed by the broadcasting arbitrator, establishing these obligations in a commission that would take responsibility for monitoring, arbitrating, hearing complaints, reporting, and otherwise ensuring transparency, equity and fairness in political broadcasting during elections. In particular, advertising should be recognized and defined in law as a commercial transaction between a broadcaster and the advertiser, whether that advertiser is a government, corporation, independent interest group, charity or political party.

The establishment of a new process for the administration of all paid political advertising would make it possible to tackle several areas of potential unfairness. First, there are invisible subsidies and tax benefits for corporate and other special-interest organizations that engage in "advocacy" advertising as a means of "nonpartisan" political communication during elections, so all paid messages that are noncommercial in nature must be regarded as political advertising. Since there is at present no uniformity or regularity in the monitoring and application of advertising standards to commercial and political advertising, the public's expectation that honesty and integrity are maintained in all advertising is not assured. If this issue is not addressed, the public will be increasingly confused about the standards and complaints procedures appropriate to emerging political advertising practices. For example, to whom do you complain about a false statement made in a political advertisement?

Second, the new commission should ensure an open environment while harmonizing the standards applied to broadcast advertising. These objectives can be achieved by moving the legislation concerning false and misleading advertising from the *Competition Act* to the *Broadcasting Act*, and making the guidelines and procedures for violations of the Act apply to all paid advertisements, whether they are for products, services or the promotion of political views.

Third, since there also appears to be a potential abuse in the current confused and unmonitored system of advertising regulation, the commission should be instructed to establish, administer and publicize during the election period guidelines concerning fairness, equity and community standards in political advertising in its broadest sense, including, therefore, government advertising and noncommercial messages of corporations and third-party interest groups.

Fourth, the commission should have the power both to set and adjust the total time allocation for political advertising during the election period in order to accommodate all demands for paid advertising. This time should be considered as a special allocation in addition to the normal quota for commercial advertising set by the CRTC, so that no bumping of certified commercial advertising takes place during the election period. In pursuit of these goals, the commission should further be obliged to monitor, arbitrate and report to both the chief electoral officer and the CRTC the full details of expenditures for time allocations and complaints about all political advertising in the election period, so that these are matters of public record. The commission must furthermore have the power to establish, administer and publicize its own guidelines and to oversee preclearance, review and complaints procedures for broadcast advertising in the pre-election and election periods.

Fifth, the commission's administrative procedures should ensure that all advertisements that are to be aired during the month preceding polling day should receive a preclearance certificate from a Political Advertising Standards Council (PASC). The PASC should be constituted like other standards councils as a nonpartisan body, which adjudicates compliance with the guidelines approved by the commission or the CRTC as they pertain to political advertising. Membership of the council should be diverse but include representatives approved by all political parties and representatives of public and private broadcasters. The PASC would preview all paid advertisements to be run during the month before polling day (storyboards would be acceptable) and would grant a preclearance certificate. This certificate should be presented to the broadcaster before the airing of any advertisement in this period.

In the case of commercial and government informational advertising, advertisements would be classed as "nonpolitical" in that their messages promote a product, program or service. This certification would also entitle private advertisers to claim the usual tax concessions associated with business expenditures on advertising, in accordance with the *Income Tax Act*. All other advertisements would be classified as "political," and would be accounted for in the special time allocation set by the commission. These expenditures should not be eligible for tax grants, concessions or rebates under the *Income Tax Act* or the *Canada Elections Act*. The PASC would ensure that all advertisements so certified clearly identify the agency or party that purchased the time for the advertisement.

The commission should also ensure an open environment through careful monitoring, accounting and reporting of all media buys on a national and regional basis; indeed, these procedures are essential to maintaining public confidence. The commission must itself make public its allocations and the results of its arbitration activities, and be equipped to respond to complaints. However, since preclearance implies the public disclosure of both message- and media-buying strategies, it is likely that the existence of a PASC would itself inhibit any particular party or organization from achieving unfair strategic advantage through surprise, deception or other illicit means. With regard to equity considerations, the commission should expect each station to be accountable for its media buys, while striving to ensure that no single political party or view achieves predominance in the media through the ability to finance advertising. Monitoring, arbitrating and publishing the media buying plans is probably the best way to ensure that individual broadcasters or targeted strategies do not create de facto inequities in their allocations, but a maximum of 30 percent of any station's time should be granted to any one party or organization.

These proposals are offered as guidelines for establishing a fairer, more democratic and diverse political environment; they are also offered to stimulate political discourse during election campaigns in Canada.

APPENDIX A

Table 5.A1
Election dates 1867–1988

1988	November 21	1930	July 28
1984	September 4	1926	September 14
1980	February 18	1925	October 29
1979	May 22	1921	December 6
1974	July 8	1917	December 17
1972	October 30	1911	September 21
1968	June 25	1908	October 26
1965	November 8	1904	November 3
1963	April 8	1900	November 7
1962	June 18	1896	June 23
1958	March 31	1891	March 5
1957	June 10	1887	February 22
1953	August 10	1882	June 20
1949	June 27	1878	September 17
1945	June 11	1874	January 22
1940	March 26	1872	July 20–October 12
1935	October 14	1867	August 7–September 20

Source: Black (1984).

APPENDIX B

Table 5.B1
Election spending 1988

	PC		Liberal		NDP	
	$	%	$	%	$	%
Advertising	721 557	9*	812 365	12	155 872	2
Broadcasting						
Radio	1 554 667	20	1 023 465	15	476 998	7
Television	2 440 503	31	2 024 456	30	2 495 316	35
Total campaign spending	7 921 738	—	6 839 875	—	7 060 563	—
Reimbursement	1 782 391	—	1 538 972	—	1 588 627	—

Other parties total campaign spending (breakdowns not available)	$
Communist Party of Canada	37 001
Confederation of Regions	6 868
Green Party of Canada	1 857
Libertarian Party	163 955
Parti Rhinocéros	5 730
Party for Commonwealth	55 073
Reform Party of Canada	112 367
Social Credit	3 462

Source: Canada, Elections Canada (1988b).

*Indicates percentage of monies spent in category before reimbursement. The percentages do not total 100% because expenditures unrelated to advertising are omitted.

Table 5.B2
Election spending 1984

	PC		Liberal		NDP	
	$	%	$	%	$	%
Advertising	206 651	3*	763 482	12	153 846	3
Broadcasting						
Radio	1 236 075	19	1 069 248	17	494 466	10
Television	1 757 944	28	1 695 186	27	1 158 150	24
Total campaign spending	6 388 941	—	6 292 983	—	4 730 723	—
Reimbursement	1 437 512	—	1 415 921	—	1 064 413	—

Other parties total campaign spending (breakdowns not available)	$
Party for Commonwealth	12 068
Communist Party of Canada	32 118
Confederation of Regions	34 649
Green Party of Canada	15 983
Libertarian Party	45 818
Parti Rhinocéros	3 371
Social Credit	5 155
Union Populaire/Parti Nationaliste	56 161

Source: Canada, Elections Canada (1984).

* Indicates percentage of monies spent in category before reimbursement. The percentages do not total 100% because expenditures unrelated to advertising are omitted.

Table 5.B3
Election spending 1980

	PC		Liberal		NDP	
	$	%	$	%	$	%
Advertising	578 246	13*	402 504	10	425 943	14
Broadcasting						
Radio	651 541	15	578 597	15	233 105	8
Television	1 876 284	43	1 612 532	42	1 167 232	38
Total campaign spending	4 407 207	—	3 846 223	—	3 086 176	—
Reimbursement	977 835	—	909 923	—	677 481	—

Other political parties	$	%
Social Credit		
Advertising	12 409	13
Broadcasting		
Radio	3 586	4
Television	1 974	2
Total campaign spending	98 510	—
Reimbursement	1 749	—
Total spending by other registered parties		
Marxist-Leninist Party	68 365	—
Communist Party of Canada	2 872	—
Libertarian Party	15 344	—
Parti Rhinocéros	9 167	—
Union Populaire	7 434	—

Source: Canada, Elections Canada (1980), as cited in Seidle and Paltiel (1981, 254).

*Indicates percentage of monies spent in category before reimbursement. The percentages do not total 100% because expenditures unrelated to advertising are omitted.

Table 5.B4
Election spending 1979

	PC		Liberal		NDP	
	$	%	$	%	$	%
Advertising	267 209	7*	576 168	15	314 613	14
Broadcasting						
Radio	939 272	24	563 029	14	247 616	11
Television	1 539 020	40	1 295 208	33	770 851	35
Total campaign spending	3 845 217	—	3 912 826	—	2 190 093	—
Reimbursement	793 967	—	718 020	—	496 350	—

Other parties total campaign spending	$
Communist Party of Canada	3 999
Libertarian Party	13 329
Marxist-Leninist Party	31 118
Parti Rhinocéros	8 634
Social Credit	109 402
Union Populaire	0

Source: Canada, Elections Canada (1980), as cited in Seidle and Paltiel (1981, 252).

*Indicates percentage of monies spent in category before reimbursement. The percentages do not total 100% because expenditures unrelated to advertising are omitted.

APPENDIX C

Table 5.C1
Comparative television free time for the election years 1957, 1958, 1962, 1963, 1965, 1974, 1984, 1988
(in minutes)

Political party	1957	1958	1962	1963	1965 CBC-TV (Eng./Fr.)	1965 All private TV stations
		(CBC English and French TV)				
Progressive Conservative	105	120	135	105	102	58
Liberal	120	105	105	90	123	47
CCF/NDP	75	75	75	52.5	65	16
Social Credit	60	60	45	52.5	35	26
Créditiste	—	—	—	—	30	—
Total free time minutes	360	360	360	300	355	147

	1974 Total [CBC-TV (Eng.) ; CTV] (%)		1984 (CBC-TV, Eng./Fr. ; CTV) (%)		1988 (CBC-TV, Eng./Fr. ; CTV) (%)	
Progressive Conservative	123 [70/53]	32*	64.9	31	101	47
Liberal	123 [70/53]	32	87	41	46	21
NDP	69 [42/27]	18	34.7	16	35	16
Social Credit	56 [28/28]	15	—		2	0.9
Parti Rhinocéros	—		4.9	2	4	2
Communist Party of Canada	7	2	2.75	1	2	0.9
Marxist-Leninist Party	7	2	—		—	
Libertarian Party	—		2.75	1	3	1
Pro-Life Party	—		2.75	1	—	
Green Party of Canada	—		2.75	1	2	0.9
Confederation of Regions	—		2.75	1	2	0.9
United Canada Concept	—		2.75	1	—	
L'Action des hommes d'affaires	—		2.75	1	—	
Parti Nationaliste du Québec	—		—		3	1
Party for Commonwealth	—		—		2	0.9
CHP of Canada	—		—		2	0.9
Canada Party	—		—		2	0.9

Table 5.C1 (cont'd)

Political party	1974	1984	1988
Reform Party of Canada	—	—	2 (0.9)
Student Party of Canada	—	—	2 (0.9)
Western Canada Concept	—	—	2 (0.9)
Western Independence Party	—	—	2 (0.9)
Total free time minutes	385	210.75	214

Sources: 1957, 1958, 1962, 1963, 1965: Canada, Committee (1966, 387, 389, 399); 1974: Fletcher (1975, 279); 1984: Canada, Elections Canada (1984, 89); 1988: Canada, Elections Canada (1989, 77–78).

*Percentage of free time allocated, to nearest number, based on total free time minutes.

APPENDIX D

Table 5.D1
Paid time made available to political parties for election advertising 1979–88
(in minutes)

Political party	1988	%	1984	%	1980	%	1979	%
Progressive Conservative	195	48*	129	31	143	36	134	34
Liberal	89	22	173	41	137	35	155	40
NDP	67	16.5	69	16.5	64	16	63	16
Parti Rhinocéros	7	2	8	2	6	1.5	—	—
Libertarian Party	5	1.2	5.5	1	6	1.5	—	—
Green Party of Canada	4	1	5.5	1	—	—	—	—
Confederation of Regions	4	1	5.5	1	—	—	—	—
Party for Commonwealth	4	1	—	—	—	—	—	—
Social Credit	3	0.7	—	—	22	6	22	6
Communist Party of Canada	3	0.7	5.5	1	6	1.5	8	2
Pro-Life Party	—	—	5.5	1	—	—	—	—
L'Action des hommes d'affaires du Canada	—	—	5.5	1	—	—	—	—
United Canada Confederation Party	—	—	5.5	1	—	—	—	—
Marxist-Leninist Party	—	—	—	—	6	1.5	8	2
CHP of Canada	3	0.7	—	—	—	—	—	—
Canada Party	3	0.7	—	—	—	—	—	—
Reform Party of Canada	3	0.7	—	—	—	—	—	—
Student Party of Canada	3	0.7	—	—	—	—	—	—
Western Canada Concept	3	0.7	—	—	—	—	—	—
Western Independence Party	3	0.7	—	—	—	—	—	—
Total paid time	405		417.5		390		390	

Sources: 1979: CRTC (1979); 1980: CRTC (1980); 1984: CRTC (1984); 1988: Canada, Elections Canada (1989).

*Percentage based on total paid time available. Figures to the nearest number.

APPENDIX E

Table 5.E1
Cost of television advertising time for election periods 1968–88
(Network/30-second spot)

	CBC-TV[a] ($)	CTV-TV[b] ($)
June 1968	1 635 (averaged)	1 890
October 1972	1 512	2 375
July 1974	1 154	2 650
May 1979	2 900	5 480
February 1980	3 100	6 030
August 1984	5 500	9 200
November 1988	n.a.	12 279

Source: Canadian Advertising Rates and Data. Individual volumes from the years 1968 to 1988.
[a] CBC: A time rate 6–11 PM.
[b] CTV: AAA/AA time rate 7–11 PM.

Note: The above figures do not reflect production costs, nor do they account for advertising packages consisting of multiple-run ads.

n.a. = not available.

ABBREVIATIONS

Alta. L.R. (2d)	Alberta Law Reports, Second Series
am.	amended
c.	chapter
en.	enacted
Q.B.	Court of Queen's Bench
R.S.C.	Revised Statutes of Canada
S.C.	Statutes of Canada
s(s).	section(s)

NOTES

Editor's Note: This study, completed in December 1991, has been heavily edited to reduce overlap with other papers and to remove substantial sections that were prepared as background for the Royal Commission but were not needed to advance the study's central arguments. Much of the editorial work was done under my supervision by Todd Harris and Claudia Forgas, with the assistance and cooperation of the senior author.

1. *Paid time* is defined as "time bought and paid for by, or on behalf of, parties or candidates or advocacy groups, and largely under the editorial control of the advertiser."
   Free time is defined as "time given free of charge by the licensee to the party or candidate, and largely under the editorial control of the party or candidate" (CRTC 1987b, 10).
2. This price does not account for nor reflect advertising packages of multiple run [advertisements], in which case the cost per [advertisement] would be lower.

INTERVIEW

Coleman, John, Canadian Advertising Foundation, Toronto, 15 January 1991.

BIBLIOGRAPHY

Advertising Standards Council. 1982. *Organization and Procedures of the Advertising Standards Council.* Toronto.

American Academy of Advertising. Advertising and Government Panel. 1979. *Advertising and Government Regulation: A Report by the Advertising and Government Panel of the American Academy of Advertising.* Report prepared by Roy Ashmen et al. Cambridge, Mass.: Marketing Science Institute.

Barrett, Tom. 1988. " 'Humorous' Ads Compare Broadbent to Marx, Ayatollah." *Gazette* (Montreal), 25 October.

Bauch, Hubert. 1980. "TV Ads: Parties Switch to the Offensive." *Gazette* (Montreal), 19 January.

Baum, Daniel J. 1970. "Controversial Broadcasting in Canada." *Osgoode Hall Law Journal* 8:159–70.

Bird, Roger, ed. 1988. *Documents of Canadian Broadcasting.* Ottawa: Carleton University Press.

Bittner, John. 1982. *Broadcast Law and Regulation.* Englewood Cliffs: Prentice-Hall.

Black, Derek. 1984. *Winners and Losers.* Toronto: Methuen.

Blais, André, and Elisabeth Gidengil. 1991. *Making Representative Democracy Work: The Views of Canadians.* Vol. 17 of the research studies of the Royal Commission on Electoral Reform and Party Financing. Ottawa and Toronto: RCERPF/Dundurn.

Blankenship, A.D., Chak Rapani and W.H. Pool. 1985. *A History of Marketing Research in Canada.* Toronto: Marketing Research Society.

Board of Broadcast Governors (BBG). 1961. "Political and Controversial Broadcasting Policies." Circular No. 51, 18 December. Ottawa.

———. 1962a. "Network Free Time." Circular No. 61, 30 April. Ottawa.

———. 1962b. "Unnecessarily Theatrical." Circular No. 57, 12 March. Ottawa.

———. 1963. "Roleplaying." Circular No. 82, 11 March. Ottawa.

———. 1965. "Federal Election Campaign – 1965." 13 September. Ottawa.

———. 1967. "Commercial Content of Political Broadcasts." Circular No. 140, 28 April. Ottawa.

Boyer, J. Patrick. 1982. "Government Advertising: Some Wheat, Too Much Chaff." *Business Quarterly* 47 (4): 34–39.

———. 1983. *Money and Message: The Law Governing Election Financing, Advertising, Broadcasting and Campaigning in Canada.* Toronto: Butterworths.

Brennan, Timothy J. 1989. "The Fairness Doctrine as Public Policy." *Journal of Broadcasting and Electronic Media* 33 (Fall): 419–40.

Broadcasting. 1990. "FCC's Repeal of Fairness Doctrine Survives Supreme Court." 15 January, 56–57.

Camp, Dalton. 1970. *Gentlemen, Players and Politicians.* Toronto: McClelland and Stewart.

Campbell, Murray. 1988. "TV Generation Zapping the Election Process." *Globe and Mail,* 7 November.

Canada. *An Act to amend the Canada Elections Act,* S.C. 1980–81–82–83, c. 96.

———. *An Act to amend the Canada Elections Act (No. 3),* S.C. 1980–81–82–83, c. 164.

———. Bill C-79, *An Act to amend the Canada Elections Act,* 2nd Session, 33rd Parliament, 1986–87.

———. *Broadcasting Act,* S.C. 1958, c. 22, ss. 11(1)(*f*) and (*i*), 17.

———. *Broadcasting Act,* S.C. 1967–68, c. 25, ss. 16, 28.

———. *Broadcasting Act,* R.S.C. 1985, c. B-9.

———. *Broadcasting Act,* S.C. 1991, c. 11.

———. *Canada Elections Act,* S.C. 1960, c. 39.

———. *Canada Elections Act,* R.S.C. 1970, c. 14 (1st Supp.), s. 13.7, en. 1973–74, c. 51, s. 4(1); s. 61.2, en. 1973–74, c. 51, s. 7; s. 70.1, en. 1973–74, c. 51, s. 12; am. 1980–81–82–83, c. 164, s. 14; s. 99.1, en. 1973–74, c. 51, s. 14; am. 1977–78, c. 3, s. 58; re-en. 1980–81–82–83, c. 164, s. 17.

———. *Canada Elections Act,* R.S.C. 1985, c. E-2; am. R.S.C. 1985, c. 27 (2nd Supp.); am. 1989, c. 28.

————. *Canadian Broadcasting Act*, S.C. 1936, c. 24, s. 22.

————. *Canadian Charter of Rights and Freedoms*, ss. 2(*b*), 3, Part I of the *Constitution Act, 1982*, being Schedule B of the *Canada Act 1982* (U.K.), 1982, c. 11.

————. *Canadian Radio Broadcasting Act*, S.C. 1932, c. 51.

————. *Competition Act*, R.S.C. 1985, c. C-34; am. R.S.C. 1985, c. 19 (2nd Supp.).

————. *Election Expenses Act*, S.C. 1973–74, c. 51.

————. *Food and Drugs Act*, R.S.C. 1985, c. F-27.

————. *Income Tax Act*, R.S.C. 1952, c. 148.

Canada. Committee on Election Expenses. 1966. *Report*. Ottawa: Queen's Printer.

Canada. Consumer and Corporate Affairs Canada. Director of Investigation and Research. 1990a. *Misleading Advertising Bulletin*, No. 2. Ottawa: CCAC.

————. 1990b. Marketing Practices Branch. Selected articles from the *Misleading Advertising Bulletin* (1976–89). Ottawa: CCAC.

Canada. Elections Canada. 1979. *Report of the Chief Electoral Officer Respecting Election Expenses, Thirty-First General Election*. Ottawa: Minister of Supply and Services Canada.

————. 1980. *Report of the Chief Electoral Officer Respecting Election Expenses, Thirty-Second General Election*. Ottawa: Minister of Supply and Services Canada.

————. 1984. *Report of the Chief Electoral Officer of Canada as per subsection 59(1) of the Canada Elections Act*. Ottawa: Minister of Supply and Services Canada.

————. 1985. *Report of the Chief Electoral Officer Respecting Election Expenses, Thirty-Third General Election*. Ottawa: Minister of Supply and Services Canada.

————. 1988a. *Guidelines Respecting Election Expenses of Registered Political Parties*. Ottawa: Elections Canada.

————. 1988b. *Report of the Chief Electoral Officer Respecting Election Expenses, Thirty-Fourth General Election*. Ottawa: Minister of Supply and Services Canada.

————. 1989. *Report of the Chief Electoral Officer of Canada as per subsection 195(1) of the Canada Elections Act*. Ottawa: Minister of Supply and Services Canada.

Canada. Health and Welfare Canada. Health Protection Branch. 1990. *Drugs Directorate Guidelines*. Ottawa: Health and Welfare Canada.

Canada. House of Commons. Special Committee on Election Expenses. 1971. *Report*. Ottawa: Queen's Printer.

Canada. Royal Commission on Broadcasting. 1957. *Report*. Ottawa: Queen's Printer.

Canada. Royal Commission on Radio Broadcasting. 1929. *Report*. Ottawa: King's Printer.

Canada. Task Force on Broadcasting Policy. 1986. *Report*. Ottawa: Minister of Supply and Services Canada.

Canadian Advertising Foundation. 1986. *The Canadian Code of Advertising Standards*. Toronto.

Canadian Advertising Rates and Data. Various years.

Canadian Association of Broadcasters. 1986. *Broadcast Advertising and Children*. Ottawa.

Canadian Broadcasting Corporation (CBC). 1944. *Political and Controversial Broadcasting Policies and Rules*. Ottawa.

———. 1989. *Advertising Standards*. Ottawa.

Canadian Press. 1990. "Election Spending Limits for Interest Groups Denied." *Globe and Mail*, 9 May.

Canadian Radio-Television Commission. 1968a. "Canadian Elections of June 25, 1968." Circular No. 149, 16 May. Ottawa.

———. 1968b. "June 25, 1968 Federal Election Campaign." Circular No. 151, 6 June. Ottawa.

———. 1972. "Canadian Election to be Held on October 30, 1972." Circular No. 179, 26 September. Ottawa.

———. 1974. "Broadcasting Guide for Elections." Circular No. 197, 14 May. Ottawa.

Canadian Radio-television and Telecommunications Commission (CRTC). 1978a. *Broadcast Advertising Handbook, Regulations, and Guidelines on Broadcast Advertising*. Ottawa: Minister of Supply and Services Canada.

———. 1978b. "Notice to Broadcasters – Federal General Elections." Public Announcement, 17 April. Ottawa.

———. 1979. "Federal General Elections – Broadcasting Guide for Federal General Elections." Circular No. 245, 21 March. Ottawa.

———. 1980. "Broadcast Guidelines: Federal General Elections February 18." Circular No. 257. Ottawa.

———. 1984. "Allocation of Federal Election Broadcasting Time." Circular No. 299, 20 July. Ottawa.

———. 1986. "Broadcast Advertising of Alcoholic Beverages and Food and Drugs." Public Notice 1986–247. Ottawa.

————. 1987a. "Regulations Respecting Television Broadcasting." Public Notice 1987–8, 9 January. Ottawa.

————. 1987b. "Election Campaign Broadcasting." Public Notice 1987–209, 23 September. Ottawa.

————. 1988a. "Federal General Election: Guidelines for Broadcast Licenses." Circular No. 351, 4 October. Ottawa.

————. 1988b. "A Policy with Respect to Election Campaign Broadcasting." Public Notice 1988–142, 2 September. Ottawa.

Caplan, Gerald, Michael Kirby and Hugh Segal. 1989. *Election: The Issues, the Strategies, the Aftermath.* Scarborough: Prentice-Hall Canada.

Clark, Harold D., Jane Jenson, Lawrence LeDuc and Jon H. Pammett. 1984. *Absent Mandate: The Politics of Discontent in Canada.* Toronto: Gage.

Clarkson, Stephen. 1981. "The Defeat of the Government, the Decline of the Liberal Party, and the (Temporary) Fall of Pierre Trudeau." In *Canada at the Polls, 1979 and 1980,* ed. Howard R. Penniman. Washington, DC: American Enterprise Institute for Public Policy Research.

Congressional Digest. 1987a. "Broadcasting Fairness Doctrine." (October): 227–31.

————. 1987b. "Recent Action in Congress." (October): 232–33.

Coolican, Murray. 1980. "Watch Those (Government) Ads!" *Maclean's,* 13 October.

Courtney, John C. 1981. "Campaign Strategy and Electoral Victory: The Progressive Conservatives and the 1979 Election." In *Canada at the Polls, 1979 and 1980,* ed. Howard R. Penniman. Washington, DC: American Enterprise Institute for Public Policy Research.

Crandell, Evelyn. 1979. *Complaints Report: Advertising Standards Council.* Toronto.

Davey, Keith. 1986. *The Rainmaker.* Toronto: Stoddart.

Editorial Research Reports. 1987. "At Issue: Is the Fairness Doctrine Fair?" 4 December, 640–41.

Esbin, Sheldon. 1979a. "A Compliance Test for False or Misleading Ads." *Marketing* (21 May): 18–19.

————. 1979b. "In Search of the 'Credulous Man': A Lawyer Looks Through the Haze of Canadian Legislation on False and Misleading Advertising." *Marketing* (14 May): 10.

Financial Times of Canada. 1988. "The Financial Times/Decima Poll – 56% Endorse the Use of Political Advertising by Business." 19 December.

Fletcher, Frederick J. 1975. "The Mass Media in the 1974 Canadian Elections." In *Canada at the Polls: The Canadian General Election of 1974,* ed. Howard R. Penniman. Washington, DC: American Enterprise Institute for Public Policy Research.

———. 1981. "Playing the Game: The Mass Media and the 1979 Campaign." In *Canada at the Polls, 1979 and 1980: A Study of the General Elections*, ed. Howard R. Penniman. Washington, DC: American Enterprise Institute for Public Policy Research.

———. 1987. "Mass Media and Parliamentary Elections in Canada." *Legislative Studies Quarterly* 12 (August): 341–72.

———. 1988. "The Media and the 1984 Landslide." In *Canada at the Polls, 1984: A Study of the Federal General Election*, ed. Howard R. Penniman. Washington, DC: American Enterprise Institute for Public Policy Research.

———. 1990. "Polling and Political Communication: The Canadian Case." Paper presented to the International Association for Mass Communication Research, Yugoslavia.

Frizzell, Alan, and Anthony Westell. 1985. *The Canadian General Election of 1984: Politicians, Parties, Press and Polls*. Ottawa: Carleton University Press.

Gilsdorf, William. 1981. "Getting the Message Across: Media Strategies and Political Campaigns." In *Communication Studies in Canada*, ed. Liora Salter. Toronto: Butterworths.

Ginsberg, Douglas. 1979. *Controversial Issues in Advertising: The Problem of Issue Definition in Regulation of Broadcasting*. St. Paul: West.

Globe and Mail. 1980. "Call It Propaganda." 10 October.

———. 1988a. "Party Ads Woo Voters Tomorrow." 22 October.

———. 1988b. "Last Ad Blitz Costing P.C.'s $2 Million." 16 November.

———. 1990. "Canadian Political Ads Expected to Turn Nastier." 12 November.

Goar, Carol. 1980. "$6 Million Worth of Spit and Polish." *Winnipeg Free Press*, 9 January.

Graham, Ron. 1985. "The Unlikely Godfather Norman Atkins." *Saturday Night* (May): 17–29.

———. 1987. *One-Eyed Kings: Promises and Illusions in Canadian Politics*. Don Mills: Totem Books.

Gwyn, Richard. 1962. "Admen and Scientists Run This Election." *Financial Post*, 28 April.

Hiebert, Janet. 1989–90. "Fair Elections and Freedom of Expression Under the Charter." *Journal of Canadian Studies* 24 (4): 72–86.

Hogg, Peter. 1985. *Constitutional Law in Canada*. 2d ed. Toronto: Carswell.

Irvine, William P. 1981. "Epilogue: The 1980 Election." In *Canada at the Polls, 1979 and 1980: A Study of the General Elections*, ed. Howard R. Penniman. Washington, DC: American Enterprise Institute for Public Policy Research.

Isberg, Seymour. 1981. "Spend and Win? Another Look at Federal Election Expenses." *Optimum* 12 (4): 5–15.

Kline, Stephen. 1988. "The Limits to the Imagination." In *Cultural Politics in America*, ed. Sut Jhally and Ian Angus. New York: Routledge.

Kopvillem, Peeter. 1988. "Prime Time for a Blitz of Ads: Commercials, Not Policy, Prevail." *Maclean's* (31 October): 21, 22.

LaCalamita, John. 1984. "The Equitable Campaign: Party Political Broadcasting Regulation in Canada." *Osgoode Hall Law Journal* 22: 543–79.

Laxer, James. 1976. *The Big Tough Expensive Job*. Erin: Porcepic Press.

Lee, Robert Mason. 1989. *One Hundred Monkeys: The Triumph of Popular Wisdom in Canadian Politics*. Toronto: Macfarlane, Walter and Ross.

Leiss, William, Stephen Kline and Sut Jhally. 1990. *Social Communication in Advertising*. 2d ed. Scarborough: Nelson Canada.

McCall-Newman, Christina. 1982. *Grits: An Intimate Portrait of the Liberal Party*. Toronto: Macmillan of Canada.

MacDonald, L. Ian. 1980. "Feds Show They Are Masters of Subliminal Advertising." *Gazette* (Montreal), 8 August.

———. 1984. *Mulroney: The Making of the Prime Minister*. Toronto: McClelland and Stewart.

McKenzie, Robert. 1988. "Liberals' French TV Ads Blast Mulroney's 'Lies.' " *Toronto Star*, 24 October.

Magnet, Joseph Elliot. 1985. *Constitutional Law in Canada: Canadian Charter of Rights and Freedoms, Volume 2*. 2d ed. Toronto: Carswell.

Marketing. 1984. "Turner Is the Product That Liberal Ads Will Sell." 6 August.

———. 1988a. "All's *Not* Well That Ends Well." 28 November.

———. 1988b. "It's Advertising Big Sell." 10 October.

Meadow, Robert J. 1981. "The Political Dimensions of Nonproduct Advertising." *Journal of Communication* 31 (3): 69–82.

Meeske, Milan D. 1974. "Editorial Advertising and the First Amendment." *Journal of Broadcasting* 17 (4): 417–26.

Meisel, John. 1962. *The Canadian General Election of 1957*. Toronto: University of Toronto Press.

Moon, Barbara. 1962. "The Back-Room Conspiracy." *Maclean's* (28 July), 15, 41–44.

Morton, Desmond. 1986. *The New Democrats, 1961–1986: The Politics of Change.* Toronto: Copp Clark Pitman.

Muncie, Colin. 1984. "The Selling of Brian, John and Ed." *Marketing,* 10 September.

National Citizens' Coalition Inc./Coalition nationale des citoyens inc. v. Canada (Attorney General) (1984), 32 Alta. L.R. (2d) 249 (Q.B.).

Newman, Peter C. 1968. *The Distemper of Our Times.* Winnipeg: Greywood.

———. 1973. *Renegade in Power: The Diefenbaker Years.* Toronto: McClelland and Stewart.

Nolan, Michael. 1984. "A Special Challenge for Canada's Media." *Globe and Mail,* 23 July.

Ontario. Commission on Election Contributions and Expenses. 1982. *Canadian Election Reform: Dialogue on Issues and Effects, December 1982.* Toronto: The Commission.

Ontario. Commission on Election Finances. 1988. *A Comparative Survey of Election Finance Legislation 1988.* Toronto: The Commission.

Paltiel, Khayyam Z. 1974. "Party and Candidate Expenditures in the Canadian General Election of 1972." *Canadian Journal of Political Science* 7:341–52.

———. 1975. "Campaign Financing in Canada and Its Reform." In *Canada at the Polls: The General Election of 1974,* ed. Howard R. Penniman. Washington, DC: American Enterprise Institute for Public Policy Research.

———. 1988. "The 1984 Federal General Election and Developments in Canadian Party Finance." In *Canada at the Polls, 1984: A Study of the Federal General Election,* ed. Howard R. Penniman. Washington, DC: American Enterprise Institute for Public Policy Research.

Penniman, Howard R., ed. 1975. *Canada at the Polls: The General Election of 1974.* Washington, DC: American Enterprise Institute for Public Policy Research.

———, ed. 1981. *Canada at the Polls, 1979 and 1980: A Study of the General Elections.* Washington, DC: American Enterprise Institute for Public Policy Research.

———, ed. 1988. *Canada at the Polls, 1984.* Washington, DC: American Enterprise Institute for Public Policy Research.

Persky, Stan. 1990. "When It Came to the Crunch, Volvo Ads Were Misleading." *Vancouver Sun,* 24 November.

Philcox, Brian. 1989. "The Public Has a Right to Know What's for Sale." *Globe and Mail,* 16 January.

Poirier, Patricia. 1988. "Parties Blanket Francophones with $4 Million in Election Ads." *Globe and Mail*, 24 October.

Qualter, Terence H. 1970. *The Election Process in Canada*. Toronto: McGraw-Hill.

Robinson, Jennifer. 1988. "Slick Television Ad Campaign Under Way to Sell Parties to Canadians." *Gazette* (Montreal), 24 October.

Romanow, Walter I., Walter C. Soderlund and Richard G. Price. 1991. "Negative Political Advertising: An Analysis of Research Findings in Light of Canadian Practice." In *Political Ethics: A Canadian Perspective*, ed. Janet Hiebert. Vol. 12 of the research studies of the Royal Commission on Electoral Reform and Party Financing. Ottawa and Toronto: RCERPF/Dundurn.

Rose, Jonathan. 1990. "Ethics and Advertising by Political Parties and Interest Groups: A Background Study of Some Key Issues." Issue paper prepared for the Royal Commission on Electoral Reform and Party Financing. Ottawa.

Sears, Val. 1988. "Tories Plan to Step Up 'Liar' Ads on Turner." *Toronto Star*, 2 November.

Seib, Philip. 1987. *Who's in Charge? How the Media Shape News and Politicians Win Votes*. Dallas: Taylor.

Seidle, F. Leslie. 1985. "The Election Expenses Act: The House of Commons and the Parties." In *The Canadian House of Commons: Essays in Honour of Norman Ward*, ed. John C. Courtney. Calgary: University of Calgary Press.

Seidle, F. Leslie, and Khayyam Zev Paltiel. 1981. "Party Finance, the Election Expenses Act, and Campaign Spending in 1979 and 1980." In *Canada at the Polls, 1979 and 1980: A Study of the General Elections*, ed. Howard R. Penniman. Washington, DC: American Enterprise Institute for Public Policy Research.

Shwartz, Tony. 1973. *The Responsive Chord*. New York: Anchor.

Simpson, Jeffrey. 1988. *Spoils of Power: The Politics of Patronage*. Toronto: Collins.

Singer, Murray, and Fernanda Ferreira. 1982. *Empirical Research on Misleading Advertising: A Review, 1982*. Ottawa: Consumer and Corporate Affairs Canada, Marketing Practices Branch.

Smyka, Mark. 1979. "This Time the 'Products' Are Political Leaders." *Marketing* (2 April).

Soderlund, Walter C., Walter I. Romanow, E. Donald Briggs and Ronald H. Wagenberg. 1984. *Media and Elections in Canada*. Toronto: Holt, Rinehart and Winston of Canada.

Strauss, Marina. 1990. "Government Must Restrain Ad-Lib Claims." *Globe and Mail*, 30 November.

Stridsberg, Albert. 1977. *Controversial Advertising: How Advertisers Present Points of View on Public Affairs*. New York: Communication Arts Books, Hastings House.

Sutter, Stan. 1989. "Elections: Violating the Spirit of Fair Play." *Marketing*, 24 April.

Swinton, K. 1977. "Advertising and Canadian CATV – A Problem in International Communication Law." *Osgoode Hall Law School* 15:543–90.

Tatham, Cautley. 1984. "Ad Industry One of the Losers in This Campaign." *Marketing*, 17 September.

Telecaster Committee of Canada. 1980. Pamphlet.

———. 1990. *Agency Kit*.

Toronto Star. 1984. "The Selling of a Leader: Do TV Ads Work?" 1 September.

———. 1988a. "Are Ad Blitzes Eroding Democracy?" 29 November.

———. 1988b. "Coming at You Starting Sunday: $6 Million in TV Ads on Election." 19 October.

Vancouver Sun. 1988. "Is Ordinary Ed Out of Time?" 15 November.

Vandal, N. Jill (Carruthers). 1982. *The Use of Communications Research in the Determination of Misleading and Deceptive Advertising*. Ottawa: Consumer and Corporate Affairs Canada, Marketing Practices Branch.

Vipond, Mary. 1989. *The Mass Media in Canada*. Toronto: James Lorimer and Company.

Wearing, Joseph. 1981. *The L-Shaped Party: The Liberal Party of Canada, 1958–1980*. Toronto: McGraw-Hill Ryerson.

Whitaker, Reginald. 1977. *The Government Party: Organizing and Financing the Liberal Party of Canada, 1930–58*. Toronto: University of Toronto Press.

White, Theodore. 1961. *The Making of the President, 1960*. New York: Atheneum.

Wills, Terrance. 1988. "Election Expected to Be the Costliest Ever." *Gazette* (Montreal), 27 August.

Wilson, Rob. 1984. "P.M. Race a Bonanza for Dailies." *Marketing*, 30 July.

Winsor, Hugh. 1984. "The Tories' Master Chef with a Recipe for Victory." *Globe and Mail*, 10 September.

Winter, James P. 1990. *The Silent Revolution: Media, Democracy, and the Free Trade Debate*. Ottawa: University of Ottawa Press.

Young, Walter D. 1981. "The New Democratic Party in the 1979 Federal General Election." In *Canada at the Polls, 1979 and 1980*, ed. Howard R. Penniman. Washington, DC: American Enterprise Institute for Public Policy Research.

Zarry, P., and R. Wilson, eds. 1981. *Advertising in Canada: Its Theory and Practice*. Toronto: McGraw-Hill Ryerson.

6

THE CBC
NORTHERN SERVICE
AND
THE FEDERAL
ELECTORAL PROCESS
Problems and Strategies
for Improvement

Lorna Roth

I THINK ONE OF THE PROBLEMS we've had with the CBC is that they get into some of the larger communities, but they don't reach some of the very small ones, and I guess my problem is that those people who live in those very small communities are Canadians too. And to me every Canadian should have the same access to information as every other. CBC doesn't go there to cover issues because of budget constraints. The thing is, though, that this would never do in the other two-thirds of Canada. I mean this is one-third of Canada. And if you were to take this and transplant it into Quebec and Ontario and do exactly what's being done in the North in Quebec or Ontario, you'd have an almighty scream coming out of parliamentarians that would just horrify the House. That doesn't ever happen up here because there isn't that representation. I think there are some improvements that can be made.

(Pat McMahon, mayor of Yellowknife, 11 December 1990)

INTRODUCTION AND METHODOLOGICAL COMMENTS
This study explores the roles and performance of CBC Northern Service radio and television programming in the context of the federal election

of 1988. It also addresses the perceptions of and reactions to electoral coverage programming by CBC Northern Service target audiences in the Northwest Territories and northern Quebec.[1] It was undertaken in response to a series of complaints about Northern-based election campaign coverage outlined at the hearings of the Royal Commission on Electoral Reform and Party Financing (RCERPF) in Yellowknife, Northwest Territories (24 May 1990) and Iqaluit, Northwest Territories (23 July 1990). The principal object of this study is to discern the relevance of these complaints and provide suggestions for improvements in the CBC Northern Service's coverage of federal elections. Methods employed include the analysis of relevant documentation, the collection of field data through interviews and questionnaires, and the critical examination of all aspects of key issues as initially outlined by northern residents.

Evidence from field work and documentation indicates there are legitimate grounds to formally separate the mandate of the CBC Northern Service from that of the CBC service in the rest of the country in regard to the conduct of each during federal elections. To this end, I have formulated a set of recommendations designed to improve the quantity and quality of election coverage by the CBC Northern Service. Furthermore, given that native broadcasters are now allowed to accept advertising (CRTC 1990) and that Television Northern Canada (TVNC) is expected to be operational by January 1992, I have also commented on the complementary role which native media may play in federal elections.

Methodologically, my first steps were to examine the relevant hearing transcripts and briefs, as well as other pertinent documentation related to northern media coverage, and to place these within appropriate historical contexts. The documentation examined includes the *Canada Elections Act*, CRTC regulations and complaint files, and the CBC's internal election coverage policies and available documentation.

Following this, I proceeded to conduct a total of 56 on-site and telephone interviews with CBC management personnel across the North and in Ottawa, northern complainants and witnesses from the RCERPF hearings, other key northern residents, including federal party candidates and campaign managers from the 1988 election, Native Communications Societies executive directors, and TVNC board members. (See complete list at the end of this study.) Interviews with communications and cultural department personnel within the Northwest Territories (NWT), including the TVNC/NWT liaison person, were also undertaken. Questionnaires were sent to northern Native Communications Societies and follow-up telephone interviews were done with those executive directors who did not return them on schedule.

All these interviews were initially structured around formal questionnaires (see appendix A), but as time progressed it became apparent
that interviewees were more comfortable with the unstructured,
exploratory interview. I also found this to be a productive method
which generated more information than the formal questionnaire.

This study is structured as follows. First, the CBC Northern Service
is placed within its territorial context by discussing the demographics
and political context of the North. This is followed by a history of the
development of CBC Northern Services and an outline of the present
configuration of northern broadcast media. Then specific complaints,
and the CBC Northern Service's response to them, are addressed. The
study concludes with a set of recommendations.

THE NORTHERN DEMOGRAPHIC AND POLITICAL CONTEXT

> It's hard to be on the ground during an election period. By the time
> you've spoken at one end of the country, the other end forgets what
> you said and you've got to start all over again.
>
> (Abe Ookpik, Iqaluit, 4 January 1991)

The Northwest Territories, the Yukon and northern Quebec represent
more than one-third of Canada's total land mass and span four time
zones (see appendix B for map). Northern parts of other provinces,
including Labrador, experience similar problems of inadequate communications reception as does the Far North. However, for the purposes of this study, I have limited my consideration of the North
to those communities and territories which are recipients of CBC
Northern Services.

CBC figures indicate that in the North it serves a population of
approximately 100 000, split among three racial groups – Inuit, Dene and
non-native, approximately half of whom are persons of Aboriginal
descent (CBC 1990c, 6). In the Yukon, the majority of the population is
non-native. Of 23 505 people living there, only 3 280 (14 percent) are
native in ancestry. In the Northwest Territories, the total population is
52 238, of which 27 175 (52 percent) are Aboriginal. Northern Quebec's
native population ratio is even higher at 90 percent of the total. Whereas
47 percent of the overall Canadian population is under the age of 30,
the population of the North is still very young, with 60 percent under
age 30 (Canada, Statistics Canada 1987a, 1987b).

Linguistically, the North is very complex. In the Northwest Territories,
there are nine official languages, seven of which are Aboriginal. They
are: Inuktitut, North and South Slavey, Chipewyan, Dogrib, Gwich'in

and Inuvialuktun. The other two are English and French. There are still some unilingual native-language speakers (mostly elders) in the territories, but the trend for younger people is to speak in English. In northern Quebec, the area covered by the northern Quebec Regional CBC Service, three native languages are spoken: Inuktitut, Cree and Attikamek. The Yukon language situation is quite different. Aside from Old Crow, where the Gwich'in language is still fluently spoken, the remaining six languages are not frequently spoken and most native peoples within the Yukon converse in English (Canada, Statistics Canada 1987a, 1987b).

Both the NWT and the Yukon have elected legislatures. In the Yukon, 16 MLAs are elected along traditional party lines. The Yukon currently has a New Democratic Party (NDP) government headed by Tony Penikett.

The NWT does not operate according to conventions of southern party politics. Rather, it elects a 24-seat legislature which practises "nonpartisan government" and bypasses many of the party traditions followed in the South (Dacks 1986).

> Party organization at the level of territorial constituencies has either been non-existent or rudimentary. Candidates contest the territorial elections as independents. At the start of the first session of the Assembly, the members meet as a "caucus of the whole" to elect from their number those who will sit on the Executive Council. Subsequently, the MLAs elected to the Executive Council nominate several of their colleagues on the Council as candidates for the position of government leader. The full Assembly then elects the leader. A formal vote is required because the absence of parties makes it impossible to use the process for selecting a first minister which is ordinarily applied in a parliamentary system. (Dacks 1986, 351)

The present leader of the NWT legislature is Denis Patterson.

The nonpartisan political practices within the Northwest Territories emerge from very different traditions than those that laid the foundations for the partisan practices of the federal system of government. Special consideration of these is important because this factor is at the basis of the complaints from the NWT population that independent candidates should be, but are not yet, eligible for broadcast access time.

Federally, the Northwest Territories comprises two ridings: the Western Arctic, represented in Parliament by Ethel Blondin (Liberal), and Nunatsiaq, Canada's largest riding. The latter contains 2.6 million square kilometres and 41 small communities. It is currently represented by Jack Anawak (Liberal). The Yukon has only one riding, represented by Audrey McLaughlin, national NDP leader. Northern Quebec is represented by two MPs, neither of whom at the time of this writing has ever visited the northern communities in their constituencies and whose electorate is mainly in the South. The Inuit of northern Quebec, in their RCERPF intervention in Kuujjuaq (24 July 1990), requested a change in the electoral boundaries in the hope that a single riding would cover all of the region north of the 55th parallel. This is supported in a letter to the Commission dated 24 July 1990 by Charles A. Langlois, MP for the present riding of Manicouagan.

The Abitibi riding, in which the James Bay Cree live, is one in which there is very little contact between Aboriginal peoples and their federal MP, Guy St-Julien. The Cree people with whom I spoke indicated that when they have a problem related to a federal issue, they prefer to go directly to the federal Minister of Indian Affairs rather than through their MP. To date, it appears as if the operation of the federal system in northern Quebec has resulted in the marginalization of Aboriginal peoples from participating in federal democratic politics and practices. The boundary problem, coupled with very limited media coverage relevant to northern native interests in general, and a specific absence of electoral coverage, has contributed to this process.[2]

CBC AND OTHER CANADIAN NORTHERN MEDIA: A HISTORICAL PROFILE

Until the formation of the CBC Northern Service in 1958, the only available radio broadcast service in the North was provided by the Canadian Armed Forces and the federal Department of Transport, with some program assistance from the CBC (Canada, Committee 1965, 189). The take-over of the military and community radio stations by the CBC Northern Service was precipitated by the federal government's concern over the assurance of a Canadian presence and sovereignty in the Far North. In the mid-fifties, shortwave radio broadcast reception was notoriously poor and the federal government became alarmed by the fact that Northerners were isolated from the main flow of national life.

Furthermore, in many areas, Soviet and (less frequently) American broadcasts were received more clearly and with more up-to-date programs than the local stations. The Commissioner of the Yukon had expressed his concern in 1957 when he suggested "it would not be surprising if the operators of the Soviet radio service looked upon our northland 'as an interesting battle-ground of Soviet and American ideologies through the medium of radio, while Canadian viewpoints are totally absent'" (Canada, Royal Commission 1957, 213). It was, therefore, critical to federal government sovereignty interests that a relevant Canadian radio service be structured for the North that would reflect southern Canadian interests. Because it was impossible to develop a conventional land-line system for the Eastern Arctic, due to its insurmountable geographic and atmospheric barriers, early federal broadcasting initiatives focused upon the Western Arctic. The East would have to await the advent of satellite technology before broadcast reception service could be improved.

In 1958, the CBC Northern Service took over transmitters in Yellowknife, Whitehorse and Dawson City (CBC 1972, 44). Although some programming was designed specifically for the North, stations still had to rely mainly on the shortwave service from Sackville, New Brunswick for their news broadcasts and various topical programs.

In 1960, the first Inuktitut broadcasts occurred, and in 1961 the concept of a sub-regional production centre, which would feed smaller stations with regional programming, was established (CBC 1978, 2). By May 1972, shortwave service was broadcasting 16.4 percent of its programs to the North in Inuktitut (Roth 1983).

By the 1970s, as radio broadcasting equipment became more accessible and less expensive, many small native communities established community radio stations, often with the assistance of the CBC. Alternatively, the CBC provided access to its local transmitters and arranged affiliate agreements with local communications groups. By 1980 there were at least 150 native community radio stations in Canada (Stiles and Litwack 1986, 21). In 1973, the CBC began delivery of live television broadcasts into 17 northern communities as a result of the activation of the Anik satellite. The same year, the CBC's proposed Northern Broadcasting Plan, which would have expanded its service to include northern television production with some input from native people, was rejected by the federal Cabinet. As a consequence, the CBC allocated some of its resources to produce a modest amount of northern content within its television schedule. This basically took the form of northern public service announcements between scheduled programs, but later included a 15-minute Inuktitut-language program, Taqravut, produced in Montreal with the borrowed resources of the Montreal shortwave radio team (Roth 1983, 29). In 1974, the CBC began to implement the federally funded Accelerated Coverage Plan which further distributed receiver dishes across the North to all communities with a population of 500 or more. The governments of the Northwest Territories and the Yukon supplied relay transmitters in all other smaller communities, so that by the end of the 1970s, CBC radio and television were available in all northern communities with more than 50 people (ibid., 82).

Currently, there are sub-regional radio production centres in Whitehorse, Yellowknife, Inuvik, Kivalliq (Rankin Inlet) and Iqaluit, supported by bureaus in Kuujjuaq, Montreal and Ottawa. Radio programming is rooted in the North and broadcasts much of its schedule in the native languages. Television production centres are located in Yellowknife, with field production bureaus in Whitehorse and Iqaluit, and limited access to production facilities in Ottawa and Montreal.[3]

Native content on CBC northern television, in contrast to radio, is severely limited due to budget constraints. The CBC Northern Service at present produces about 50 hours of original programming each year (CBC 1990c, 5). Its half-hour program, Focus North, is produced in Yellowknife and is broadcast once a week in English. There are only three native-language programs. These are: Aqsarniit, a 19-minute Inuktitut program; Denendeh'keh, a 16-minute program in various Dene languages; and Maamuitaau, a 27-minute Cree program, all of which are broadcast weekly (ibid., 9). Essentially, the "quantity of CBC regional programming available to northern residents remains less than 10% of what the CBC provides in any other region of the country" (ibid.). It is important to note existing available times because these are the regional time-slots that might be used for electoral broadcasting purposes in the future (see appendix C for existing CBC Northern Service schedules).

The CBC proposed the establishment of a pan-Arctic daily news program in May 1990 (1990c), but with the 1991 CBC budget cuts the possibility of financing this undertaking is, unfortunately, tenuous. From both the native people's and management's perspectives, the CBC Northern Service has taken too long to incorporate native programming and has not dedicated enough resources to the development of native television production.

Since the late 1960s, after the passing of the Telesat Act (1969), native people in the North have argued for control of their own media infrastructures for the production of native-oriented radio and television (Telesat Canada 1979). In the late 1970s, several native groups were given the opportunity to experiment with the technical and native-language programming potential of the Anik B satellite. In particular, the Inuit of northern Quebec and the Northwest Territories benefited from these access experiments by getting media production and distribution training. As a result of having participated in the Inukshuk and Naalakvik projects from 1978 to 1981, the Inuit proved to the federal authorities that they were capable of organizing, operating and managing a broadcasting undertaking with a significant budget. In 1981, the Inuit Broadcasting Corporation was issued a licence to become a television broadcasting undertaking.[4] They negotiated with the CBC Northern Service and gained access to their transponder for approximately five hours per week for Inuktitut programming.[5]

Since 1981 a powerful native broadcasting lobby has been mounted. In 1983 the Northern Broadcasting Policy was announced and was accompanied by a federal program called the Northern Native Broadcast Access Program (NNBAP). The policy laid out the framework for native media development and included the notion of fair access to broadcasting production and distribution facilities and called for participation of native people in future broadcasting policy development. The NNBAP was to provide 13 regional Native Communications Societies with $40.3 million over the next four years to help develop and sustain the production of 20 hours of native-language radio and five hours of television programming per week.

The Native Communications Societies (NCSs) complement the CBC's programming by filling in the native-language gaps and by providing cultural perspectives targeted toward native, and in some cases, non-native audiences. For example, Northern Native Broadcasting, Yukon, broadcasts mostly in English and has negotiated a distribution arrangement with CBC Newsworld and some of the provincial educational services. Audience reach for its program "Nedaa – Your Eye on the Yukon" is quite extensive and national in scope. In general, NCSs have been evaluated as a highly successful and productive government program (Abrahamson et al. 1986).

A list of the Native Communications Societies within the regions addressed in this study follows.[6] (See appendix D for geographic locations.)

Location	Name of NCS	Output
Whitehorse	Northern Native Broadcasting, Yukon	Radio and television
Yellowknife	NCS of the Western NWT	Radio and newspaper
Inuvik	Inuvialuit NCS	Television
Iqaluit	Inuit Broadcasting Corporation	Television
Salluit, Quebec	Taqramiut Nipingat Inc.	Radio and television
Mistinnini	James Bay Cree NCS	Radio
Huron Village	Société de Communication Atikamekw Montagnais	Radio

In 1990, some very severe cut-backs were announced. Funding for the NNBAP was reduced by 16 percent and another native communications program which sponsored native print media and community radio was cut by 100 percent. The 1990–91 NNBAP budget, after seven years of operation and several prior budget cuts, is $12.3 million. These budget constraints have resulted in the drastic reorganization of native communications in this country and have precipitated the need for alternative sources of revenue in order to maintain production levels. All NCSs have had to cut back considerably on production and staffing.

In September 1990, the CRTC announced its new Native Broadcasting Policy (Public Notice CRTC 1990-89) which permits NCSs to accept advertising. This no doubt will ameliorate some of their problems. New advertising possibilities will also have major ramifications during federal and territorial elections.

Beyond the CBC Northern Services and those of the Native Communications Societies, private broadcasting exists in the Western Arctic and the Yukon, although there are no private radio stations in the Eastern Arctic or northern Quebec. In Whitehorse, there is a private radio station (CKRW) which is distributed by satellite to most of the other Yukon communities. Yellowknife also has a private radio station (CJCD) available in the town and in Hay River, NWT, some 200 kilometres south. By contrast, in the Eastern Arctic the CBC provides the only radio service and is, therefore, in a particularly critical and responsible position to provide access to a diverse range of information and entertainment programming. There are no private radio or television stations producing programs in northern Quebec, although there are many local community radio stations.

In 35 northern communities, Canadian Satellite Communications Inc., known as CANCOM, television services are now available on a user-pay basis. Programming menus are typical: basic Canadian services along with ABC, CBS, NBC and PBS from Detroit; CHCH, Hamilton; TVA, Montreal; ITV, Edmonton; BCTV, Vancouver; and pay channels.

The final element of the northern broadcasting configuration consists of a planned dedicated northern satellite service called Television Northern Canada (TVNC), which is due to begin operations in January 1992. TVNC is a consortium of six northern Aboriginal broadcasters (Northern Native Broadcasting, Yukon, Inuvialuit Native Communications Society, Native Communications Society of the Western NWT, Inuit Broadcasting Corporation, Taqramiut Nipingat Inc. and OkalaKatiget Society), Yukon College and the Government of the Northwest Territories, with the common goal of producing culturally relevant and educational television to a pan-Arctic audience. It will be a significant addition to the northern media resource pool, and will no doubt be involved in distribution of campaign messages and coverage during the next federal election. Those interviewed suggest that TVNC and NCS electoral coverage in native languages and in English will complement CBC Northern Services in the future.

CONSTITUENTS' COMPLAINTS ABOUT NORTHERN MEDIA SERVICES DURING THE 1988 FEDERAL ELECTION

The RCERPF testimonial documentation and my field research have identified the problems of both the CBC northern radio and television service and other media coverage and practices in the Northwest Territories during the 1988 election.

These are the major complaints received by the Commission about the CBC Northern Service:

- lack of access by all political candidates to free air time;
- limitation of electoral coverage to CBC journalistic control through news and current affairs programming;
- dissatisfaction with the amount of appropriate native-language coverage of election issues, particularly in the Western Arctic where seven Aboriginal languages are spoken and where CBC radio mainly broadcasts in Dogrib, Chipewyan and Slavey;
- dissatisfaction with the CBC's policy of not allowing Inuit Broadcasting Corporation to sell advertising time while accessing the CBC's satellite channel;[7]
- the lack of consistency in the quality of radio coverage of the election in different regions of the North, i.e., most complaints were made about radio coverage in the Western Arctic while there seems to be a fair degree of satisfaction in the Eastern Arctic;
- the desire for the CBC Northern Service, as well as Elections Canada, to take a more proactive role in educating native people about electoral processes, given that literacy levels in the North are low and that radio in particular is identified by Northerners as the most constructive way of developing an informed constituency.

In conjunction with these complaints, the Commission received other critical comments about the broader media framework of northern electoral processes. Specifically, these comments touched upon:

- a lack of variety of other northern-based media channels from which to buy advertising time to balance out the CBC's policy of not supplying free air time (particularly in the Eastern Arctic, where the CBC is the only radio service);
- the logistical complexity of negotiating political advertising air time through southern political party representatives and the consequent goal of organizing access times regionally within the North;
- the inability to use electronic fax machines to substitute for travel to register as an official candidate;
- the way in which "independent" candidates are bypassed in all rules about access time for paid political advertising in the North

where the political culture is based on independent candidate, nonpartisan politics;
- the "unfair" and "inequitable" formula for assigning advantageous amounts of broadcasting access time to incumbent parties on the basis of the results of prior elections; and
- the high costs of transportation between northern communities, perceived to be necessary for campaigning in light of constrained access to media advertising.

Although some of these complaints require a detailed background to understand, others can be explained by examining the CBC Northern Service's policies, elaborated within the next section of this study.

THE CBC NORTHERN SERVICE AND THE 1988 FEDERAL ELECTION

Policies

To better understand the CBC's performance during the 1988 election, it is important to map out the corporate policy perspective within which CBC Northern Service management was operating. Of note is the fact that the CBC has a specific policy regarding remote areas which states: "Where a CBC station serves a community, constituency or part of a constituency which does not receive adequate service by other media, the Corporation will consider offering limited local free time so that the candidates can discuss the issues in the election" (CBC 1985, 10).

In a telephone conference prior to the start of the 1988 campaign, CBC Northern Service managers decided not to apply this policy, but rather to operate with an alternate approach. As an outcome of this internal consultation, four key decisions form the framework within which CBC Northern Services covered the 1988 election. These were:

- No free political access time was to be given by any of the northern sub-regional production centres to any political candidate.
- There could be paid political advertising, but it was not the CBC's responsibility to inform candidates of the procedures for gaining access to this service. This was the responsibility of the political parties.
- If any community station gave access to one candidate, it would be required to give equitable access to all others.
- The election was to be covered journalistically through news and current affairs programming.

The management consensus to cover the electoral issues and

campaigns journalistically was based on the grounds that there were only three ridings in the coverage area and that "candidates and issues tend to receive a proportionately greater amount of attention in regular news and current affairs programming than is the case in the southern constituencies" (letter from Michael McEwen to Pierre Lortie; see CBC, 1 August 1990b, 2).

In his explanatory letter (about the rationale for the CBC's position in the North) to RCERPF chairman Pierre Lortie, Michael McEwen, executive vice-president of the CBC, expanded upon this view:

> The Northern Service typically facilitates all-candidate special broadcasts during election campaigns. These broadcasts involve interviews and debates with all the candidates for each of the Yukon, Western Arctic and Nunatsiaq constituencies. In this context, the program formats have allowed candidates to make "statements" on identified issues, a direct parallel to conventional free time broadcasts. (As a point of interest, the candidates may, if they choose, use Aboriginal languages during their statement time.)
>
> In addition, many northern communities have a "community access" capability on their local radio rebroadcast transmitters and undertake local programming during certain periods each day. The CBC is aware that candidates are permitted access to this community time, either to make statements or to participate in phone-in programs. This local radio access opportunity has proved very effective in reaching voters within the individual communities and, in our experience, most candidates are aware of its value.
>
> Finally, I should note that paid time is made available to the political parties on our Northern Service radio and television stations, at quite modest rates. These messages can be targeted to specific areas, and broadcast in English, French and/or native languages. While none of the parties took advantage of this opportunity during the last federal election, they have done so in the past. (CBC, 1 August 1990b, 2–3)

According to the CBC's submission to the Commission, it is "generally satisfied with the current method of allocating both free time and purchased time" (CBC 1990a, 15). Important to northern constituents is the stipulation that "free time messages should continue to be carried only on a full network basis (unlike paid time, which can be bought on a market by market basis) and, also, that the law should specifically require that both free and paid time messages be in the language of the carrying network" (ibid., 17). The document further specifies:

"As 'registered political parties' must, inherently, have a national scope, this approach would seem to be reasonable" (ibid.).

In the CBC's verbal testimony before the Commission, Michael McEwen reiterated the Corporation's position on its role concerning free time, arguing that it should be reactive rather than proactive. He said, in part: "We feel it would be more practical if the parties were required to approach the broadcaster to negotiate free time arrangements, rather than us having to seek them out" (Canada, RCERPF Public Hearings, Ottawa, 13 June 1990).

Individual northern managers concurred with this opinion. In the East and West, as well as at the Northern Service Ottawa headquarters, it was clear that free and paid political advertising time are perceived by management as intrusive and disruptive to regular non-commercial radio services. Several managers suggested that if they were required by law to accept electoral advertising, they would prefer to have it scheduled at pre-slotted times. They said they favoured free time over paid commercials because they felt it was fairer and started all candidates off on a "level playing field." Moreover, they stressed their preference for only one kind of advertising per election, either free time or commercial time but not both, because of their perception that the audience would find both overwhelming in impact.

CBC Radio Coverage of the 1988 Federal Election

As I travelled and interviewed residents, former candidates and campaign team members throughout the Northwest Territories for two weeks during December 1990, it was clear that those who had not directly participated in the campaigns had a tendency to confuse the 1984 with the 1988 election. Nonetheless, campaign workers did have very distinct and informed comments to make about CBC radio electoral coverage.

According to the information I collected, there was a definite difference in quality of radio journalism between the East and the West. Interviewees said they would like to see more consistency of standards applied to CBC coverage in the future. The Western Arctic manager who had administered the 1988 electoral coverage is no longer an employee of CBC Northern Services, so information about Yellowknife coverage (from the CBC's perspective) is not as extensive as that in the East, where the manager was available for an interview. But from the other interviews in Yellowknife it became clear that coverage had not been as thorough as in the East. This was a problem for candidates and their teams, who expect standardized quality across the North. Many people, reasonably, argued that quality of coverage should not be dependent on the personal qualities of local or regional management teams, but should be based on a clear set of guidelines and expectations consistently applied across all of the CBC's Northern Service.

In the Eastern Arctic, the CBC is the only radio outlet and therefore has the weighty responsibility of assuring accurate and focused coverage across a very large territory. In this region, the CBC's manager appears to have taken a fair and proactive role in informing the Aboriginal publics about electoral practices and processes. With 12 hours of Inuktitut programming, including news, on air per day – nine hours from Iqaluit and three from Kivalliq/Rankin Inlet – the CBC used a bilingual announcer to sight-translate into Inuktitut such topical information as the history of the parliamentary system, the nature of political parties, voting procedures, who the candidates were and what they represented, and other pertinent subjects (Craig Mackie, Yellowknife, 11 December 1990).

Several phone-in shows also took place, including a cooperative debate/phone-in show in Inuktitut between the CBC and the Inuit Broadcasting Corporation (IBC) with all four candidates in the IBC television studio. Inuktitut sound was broadcast on television, and simulcast on CBC radio in English. In the East, Craig Mackie, CBC area manager, met with the campaign managers to attempt to balance their needs with those of the CBC as the national, responsible public broadcaster.

In the West, however, constituents were not nearly as satisfied with the level of cooperation from the CBC radio manager at the time. I was told by several of the major parties' team members and others that the coverage was "shockingly terrible" in the Western Arctic. They stated that it was far too controlled by journalists and that the few features and news clips that were done were mediocre and not terribly informative. Moreover, there was a consensus that the service in the Western Arctic was not as proactive in terms of educating native peoples about electoral processes as it was in the East. (This might be due to the complexity of producing multilingual programming.)

In native-language coverage in the West, a key point stood out: that CBC Western Arctic should try to be equitable in its native-language programming. By this is meant that in order to extend native audience reach, the CBC should make every arrangement possible to equitably broadcast information in all nine official languages.

Other Western Arctic residents suggested that CBC radio and television organize live debates by satellite uplink where possible, or by telephone in each constituency, so that candidates travelling in the regions could participate without having to spend huge amounts of money getting to Yellowknife. This would attract and educate listeners/viewers about the political issues involved, they argued.

The CBC's policy in 1988 not to carry free political broadcasts, a legitimate decision made by each licensed broadcasting undertaking, had a significant impact on the candidates' campaigns in the Eastern Arctic. A small amount of free time on the northern airwaves would have reduced the prohibitive expenditure required to travel to the communities to campaign. Broadcasting is the only guaranteed message-delivery alternative in the North. Depriving northern candidates of this vehicle creates unnecessary hardships in constituencies which are already complex linguistically, politically, socially and economically. Campaign budget restrictions are clearly not designed with the North in mind.

The general complaint about having the issues covered only by journalists lay in the difference between self-representation and representation by others. The candidates wanted the opportunity to speak in their own voices, outline their own agendas and raise their own issues, and they were frustrated by not being able to reach their constituents verbally with their own platforms. This is particularly important in light of the low literacy levels and the oral tradition among Aboriginal peoples in the North.

The opportunity for individuals to generate their own political agendas and policies by representing themselves "on their feet" and promoting what they consider to be their own assets is important to the candidates. There is a major difference in control, impact and potential influence between self-representation and representation by others. The CBC's journalistic coverage carried with it the power to control the information about each candidate so that journalists could choose which messages were emphasized and which were minimized (journalist as gatekeeper). Journalists could influence viewers' opinions in very subtle ways: by the kinds and content of the questions asked and the selection of sound bites, for instance, as well as in their interpretation of election issues. This is not to question the legitimacy of journalists' attempts to present balanced views, equitably distributing attention to each of the party candidates. It is merely to point out the distinctions between self-representation and journalistic representation, and the frustration on the part of the candidates in not feeling they were permitted an open platform from which to speak in their own voices.

Although I could not get a straight answer to my questions about it, I suspect part of the reason the CBC Northern Service made the decision not to encourage paid political advertising was because audiences, uninformed about *Canada Elections Act* broadcasting requirements favouring incumbent parties, might have got the idea that the CBC favoured the Conservative party over the others, because Conservative candidates would have been eligible for the largest segment of broadcasting time. To avoid the impression of providing inequitable advertising time, the CBC did not encourage advertising at all, although had it been organized through the proper channels, the CBC would have carried it, as Mr. McEwen stated.

Present federally regulated broadcasting access rules appear to favour the incumbent parties by allotting time on the basis of two criteria: the number of seats a party had in the House of Commons and the percentage of its popular support, both at the time of the last election. My interviews with CBC Northern Service management staff confirmed my impression that the unequal time that would have been allocated to the parties in accordance with the *Canada Elections Act* would have made it appear that the CBC was biased in favour of the Conservative party, especially in light of the unique context of the North.[8]

CBC Northern Service Television Coverage

Due to financial constraints and the fact that there is only one half-hour pan-Arctic television program per week, Focus North, CBC television coverage consisted of a single half-hour election debate covering the three constituencies. There was no live television coverage. The debate was taped in Whitehorse, Yellowknife and Iqaluit at different times and segments highlighting the key points were edited together for the election "special." People complained about the lack of opportunity to get their own points across, and several said the debate format was too controlled and stilted.

But mainly, viewers criticized the form and narrowness of questioning in the debate. Each candidate was asked to respond to the same question. The debate was designed as an interaction between each candidate and the journalists, but there was no conversation among the candidates to show the audience how each person might operate "on their feet, so to speak. There was no mud-slinging allowed" (Peter Ittinuar, Rankin Inlet, 27 December 1990). Many people suggested that in future some one-on-one interaction be permitted to take place among the candidates. It would make a much more compelling program, they argued.

CBC Northern Service television management staff are hoping to increase their production quota in the future. They are, in theory at least, planning to produce a daily pan-Arctic news program and believe that until a budget is forthcoming for this program, they will never be able to do fair and equitable television coverage of an election in the

North. Brian Cousins, regional director of the CBC Northern Service, said in response to my question about whether he would support the CBC Northern Service being given a special status for federal elections: "Before we become a special status broadcasting undertaking for the purposes of federal election coverage, I would prefer to become an equal status broadcasting undertaking on a daily basis" (Brian Cousins, Ottawa, 7 December 1990).

EQUALIZING THE NORTHERN MEDIA/ELECTION RELATIONSHIP

The Case for Special Status for the CBC Northern Service

> Our tax money is the same as Mulroney's tax money. Why shouldn't we Northerners have the same information rights as everyone else in this country?
>
> (Bert Rose, Iqaluit, 18 December 1990)

In almost every northern brief submitted to the RCERPF, the problems of communications over vast distances were prominent. The high costs of transportation were criticized, and better and more widely accessible communications during a northern election campaign were proposed. "Getting the message across to the public" was the single most popular response from candidates and their campaign teams to the question about their greatest difficulty during the 1988 election. It was consistently argued across the constituencies that the remoteness of the North from the southern, centralist bias of media coverage for federal elections has had an escalating tendency to marginalize northern residents from the electoral process.

As Senator Len Marchand notes in his discussion paper "Aboriginal Electoral Reform" (1991), Aboriginal peoples have only recently attained the right to vote in a federal election (1960) and their participation has not been facilitated by the extension of southern-reasoned rules into the North (ibid.). Marchand specifies three components of federal elections which deter active Aboriginal participation and representation: "First, the electoral legislation which determines the distribution and allocation of electoral boundaries has failed to accommodate the demographic distribution of Aboriginal People. Second, the political parties have historically not been receptive to increasing Aboriginal participation. Finally, electoral administration has failed to accommodate the unique socioeconomic and cultural circumstances of Aboriginal People" (ibid., 7).

In my northern field work I have found ample evidence of each of these factors at work within the media regulatory framework and practices as they pertain to the electoral process. Existing broadcasting regulations make it logistically difficult to get access to either free or paid political advertising for northern election candidates. Paid political advertising would have been available on the CBC had the candidates been appropriately informed by the national headquarters of their respective parties.

Unfortunately, most of the national parties assumed incorrectly that their candidates would be familiar with the exact procedures or, alternatively, they chose to ignore the regional candidates of the North. In practice, only one of all the NWT-based candidates in the 1988 election, Peter Kusagak (NDP candidate for Nunatsiaq), was aware of the process. All other candidates and their managers with whom I spoke assumed it was the exclusive role of the CBC Northern Service to inform candidates of their rights to paid broadcasting access. Kusagak happened to find out about the appropriate procedure because his manager, brought from Vancouver to assist in his campaign, knew the system from past experience in urban regions. The NDP did attempt to organize paid political advertising, but according to Kusagak, "The process stopped us. We had no time to go through that logistical nightmare of a procedure. We would have needed a much longer campaign period" (Peter Kusagak, Iqaluit, 17 December 1990).

The present method of getting paid political advertising time is extremely awkward and time-consuming for northern candidates. It involves contacting the party headquarters' agent in the South, who deals with requests for time and, when applicable, negotiates specific time slots with the CBC's Federal Election Broadcasting Time Allocation Committee at the Commercial Acceptance Office. Once this has been organized, the northern candidate is notified and is expected to produce a completed ad for broadcasting at a specific time. It is then sent south for pre-clearance, and finally delivered north to the station for broadcasting. As noted elsewhere in this study, the CBC does not feel it is its responsibility to inform candidates of this procedure. It, therefore, reacts to the request for broadcasting by candidates after they become informed of the process by their own national party (Fran Cutler and Brian Cousins, Ottawa, 7 December 1990).

Since parties are focused on national and mainstream issues, the North is often left out of the process. This aspect of access is falsely perceived by some to be a denial or lack of cooperation on the part of the CBC. Rather, it is a problem in communications between the party headquarters and/or their advertising agencies and the candidates in the North and other remote regions. Likely it results from an uncertain and inconsistent interaction that is focused on a national, centralist political party bias. Too often, it unintentionally results in ignoring the specific conditions of northern and isolated regions. The physical dimension of the Northwest Territories, plus its political nonpartisan tradition, the complex linguistic structures in the West, and the dependence in the East on a single radio outlet during the 1988 election, characterize the uniqueness of the North as a site for a federal election campaign. Yet during this time, there were no specific exceptions made to any of the rules which govern electoral practices elsewhere in the country. Policies originating in the South, which assume a similar framework "established for a 10 block constituency in Toronto will work for a 2.6 million square kilometres in Nunatsiaq" (Fred Coman, Iqaluit, 17 December 1990), were implemented without modification in the North.

Take, for example, the absence of a time allocation for independent candidates for the purposes of paid political advertising on broadcasts. Since the Northwest Territories has a tradition of nonpartisan politics, people base their vote for candidates on personal record and familiarity with the candidate's ways of doing things. This means partisan affiliation is not a criterion for broadcasting access times during a Territorial election. So, when the federal election process of political party advertising is imported into the North, most northern peoples don't quite understand why independent candidates do not qualify for air time under the broadcasting regulatory framework. Furthermore, Aboriginal peoples don't always understand the distinctions between the different parties, their policies, and federal electoral practices in general. For example, many people suggested that photo-ballots be used so that illiterate people will be able to positively identify the candidate of their choice. I was also told that names should be placed horizontally on the ballot slip rather than vertically because people tend to choose the name at the top of the list (Abe Ookpik, Iqaluit, 4 January 1991). These problems are not nearly so predominant elsewhere as in the North.

The particular set of historical and political conditions in the Northwest Territories and northern Quebec requires cross-cultural sensitivity and policies that aid the participation and representation of native and remote populations in the electoral process. Without special conditions to address the specific needs of Northerners in relation to the rest of the country, federal politicians risk the danger of bypassing the interests and concerns of native constituents. To make federal politics more relevant to and representative of Aboriginal peoples, especially those who are either unilingual in their native language or isolated from easy access to electoral information, it is important to realize that much native-language electoral education and discussion is required. This is necessary to enable people to participate as candidates and/or to make informed democratic decisions based on accurate information, not hearsay or intuition.

CONCLUDING COMMENTS

In the next federal election, individual Native Communications Societies will be entitled to carry free and/or paid Aboriginal-language election ads. As well, if it becomes operational on schedule, Television Northern Canada will be in a position to broadcast free and/or paid political advertising and will provide complementary coverage from a native perspective to that of the CBC Northern Service. Also, before the next federal election, the status of the CBC Northern Service's draft plans to establish a daily television news program will be clearer. If plans are approved, CBC northern television operations might be able to expand election coverage capability on television.

Although all these opportunities for improved access to electoral campaign coverage will probably be available for the next election, the medium which is still most consistent with the existing oral traditions of native peoples, and which has already demonstrated its potential to target multilinguistic native and non-native audiences, is CBC Northern Service radio. It is, to date, the only service with the capacity to program pan-Arctic broadcasts in all the nine official languages of the NWT. It is also the service of the national public broadcaster and, as such, carries with it the obligation to "provide radio and television services incorporating a wide range of programming that informs, enlightens and entertains" (*Broadcasting Act* (1991), section 3(1)(*l*)); "reflect Canada and its regions to national and regional audiences, while serving the special needs of those regions" (section 3(1)(*m*)(ii)); "actively contribute to the flow and exchange of cultural expression" (section 3(1)(*m*)(iii)); "contribute to shared national consciousness and identity" (section 3(1)(*m*)(vi)); "be made available throughout Canada by the most appropriate and efficient means and as resources become available for the purpose" (section 3(1)(*m*)(vii)); "reflect the multicultural and multiracial nature of Canada" (section (3)(1)(*m*)(viii)).

In concluding this study I am recommending that the CBC Northern Service's federal election mandate, obligations and budget be strengthened and adapted to the special sociopolitical and cultural conditions in the North. In calling for a special status for the CBC Northern Service during a federal election period, I am asking for a fairer and more equitable portion of electoral resources to be allocated to northern and remote regions of this large country to enable its geographically isolated residents to take a more informed and active role in the democratic process. To equalize the CBC Northern Service with that of the rest of the country, the CBC requires a modified regulatory framework within which to operate.

From the testimony of Michael McEwen at the RCERPF hearings on 13 June 1990, it is clear that the CBC has the will to make these changes. What is needed now is a new and more flexible regulatory framework, adapted to northern conditions, within which the CBC Northern Service can work.

Here is an exchange between one of the Commissioners, Lucie Pépin, and Michael McEwen at this hearing:

> **Mrs. Pépin:** Given that their only means of communicating with constituents in this region is through the CBC, couldn't the laws and regulations for this region be amended or adjusted to permit candidates to make contact more easily with the voters? It seems that communication is very difficult here.
>
> We have had many representations in this regard which reflected very negatively upon CBC services. [translation]
>
> **Mr. McEwen:** Yes, I am very aware of that. I would like to see the law amended so that perhaps we could be more proactive in those areas. The North is a special circumstance. (Canada, RCERPF Public Hearings, Ottawa, 13 June 1990)

KEY RECOMMENDATIONS TO THE COMMISSIONERS

Most of the initial complaints that formed the foundation for this study were found to be widespread and legitimate. They indicate a strong need to restructure the way in which election coverage is organized, managed and adapted to the specific information needs in the Canadian North. Key recommendations to the Commissioners are:

1. Broadcasting time for federal elections should be allocated using a new and fairer formula to allow reasonable access to all major and minor parties, as well as to independent candidates.
2. This time should be divided into equal amounts of free and paid political advertising time, with each party and independent candidate being entitled to equal amounts of each. Ten to 15 minutes of both free and paid advertising time for each candidate is recommended.
3. For a federal election, to equalize service standards in the North and South, the CBC Northern Service should be given a special status and mandate different from that of the CBC's national service. This status should be officially enshrined in Canada's new *Broadcasting Act*

(1991), the *Canada Elections Act,* and the CRTC rules and regulations. Should a budget be required to effectively implement this new mandate, funding should be made available. This special status should require the CBC Northern Service to:

a. Conduct a northern federal election in a manner comparable to a by-election elsewhere in Canada, with broadcasting controls only on campaign expenditure limits and equal time allocations for all qualifying parties and independent candidates.
b. Allocate a minimum equal amount of free access during prime times, and sell time for paid political advertising during other times.
c. Equitably divide its portion of the 6.5 allowable hours of channel time for advertising among all major and minor parties as well as independent candidates. Cluster all free political time and announce when the broadcast will occur.
d. Negotiate and allocate the limited amount of free and paid access time for each candidate at each sub-regional production centre rather than require each candidate to negotiate for access time through party and CBC headquarters.
e. Continue to cover electoral candidates and issues journalistically, ensuring time for phone-in shows.
f. Organize at least one television debate per constituency to allow for both one-on-one interaction between the candidates and responses to questions posed by journalists. This will enable listeners/viewers to see candidates react spontaneously to questions for which they might not have been prepared. If all candidates are not able to be in one place simultaneously, telephone hook-ups should be used.
g. Take its education mandate, as set out in the *Broadcasting Act* (1991, section 3(1)) very seriously, taking account of the fairly recent enfranchisement and low literacy levels of native peoples. The mandate should also be applied equitably across the Northwest Territories. Everyone interviewed who wasn't affiliated with the CBC expected and wanted the CBC Northern Service, as well as Elections Canada, to take a more proactive role in offering electoral education in native languages prior to a federal election.
h. Be equitable in its native-language radio programming. In order that a candidate's message can reach the entire constituency, the CBC Northern Service should be required during an election campaign to equitably provide some electoral coverage in all nine official languages of the Northwest Territories.
4. The fact that Television Northern Canada and Native Communications Societies will be able to accept paid political advertisements

during the next election, and will therefore multiply the number of possible venues for campaigning, should not decrease the public service obligations, effort or budget that the CBC Northern Service should dedicate to publicizing information and encouraging electoral participation.

5. CBC Northern Television News Service should be allocated the human and material resources for organizational expansion as in its draft plan (1990c) to provide for daily pan-Arctic coverage of relevant northern political issues in an ongoing fashion. This will aid the political development of native peoples so that during election periods the constituents will already be informed and motivated to participate more actively in the electoral process.

6. The CBC should be encouraged to cover some aspects of the northern electoral campaign on a national basis so the rest of the country can become aware of the conditions and constraints within which northern residents vote.

7. To implement some of the above recommendations, it would be necessary to change the requirement that northern advertising time allocation be controlled by party headquarters' representatives. This would require only minimal adjustment. The CBC Northern Service in conjunction with the CBC, party agents, and the federal broadcasting arbitrator could work out a minimal amount of paid political advertising time to be divided among northern candidates for regional broadcasting. This could be subtracted from the channel's total allocation of 6.5 hours. Since this requirement only pertains to the CBC in the North, only a small amount of regional broadcasting time per constituency per election, over and above the journalistic coverage, would be affected. This could easily be organized in one meeting between the CBC, a Northern Service representative, the party headquarters' agents, and someone appointed to represent the interests of the independent candidates. Negotiation and allocation of appropriate broadcasting times might be mediated in the North by the chief returning officer of each constituency, along with a CBC Northern Service representative, appointed to deal with election coverage logistics. For example, if the CBC does not have the time to elaborate the procedures for allotting free and paid advertising time to candidates, the chief returning officer or her/his appointee might be delegated the task, so all candidates start off with an equal amount of information, and equal opportunity to represent their platforms and positions in a democratic fashion.

APPENDIX A
NORTHERN QUESTIONNAIRE

(This questionnaire was used as the basis of interviews with key northern residents, including CBC management and communications and cultural personnel in the North. A similar questionnaire was sent to northern Native Communications Societies with the letter and note added.)

To: All Native Communications Societies

From: Lorna Roth, Consultant for the Royal Commission on Electoral Reform and Party Financing

Re: Study entitled: The CBC Northern Service and the Federal Electoral Process: Problems and Strategies for Improvement

Hi,

I have been commissioned by the Electoral Reform Commission to look into the ways in which **CBC Northern Service** coverage of *federal* (**not provincial**) elections can be improved in the future.

During the 1988 election, a number of coverage problems associated with CBC Northern Service, were identified and discussed. These include: lack of access by all political candidates to "enough" free air time; limitation of coverage of election issues to news features; lack of availability of other northern-based media channels from which to buy advertising time to balance out CBC's policy of not supplying free air time; dissatisfaction with the amount of appropriate native-language coverage of election issues; dissatisfaction with CBC's policy of not allowing Inuit Broadcasting Corporation to sell advertising time while accessing CBC's satellite channel, and others.

Unfortunately, my budget does not allow me to visit each of your Societies to do on-site interviews, so I would very much appreciate it if you could answer the enclosed questionnaire and return it to me in the self-addressed and stamped envelope which I am enclosing.

Because I would like to focus my study on means of improvement for the future, I would like you to feel free to include as many reasonable and "do-able" suggestions as possible.

I very much appreciate your immediate attention to this matter and look forward to hearing from you as soon as possible.

Thanks and have a good Christmas holiday.

Sincerely yours,

Lorna Roth

Encl.

P.S. If you know anyone else interested in making comments to help in the research, please do not hesitate to pass a copy of this to them too.

Note: If you prefer to speak answers to these questions into a tape cassette recorder, feel free to do so and then just mail me the cassette. If you choose to do this, though, please don't forget to announce the number of each question before you answer it. Thanks and I look forward to hearing your responses.

A Study Commissioned by the Royal Commission on Electoral Reform and Party Financing
Principal Researcher: Lorna Roth

Northern Questionnaire

Name of Individual/Group/Organization _____

Date_____

Address and Phone No. _____

_____

1. In your opinion, does the CBC do an adequate job of explaining the electoral process to its northern *television* viewers?

   Yes ☐   No ☐

   Comments _____

2. In your opinion, does the CBC do an adequate job of explaining the electoral process to its *radio* listeners?

   Yes ☐   No ☐

   Comments _____

3. Do you think that it *should* be part of the CBC's role to explain the electoral process to its audiences?

   Yes ☐   No ☐

   Comments _____

4. Is the CBC coverage broadcast in languages appropriate to its audiences?

   Yes ☐   No ☐

   Comments _____

5. In the 1988 federal election, do you think that the CBC adequately covered the issues?

   a. Local issues: Yes ☐   No ☐

   Comments _____

   b. Regional issues: Yes ☐   No ☐

   Comments _____

   c. National issues: Yes ☐   No ☐

   Comments_____

6. What did it do well? What was outstanding about the coverage?

_____

7. What aspects need improvement for the next federal election?

_____

8. What are your suggestions for improvement?

_____

9. In the 1988 federal election, do you think that the CBC adequately covered the candidates' political positions?

Yes ☐   No ☐

Comments _____

10. Did the CBC devote _enough_ time to its coverage in the 1988 federal election?

Yes ☐   No ☐

Comments _____

11. How much _more_ time would you have wanted CBC to devote and why?

_____

12. If you had control over the CBC Northern Service policy regarding federal election coverage, how would you change it? Please be specific.

_____

13. In your opinion, is there a need for more paid political broadcasting?

a. On national CBC Northern Service television? Yes ☐   No ☐

Comments _____

b. On regional and/or local access television? Yes ☐   No ☐

Comments _____

c. On regional radio? Yes ☐   No ☐

Comments _____

d. On local radio? Yes ☐   No ☐

Comments _____

14. Would you have a limit on the amount of paid political broadcasting?

a. On television? Yes ☐   No ☐

Comments _____

b. On radio? Yes ☐   No ☐

Comments _____

15. What would you suggest as a limit for each, and explain your reasons?

_____

16. In your opinion, is there a need for more free time political broadcasting?

    a. On television? Yes ☐   No ☐

    Comments _____

    b. On radio? Yes ☐   No ☐

    Comments _____

17. How would you fairly allocate this time, i.e., on the basis of what criteria? (At present, it is allocated on the basis of the number of existing seats held by each political party in the House of Commons and the percentage of the popular vote each party won during the previous election.)

    _____

18. Would you like to hear more phone-in shows during election time?

    Yes ☐   No ☐

    Comments _____

19. Would you like to watch more "all-candidate" debates during election time?

    Yes ☐   No ☐

    Comments _____

20. Please describe _other_ television and radio show formats which could be informative re election information coverage and public education regarding federal elections.

    _____

21. At the present time, CBC Northern Service is considered a _regional_ service and is treated in the same manner as are all other regional services of the CBC. Do you think that for the purposes of the federal election, CBC Northern Service should take on a "special status" so that "special" northern considerations, such as difficulty in transportation, communication and linguistic diversity could be better addressed?

    Yes ☐   No ☐

    Comments _____

22. If you answered "Yes" to question 21, what arguments would you use to convince the CBC of the need to give Northern Service this "special status"? (Your responses to this question will be very helpful to me in laying out the framework for "special status" arguments to the CBC, so I would appreciate your thoughts on this one.)

    _____

23. In your opinion, does CBC coverage do a convincing job of influencing voters to go out and vote?

    Yes ☐   No ☐

    Comments _____

24. Do you see Native Communications Societies' service as complementing that of the CBC in providing relevant information about federal elections to your audiences?

    Yes ☐   No ☐

    Comments _____

25. Would you like to see NCSs permitted to broadcast paid political advertisements?

    Yes ☐   No ☐

    Comments _____

26. Would you like to see NCSs permitted to broadcast free political announcements?

    Yes ☐   No ☐

    Comments _____

27. When Television Northern Canada (TVNC) begins broadcasting, do you see TVNC as playing a role in televising information about the federal election process, parties and candidates?

    Yes ☐   No ☐

    Comments _____

    a. How would this role be different from what CBC Northern Service is presently doing?

    _____

28. How would you organize the fair allocation of time to each party and candidate using TVNC? What criteria would you use?

    _____

29. Would you like to see TVNC provide a venue for free political broadcasts in appropriate native languages?

    Yes ☐   No ☐

    Comments _____

30. Would you like to see TVNC provide a venue for paid political advertisements in appropriate native languages?

    Yes ☐   , No ☐

    Comments _____

31. Do you think that there would be more native participation in federal elections if NCSs and TVNC were to broadcast information about the electoral process?

    Yes ☐   No ☐

    Comments _____

32. What innovations would you like to see in TVNC and NCS productions of electoral coverage?

    _____

33. What innovations would you like to see in CBC Northern Service coverage of federal elections?

    _____

34. Do you think that if CBC Northern Service was able to produce a daily news program across the North that its election coverage would be improved?

    Yes ☐   No ☐

    Comments _____

35. CBC Northern Service radio management believes that due to the size of the 3 constituencies in the North and the fact that they do 12 hours of native-language radio per week, issues and candidates are adequately covered through news and backgrounders about candidates in regular programming. Do you agree?

    Yes ☐   No ☐

    Give your reasons _____

36. What electoral reforms would you like to see implemented in the North in relation to broadcasting practices?

    _____

37. Other comments _____

    _____

    _____

    _____

APPENDIX B

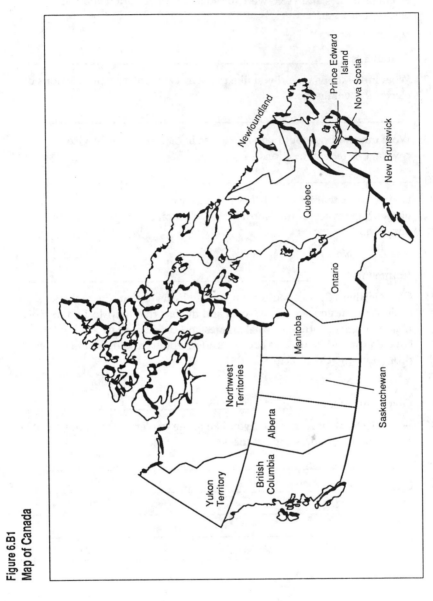

Figure 6.B1
Map of Canada

Source: Native Citizens Directorate of the Department of the Secretary of State, Ottawa, 1985.

APPENDIX C
EXISTING CBC NORTHERN SERVICE SCHEDULES

Figure 6.C1
Northern Québec Shortwave Schedule
Horaire Ondes-Courtes Service du Nord-Québec

Fall–Winter 90–91
Automne–hiver 90–91

	Monday lundi	Tuesday mardi	Wednesday mercredi	Thursday jeudi	Friday vendredi	Saturday samedi	Sunday dimanche
7:00	Radiojournal					The World Report	News
	Winschgaoug* (Cree program/Émission en cri)					Good Morning Québec	Morning Show
8:00	Radiojournal					The World Report	
						Good Morning Québec	Morning Show / The Food Show
9:00	News					The World Report	
	Salluit Inuktitut (TNI)*					The House	Sunday Morning
10:00	Bulletin réseau					News	
	Enoo Etoon (JBCC)*					Basic Black	Sunday Morning
11:00	Bulletin réseau					News	
	Ici comme ailleurs					Basic Black / Double Exposure	Sunday Morning
12:00	Radiojournal					News/Sports	Radiojournal
	Eyou Dipajimoon (Cree program/Émission en cri)*					Quirks and Quarks	Aujourd'hui la science/Politique
13:00	Tamai Noon/Kivalliq Today					News / The Media File / Inside Track	Bulletin réseau / N'Doheenoo (JBCC)*
14:00	News/Weather			Tamai Noon Kivalliq Phone-In		Bulletin réseau	Bulletin réseau
	Salluit Inuktitut (TNI)*					Double Expresso	Miyupimaatissium (JBCC)*
15:00	Bulletin réseau					Bulletin réseau	
	Enoo Emoo Ahbee (JBCC)*					Double Expresso	Miyupimaatissium (JBCC)*
16:00	News/Weather					Bulletin réseau	News
	Tuttavik (Kuujjuaq)*					Double Expresso or Chambre des communes	Sunday Matinee
17:00	Canada at Five					Bulletin réseau	News/Sports
		Alliq (Iqaluit)* (17:10) Inuktitut News* (17:45)				Tournée d'Amérique	Cross Country Checkup
18:00	The World at Six					Radiojournal	
						Boréal Hebdo	
19:00	As It Happens					News/Sports	Bulletin réseau
						Coast to Coast	Sport/Boréal Hebdo
20:00	News					News/Sports	News/Sports
	Salluit Inuktitut (TNI)*					Finkleman's 45's	Qaggiavut*
21:00	Tusaajaksat (Rankin Inlet)*					News/Sports	News/Weather
						Finkleman's 45's	
22:00	News/Sports					News/Sports	Two New Hours
	The Best of Morningside					A propos	
23:00	News/Late Evening Information					News/Sports	News
	Sinnaksautit (Iqaluit)*					Saturday Night Blues	
00:00	News/Weather					News	Jazz Beat
	That Time of Night					Saturday Night Blues	
1:00	News					News	News

CBC Northern Service – Québec, P.O. Box 6000, Montréal, Québec, Canada H3C 3A8 (514) 597-4370
Effective October 90. All times Eastern. (Programs subject to change.)

Radio-Canada, Service du Nord-Québec, c.p. 6000, Montréal, Québec, Canada H3C 3A8 (514) 597-4370
En vigueur octobre 90. Cet horaire est établi à l'heure de l'est. (Sous réserve de modifications.)

KHZ: Fréquence/Frequency
9625 (0658 - 0109)

*Includes Native language content.

Figure 6.C2
CBC Radio in Nunavik, Québec
English/Inuktitut program schedule

Fall–Winter   90–91

Time	Monday	Tuesday	Wednesday	Thursday	Friday	Saturday	Sunday
6:00	World Report					News	
	Québec A.M.					Saturday A.M.*	Sunday A.M.*
7:00	World Report					World Report/Sports	News
	Qulliq* (Iqaluit)					Saturday A.M.*	Sunday A.M.*
8:00	World Report					World Report/Sports	
						Nitjautiit*	Sunday A.M.* / The Food Show
9:00	News					World Report/Sports	
	Salluit Inuktitut (TNI)*					The House	Sunday Morning
10:00	News					News	
	Morningside					Basic Black	Sunday Morning
11:00	News					News	
						Basic Black / Double Exposure	Sunday Morning
12:00	News					News/Sports	
	Inuktitut News – Tamai Noon* (Iqaluit)			Tamai Noon		Quirks and Quarks	North by Northwest (Iqaluit)
13:00	Tamai Noon/Kivalliq Today			Kivalliq Phone-In		News/Sports	
						The Media File	Air Farce
14:00	News/Weather					Inside Track / News/Sports	Musical Friends
	Salluit Inuktitut (TNI)*					The Radio Show	
15:00						News/Sports	
	Tausunni* (Iqaluit)					The Radio Show	Variety
16:00	News/Weather					News/Sports	News
	Tuttavik (Kuujjuaq)*					Swinging on a Star	Sunday Matinee
17:00	Canada at Five					News/Sports	
	Alliq* (17:10)					Saturday Spotlight	Cross Country Checkup
18:00	Inuktitut News* (17:45)					Radiojournal	
	The World at Six					Boréal Hebdo	
19:00	As It Happens			Alliq		News/Sports	Bulletin réseau
						Coast to Coast	Sport/Boréal Hebdo
20:00	News					News/Sports	
	Salluit Inuktitut (TNI)*					Finkleman's 45's	Qaggiavut*
21:00	Tusaajaksat (Rankin Inlet)*					News/Sports	News/Weather
						Finkleman's 45's	
22:00	News/Sports					News/Sports	Two New Hours
	The Best of Morningside					A propos	
23:00	News/Late Evening Information					News/Sports	
	Sinnaksautit (Iqaluit)*					Saturday Night Blues	
00:00						News/Sports	
	Brave New Waves					Saturday Night Blues	Brave New Waves
1:00						News/Weather	
2:00						Night Lines	
3:00							

Figure 6.C3
La radio au Service du Nord-Québec

Automne–hiver   90–91

	lundi	mardi	mercredi	jeudi	vendredi	samedi	dimanche
6:00	Radiojournal				Radiojournal	Bulletin réseau	
	CBF Bonjour					Le carrousel du samedi matin	Le matin de la fête
7:00	Radiojournal				Radiojournal	Bulletin réseau	
						Le carrousel du samedi matin	Le matin de la fête
8:00	Radiojournal	Winschgaoug (Émission en cri)			Radiojournal	Radiojournal	
						Le carrousel du samedi matin	Le matin de la fête
9:00	Radiojournal				Radiojournal	Bulletin réseau	Radiojournal
		Tout compte fait	Ici comme ailleurs			Le carrousel du samedi matin	Dimanche magazine
10:00	Bulletin réseau				Bulletin réseau	Bulletin réseau	
	Enoo Etoon (SCCBJ)					Hebdo radio CBF	Dimanche rmagazine
11:00	Bulletin réseau				Bulletin réseau	Bulletin réseau	
	Ici comme ailleurs					Hebdo radio CBF	Signes des temps
12:00	Radiojournal				Radiojournal	Radiojournal	
	Eyou Dipajimoon (Émission en cri)					Les affaires et la vie	Aujourd'hui la science/Politique
13:00	Bulletin réseau				Bulletin réseau	Bulletin réseau	
	Par quatre chemins					Les affaires et la vie	N'Doheenoo (SCCBJ)
14:00	Bulletin réseau				Bulletin réseau	Bulletin réseau	
	Et Quoi Encore					Double expresso	Miyupimaatissium (SCCBJ)
15:00	Bulletin réseau				Bulletin réseau	Bulletin réseau	
	Enoo Emoo Ahbee (SCCBJ)					Double expresso	Miyupimaatissium (SCCBJ)
16:00	Bulletin réseau				Bulletin réseau	Bulletin réseau	
						Double expresso ou Chambre des communes	Multipiste
17:00	Bulletin réseau	Montréal express			Bulletin réseau	Bulletin réseau	
						Tournée d'Amérique	Débats à l'Assemblée nationale/Multipiste
18:00	Radiojournal					Radiojournal	
	Les Actualités						
	D'un soleil à l'autre					Boréal hebdo (Magazine autochtone)	Dialogue
19:00	Bulletin réseau				Bulletin réseau	Bulletin réseau	
	275 — Allô					Hebdo sport ou Hockey	Sports/Boréal Hebdo
	Les contes classiques (19:30–19:40)						
20:00	Bulletin réseau				Bulletin réseau	Bulletin réseau	
	L'aventure (19:40–21:00)					Hebdo sport ou Hockey	Entre parenthèses
21:00	Bulletin réseau				Bulletin réseau	Bulletin réseau	
						Ici Vancouver ou Hockey	Entre parenthèses
22:00	Radiojournal	Du jour au lendemain			Radiojournal	Bulletin réseau	
		Nouvelles du sport (22:55–23:00)				Ici Vancouver ou Hockey	Émergences
23:00	Bulletin réseau				Bulletin réseau	Bulletin réseau	
	Par quatre Chemins					Ici Vancouver	Émergences/ Sports
00:00	Réseau FM français (jusqu'à 6:00)						

Radio-Canada, Service du Nord-Québec, c.p. 6000, Montréal, Québec, Canada H3C 3A8 (514) 597-4370
En vigueur octobre 90. Cet horaire est établi à l'heure de l'est (sous réserve de modifications).
Fréquences Chisasibi — 103.5 mHz; Wemindii — 103.5 mHz; Waskaganish — 103.5 mHz; Mistassini — 100.7 mHz; Waswanipi — 101.5 mHz; Manouane — 103.5 mHz; Obedjiwan — 92.9 mHz; Weymontachie — 1340 kHz; Whapmagoostui — 96.5 mHz.

Figure 6.C4
CBC Yukon

	Monday	Tuesday	Wednesday	Thursday	Friday	Saturday	Sunday
6:00	World Report					News	
						Saturday A.M.	Musicale
7:00	World Report					World Report	News
			Yukon Morning			Saturday A.M.	Musicale
8:00	World Report					World Report	
						North By Northwest	Musicale
							Food Show
9:00	News					World Report	
						The House	Sunday Morning
10:00	News					News	
			Morningside			Basic Black	Sunday Morning
11:00	News					News	
						Basic Black	Sunday Morning
						Double Exposure	
12:00	News					News/Sports	
			Radio Noon			Quirks and Quarks	Sunday Magazine
13:00	News					News/Sports	
						The Media File	Sunday Matinee
						Inside Track	
14:00	News					News/Sports	
						The Radio Show	
15:00	News		Gabereau			News/Sports	Cross Country Checkup
						The Radio Show	
16:00	News					News/Sports	News
						Swinging on a Star	Air Farce
			Home Run				Musical Friends
17:00	Canada at Five					News/Sports	
						Country Style	Musical Friends
18:00			The World at Six			News/Sports	Gilmour's Albums
19:00						Coast to Coast	
			As It Happens			News/Sports	News
						Coast to Coast	Open House
20:00	News					News/Sports	
			Ideas			A propos	People Speak Gwich'in
21:00	News					News/Sports	Local French Access
						A propos	
22:00	News/Sports		R.S.V.P.			News/Sports	
						Finkleman's 45's	Speaking Volumes
							Vanishing Point
23:00	News/Sports					News/Sports	News
						Finkleman's 45's	Jazz Beat
00:00	News		Mostly Music			News/Sports	
						Saturday Night Blues	Jazz Beat
1:00	News					News	
		Brave New Waves (until 6:00)		Nightlines (until 6:00)			Brave New Waves

Subject to change.

Effective: September 1989.

APPENDIX D
LOCATIONS OF NATIVE COMMUNICATIONS SOCIETIES
IN NORTHERN CANADA

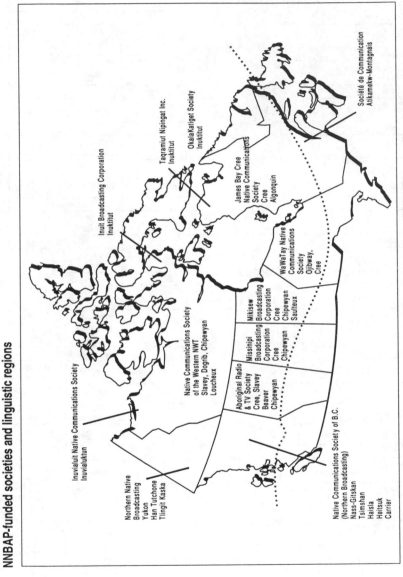

Figure 6.D1
NNBAP-funded societies and linguistic regions

Source: Native Citizens Directorate of the Department of the Secretary of State, Ottawa, 1985.

········· NNBAP boundary line

APPENDIX E
GLOSSARY OF TERMS AND ACRONYMS

Accelerated Coverage Plan	A 1974 post-satellite CBC policy designed to extend broadcasting service to all communities in Canada with a population of 500 or more.
CANCOM	Canadian Satellite Communications Inc. Provides television services, primarily channels from southern Canada and the United States, on a user-pay basis to 35 northern communities.
CBC	Canadian Broadcasting Corporation, Canada's national public broadcasting service.
CRTC	Canadian Radio-television and Telecommunications Commission, Canada's broadcasting regulatory agency.
IBC	Inuit Broadcasting Corporation, a Native Communications Society, licensed in 1981 to operate a pan-Arctic Inuktitut-language television service.
Inukshuk Project	An experimental (interactive video/audio) Anik-B satellite access project undertaken by the Inuit in the NWT between the years 1978 and 1981, which helped establish their credibility as capable television broadcasters.
MLA	Member of the Legislative Assembly
MP	Member of Parliament
Naalakvik Project	An experimental Anik-B satellite access project similar to the Inukshuk project that took place in northern Quebec.
NBP	Northern Broadcasting Policy
NCS	Native Communications Society
NDP	New Democratic Party, one of Canada's three larger political parties.
NNBAP	Northern Native Broadcast Access Program, a Secretary of State broadcasting support program, which began in 1983 as an implementation vehicle for the Northern Broadcasting Policy. NNBAP initially provided funding to 13 regional Native Communications Societies to produce five hours of native-language television and 20 hours of radio per week. It has subsequently been cut back, but still supports the broadcasting infrastructure for most native-perspective broadcasting in Canada's North.
NWT	Northwest Territories
TNI	Taqramiut Nipingat Incorporated, a northern Quebec Inuit-controlled Native Communications Society that produces

and broadcasts radio and television programming to northern Quebec residents.

TVNC   Television Northern Canada, a consortium of six northern Aboriginal broadcasters, the NWT government, and Yukon College, which will control a dedicated northern satellite transponder to distribute native programming across the North. It is expected to begin operations in January 1992.

ABBREVIATIONS

c.   chapter

R.S.C.   Revised Statutes of Canada

S.C.   Statutes of Canada

s(s).   section(s)

NOTES

This study was completed in May 1991.

I would like to thank all the "Northerners" (in the North and South) who generously donated their time and hospitality in helping me to gather the information for this analysis. In particular, I would like to thank Fred Fletcher for his patience and support in helping me complete this study, and Kathleen McBride, at the RCERPF office, who cheerfully and immediately responded to all of my requests for documentation. I would also like to thank the CBC Northern Service management in Ottawa and across the North for their cooperation in the completion of this research, even though it took some time "getting access." I would also like to acknowledge Valerie Alia, with whom I conferred frequently during the preparation of this document, for her intelligent comments and cheerful spirits. Finally, I would like to acknowledge Richard Ashby for his thorough assistance in document analysis and for his perseverance during the telephone interview stage of this study.

1. This study deals explicitly with problems and suggested resolutions within the NWT and northern Quebec, two representative Canadian regions which most directly experience the difficulties of transportation and communication during a federal election. It does not deal with the Yukon, which is addressed in the work of Valerie Alia (in Volume 9 on Aboriginal issues). Her study emphasizes Aboriginal participation and media coverage. Nor does my study elaborate details of the situation in the northern parts of the provinces, with the exception of Quebec, where the CBC Northern Service Quebec operates. This is because the northern parts of the other provinces do not comprise the target regional audience of CBC Northern Services, despite the fact that they experience similar problems of communications

and transportation during federal elections. This essentially means that candidates from northern parts of the provinces have to follow the same methods of accessing advertising on CBC national air time as would someone living in Toronto. There is a case to be made, based on testimony to the Commission during the Thompson and Saskatoon hearings, that the northern parts of the provinces should be considered exceptions and should benefit from the restructuring of election advertising procedures which I suggest in this study.

2. Although northern Quebec boundary issues are important, they are not particularly pertinent to this study. Some election impact media research in northern Quebec was undertaken, but was very limited in scope and not very informative, due to the fact that there were no complaints about media services registered from this region.

3. Interestingly, CBC Northern Service broadcasting spills over into the northern parts of many provinces, even though these are not their target audiences. In a recent note to me, Brian Cousins, Regional Director, CBC Northern Service, described the CBC Northern Service's audience reach within the northern parts of the provinces:

> With respect to *television*, 100 000-plus people in northern and interior British Columbia receive CBC North. Fortunately for them, our western CBC North feed includes regional news from CBC Vancouver. There are also about 7 or 8 communities in northern Alberta and Saskatchewan which receive CBC North television because extension of our provincial microwave networks in those provinces would be too costly. In addition, there are a few communities in northern Manitoba and northern Ontario which receive CBC's Montreal English television service via satellite for the same reason. Two or three northern Ontario communities have been using CBC North but are likely to switch to the Montreal feed.
>
> Northern Service radio serves Atlin and Cassiar in northern BC from Whitehorse and Fort Chipewyan in northern Alberta from Yellowknife.
>
> Nunavik communities receive most of their CBC programming from our Iqaluit station including a daily hour long program originating in our Kuujjuaq bureau.
>
> Except for the above, CBC regional offices in Vancouver, Edmonton, Regina (La Ronge), Winnipeg (Thompson), Toronto (Thunder Bay and Sudbury), Montreal and St. John's (Happy Valley) are responsible for CBC coverage in their respective northern regions.
>
> As noted in your memo, our region does not provide significant federal election coverage in the northern parts of the provinces.
>
> Our Iqaluit bureau and Montreal production centre provided only limited reports about campaigns on the northern Quebec constituencies during the last federal election owing, in part, to the fact that

those constituencies are dominated by "southern" populations. Our election night coverage from Iqaluit included results from those ridings which stretch into Nunavik.

Our Yukon station did not provide coverage of northern BC ridings leaving this to CBC and CTV television from Vancouver, which did.

Our Yellowknife station provided only occasional election night reports of the Alberta constituency which includes Fort Chipewyan as well as the election results for that constituency in the next day's morning program. With respect to this riding, our Yellowknife station anticipates providing a riding and candidate profile prior to the election date in co-operation with our Edmonton station. (Brian Cousins, fax to Lorna Roth, 10 May 1991)

4. The Northern Native Broadcasting, Yukon Native Communications Society was also issued a licence in 1981 to operate a regional radio service.

5. In 1983, IBC began broadcasting approximately five hours per week. It increased its hours between 1983 and 1990 but has had to decrease its air time since the federal government cut-backs to native broadcasting in March 1990. As of May 1991, IBC was airing 4.5 hours of programming per week. Television Northern Canada became operational in January 1992. Since then, and due to increased private funding, IBC has been able to offer an additional half-hour of overall air time per week.

6. The executive director of the OkalaKatiget Communications Society in Labrador was interviewed for this study despite the fact that Labrador does not receive CBC Northern Service broadcasting. The decision to interview Ken Todd was made because of the similarity of circumstances regarding remoteness and marginalization of local and regional Labrador populations from mainstream media and political activities.

7. The change in the CRTC policy regarding the right of Native Communications Societies to advertise as well as the operation of Television Northern Canada readily addresses this complaint. For the next election, all NCSs will be able to advertise.

8. In the 1988 election, of the 6.5 hours allotted to each major broadcaster for election coverage, the following entitlements were assigned to the major parties: Conservative – 195 minutes; Liberal – 89 minutes; New Democratic Party – 67 minutes. The minor parties' allocations were: Parti Rhinocéros – seven minutes; Parti Nationaliste du Québec – six minutes; Libertarian Party of Canada – five minutes; Green Party of Canada – four minutes; Confederation of Regions Western Party – four minutes; Party for the Commonwealth of Canada – four minutes. All other parties – Social Credit, Communist, Christian Heritage, Western Canada Concept, Reform, Canada, Student, and Western Independence – received three minutes each (CRTC 1988a).

INTERVIEWS

CBC Northern Service

Aubin, Suzanne, Acting Area Manager, Northern Quebec Service Office (Montreal).

Awa, Simon, Operations Manager, Eastern Arctic (Iqaluit) Office.

Boyles, Jim, Area Manager, Yukon Office.

Cousins, Brian, Regional Director, Ottawa Office.

Cutler, Fran, Radio Program Director, Ottawa Office.

Kusagak, Josie, Area Manager, Kivalliq (Rankin Inlet) Office.

Mackie, Craig, Area Manager, Yellowknife Office.

McNaughton, Dave, Acting Area Manager, Western Arctic (Inuvik) Office.

Nayle, Peter, Area Manager, Eastern Arctic (Iqaluit) Office.

Wilson, Marie, Director of Television, Yellowknife Office.

Native Communications Societies

Goose, Louie, Inuvialuit Native Communications Society.

Gunn, Linda, Inuit Broadcasting Corporation.

Gyberson, Gerry, Television Northern Canada Coordinator.

Hervieux, Bernard, Société de Communication Atikamekw Montagnais.

Kane, Ken, Northern Native Broadcasting, Yukon.

Kuptama, Rosemary, former president, Inuit Broadcasting Corporation.

Longchap, John, James Bay Cree Native Communications Society.

MacQuarrie, Catherine, Native Communications Society of the Western Northwest Territories.

Todd, Ken, OkalaKatiget Society.

Parliament of Canada

Anawak, Jack, member of Parliament, Nunatsiaq riding.

Blondin, Ethel, member of Parliament, Western Arctic.

Marchand, Len, Senator.

In the Western Arctic

Barkley, Dorothy, Liberal party organizer, Western Arctic riding.

Cotterill, Ewen, Liberal party organizer, Western Arctic riding.

Crass, Peter, director of television and radio, Government of the Northwest Territories.

Gilday, Dave, Assistant Deputy Minister, Communications and Culture, NWT.

Hauser, Don, Sales Manager, CJCD radio station.

Lake, Ricki, New Democratic Party organizer.

MacQuarrie, Bob, teacher, election consultant.

McMahon, Pat, Mayor of Yellowknife.

Nerysoo, Richard, Speaker of the Legislative Assembly, NWT Council.

Pepper, Mary, President, New Democratic Party, Western Arctic.

Porter, Dave, Deputy Minister of Communications and Culture, NWT.

Sorenson, Linda, campaign manager for Ethel Blondin, 1988 election.

Spitzer, Elouise, lawyer.

Stevens, Sam, Administrator, NWT Justice of the Peace program.
Vertes, John, President, Progressive Conservative party, NWT.
Walsh, Wayne, President, Young Liberals of the Northwest Territories.
Whipp, Steven, New Democratic Party organizer.

In Nunatsiaq

Bell, Jim, copy editor, *Nunatsiaq News.*
Coman, Fred, campaign manager for Bryan Pearson, Progressive Conservative candidate, 1988.
Coman, Mickey, campaign manager for Bryan Pearson, Progressive Conservative candidate, 1988.
Cunningham, Duncan, Baffin Regional Inuit Association.
Harper, Kenn, author and Northern historian.
Ittinuar, Peter, CBC-Rankin Inlet; former MP, Nunatsiaq riding.
Kilabuk, Meeka, Baffin Regional Council.
Kinnear, Cherie, Iqaluit Chamber of Commerce.
Kusagak, Peter, New Democratic Party candidate, 1988 election.
Mongeau, Ron, President, New Democratic Party, Nunatsiaq riding.
Ookpik, Abe, former MLA, NWT council.
Parent, Gilles, Chamber of Commerce, Iqaluit.
Rennie, Gordon, manager, Northern Store, Iqaluit.
Rose, Burt, Director, Arctic College, Iqaluit campus.
Spence, Matthew, Editor-in-chief, *Nunatsiaq News.*
Woodhouse, Al, Liberal party organizer.

BIBLIOGRAPHY

Abrahamson, Gunther, Kendall Lougheed, Lorna Roth, Gail Valaskakis and Tom Wilson (Lougheed and Associates). 1986. *Report on the Native Communications Program and the Northern Native Broadcast Access Program.* Ottawa: Dept. of Secretary of State, Program Evaluation Directorate.

Assembly of First Nations. 1990. Brief to the Royal Commission on Electoral Reform and Party Financing. Ottawa.

Canada. *Broadcasting Act*, S.C. 1967–68, c. 25.

———. *Broadcasting Act*, S.C. 1991, c. 11, s. 3.

———. *Canada Elections Act*, R.S.C. 1985, c. E-2, Schedule III.

———. *Telesat Act*, R.S.C. 1970, c. T-4.

Canada. Broadcasting Arbitrator. 1989. "Report of the Broadcasting Arbitrator to the Chief Electoral Officer." In *Report of the Chief Electoral Officer of Canada as per Subsection 195(1) of the Canada Elections Act.* Ottawa: Minister of Supply and Services Canada.

Canada. Committee on Broadcasting. 1965. *Report.* Ottawa: Queen's Printer.

Canada. Royal Commission on Broadcasting. 1957. *Report.* Ottawa: Queen's Printer.

Canada. Royal Commission on Electoral Reform and Party Financing. 1990. Summaries and transcripts of hearings held at Saskatoon (17 April), Thompson (20 April), Whitehorse (14 May), Yellowknife (24 May), Ottawa (13 June), Iqaluit (23 July), and Kuujjuaq (24 July).

Canada. Statistics Canada. 1987a. *Population and Dwelling Counts, Provinces and Territories: Northwest Territories.* 1986 Census. Cat. 92-120. Ottawa: Minister of Supply and Services Canada.

———. 1987b. *Population and Dwelling Counts, Provinces and Territories: Yukon.* 1986 Census. Cat. 92-119. Ottawa: Minister of Supply and Services Canada.

Canadian Broadcasting Corporation (CBC). 1972. *CBC: A Brief History and Background.* Ottawa: CBC Information Services.

———. 1978. *Background and Historical Mileposts in the Operations of* CBC *Northern Service.* Ottawa: CBC Northern Service.

———. 1985. *Regulations Governing Party Political Broadcasts.* March. Ottawa: CBC.

———. 1990a. Brief to the Royal Commission on Electoral Reform and Party Financing. Ottawa.

———. 1990b. Correspondence from Michael McEwen to Pierre Lortie, 1 August and 15 October.

———. 1990c. "Northern Television Development Study (Draft)." Ottawa: CBC Northern Service.

Canadian Radio-television and Telecommunications Commission (CRTC). 1988a. "Allocation of Federal Election Broadcast Time." Circular No. 352. Ottawa: CRTC.

———. 1988b. "Federal General Election – Guidelines for Broadcast Licensees." Circular No. 351. Ottawa: CRTC.

———. 1990. "Native Broadcasting Policy." Public Notice CRTC 1990-89. Ottawa: CRTC.

CTV Television Network. 1989. "A Report to the CRTC Regarding Coverage of the 1988 Federal General Election." Toronto.

Collin, Ken. 1990. Brief to the Royal Commission on Electoral Reform and Party Financing. Ottawa.

Dacks, Gurston. 1986. "Politics on the Last Frontier: Consociationalism in the Northwest Territories." *Canadian Journal of Political Science* 19:345–61.

Diamond, Edwin, and Stephen Bates. 1984. *The Spot: The Rise of Political Advertising on Television.* Cambridge: MIT Press.

Frizzell, Alan, Jon H. Pammett and Anthony Westell. 1989. *The Canadian General Election of 1988.* Ottawa: Carleton University Press.

Gilsdorf, Bill. 1981. "Getting the Message Across: Media Strategies and Political Campaigns." In *Communication Studies in Canada*, ed. Liora Salter. Toronto: Butterworths.

Jennings, M. Kent, and L. Harmon Zeigler, eds. 1966. *The Electoral Process.* Englewood Cliffs: Prentice-Hall.

Kraus, Sidney, and Dennis Davis. 1976. *The Effects of Mass Communication on Political Behavior.* University Park: Pennsylvania State University Press.

Lortie, Pierre. 1990. "Notes for the Opening Remarks of Pierre Lortie, Chairman, Royal Commission on Electoral Reform and Party Financing at the First Public Hearing of the Commission," 12 March. Ottawa.

Marchand, Senator Len. 1991. "Aboriginal Electoral Reform – A Discussion Paper." Background paper presented to the Royal Commission on Electoral Reform and Party Financing. Ottawa.

Mayes, Robert G. 1972. "Mass Communication and Eskimo Adaptation in the Canadian Arctic." Master's thesis, McGill University.

Meadow, Robert G. 1980. *Politics as Communication.* Norwood: Ablex Publishing.

Penniman, Howard R., ed. 1981. *Canada at the Polls, 1979 and 1980: A Study of the General Elections.* Washington, DC: American Enterprise Institute for Public Policy Research.

Roth, Lorna. 1983. "The Role of Communication Projects and Inuit Participation in the Formation of a Communication Policy for the North." Master's thesis, McGill University.

Sabato, Larry J. 1981. *The Rise of Political Consultants: New Ways of Winning Elections.* New York: Basic Books.

Stiles, Mark, and William Litwack. 1986. *Native Broadcasting in the North of Canada.* Report 54. Ottawa: Canadian Commission for UNESCO.

Telesat Canada. 1979. *Ten Years and Counting.* Ottawa: Telesat Canada Information Department.

Valaskakis, Gail, Ron Robbins and Tom Wilson. 1981. *The Inukshuk ANIK B Project: An Assessment.* Report commissioned by the Inuit Tapirisat of Canada. Ottawa: ITC.

CONTRIBUTORS TO VOLUME 21

France Abran — Université de Montréal
Catherine M. Bolan — York University
Rovin Deodat — Simon Fraser University
Peter Desbarats — University of Western Ontario
William O. Gilsdorf — Concordia University
David Hogarth — Concordia University
Stephen Kline — Simon Fraser University
William Leiss — Simon Fraser University
Lorna Roth — Concordia University
Arlene Shwetz — Simon Fraser University
David R. Spencer — University of Western Ontario
Pierre Trudel — Université de Montréal

ACKNOWLEDGEMENTS

The Royal Commission on Electoral Reform and Party Financing and the publishers wish to acknowledge with gratitude the permission of the following to reprint and translate material:

Canadian Broadcasting Corporation/Radio Canada; Éditions Yvon Blais; *Financial Post*; *The Gazette* (Montreal); *The Globe and Mail*; Richard Gwyn; Harvard University Press; *Journal of Canadian Studies*; Dr. Michael Nolan, University of Western Ontario; *North Carolina Law Review*; University of Calgary Press.

Care has been taken to trace the ownership of copyright material used in the text, including the tables and figures. The authors and publishers welcome any information enabling them to rectify any reference or credit in subsequent editions.

Consistent with the Commission's objective of promoting full participation in the electoral system by all segments of Canadian society, gender neutrality has been used wherever possible in the editing of the research studies.

THE COLLECTED RESEARCH STUDIES*

---

* The titles of studies may not be final in all cases.

ROBERT A. HACKETT, WITH THE ASSISTANCE OF JAMES MACKINTOSH, DAVID ROBINSON AND ARLENE SHWETZ	Smaller Voices: Minor Parties, Campaign Communication and the News Media
EILEEN SAUNDERS	Mass Media and the Reproduction of Marginalization

VOLUME 23
Canadian Political Parties in the Constituencies: A Local Perspective

R.K. CARTY	Canadian Political Parties in the Constituencies: A Local Perspective

Commission Organization

Chairman
Pierre Lortie

Commissioners
Pierre Fortier
Robert Gabor
William Knight
Lucie Pépin

Senior Officers

Executive Director
Guy Goulard

Director of Research
Peter Aucoin

Special Adviser to the Chairman
Jean-Marc Hamel

Research
F. Leslie Seidle,
  Senior Research Coordinator

Legislation
Jules Brière, Senior Adviser
Gérard Bertrand
Patrick Orr

Coordinators
Herman Bakvis
Michael Cassidy
Frederick J. Fletcher
Janet Hiebert
Kathy Megyery
Robert A. Milen
David Small

Communications and Publishing
Richard Rochefort, Director
Hélène Papineau, Assistant
  Director
Paul Morisset, Editor
Kathryn Randle, Editor

Assistant Coordinators
David Mac Donald
Cheryl D. Mitchell

Finance and Administration
Maurice R. Lacasse, Director

Contracts and Personnel
Thérèse Lacasse, Chief

Editorial, Design and Production Services

Printed and bound in Canada by
Best Gagné Book Manufacturers